BY THE NUMBERS

BY THE NUMBERS

NUMBERS

Publishing

Robert S. Lazich, Editor

A Statistical Guide to the Publishing Industry

GALE

DETROIT • NEW YORK • TORONTO • LONDON

Robert S. Lazich, *Editor*

Editorial Code & Data Inc. Staff

Monique S. Darnay, Susan M. Turner, and David Smith, *Contributing Editors*
Sherae R. Carroll, *Data Entry Associate*
Joyce Piwowarski, *Programmer/Analyst*
Kenneth J. Muth, *Manager, Technical Operations*

Gale Research Staff

Kristin Mallegg, *Coordinating Editor*
Mary Beth Trimper, *Production Director*
Shanna Heilveil, *Production Assistant*
Michelle DiMercurio, *Art Director*
Barbara J. Yarrow, *Graphic Services Supervisor*
Cynthia Baldwin, *Product Design Manager*

The paper used in this publication meets the minimum requirements of American National Standard for Information Sciences—Permanence Paper for Printed Library Materials, ANSI Z39.48-1984.

ISBN 0-7876-1860-8
ISSN 1096-4967
10 9 8 7 6 5 4 3 2 1

Printed in the United States of America

TABLE OF CONTENTS

CHAPTER 2 - PUBLISHING OVERVIEW continued:

CHAPTER 3 - PUBLISHING: MARKET BY MARKET continued:

Introduction

By the Numbers: Publishing is a compilation of statistical information on the publishing industry. *Publishing* features:

- More than 550 tabulations of data, many with graphics
- Comprehensive coverage of the subject in 15 chapters
- National and international scope
- Market, market share, and technological data
- Selected Data Index for rapid access to facts and figures
- Timelines for tracking events from ancient times to the present
- Glossary of terms used
- Source listing with table references
- Keyword index for rapid access to contents

Most importantly, *Publishing* provides a handy, single-volume desktop reference to the most important industry spawned by the invention of movable type in the 15th century—which has continued strong in the face of all manner of technological change, including the advent of radio, films, television, and (most recently) electronics. Those seeking to get a perspective on the various participants in the "information revolution" will find this book, along with its companion, *By the Numbers: Electronic and Online Publishing*, a valuable reference tool.

Overview of the Field

Coverage of the publishing industry in this book is restricted largely to the print segment, with some exceptions:

- Music publishing is predominantly on electronic media but is included here.

- Audio books are included.

- Federal statistics, presented throughout the book, are based on the reporting of "establishments" to the Federal government. The statistics, consequently, do not differentiate between the print and electronic activities of a book publisher, a newspaper, or a magazine. When using Federal statistics, differences between print and other media are not easily made except at the product level.

Publishing naturally divides into segments. Book publishing is the oldest. It goes back to the dawn of history. Newspapers and magazines are more recent innovations. Specialized publishing activities have emerged in modern times, including the distribution of music on records, tapes, and disks; the publishing of catalogs for selling all manner of products; and the greeting cards industry. Information on each of these major activities is presented as a chapter. Smaller specialized segments are brought together in one place (Chapter 3); these include many product categories of book publishing as well as such categories as calendars, maps, trading cards, yearbooks, and yellow pages. Newspapers, periodicals, book publishing, in that order, represent the largest segments of publishing, narrowly construed.

Publishing rests upon the printing industry. That segment, in turn, uses a variety of products, most notably paper and ink. These secondary and tertiary activities underlying publishing are also profiled in chapters of their own. Commercial lithographic printing is the dominant segment of this group.

From a statistical point of view, printing and publishing consists of more than 61,000 companies employing nearly 1.5 million people, with annual shipments of $213 billion (projected for 1998). If commercial printing categories are excluded, the industry has nearly 20,000 companies, more than 866,000 employees, and shipments in 1998 of $135 billion.

The Publishing Industry

Industry Segment	Companies 1992	Employment in 1992	Shipments - 1992 ($ mil)	Shipments - 1998 ($ mil)
Book publishing	2,504	79,600	16,731.1	23,232.3
Book printing	557	50,900	4,687.9	5,741.2
Book binding and related	1,071	27,700	1,321.3	1,655.5
Miscellaneous publishing	3,159	65,400	10,977	15,964.5
Newspapers	6,762	417,000	34,124.3	42,305.1
Periodicals	4,390	116,200	22,033.9	27,259.5
Greeting cards	157	22,800	4,195.6	5,370.0
Manifold business forms	644	47,900	7,435.9	8,598.5
Blank books and binders	376	39,100	3,788.1	4,540.9
Commercial printing - lithography	28,489	439,900	43,588.2	56,495.2
Commercial printing - gravure	401	21,500	3,560.5	3,926.9
Commercial printing nec	8,570	107,300	9,290.2	11,385.7
Typesetting	2,481	26,100	1,611.9	1,925.6
Platemaking services	1,558	38,700	3,451.5	4,240.2
Total - Publishing only	19,638	866,600	105,295.2	77,973.6
Total - Commercial printing and below	41,499	633,500	61,502.3	77,973.6
Total	61,137	1,500,100	166,797.5	212,641.1

Scope and Organization

Publishing covers the industry by major segments, beginning with a broad view of the industry as a whole and followed by segments treated in more detail. *Publishing* has 15 chapters, outlined below. Chapters are organized by topic. Within a topical subdivision, tables are sorted alphabetically, although in some cases more general subjects are placed first. In many cases, tables have been titled so that their content is signalled by the first word or phrase of the title.

Chapter 1. Selected Data Index. The Data Index presented here provides "factoids" drawn from the rest of the book and arranged alphabetically by topics. The objective is to provide a rapid look-up tool for the casual user, reference librarian, journalist, or analyst attempting to get a quick grasp of the field in numbers. Each item is described in abbreviated form. Values, their denomination (e.g., %, $ mil), and year of reporting are presented. A table reference points to a place in *Publishing* where more information may be available. It is anticipated that this "database" will be increased and updated in each new edition of *Publishing*.

Chapter 2. Publishing Overview. This chapter presents information on the publishing industry as a whole. The chapter begins with a presentation of *Industry Statistics* drawn, with the exception of the first table, from the *Economic Census* of the U.S. Department of Commerce. *State Summaries* are presented, showing the entire industry, to the extent reported, for each state. The *Miscellaneous Publishing* topic presents additional census data for an industry classification that is not usually reported under that designation in other sources. Other general topics covered are *Sales and Distribution*, *Companies*, *Costs and Margins*, *Mergers and Acquisitions*, and *Foreign Markets*. More detailed information will be found in *Chapter 3, Publishing: Market by Market* and in chapters that deal with an industry segment.

Chapter 3. Publishing: Market by Market. This chapter presents statistics in tabular or text format on 19 categories of publishing: *Audio Books, Business Books, Calendars, Children's Books, Comic Books, Cookbooks, Detective Novels, Electronic Publishing, Libraries, Maps, Professional Books, Religious Books, Romance Novels, Textbooks, Trading Cards, Translations, University Presses, Yearbooks*, and *Yellow Pages*.

Chapter 4. Book Publishing. Book publishing continues to be one of the three major "anchors" of the publishing industry (along with newspapers and magazines). This chapter presents data on this segment. Specific products are covered in *Chapter 3, Publishing: Market by Market*. Information on awards and bestsellers is presented in the chapter on *Awards, Bestsellers, and Picks*. In this chapter, coverage includes *Industry Statistics, Sales and Distribution, Retailing, Wholesaling, Book Fairs, Buyers, Consumer Spending, Production*, and *Foreign Markets*.

Chapter 5. The Catalog Industry. This chapter presents selected data on the Catalog industry, a significant producer of printed products that are intended to be used in product selection and acquisition by distant buyers. Topics covered include *Sales and Distribution, Companies, Catalog Users*, and *Foreign Markets*. Electronic dissemination of this type of material is covered under the topic of *Electronic Publishing* in Chapter 3 and, in much more detail, in Gale's *By the Numbers: Electronic and Online Publishing*.

Chapter 6. The Greeting Cards Industry. A highly specialized and distinct segment of publishing is the Greeting Cards industry, profiled in this chapter under the topics of *Industry Statistics* and *Sales Statistics*—the first covering information as reported by the Federal government and the second data published on the industry in other sources.

Chapter 7. Magazine Publishing. This chapter presents data on all periodicals except newspapers and serial reference publications. The popular magazine categories are included along with academic journals, business and computer magazines, and other periodicals. Coverage of online magazines is incidental. For a full treatment of that subject, please see Gale's *By the Numbers: Electronic and Online Publishing*. Topics included here are *Industry Statistics*, *Sales and Distribution*, *Publishers*, *Magazine Categories*, *Academic Publishing*, *Advertising*, *Business Magazines*, *Computer Magazines*, *Consumer Magazines*, and *Foreign Markets*.

Chapter 8. Music Publishing. With the exception of audio books (covered in Chapter 3), the publishing of music is the most important non-print segment of the Publishing industry—although electronic publishing is a growing contender. Music publishing is covered in this chapter under the topics of *Sales and Distribution*, *Bestsellers*, *Companies*, *Costs*, *Royalties*, and *Foreign Markets*.

Chapter 9. Newspaper Publishing. This major segment of publishing is profiled under the topics of *Industry Statistics*, *Trends*, *Sales and Markets*, *Companies*, *Rankings*, *Circulation*, *Reader Profiles*, and *Foreign Markets*. Related information, on magazines and journals, is presented in Chapter 7. For a full treatment of electronic newspapers, please see Gale's *By the Numbers: Electronic and Online Publishing*.

Chapter 10. The Printing Industry. Publishing, like many other industries, is a multi-tiered activity. The Printing Industry, profiled in this chapter, is the most important second tier, supporting the primary publishers. *Chapter 11, Suppliers of the Industry*, provides additional data on a third tier. Topics covered here include *Markets*, *Companies*, *Employment*, *Book Printing*, *Business Forms* (which is actually a primary industry), *Commercial Printing*, *Digital Printing*, *Typesetting*, *Capital Expenditures*, *Mergers and Acquisitions*, *Print-on-Demand*, and *Foreign Markets*.

Chapter 11. Suppliers of the Industry. This chapter covers industrial sectors that support publishing activities. Included are *Industry Statistics*, *Bookbinding*, *Chemicals*, *Computer Equipment*, *Ink*, *Machinery*, *Paper*, and *Photographic Equipment*. The printing industry is covered separately in Chapter 10.

Chapter 12. Employment, Compensation, and Positions. Information on employment, occupations, income, and wages is presented throughout this book under the topic of *Industry Statistics* in a number of chapters, including occupational growth to the year 2005. The tables in this chapter are from trade sources and presented in one place to give additional career-related information.

Chapter 13. Crime and Censorship. The ten tables in this chapter provide a glimpse of illegal activities—primarily piracy of electronic and tape products—and some information about the censorship of printed products.

Chapter 14. Awards, Bestsellers, Picks. This chapter presents tabulations of award winners, lists of bestsellers, and "picks" of favorites by different groups or authorities.

Chapter 15. Time Lines. This chapter provides a chronology for technological developments covered in the rest of *Publishing*.

Geographic Areas Covered. Publishing covers the industry the world over. Most of the tabular materials are related to the U.S. market. Most U.S. coverage is at the national and state levels.

Period Covered. Most of the information presented in *Publishing* is from the 1993-1997 period. The timelines present some historical milestones, including dates for developments in recent decades.

Sources

Publishing is drawn largely from periodicals literature and from electronic databases accessible by way of the Internet. Magazines, newspapers, governmental publications, press releases, and online files were consulted. Source notes beneath each table identify the original publication. In many cases, *Publishing* shows only a fraction of all the information available from a source and, of necessity, omits meaningful analysis and commentary that the statistical tabulation was meant to illustrate. It is recommended that the user consult the original sources when delving more deeply into a particular topic of interest.

All sources are shown in *Appendix II - Listing of Sources*. The number of the table drawn from the source is shown for easy reference.

Appendices and Index

The presentation of data in Chapters 1 through 15 is followed by two appendices: *Appendix I - Abbreviations and Acronyms* and *Appendix II - Listing of Sources*. The *Keyword Index* provides references to all subjects, issues, and organizations covered. Index entries feature both page and table references. Cross references are also provided.

Comments and Suggestions

Although every effort has been made to ensure the accuracy and timeliness of the data in *Publishing,* errors and omissions may occur. Notification of changes or additions deemed appropriate by users of this edition are appreciated. Comments and suggestions for the improvement of *Publishing* are welcome. Please contact:

> *By the Numbers: Publishing*
> Gale Research
> 835 Penobscot Building
> Detroit, MI 48226-4094
> Phone: (313)961-2242
> Toll-free: 800-347-GALE
> Fax: (313)961-6851

BY THE
NUMBERS

Chapter 1
SELECTED DATA INDEX

This chapter presents a selection of facts and forecasts drawn from the balance of *Publishing*. The extracts are arranged under keywords and presented alphabetically. The aim of the chapter is to provide the user rapid answers to questions that might arise in the study of new technological areas or emerging markets without the need to consult the index and to find a table. The data index is also useful for locating tables, of course.

Each line of the data index is either a keyword (*Greeting cards*), a secondary descriptive header (*Greeting card sales*), or a description (*Sales*). Descriptions are followed by a value (e.g., *6.85*), a denomination (*$ bil*), a year for which the value is reported (*1996*), and a table reference. Descriptions are somewhat abbreviated to fit the index. For full context, please consult the table reference.

A description may occur more than once under different keyword references. The descriptor *Magazine advertisers*, for instance, appears under the keywords *Advertising* and *Magazines*.

Selected Data Index

	Value	Denomination	Year	Ref.
Advertising				
Magazine advertisers				
Top magazine advertiser: General Motors Corp.	456.4	$ mil	1996	320
Second magazine advertiser: Phillip Morris Co.	343.1	$ mil	1996	320
Minority publications ad spending				
African American press	860.0	$ mil	1996	315
African American press increase from 1995	3.0	%		315
Gay/lesbian press	73.7	$ mil	1996	315
Gay/lesbian press increase from 1995	19.6	%		315
Hispanic press	186.5	$ mil	1996	315
Hispanic press increase from 1995	11.0	%		315
Newspaper advertisers				
Top growth of advertising: Circuit City Stores	3,299.1	%		407
Second in growth of advertising: Travelers Group	143.8	%		407
Web advertiser spending				
Top in ad spending: Microsoft	2,905.7	$ mil	1996	159
Second in ad spending: Netscape	2,172.9	$ mil	1996	159
Audio books				
Audio book sales				
Sales	0.25	$ bil	1989	113
Sales	1.60	$ bil	1996	113
Baseball cards				
Baseball card sales				
Sales	250	mil	1988	182
Sales	1,100	mil	1992	182
Book manufacturing				
Book manufacturing employment				
Writers and editors (% of all in this sector)	7.7	%	1994	199
Sales and related workers (% of all in this sector)	5.8	%	1994	199
Computer programmers (% of all in this sector)	1.1	%	1994	199
Book market				
Book market -- U.S./Latin America				
Top market: Mexico	48	$ mil	1995	257
Second in market share: Spain	34	$ mil	1995	257
Book production				
Book shipments				
Value of shipments	7,740.0	$ mil	1982	195

Continued. Column headed 'Ref.' shows table number where more information may be available.

	Value	Denomi-nation	Year	Ref.
Value of shipments (projected)	23,232.3	$ mil	1998	195
Book publishing				
Book publishing employment				
Total employment	67.1	000	1982	193
Total employment (projected)	88.3	000	1998	193
Books				
Book buyers				
Buyers with income < $30,000	32	%		235
Buyers with income > $75,000	26	%		235
Buyers with income between $60,000 and $74,999	8	%		235
Book market				
Top market share: United States	25.49	$ bil	1995	255
Second in market share: Japan	10.47	$ bil	1995	255
Third in market share: Germany	9.95	$ bil	1995	255
Book publishing employment				
Top employment: New York	25.60	%		202
Second in employment: California	8.50	%		202
Third in employment: New Jersey	7.90	%		202
Book publishing revenues				
Top book publisher in revenues: Time Warner Inc.	2,010.5	$ mil	1995	98
Second publisher in revenues: Hearst Magazines	901.7	$ mil	1995	98
Book publishing sales				
Top publisher in sales: Bertelsmann	4,766	$ bil		94
Second publisher in sales: Warner Books	3,722	$ bil		94
Book purchases				
Place of purchase: Chain bookstores	26	%		228
Place of purchase: Independent bookstores	20	%		228
Place of purchase: Used bookstores	4	%		228
Book sales				
Book sales in units	2.04	bil	1991	204
Book sales in units	2.13	bil	1994	204
Book sales in units	2.27	bil	1997	204
Book sales -- retail				
Top sales growth: Membership discount stores	208	%	1991-1995	223
Second in sales growth: Bookstores, used	96	%	1991-1995	223
Third in sales growth: Mail order, clubs	49	%	1991-1995	223
Book sales by region				
Pacific (as % of world sales)	20	%		203
South Atlantic (as % of world sales)	18	%		203
Mid-Atlantic (as % of world sales)	17	%		203
Book spending growth				
Growth in adult trade	5.0	%	1991-1996	205

Continued. Column headed 'Ref.' shows table number where more information may be available.

	Value	Denomination	Year	Ref.
Growth in juvenile trade	2.2	%	1991-1996	205
Growth in mass market	3.1	%	1991-1996	205
Projected growth in adult trade	4.4	%	1996-2001	205
Projected growth in juvenile trade	3.9	%	1996-2001	205
Projected growth in mass market	4.5	%	1996-2001	205
Book types				
Most popular: Fiction	50.9	%		247
Second in popularity: Cooking/crafts	10.4	%		247
Third in popularity: Non-fiction	10.2	%		247
Influential books				
Most influential based on survey: *The Bible*	79.8	%		562
Second most influential: *Baby and Child Care*	4.7	%		562
Catalogs				
Catalog distribution				
% of population receiving in northeast U.S.	90.8	%		258
% of population receiving in western U.S.	91.6	%		258
Catalog sales				
Top sales: Dell Computer Corp.	7,554	$ mil	1996	267
Second in sales: Gateway 2000	5,035	$ mil	1996	267
Catalogs: reasons for shopping				
Top reason men shop: Convenience	40	%		272
Top reason women shop: Convenience	50	%		273
Second reason men shop: Variety	19	%		272
Second reason women shop: Variety	20	%		273
CD-ROM				
CD-ROM production				
Top production: United States	65	%	1996	150
Second in production: Germany	10	%	1996	150
Children's books				
Children's book purchases				
Mother purchases at chain stores	45.0	%		130
Child purchases at chain stores	15.4	%		130
Children's book sales				
Top title: *The Poky Little Puppy*	14	mil		121
Second best selling title: *The Tale of Peter Rabbit*	9.3	mil		121
Children's book spending				
Consumer spending	2,231.1	$ mil	1995	123
Consumer spending (projected)	3,022.3	$ mil	2000	123
Christian books				
Christian book purchases				
Purchases by 18-29 year olds	35.7	%		167
Purchases by 30-39 year olds	48.0	%		167

Continued. Column headed 'Ref.' shows table number where more information may be available.

	Value	Denomi-nation	Year	Ref.
Purchases by 60 years old and up	50.0	%		167
Christian book sales				
Top bible translation: New International	40.0	%		170
Second in sales: King James	20.0	%		170
Circulation				
Computer magazine circulation				
Top in circulation: *PC Magazine*	1.0	$ mil	1994	327
Second in circulation: *PC World*	0.9	$ mil	1994	327
Magazine circulation				
Top in paid circulation: *Reader's Digest*	15.1	$ mil	1995	335
Second in paid circulation: *TV Guide*	13.2	$ mil	1995	335
Newspaper circulation				
Top daily circulation: Japan	71.7	mil		420
Second in circulation: United States	60.2	mil		420
Comic books				
Comic book market				
Market value	500	$ mil	1991	134
Market value	2,000	$ mil	1994	134
Comic book producer				
Top producer: Marvel Comics	41	%	1996	138
Second producer: DC Comics	25	%	1996	138
Computer magazines				
Computer and Internet magazine ad revenue				
Top in ad revenue: *PC Magazine*	318.1	$ mil	1996	326
Second in ad revenue: *PC Week*	239.5	$ mil	1996	326
Computer magazine circulation				
Top in circulation: *PC Magazine*	1.0	$ mil	1994	327
Second in circulation: *PC World*	0.9	$ mil	1994	327
Consumer magazines				
Consumer magazine ad revenue				
Top in ad revenue: *People*	525.6	$ mil	1996	333
Second in ad revenue: *Sports Illustrated*	522.2	$ mil	1996	333
Digital				
Digitally printed products				
Top product based on survey: Reports	72	%		461
Second product based on survey: Manuals	68	%		461
Distribution				
Catalog distribution				
% of population receiving in northeast U.S.	90.8	%		258
% of population receiving in western U.S.	91.6	%		258
In-flight magazine distribution				
Top in distribution (tie): *Sky* and *Hemispheres*	500,000			330

Continued. Column headed 'Ref.' shows table number where more information may be available.

	Value	Denomination	Year	Ref.
Second in distribution: *US Airways*	440,000			330
Editors				
Editor salaries				
Salary for supervising one magazine	51,100	$		511
Salary for supervising more than one magazine	47,600	$		511
Employment				
Book manufacturing employment				
Writers and editors (% of all in this sector)	7.7	%	1994	199
Sales and related workers (% of all in this sector)	5.8	%	1994	199
Computer programmers (% of all in this sector)	1.1	%	1994	199
Book publishing employment				
Top employment: New York	25.60	%		202
Second in employment: California	8.50	%		202
Third in employment: New Jersey	7.90	%		202
Total employment	67.1	000	1982	193
Total employment (projected)	88.3	000	1998	193
Editor salaries				
Salary for supervising one magazine	51,100	$		511
Salary for supervising more than one magazine	47,600	$		511
Greeting card industry employment				
Total employment	20.8	000	1982	277
Total employment	23.2	000	1994	277
Periodicals industry employment				
Total employment	81,000		1982	294
Total employment (projected)	112,000		1998	294
Wages per hour	57	$	1982	294
Wages per hour (projected)	120	$	1998	294
Publishing employment -- United States				
Total	1.5	mil	1992	17
Commercial printing, lithographic	439,900		1992	17
Newspapers	417,000		1992	17
Periodicals	116,200		1992	17
Establishments				
Publishing establishments -- United States				
Total	63,763		1992	17
Commercial printing, lithographic	29,344		1992	17
Newspapers	8,679		1992	17
Periodicals	4,699		1992	17
Publishing establishments by state				
California (% of all of this type in U.S.)	12.848	%	1992	22
New York (% of all of this type in U.S.)	8.185	%	1992	50
Texas (% of all of this type in U.S.)	6.259	%	1992	61

Continued. Column headed 'Ref.' shows table number where more information may be available.

	Value	Denomi- nation	Year	Ref.
General interest magazines				
General interest magazine ad revenue				
Top in ad revenue growth: *Marie Claire*	124.3	%	1996	334
Second in ad revenue growth: *InStyle*	104.5	%	1996	334
Third in ad revenue growth: *Martha Stewart Living*	97.1	%	1996	334
Greeting cards				
Greeting card consumption				
Per capita consumption ages 55 to 64	57	%	1996	286
Per capita consumption ages 19 to 24	9	%	1996	286
Greeting card industry employment				
Total employment	20.8	000	1982	277
Total employment	23.2	000	1994	277
Greeting card sales				
Sales	2.10	$ bil	1980	288
Sales	6.85	$ bil	1996	288
In-flight magazines				
In-flight magazine distribution				
Top in distribution (tie): *Sky* and *Hemispheres*	500,000			330
Second in distribution: *US Airways*	440,000			330
Juvenile books				
Juvenile book market share				
Top segment: Fiction	50.0	%		128
Second in market share: Coloring/activity	25.0	%		128
Magazines				
Magazine advertisers				
Top magazine advertiser: General Motors Corp.	456.4	$ mil	1996	320
Second magazine advertiser: Phillip Morris Co.	343.1	$ mil	1996	320
Magazine circulation				
Top in paid circulation: *Reader's Digest*	15.1	$ mil	1995	335
Second in paid circulation: *TV Guide*	13.2	$ mil	1995	335
Magazine revenues				
Newsweekly revenues	4.7	$ bil	1996	310
Home service & home category revenues	1.6	$ bil	1996	310
Magazine sales				
Sales of tabloids	24.8	%		305
Sales of family and home type	22.5	%		305
Sales of TV and movie type	21.9	%		305
Top in single-copy sales: *TV Guide*	4.0	mil	1996	338
Second in single-copy sales: *Family Circle*	2.3	mil	1996	338
Online magazine readers				
Top magazine (readers per year): *Hotwired*	3	mil		153
Second magazine (readers per day): *Mr. Showbiz*	23,000			153

Continued. Column headed 'Ref.' shows table number where more information may be available.

	Value	Denomi-nation	Year	Ref.
Mail order				
Mail order sales				
Top company in sales: United Services Auto. Assoc.	6,634.0	$ mil		264
Second in sales: Time Warner	5,595.6	$ mil		264
Market share				
Book market				
Top market share: United States	25.49	$ bil	1995	255
Second in market share: Japan	10.47	$ bil	1995	255
Third in market share: Germany	9.95	$ bil	1995	255
Book market -- U.S./Latin America				
Top market: Mexico	48	$ mil	1995	257
Second in market share: Spain	34	$ mil	1995	257
Juvenile book market share				
Top segment: Fiction	50.0	%		128
Second in market share: Coloring/activity	25.0	%		128
Music market share				
Market share in Europe	34	%	1996	376
Market share in North America	33	%	1996	376
Minorities				
Minority publications ad spending				
African American press	860.0	$ mil	1996	315
African American press increase from 1995	3.0	%		315
Gay/lesbian press	73.7	$ mil	1996	315
Gay/lesbian press increase from 1995	19.6	%		315
Hispanic press	186.5	$ mil	1996	315
Hispanic press increase from 1995	11.0	%		315
Music				
Album sales				
Top title in sales: *Jagged Little Pill*	7.38	mil	1996	364
Second in sales: *Falling Into You*	6.13	mil	1996	364
Music market share				
Market share in Europe	34	%	1996	376
Market share in North America	33	%	1996	376
Music piracy				
Top country: Russia	222.3	$ mil		524
Second country: China	145.0	$ mil		524
Music sales				
Sales by genre: rock	33	%	1996	362
Sales by genre: country	15	%	1996	362
Online music sales				
Estimated sales of online music	47	$ mil	1997	379
Estimated sales of online music	1,640	$ mil	2002	379

Continued. Column headed 'Ref.' shows table number where more information may be available.

	Value	Denomination	Year	Ref.
Printed music				
Retail revenues	330.36	$ mil	1991	361
Retail revenues	425.00	$ mil	1996	361
Wholesale revenues	181.51	$ mil	1991	361
Wholesale revenues	228.00	$ mil	1996	361
Newspapers				
Newspaper advertisers				
Top growth of advertising: Circuit City Stores	3,299.1	%		407
Second in growth of advertising: Travelers Group	143.8	%		407
Newspaper circulation				
Top daily circulation: Japan	71.7	mil		420
Second in circulation: United States	60.2	mil		420
Newspaper industry				
Total employment	94.0	000	1982	381
Total employment (projected)	130.3	000	1998	381
Wages per hour	7.62	$	1982	381
Wages per hour (projected)	16.11	$	1998	381
Online magazines				
Online magazine readers				
Top magazine (readers per year): *Hotwired*	3	mil		153
Second magazine (readers per day): *Mr. Showbiz*	23,000			153
Paper				
Lightweight coated stock use				
Magazines	67.9	%		502
Catalogs	26.4	%		502
Inserts	3.8	%		502
Supercalendered stock use				
Inserts	50.0	%		503
Catalogs	31.3	%		503
Magazines	6.3	%		503
Periodical production				
Periodical shipments				
Value of shipments	11,478.0	$ mil	1982	295
Value of shipments (projected)	27,259.5	$ mil	1998	295
Periodicals industry				
Value of shipments	11,478.0	$ mil	1982	295
Value of shipments (projected)	27,259.5	$ mil	1998	295
Periodicals industry employment				
Total employment	81,000		1982	294
Total employment (projected)	112,000		1998	294
Wages per hour	57	$	1982	294
Wages per hour (projected)	120	$	1998	294

Continued. Column headed 'Ref.' shows table number where more information may be available.

	Value	Denomination	Year	Ref.
Periodicals shipments				
Shipments as % of U.S.: New York	43.70	%		302
Shipments as % of U.S.: California	8.90	%		302
Shipments as % of U.S.: Illinois	6.50	%		302
Piracy				
Music piracy				
Top country: Russia	222.3	$ mil		524
Second country: China	145.0	$ mil		524
Software piracy				
Top country: United States	2,361	$ mil		526
Second country: Japan	1,190	$ mil		526
Video piracy				
Top country: Russia	312	$ mil		527
Second country: Italy	294	$ mil		527
Printers				
Printing sales growth				
Top in sales growth: The Peerless Group	2,510	%	1994-1996	437
Second in sales growth: Express Press	300	%	1994-1996	437
Purchasing				
Book buyers				
Buyers with income < $30,000	32	%		235
Buyers with income > $75,000	26	%		235
Buyers with income between $60,000 and $74,999	8	%		235
Book purchases				
Place of purchase: Chain bookstores	26	%		228
Place of purchase: Independent bookstores	20	%		228
Place of purchase: Used bookstores	4	%		228
Book spending growth				
Growth in adult trade	5.0	%	1991-1996	205
Growth in juvenile trade	2.2	%	1991-1996	205
Growth in mass market	3.1	%	1991-1996	205
Projected growth in adult trade	4.4	%	1996-2001	205
Projected growth in juvenile trade	3.9	%	1996-2001	205
Projected growth in mass market	4.5	%	1996-2001	205
Book types				
Most popular: Fiction	50.9	%		247
Second in popularity: Cooking/crafts	10.4	%		247
Third in popularity: Non-fiction	10.2	%		247
Children's book purchases				
Mother purchases at chain stores	45.0	%		130
Child purchases at chain stores	15.4	%		130
Children's book spending				
Consumer spending	2,231.1	$ mil	1995	123

Continued. Column headed 'Ref.' shows table number where more information may be available.

	Value	Denomi-nation	Year	Ref.
Consumer spending (projected)	3,022.3	$ mil	2000	123
Christian book purchases				
Purchases by 18-29 year olds	35.7	%		167
Purchases by 30-39 year olds	48.0	%		167
Purchases by 60 years old and up	50.0	%		167
Revenues				
Book publishing revenues				
Top book publisher in revenues: Time Warner Inc.	2,010.5	$ mil	1995	98
Second publisher in revenues: Hearst Magazines	901.7	$ mil	1995	98
Computer and Internet magazine ad revenue				
Top in ad revenue: *PC Magazine*	318.1	$ mil	1996	326
Second in ad revenue: *PC Week*	239.5	$ mil	1996	326
Consumer magazine ad revenue				
Top in ad revenue: *People*	525.6	$ mil	1996	333
Second in ad revenue: *Sports Illustrated*	522.2	$ mil	1996	333
General interest magazine ad revenue				
Top in ad revenue growth: *Marie Claire*	124.3	%	1996	334
Second in ad revenue growth: *InStyle*	104.5	%	1996	334
Third in ad revenue growth: *Martha Stewart Living*	97.1	%	1996	334
Magazine revenues				
Newsweekly revenues	4.7	$ bil	1996	310
Home service & home category revenues	1.6	$ bil	1996	310
Printed music				
Retail revenues	330.36	$ mil	1991	361
Retail revenues	425.00	$ mil	1996	361
Wholesale revenues	181.51	$ mil	1991	361
Wholesale revenues	228.00	$ mil	1996	361
Sales				
Album sales				
Top title in sales: *Jagged Little Pill*	7.38	mil	1996	364
Second in sales: *Falling Into You*	6.13	mil	1996	364
Audio book sales				
Sales	0.25	$ bil	1989	113
Sales	1.60	$ bil	1996	113
Baseball card sales				
Sales	250	mil	1988	182
Sales	1,100	mil	1992	182
Book publishing sales				
Top publisher in sales: Bertelsmann	4,766	$ bil		94
Second publisher in sales: Warner Books	3,722	$ bil		94
Book sales				
Book sales in units	2.04	bil	1991	204

Continued. Column headed 'Ref.' shows table number where more information may be available.

11

	Value	Denomination	Year	Ref.
Book sales in units	2.13	bil	1994	204
Book sales in units	2.27	bil	1997	204
Book sales by region				
Pacific (as % of world sales)	20	%		203
South Atlantic (as % of world sales)	18	%		203
Mid-Atlantic (as % of world sales)	17	%		203
Catalog sales				
Top sales: Dell Computer Corp.	7,554	$ mil	1996	267
Second in sales: Gateway 2000	5,035	$ mil	1996	267
Children's book sales				
Top title: *The Poky Little Puppy*	14	mil		121
Second best selling title: *The Tale of Peter Rabbit*	9.3	mil		121
Christian book sales				
Top bible translation: New International	40.0	%		170
Second in sales: King James	20.0	%		170
Greeting card sales				
Sales	2.10	$ bil	1980	288
Sales	6.85	$ bil	1996	288
Magazine sales				
Sales of tabloids	24.8	%		305
Sales of family and home type	22.5	%		305
Sales of TV and movie type	21.9	%		305
Top in single-copy sales: *TV Guide*	4.0	mil	1996	338
Second in single-copy sales: *Family Circle*	2.3	mil	1996	338
Mail order sales				
Top company in sales: United Services Auto. Assoc.	6,634.0	$ mil		264
Second in sales: Time Warner	5,595.6	$ mil		264
Music sales				
Sales by genre: rock	33	%	1996	362
Sales by genre: country	15	%	1996	362
Online music sales				
Estimated sales of online music	47	$ mil	1997	379
Estimated sales of online music	1,640	$ mil	2002	379
Printing sales growth				
Top in sales growth: The Peerless Group	2,510	%	1994-1996	437
Second in sales growth: Express Press	300	%	1994-1996	437
Sales -- retail				
Book sales -- retail				
Top sales growth: Membership discount stores	208	%	1991-1995	223
Second in sales growth: Bookstores, used	96	%	1991-1995	223
Third in sales growth: Mail order, clubs	49	%	1991-1995	223

Continued. Column headed 'Ref.' shows table number where more information may be available.

	Value	Denomi-nation	Year	Ref.
Software				
Software piracy				
Top country: United States	2,361	$ mil		526
Second country: Japan	1,190	$ mil		526
Textbooks				
Textbook exports				
Top value of exports: United Kingdom	41,456	000	1997	181
Second in value of exports: Canada	30,679	000	1997	181
Video				
Video piracy				
Top country: Russia	312	$ mil		527
Second country: Italy	294	$ mil		527
Web advertising				
Web advertiser spending				
Top in ad spending: Microsoft	2,905.7	$ mil	1996	159
Second in ad spending: Netscape	2,172.9	$ mil	1996	159
Web sites				
Web site hits				
Top sites (daily hits): Netscape	30.00	mil		160
Second in daily hits: Yahoo!	9.45	mil		160
World Wide Web				
Web advertiser spending				
Top in ad spending: Microsoft	2,905.7	$ mil	1996	159
Second in ad spending: Netscape	2,172.9	$ mil	1996	159
Web site hits				
Top sites (daily hits): Netscape	30.00	mil		160
Second in daily hits: Yahoo!	9.45	mil		160

Column headed 'Ref.' shows table number where more information may be available.

Chapter 2
PUBLISHING OVERVIEW

This chapter presents information on the Publishing industry not further divided by industry products or sectors. The chapter begins with a presentation of *Industry Statistics* drawn, with the exception of the first table, from the Economic Census statistics of the U.S. Department of Commerce. *State Summaries* are presented, showing the entire industry, to the extent reported, for each state. The *Miscellaneous Publishing* topic presents additional census data for an industry classification that is not usually reported under that designation in other sources. Other general topics covered are *Sales and Distribution*, *Companies*, *Costs and Margins*, *Mergers and Acquisitions*, and *Foreign Markets*. More detailed information will be found in the chapter on *Publishing: Market by Market* and in chapters that deal solely with an industry segment.

★ 1 ★

U.S. Publishing Industry

Here are a couple quick facts on the publishing industry:

- Last year, more than 11,000 new publishing firms were created, a 38 percent increase over the average 8,000 firms launched annually. Most of these new firms were founded by self-publishers, writers who publish their own works.

- Today, there are 53,000 publishers in the United States, including eight large New York companies, 15 companies a step below them, and about 300 mid-sized companies that each generate between $1 million and $10 million in sales annually. That leaves more than 52,000 small publishers publishing between one and three books annually. Most of these are self-publishers.

Source: "Desktop Publishing Wave Brings Tide of New Authors to Bookstore Shelves." *The Christian Science Monitor,* 11 June 1996, p. 13.

★ 2 ★
Industry Statistics

Companies in 1987 and 1992

Industry	Companies		% Change 1987 to 1992
	1987	1992	
Newspapers	7,465	6,762	-10.40
Periodicals	3,757	4,390	14.42
Book publishing	2,180	2,504	12.94
Miscellaneous publishing	2,136	3,159	32.38
Greeting cards	147	157	6.37

Source: 1997 *Manufacturing STATROM* [machine-readable data files]. MStat97. Editorial Code and Data Inc., Detroit, Michigan, 1997. Primary source: *Economic Census for 1992* and earlier years. The Economic Census is conducted by the Bureau of the Census, U.S. Department of Commerce, Washington DC 20233.

★3★

Industry Statistics

Employment, 1985-1998

Data for 1994 and beyond are projections. These projections have been made based on a curve-fitting algorithm and by using the least-square method. In essence, the algorithm calculates a trend line for the data using existing data points. Misc. publishing includes the publishing of atlases, maps, calendars, directories, race track programs, manuals, and sheet music.

[In thousands]

Industry	1985	1990	1991	1992	1993	1994	1995	1996	1997	1998	% change 1985 to 1998
Newspapers	411	443	428	417	410	410	428	430	431	433	4.97
Periodicals	96	115	111	116	117	116	123	126	128	130	26.48
Book publishing	71	74	77	80	83	87	84	86	87	88	19.71
Misc. publishing	52	65	65	65	67	71	-	-	-	-	-
Greeting cards	20	25	24	23	22	23	-	-	-	-	-

Source: 1997 *Manufacturing STATROM* [machine-readable data files]. MStat97. Editorial Code and Data, Inc., Detroit Michigan, 1997. Primary source: *Economic Census for 1992* and earlier years. The *Economic Census* is conducted by the Bureau of the Census, U.S. Department of Commerce, Washington, DC 20233. *Note:* A dash (-) means that data for the item were not reported.

★4★

Industry Statistics

Production Workers Employed by the Publishing Industry, 1985-1998

Data for 1994 and beyond are projections. These projections have been made based on a curve-fitting algorithm and by using the least-square method. In essence, the algorithm calculates a trend line for the data using existing data points. Misc. publishing includes the publishing of atlases, maps, calendars, directories, race track programs, manuals, and sheet music.

[In thousands]

Industry	1985	1990	1991	1992	1993	1994	1995	1996	1997	1998	% change 1985 to 1998
Newspapers	151	149	145	135	132	134	136	134	133	131	-15.14
Periodicals	16	22	21	20	20	18	21	21	22	22	26.03
Book publishing	16	17	17	19	18	19	19	19	19	20	20.41
Misc. publishing	17	22	23	24	23	25	-	-	-	-	-
Greeting cards	11	12	13	12	12	13	-	-	-	-	-

Source: 1997 *Manufacturing STATROM* [machine-readable data files]. MStat97. Editorial Code and Data, Inc., Detroit, Michigan, 1997. Primary source: *Economic Census for 1992* and earlier years. The *Economic Census* is conducted by the Bureau of the Census, U.S. Department of Commerce, Washington, DC 20233. *Note:* A dash (-) means that data for the item were not reported.

★5★

Industry Statistics

Production Hours in Publishing, 1985-1998

Data for 1994 and beyond are projections. These projections have been made based on a curve-fitting algorithm and by using the least-square method. In essence, the algorithm calculates a trend line for the data using existing data points. Misc. publishing includes the publishing of atlases, maps, calendars, directories, race track programs, manuals, and sheet music.

[In millions]

Industry	1985	1990	1991	1992	1993	1994	1995	1996	1997	1998	% change 1985 to 1998
Newspapers	266	253	252	236	224	220	228	225	221	218	-22.08
Periodicals	28	35	35	39	37	35	38	38	39	40	28.46
Book publishing	29	31	30	36	35	35	34	34	35	35	18.98
Misc. publishing	30	40	43	43	43	48	49	51	52	54	45.17
Greeting cards	18	24	23	21	21	22	22	23	23	23	23.04

Source: 1997 *Manufacturing STATROM* [machine-readable data files]. MStat97. Editorial Code and Data, Inc., Detroit, Michigan, 1997. Primary source: *Economic Census for 1992* and earlier years. The *Economic Census* is conducted by the Bureau of the Census, U.S. Department of Commerce, Washington, DC 20233. *Note:* A dash (-) means that data for the item were not reported.

★6★

Industry Statistics

Payroll in Publishing, 1985-1998

Data for 1994 and beyond are projections. These projections have been made based on a curve-fitting algorithm and by using the least-square method. In essence, the algorithm calculates a trend line for the data using existing data points. Misc. publishing includes the publishing of atlases, maps, calendars, directories, manuals, race track programs and sheet music.

[In millions of dollars]

Industry	1985	1990	1991	1992	1993	1994	1995	1996	1997	1998	% change 1985 to 1998
Newspapers	7,905	10,407	10,309	10,506	10,396	10,585	11,572	11,932	12,292	12,652	37.52
Periodicals	2,555	3,659	3,661	4,075	4,305	4,274	4,619	4,827	5,035	5,244	51.28
Book publishing	1,672	2,300	2,514	2,676	2,799	2,936	3,022	3,156	3,290	3,425	51.17
Misc. publishing	1,047	1,708	1,780	1,733	1,897	1,982	2,196	2,311	2,425	2,540	58.76
Greeting cards	398	625	609	585	610	628	680	707	733	759	47.64

Source: 1997 *Manufacturing STATROM* [machine-readable data files]. MStat97. Editorial Code and Data, Inc., Detroit, Michigan, 1997. Primary source: *Economic Census* for 1992 and earlier years. The *Economic Census* is conducted by the Bureau of the Census, U.S. Department of Commerce, Washington, DC 20233. *Note:* A dash (-) means that data for the item were not reported.

★ 7 ★

Industry Statistics

Publishing Payroll per Employee, 1985-1998

Data for 1994 and beyond are projections. These projections have been made based on a curve-fitting algorithm and by using the least-square method. In essence, the algorithm calculates a trend line for the data using existing data points. Misc. publishing includes the publishing of atlases, maps, calendars, directories, race track programs, manuals, and sheet music.

[In dollars]

Industry	1985	1990	1991	1992	1993	1994	1995	1996	1997	1998	% change 1985 to 1998
Newspapers	19,233	23,471	24,063	25,195	25,336	25,810	27,018	27,769	28,515	29,256	34.26
Periodicals	26,665	31,758	33,101	35,065	36,766	36,717	37,487	38,444	39,365	40,253	33.76
Book publishing	23,584	30,913	32,524	33,614	33,644	33,704	35,941	36,913	37,853	38,763	39.16
Misc. publishing	20,142	26,193	27,380	26,497	28,480	27,838	-	-	-	-	-
Greeting cards	19,975	25,415	25,485	25,662	27,495	27,047	-	-	-	-	-

Source: 1997 *Manufacturing STATROM* [machine-readable data files]. MStat97. Editorial Code and Data, Inc., Detroit, Michigan, 1997. Primary source: *Economic Census for 1992* and earlier years. The *Economic Census* is conducted by the Bureau of the Census, U.S. Department of Commerce, Washington, DC 20233. *Note:* A dash (-) means that data for the item were not reported.

★ 8 ★

Industry Statistics

Wages per Hour in Publishing, 1985-1998

Data for 1994 and beyond are projections. These projections have been made based on a curve-fitting algorithm and by using the least-square method. In essence, the algorithm calculates a trend line for the data using existing data points. Misc. publishing includes the publishing of atlases, maps, calendars, directories, race track programs, manuals and sheet music.

[In dollars]

Industry	1985	1990	1991	1992	1993	1994	1995	1996	1997	1998	% change 1985 to 1998
Newspapers	10.64	12.37	12.27	12.89	12.90	13.40	13.76	14.09	14.42	14.74	27.82
Periodicals	9.59	13.09	13.21	13.40	12.51	12.97	14.65	15.14	15.62	16.11	40.47
Book publishing	9.78	11.68	12.72	12.49	12.90	13.27	13.96	14.40	14.83	15.27	35.95
Misc. publishing	8.11	9.40	9.60	10.80	10.41	10.39	-	-	-	-	-
Greeting cards	9.43	10.10	10.46	10.76	11.51	11.37	-	-	-	-	-

Source: 1997 *Manufacturing STATROM* [machine-readable data files]. MStat97. Editorial Code and Data, Inc., Detroit, Michigan, 1997. Primary source: *Economic Census for 1992* and earlier years. The *Economic Census* is conducted by the Bureau of the Census, U.S. Department of Commerce, Washington, DC 20233. *Note:* A dash (-) means that data for the item were not reported.

★ 9 ★

Industry Statistics

Cost of Materials in Publishing, 1985-1998

Data for 1994 and beyond are projections. These projections have been made based on a curve-fitting algorithm and by using the least-square method. In essence, the algorithm calculates a trend line for the data using existing data points. Misc. publishing includes the publishing of atlases, maps, calendars, directories, race track programs, manuals and sheet music.

[In millions of dollars]

Industry	1985	1990	1991	1992	1993	1994	1995	1996	1997	1998	% change 1985 to 1998
Newspapers	6,585	8,087	7,606	6,874	6,907	7,018	7,598	7,827	8,056	8,285	20.52
Periodicals	5,580	6,580	6,459	6,201	6,391	5,903	6,639	6,895	7,151	7,408	24.67
Book publishing	3,021	4,466	5,001	5,338	5,807	5,827	6,081	6,378	6,674	6,971	56.66
Misc. publishing	1,200	2,267	2,470	2,477	2,592	2,803	3,044	3,239	3,433	3,628	66.94
Greeting cards	673	938	870	743	826	915	959	1,003	1,046	1,090	38.28

Source: 1997 *Manufacturing STATROM* [machine-readable data files]. MStat97. Editorial Code and Data, Inc., Detroit Michigan, 1997. Primary source: *Economic Census for 1992* and earlier years. The *Economic Census* is conducted by the Bureau of the Census, U.S. Department of Commerce, Washington, DC 20233. *Note:* A dash (-) means that data for the item were not reported.

★ 10 ★

Industry Statistics

Cost of Materials per Employee, 1985-1998

Data for 1994 and beyond are projections. These projections have been made based on a curve-fitting algorithm and by using the least-square method. In essence, the algorithm calculates a trend line for the data using existing data points.

[In dollars]

Industry	1985	1990	1991	1992	1993	1994	1995	1996	1997	1998	% change 1985 to 1998
Newspapers	16,021	18,239	17,755	16,484	16,833	17,114	17,740	18,216	18,689	19,158	16.37
Periodicals	58,244	57,115	58,400	53,364	54,579	50,714	53,884	54,915	55,908	56,864	-2.43
Book publishing	42,611	60,020	64,701	67,057	69,793	66,897	72,320	74,588	76,781	78,904	46.00
Misc. publishing	23,067	34,765	37,997	37,870	38,920	39,362	-	-	-	-	-
Greeting cards	33,814	38,142	36,410	32,588	37,198	39,440	-	-	-	-	-

Source: 1997 *Manufacturing STATROM* [machine-readable data files]. MStat97. Editorial Code and Data, Inc., Detroit, Michigan, 1997. Primary source: *Economic Census for 1992* and earlier years. The Economic Census is conducted by the Bureau of the Census, U.S. Department of Commerce, Washington, DC 20233. *Note:* A dash (-) means that data for the item were not reported.

Industry Statistics

Value Added by Manufacturing, 1985-1998

Data for 1994 and beyond are projections. These projections have been made based on a curve-fitting algorithm and by using the least-square method. In essence, the algorithm calculates a trend line for the data using existing data points. Misc. publishing includes the publishing of atlases, maps, calendars, race track programs, manuals and sheet music.

[In dollars]

Industry	1985	1990	1991	1992	1993	1994	1995	1996	1997	1998	% change 1985 to 1998
Newspapers	20,426	26,560	26,093	27,247	27,745	28,818	31,198	32,138	33,079	34,019	39.96
Periodicals	9,678	13,848	13,794	15,833	16,272	15,821	17,794	18,480	19,167	19,854	51.25
Book publishing	7,396	10,920	11,683	11,494	12,743	13,681	14,278	14,975	15,671	16,368	54.81
Misc. publishing	3,265	6,656	7,354	8,525	9,218	9,523	10,343	11,004	11,666	12,327	73.52
Greeting cards	1,895	2,828	2,925	3,394	3,482	3,660	3,835	4,010	4,186	4,361	56.55

Source: 1997 *Manufacturing STATROM* [machine-readable data files]. MStat97. Editorial Code and Data, Inc., Detroit, Michigan, 1997. Primary source: *Economic Census for 1992* and earlier years. The *Economic Census* is conducted by the Bureau of the Census, U.S. Department of Commerce, Washington, DC 20233. *Note:* A dash (-) means that data for the item were not reported.

Industry Statistics

Value Added per Employee in Publishing, 1985-1998

Data for 1994 and beyond are projections. These projections have been made based on a curve-fitting algorithm and by using the least-square method. In essence, the algorithm calculates a trend line for the data using existing data points. Misc. publishing includes the publishing of atlases, maps, calendars, directories, race track programs, manuals and sheet music.

[In dollars]

Industry	1985	1990	1991	1992	1993	1994	1995	1996	1997	1998	% change 1985 to 1998
Newspapers	49,699	59,900	60,907	65,341	67,621	70,270	72,840	74,794	76,736	78,665	36.82
Periodicals	101,024	120,206	124,723	136,256	138,957	135,923	144,419	147,182	149,843	152,407	33.71
Book publishing	104,313	146,767	151,142	144,402	153,160	157,072	169,807	175,131	180,281	185,265	43.70
Misc. publishing	62,781	102,089	113,132	130,350	138,410	133,746	-	-	-	-	-
Greeting cards	95,216	114,939	122,402	148,838	156,829	157,759	-	-	-	-	-

Source: 1997 *Manufacturing STATROM* [machine-readable data files]. MStat97. Editorial Code and Data, Inc., Detroit, Michigan, 1997. Primary source: *Economic Census* for 1992 and earlier years. The *Economic Census* is conducted by the Bureau of the Census, U.S. Department of Commerce, Washington, DC 20233. *Note:* A dash (-) means that data for the item were not reported.

★ 13 ★

Industry Statistics

Shipments in Publishing, 1985-1998

Data for 1994 and beyond are projections. These projections have been made based on a curve-fitting algorithm and by using the least-square method. In essence, the algorithm calculates a trend line for the data using existing data points. Misc. publishing includes the publishing of atlases, maps, calendars, directories, race track programs, manuals, and sheet music.

[In millions of dollars]

Industry	1985	1990	1991	1992	1993	1994	1995	1996	1997	1998	% change 1985 to 1998
Newspapers	27,015	34,642	33,702	34,124	34,651	35,837	38,797	39,966	41,136	42,305	36.14
Periodicals	15,246	20,397	20,345	22,034	22,653	21,723	24,431	25,374	26,317	27,260	44.07
Book publishing	10,196	15,318	16,596	16,731	18,616	19,419	20,267	20,255	22,244	23,232	56.11
Misc. publishing	4,437	8,875	9,762	10,977	11,807	12,332	13,394	14,251	15,108	15,965	72.21
Greeting cards	2,598	3,721	3,810	4,196	4,275	4,507	4,723	4,939	5,154	5,370	51.62

Source: 1997 *Manufacturing STATROM* [machine-readable data files]. MStat97. Editorial Code and Data, Inc., Detroit, Michigan, 1997. Primary source: *Economic Census for 1992* and earlier years. The *Economic Census* is conducted by the Bureau of the Census, U.S. Department of Commerce, Washington, DC 20233. *Note:* A dash (-) means that data for the item were not reported.

★ 14 ★

Industry Statistics

Shipments per Employee in Publishing, 1985-1998

Data for 1994 and beyond are projections. These projections have been made based on a curve-fitting algorithm and by using the least-square method. In essence, the algorithm calculates a trend line for the data using existing data points.

[In dollars]

Industry	1985	1990	1991	1992	1993	1994	1995	1996	1997	1998	% change 1985 to 1998
Newspapers	65,729	78,127	78,670	81,833	84,453	87,386	90,582	93,012	95,427	97,826	32.81
Periodicals	159,148	177,055	183,952	189,620	193,446	186,626	198,293	202,085	205,739	209,260	23.95
Book publishing	143,811	205,886	214,697	210,190	223,749	222,949	241,025	248,582	255,891	262,966	45.31
Misc. publishing	85,327	136,115	150,185	167,846	177,276	173,208	-	-	-	-	-
Greeting cards	130,553	151,248	159,410	184,018	192,545	194,276	-	-	-	-	-

Source: 1997 *Manufacturing STATROM* [machine-readable data files]. MStat97. Editorial Code and Data, Inc., Detroit, Michigan, 1997. Primary source: *Economic Census for 1992* and earlier years. The *Economic Census* is conducted by the Bureau of the Census, U.S. Department of Commerce, Washington, DC 20233. *Note:* A dash (-) means that data for the item were not reported.

★ 15 ★

Industry Statistics

Capital Investment in Publishing, 1985-1998

Data for 1994 and beyond are projections. These projections have been made based on a curve-fitting algorithm and by using the least-square method. In essence, the algorithm calculates a trend line for the data using existing data points.

[In millions of dollars]

Industry	1985	1990	1991	1992	1993	1994	1995	1996	1997	1998	% change 1985 to 1998
Newspapers	1,430	1,886	1,538	1,667	1,262	1,330	1,721	1,762	1,803	1,844	22.48%
Periodicals	340	275	223	234	290	307	279	281	283	285	-19.03%
Book publishing	232	329	331	327	282	283	352	365	378	391	40.67%
Misc. publishing	110	179	166	190	139	193	-	-	-	-	-
Greeting cards	47	132	94	86	54	71	-	-	-	-	-

Source: 1997 *Manufacturing STATROM* [machine-readable data files]. MStat97. Editorial Code and Data, Inc., Detroit, Michigan, 1997. Primary source: *Economic Census for 1992* and earlier years. The *Economic Census* is conducted by the Bureau of the Census, U.S. Department of Commerce, Washington, DC 20233. *Note:* A dash (-) means that data for the item were not reported.

★ 16 ★

Industry Statistics

Capital Investment per Employee, 1985-1998

Data for 1994 and beyond are projections. These projections have been made based on a curve-fitting algorithm and by using the least-square method. In essence, the algorithm calculates a trend line for the data using existing data points. Misc. publishing includes the printing of atlases, maps, calendars, directories, race track programs, manuals, and sheet music.

[In dollars]

Industry	1985	1990	1991	1992	1993	1994	1995	1996	1997	1998	% change 1985 to 1998
Newspapers	3,479	4,253	3,590	3,999	3,077	3,242	4,019	4,101	4,183	4,264	18.41
Periodicals	3,546	2,385	2,016	2,017	2,472	2,634	2,262	2,237	2,214	2,191	-61.84
Book publishing	3,274	4,423	4,276	4,104	3,389	3,249	4,186	4,269	4,350	4,428	26.06
Misc. publishing	2,110	2,739	2,546	2,911	2,080	2,708	-	-	-	-	-
Greeting cards	2,337	5,366	3,937	3,759	2,423	3,060	-	-	-	-	-

Source: 1997 *Manufacturing STATROM* [machine-readable data files]. MStat97. Editorial Code and Data, Inc., Detroit, Michigan, 1997. Primary source: *Economic Census for 1992* and earlier years. The *Economic Census* is conducted by the Bureau of the Census, U.S. Department of Commerce, Washington, DC 20233. *Note:* A dash (-) means that data for the item were not reported.

★17★

United States: Publishing Summary, 1992

Industry	Establish-ments	Employ-ment	Shipments ($ mil.)	Cost of materials ($ mil.)	Payroll per employee ($)
2711 - Newspapers	8,679	417,000	34,124.3	6,874.0	25,195
2721 - Periodicals	4,699	116,200	22,033.9	6,200.9	35,065
2731 - Book publishing	2,644	79,600	16,731.1	5,337.7	33,614
2732 - Book printing	623	50,900	4,687.9	1,868.4	26,733
2741 - Miscellaneous publishing	3,390	65,400	10,977.1	2,476.7	26,497
2752 - Commercial printing, lithographic	29,344	439,900	43,588.2	18,723.1	27,387
2754 - Commercial printing, gravure	431	21,500	3,560.5	1,860.9	33,777
2759 - Commercial printing, nec	8,690	107,300	9,290.2	3,790.9	24,202
2761 - Manifold business forms	922	47,900	7,435.9	3,499.9	28,042
2771 - Greeting cards	173	22,800	4,195.6	743.0	25,662
2782 - Blankbooks and looseleaf binders	553	39,100	3,788.1	1,123.9	23,839
2789 - Bookbinding and related work	1,098	27,700	1,321.3	309.3	19,816
2791 - Typesetting	2,517	26,100	1,611.9	286.3	26,345
Total	63,763	1,461,400	163,346.0	53,095.0	27,246

Source: 1997 Manufacturing STATROM [machine-readable data files]. MStat97. Editorial Code and Data, Inc., Detroit, Michigan, 1997. Primary source: 1992 Economic Census.

★ 18 ★

Alabama: Publishing Summary, 1992

The publishing industry in Alabama represented **1.059**% of all publishing establishments in the U.S. in 1992. The state's population was **1.625**% of the U.S. population. Alabama's reported employment in this sector was **0.830**% of the U.S. sector's employment. And the state's reported shipments were **0.653**% of the U.S. sector's shipments.

Industry	Establish-ments	Employ-ment	Shipments ($ mil.)	Cost of materials ($ mil.)	Payroll per employee ($)
2711 - Newspapers	132	4,100	302.5	54.4	22,585
2721 - Periodicals	42	1,000	212.0	49.7	30,200
2731 - Book publishing	27	375	(D)	(D)	-
2741 - Miscellaneous publishing	25	400	30.3	8.2	19,000
2752 - Commercial printing, lithographic	332	4,100	395.1	187.2	22,463
2759 - Commercial printing, nec	101	1,200	96.3	51.4	21,250
2761 - Manifold business forms	9	200	30.4	11.4	29,500
2782 - Blankbooks and looseleaf binders	7	750	(D)	(D)	-
Total	675	12,125	1,066.6	362.3	23,082

Source: 1997 *Manufacturing STATROM* [machine-readable data files]. MStat97. Editorial Code and Data, Inc., Detroit, Michigan, 1997. Primary source: 1992 *Economic Census*.

★ 19 ★

State Summaries

Alaska: Publishing Summary, 1992

The publishing industry in Alaska represented **0.119**% of all publishing establishments in the U.S. in 1992. The state's population was **0.231**% of the U.S. population. Alaska's reported employment in this sector was **0.103**% of the U.S. sector's employment. And the state's reported shipments were **0.049**% of the U.S. sector's shipments.

Industry	Establish-ments	Employ-ment	Shipments ($ mil.)	Cost of materials ($ mil.)	Payroll per employee ($)
2711 - Newspapers	37	1,200	55.4	12.4	18,917
2752 - Commercial printing, lithographic	39	300	24.3	8.7	28,333
Total	76	1,500	79.7	21.1	20,800

Source: 1997 *Manufacturing STATROM* [machine-readable data files]. MStat97. Editorial Code and Data, Inc., Detroit, Michigan, 1997. Primary source: 1992 *Economic Census*.

★ 20 ★

State Summaries

Arizona: Publishing Summary, 1992

The publishing industry in Arizona represented **1.543%** of all publishing establishments in the U.S. in 1992. The state's population was **1.506%** of the U.S. population. Arizona's reported employment in this sector was **1.153%** of the U.S. sector's employment. And the state's reported shipments were **0.732%** of the U.S. sector's shipments.

Industry	Establish-ments	Employ-ment	Shipments ($ mil.)	Cost of materials ($ mil.)	Payroll per employee ($)
2711 - Newspapers	110	6,300	592.3	112.7	25,905
2721 - Periodicals	72	600	59.4	20.5	26,167
2731 - Book publishing	44	375	(D)	(D)	-
2741 - Miscellaneous publishing	41	750	(D)	(D)	-
2752 - Commercial printing, lithographic	515	5,000	392.4	162.9	23,600
2754 - Commercial printing, gravure	4	375	(D)	(D)	-
2759 - Commercial printing, nec	110	1,750	(D)	(D)	-
2761 - Manifold business forms	20	700	92.6	35.0	26,286
2782 - Blankbooks and looseleaf binders	12	500	40.1	13.0	23,800
2789 - Bookbinding and related work	14	300	11.7	2.0	20,000
2791 - Typesetting	42	200	7.6	1.5	18,000
Total	984	16,850	1,196.1	347.6	24,765

Source: 1997 *Manufacturing STATROM* [machine-readable data files]. MStat97. Editorial Code and Data, Inc., Detroit, Michigan, 1997. Primary source: 1992 *Economic Census.*

★ 21 ★

State Summaries

Arkansas: Publishing Summary, 1992

The publishing industry in Arkansas represented **0.645%** of all publishing establishments in the U.S. in 1992. The state's population was **0.943%** of the U.S. population. Arkansas's reported employment in this sector was **0.809%** of the U.S. sector's employment. And the state's reported shipments were **0.305%** of the U.S. sector's shipments.

Industry	Establish-ments	Employ-ment	Shipments ($ mil.)	Cost of materials ($ mil.)	Payroll per employee ($)
2711 - Newspapers	117	3,500	188.7	42.4	16,657
2721 - Periodicals	18	175	(D)	(D)	-
2731 - Book publishing	10	375	(D)	(D)	-
2741 - Miscellaneous publishing	18	175	(D)	(D)	-
2752 - Commercial printing, lithographic	175	2,500	217.3	105.0	23,680
2759 - Commercial printing, nec	63	750	(D)	(D)	-

[Continued]

★ 21 ★

Arkansas: Publishing Summary, 1992
[Continued]

Industry	Establish-ments	Employ-ment	Shipments ($ mil.)	Cost of materials ($ mil.)	Payroll per employee ($)
2761 - Manifold business forms	7	600	91.8	32.4	32,667
2771 - Greeting cards	3	3,750	(D)	(D)	-
Total	411	11,825	497.8	179.8	20,773

Source: 1997 *Manufacturing STATROM* [machine-readable data files]. MStat97. Editorial Code and Data, Inc., Detroit, Michigan, 1997. Primary source: 1992 *Economic Census*.

★ 22 ★

State Summaries

California: Publishing Summary, 1992

The publishing industry in California represented **12.848%** of all publishing establishments in the U.S. in 1992. The state's population was **12.129%** of the U.S. population. California's reported employment in this sector was **10.682%** of the U.S. sector's employment. And the state's reported shipments were **10.627%** of the U.S. sector's shipments.

Industry	Establish-ments	Employ-ment	Shipments ($ mil.)	Cost of materials ($ mil.)	Payroll per employee ($)
2711 - Newspapers	692	52,300	4,443.4	887.0	26,683
2721 - Periodicals	646	11,100	1,923.9	512.0	33,703
2731 - Book publishing	405	6,800	1,194.9	329.1	31,618
2732 - Book printing	79	2,800	284.3	92.8	31,107
2741 - Miscellaneous publishing	473	8,500	1,965.2	355.7	28,282
2752 - Commercial printing, lithographic	4,035	47,200	4,982.8	2,151.1	28,894
2754 - Commercial printing, gravure	54	700	142.2	46.5	34,857
2759 - Commercial printing, nec	1,130	11,100	851.3	316.2	23,667
2761 - Manifold business forms	101	4,300	639.7	316.0	29,814
2771 - Greeting cards	29	300	35.7	12.6	28,333
2782 - Blankbooks and looseleaf binders	65	5,300	595.8	212.2	24,113
2789 - Bookbinding and related work	150	3,000	120.7	18.1	19,067
2791 - Typesetting	333	2,700	178.7	28.2	26,370
Total	8,192	156,100	17,358.6	5,277.5	27,905

Source: 1997 *Manufacturing STATROM* [machine-readable data files]. MStat97. Editorial Code and Data, Inc., Detroit, Michigan, 1997. Primary source: 1992 *Economic Census*.

★ 23 ★

State Summaries

Colorado: Publishing Summary, 1992

The publishing industry in Colorado represented **1.989**% of all publishing establishments in the U.S. in 1992. The state's population was **1.364**% of the U.S. population. Colorado's reported employment in this sector was **1.692**% of the U.S. sector's employment. And the state's reported shipments were **1.358**% of the U.S. sector's shipments.

Industry	Establish-ments	Employ-ment	Shipments ($ mil.)	Cost of materials ($ mil.)	Payroll per employee ($)
2711 - Newspapers	150	6,800	482.0	116.7	23,397
2721 - Periodicals	99	1,100	140.9	37.1	31,000
2731 - Book publishing	60	1,300	137.0	17.3	27,154
2732 - Book printing	13	800	53.0	21.8	21,375
2741 - Miscellaneous publishing	79	3,400	533.4	92.8	28,206
2752 - Commercial printing, lithographic	601	6,000	564.6	258.9	26,017
2759 - Commercial printing, nec	161	1,200	84.2	35.5	21,583
2761 - Manifold business forms	9	400	51.3	28.7	30,000
2771 - Greeting cards	8	1,600	159.9	37.1	23,375
2782 - Blankbooks and looseleaf binders	9	1,750	(D)	(D)	-
2789 - Bookbinding and related work	23	175	(D)	(D)	-
2791 - Typesetting	56	200	12.1	3.0	21,000
Total	1,268	24,725	2,218.4	648.9	25,311

Source: 1997 *Manufacturing STATROM* [machine-readable data files]. MStat97. Editorial Code and Data, Inc., Detroit, Michigan, 1997. Primary source: 1992 *Economic Census*.

★ 24 ★

State Summaries

Connecticut: Publishing Summary, 1992

The publishing industry in Connecticut represented **1.603**% of all publishing establishments in the U.S. in 1992. The state's population was **1.289**% of the U.S. population. Connecticut's reported employment in this sector was **1.627**% of the U.S. sector's employment. And the state's reported shipments were **1.550**% of the U.S. sector's shipments.

Industry	Establish-ments	Employ-ment	Shipments ($ mil.)	Cost of materials ($ mil.)	Payroll per employee ($)
2711 - Newspapers	91	7,200	525.7	88.4	25,833
2721 - Periodicals	108	2,600	463.5	127.2	35,769
2731 - Book publishing	63	1,300	241.5	74.3	26,769
2741 - Miscellaneous publishing	60	1,100	112.6	27.8	27,545
2752 - Commercial printing, lithographic	472	7,100	737.0	307.4	31,099

[Continued]

★ 24 ★

Connecticut: Publishing Summary, 1992
[Continued]

Industry	Establish-ments	Employ-ment	Shipments ($ mil.)	Cost of materials ($ mil.)	Payroll per employee ($)
2754 - Commercial printing, gravure	8	300	21.0	10.3	26,667
2759 - Commercial printing, nec	132	2,100	225.3	78.8	29,000
2761 - Manifold business forms	13	600	74.3	38.4	27,667
2782 - Blankbooks and looseleaf binders	7	600	103.8	17.2	24,167
2789 - Bookbinding and related work	16	375	(D)	(D)	-
2791 - Typesetting	52	500	27.0	4.2	25,200
Total	1,022	23,775	2,531.7	774.0	28,953

Source: 1997 *Manufacturing STATROM* [machine-readable data files]. MStat97. Editorial Code and Data, Inc., Detroit, Michigan, 1997. Primary source: 1992 *Economic Census.*

★ 25 ★

State Summaries

Delaware: Publishing Summary, 1992

The publishing industry in Delaware represented **0.154**% of all publishing establishments in the U.S. in 1992. The state's population was **0.271**% of the U.S. population. Delaware's reported employment in this sector was **0.121**% of the U.S. sector's employment. And the state's reported shipments were **0.088**% of the U.S. sector's shipments.

Industry	Establish-ments	Employ-ment	Shipments ($ mil.)	Cost of materials ($ mil.)	Payroll per employee ($)
2711 - Newspapers	18	900	94.8	19.0	25,111
2752 - Commercial printing, lithographic	66	700	48.2	18.2	26,000
2759 - Commercial printing, nec	14	175	(D)	(D)	-
Total	98	1,775	143.0	37.2	25,500

Source: 1997 *Manufacturing STATROM* [machine-readable data files]. MStat97. Editorial Code and Data, Inc., Detroit, Michigan, 1997. Primary source: 1992 *Economic Census.*

District of Columbia: Publishing Summary, 1992

The publishing industry in District of Columbia represented **0.417**% of all publishing establishments in the U.S. in 1992. The state's population was **0.230**% of the U.S. population. District of Columbia's reported employment in this sector was **0.700**% of the U.S. sector's employment. And the state's reported shipments were **0.678**% of the U.S. sector's shipments.

Industry	Establish-ments	Employ-ment	Shipments ($ mil.)	Cost of materials ($ mil.)	Payroll per employee ($)
2711 - Newspapers	33	3,750	(D)	(D)	-
2721 - Periodicals	84	4,600	956.0	246.3	42,304
2741 - Miscellaneous publishing	26	300	33.4	5.7	38,333
2752 - Commercial printing, lithographic	80	1,100	97.8	42.4	29,000
2759 - Commercial printing, nec	25	300	19.9	6.9	24,000
2791 - Typesetting	18	175	(D)	(D)	-
Total	266	10,225	1,107.1	301.3	38,921

Source: 1997 *Manufacturing STATROM* [machine-readable data files]. MStat97. Editorial Code and Data, Inc., Detroit, Michigan, 1997. Primary source: 1992 *Economic Census.*

Florida: Publishing Summary, 1992

The publishing industry in Florida represented **5.243**% of all publishing establishments in the U.S. in 1992. The state's population was **5.300**% of the U.S. population. Florida's reported employment in this sector was **3.734**% of the U.S. sector's employment. And the state's reported shipments were **3.064**% of the U.S. sector's shipments.

Industry	Establish-ments	Employ-ment	Shipments ($ mil.)	Cost of materials ($ mil.)	Payroll per employee ($)
2711 - Newspapers	329	22,800	2,189.3	431.8	26,535
2721 - Periodicals	281	3,400	368.7	117.3	25,618
2731 - Book publishing	90	1,400	226.2	42.5	30,214
2732 - Book printing	26	500	35.8	14.0	24,600
2741 - Miscellaneous publishing	199	2,900	225.6	54.5	20,345
2752 - Commercial printing, lithographic	1,730	16,300	1,367.7	620.0	23,405
2754 - Commercial printing, gravure	21	100	8.4	3.8	23,000
2759 - Commercial printing, nec	439	3,600	255.7	106.6	20,611
2761 - Manifold business forms	37	1,200	170.2	94.1	28,250
2782 - Blankbooks and looseleaf binders	28	1,300	120.0	25.2	22,538
2789 - Bookbinding and related work	34	375	(D)	(D)	-

[Continued]

★ 27 ★

Florida: Publishing Summary, 1992
[Continued]

Industry	Establish-ments	Employ-ment	Shipments ($ mil.)	Cost of materials ($ mil.)	Payroll per employee ($)
2791 - Typesetting	129	700	36.8	7.3	21,857
Total	3,343	54,575	5,004.4	1,517.1	24,764

Source: 1997 *Manufacturing STATROM* [machine-readable data files]. MStat97. Editorial Code and Data, Inc., Detroit, Michigan, 1997. Primary source: 1992 *Economic Census*.

★ 28 ★

State Summaries

Georgia: Publishing Summary, 1992

The publishing industry in Georgia represented **2.570%** of all publishing establishments in the U.S. in 1992. The state's population was **2.653%** of the U.S. population. Georgia's reported employment in this sector was **2.330%** of the U.S. sector's employment. And the state's reported shipments were **1.864%** of the U.S. sector's shipments.

Industry	Establish-ments	Employ-ment	Shipments ($ mil.)	Cost of materials ($ mil.)	Payroll per employee ($)
2711 - Newspapers	233	10,200	695.6	144.6	22,961
2721 - Periodicals	108	2,400	319.5	91.4	29,833
2731 - Book publishing	30	300	32.2	7.9	25,000
2732 - Book printing	14	300	35.3	15.7	32,000
2741 - Miscellaneous publishing	65	375	(D)	(D)	-
2752 - Commercial printing, lithographic	756	11,400	1,145.7	522.6	27,342
2754 - Commercial printing, gravure	18	900	170.7	72.8	36,111
2759 - Commercial printing, nec	244	2,400	239.6	106.5	24,792
2761 - Manifold business forms	36	1,400	200.4	90.5	25,286
2771 - Greeting cards	1	375	(D)	(D)	-
2782 - Blankbooks and looseleaf binders	20	800	64.1	11.9	19,625
2789 - Bookbinding and related work	51	2,400	94.5	32.4	15,625
2791 - Typesetting	63	800	46.7	5.6	25,375
Total	1,639	34,050	3,044.3	1,101.9	25,090

Source: 1997 *Manufacturing STATROM* [machine-readable data files]. MStat97. Editorial Code and Data, Inc., Detroit, Michigan, 1997. Primary source: 1992 *Economic Census*.

Hawaii: Publishing Summary, 1992

The publishing industry in Hawaii represented **0.263**% of all publishing establishments in the U.S. in 1992. The state's population was **0.456**% of the U.S. population. Hawaii's reported employment in this sector was **0.212**% of the U.S. sector's employment. And the state's reported shipments were **0.265**% of the U.S. sector's shipments.

Industry	Establish-ments	Employ-ment	Shipments ($ mil.)	Cost of materials ($ mil.)	Payroll per employee ($)
2711 - Newspapers	23	1,500	261.4	30.3	33,067
2721 - Periodicals	28	200	28.1	7.9	31,000
2741 - Miscellaneous publishing	12	200	41.7	12.0	44,000
2752 - Commercial printing, lithographic	78	1,000	86.2	31.6	29,500
2759 - Commercial printing, nec	27	200	15.2	6.1	22,000
Total	168	3,100	432.6	87.9	31,774

Source: 1997 *Manufacturing STATROM* [machine-readable data files]. MStat97. Editorial Code and Data, Inc., Detroit, Michigan, 1997. Primary source: 1992 *Economic Census*.

Idaho: Publishing Summary, 1992

The publishing industry in Idaho represented **0.369**% of all publishing establishments in the U.S. in 1992. The state's population was **0.419**% of the U.S. population. Idaho's reported employment in this sector was **0.291**% of the U.S. sector's employment. And the state's reported shipments were **0.153**% of the U.S. sector's shipments.

Industry	Establish-ments	Employ-ment	Shipments ($ mil.)	Cost of materials ($ mil.)	Payroll per employee ($)
2711 - Newspapers	60	1,700	97.3	17.1	17,471
2721 - Periodicals	21	300	29.8	8.2	25,000
2741 - Miscellaneous publishing	20	200	14.1	2.7	17,500
2752 - Commercial printing, lithographic	111	1,700	108.5	43.4	17,235
2759 - Commercial printing, nec	22	175	(D)	(D)	-
2761 - Manifold business forms	1	175	(D)	(D)	-
Total	235	4,250	249.7	71.4	17,949

Source: 1997 *Manufacturing STATROM* [machine-readable data files]. MStat97. Editorial Code and Data, Inc., Detroit, Michigan, 1997. Primary source: 1992 *Economic Census*.

Illinois: Publishing Summary, 1992

The publishing industry in Illinois represented **5.557%** of all publishing establishments in the U.S. in 1992. The state's population was **4.570%** of the U.S. population. Illinois's reported employment in this sector was **6.973%** of the U.S. sector's employment. And the state's reported shipments were **7.148%** of the U.S. sector's shipments.

Industry	Establish-ments	Employ-ment	Shipments ($ mil.)	Cost of materials ($ mil.)	Payroll per employee ($)
2711 - Newspapers	430	19,700	1,788.3	344.9	25,010
2721 - Periodicals	249	11,900	1,451.1	414.8	28,613
2731 - Book publishing	157	5,500	1,028.2	319.3	36,473
2732 - Book printing	49	2,000	186.9	76.5	30,700
2741 - Miscellaneous publishing	136	3,500	741.5	352.2	31,400
2752 - Commercial printing, lithographic	1,615	34,400	3,948.2	1,751.4	30,968
2754 - Commercial printing, gravure	25	3,600	504.8	230.3	34,028
2759 - Commercial printing, nec	519	7,600	660.4	250.8	26,684
2761 - Manifold business forms	57	3,100	519.2	279.5	30,065
2771 - Greeting cards	9	1,500	157.7	43.5	23,467
2782 - Blankbooks and looseleaf binders	39	3,200	311.3	144.3	25,719
2789 - Bookbinding and related work	71	3,300	181.6	50.4	18,970
2791 - Typesetting	187	2,600	196.5	37.7	31,731
Total	3,543	101,900	11,675.7	4,295.6	28,965

Source: 1997 *Manufacturing STATROM* [machine-readable data files]. MStat97. Editorial Code and Data, Inc., Detroit, Michigan, 1997. Primary source: 1992 *Economic Census.*

Indiana: Publishing Summary, 1992

The publishing industry in Indiana represented **1.989%** of all publishing establishments in the U.S. in 1992. The state's population was **2.225%** of the U.S. population. Indiana's reported employment in this sector was **2.422%** of the U.S. sector's employment. And the state's reported shipments were **1.447%** of the U.S. sector's shipments.

Industry	Establish-ments	Employ-ment	Shipments ($ mil.)	Cost of materials ($ mil.)	Payroll per employee ($)
2711 - Newspapers	208	10,300	621.1	118.9	21,078
2721 - Periodicals	65	1,100	131.3	40.7	26,545
2731 - Book publishing	36	750	(D)	(D)	-
2732 - Book printing	12	3,750	(D)	(D)	-

[Continued]

★ 32 ★

Indiana: Publishing Summary, 1992
[Continued]

Industry	Establish-ments	Employ-ment	Shipments ($ mil.)	Cost of materials ($ mil.)	Payroll per employee ($)
2741 - Miscellaneous publishing	44	600	54.8	13.0	20,833
2752 - Commercial printing, lithographic	607	10,300	1,100.7	429.9	26,175
2754 - Commercial printing, gravure	10	1,750	(D)	(D)	-
2759 - Commercial printing, nec	172	1,750	(D)	(D)	-
2761 - Manifold business forms	18	1,500	310.9	165.6	30,467
2771 - Greeting cards	3	750	(D)	(D)	-
2782 - Blankbooks and looseleaf binders	12	800	79.0	24.2	29,250
2789 - Bookbinding and related work	29	1,300	65.1	20.4	18,615
2791 - Typesetting	52	750	(D)	(D)	-
Total	1,268	35,400	2,362.9	812.7	24,004

Source: 1997 Manufacturing STATROM [machine-readable data files]. MStat97. Editorial Code and Data, Inc., Detroit, Michigan, 1997. Primary source: 1992 Economic Census.

★ 33 ★

State Summaries

Iowa: Publishing Summary, 1992

The publishing industry in Iowa represented **1.266**% of all publishing establishments in the U.S. in 1992. The state's population was **1.105**% of the U.S. population. Iowa's reported employment in this sector was **1.404**% of the U.S. sector's employment. And the state's reported shipments were **0.751**% of the U.S. sector's shipments.

Industry	Establish-ments	Employ-ment	Shipments ($ mil.)	Cost of materials ($ mil.)	Payroll per employee ($)
2711 - Newspapers	241	6,100	375.9	76.2	17,262
2721 - Periodicals	40	1,750	(D)	(D)	-
2731 - Book publishing	18	750	(D)	(D)	-
2732 - Book printing	10	1,750	(D)	(D)	-
2741 - Miscellaneous publishing	51	1,000	73.2	15.5	17,400
2752 - Commercial printing, lithographic	315	5,700	521.5	223.5	23,175
2754 - Commercial printing, gravure	6	750	(D)	(D)	-
2759 - Commercial printing, nec	84	750	(D)	(D)	-
2761 - Manifold business forms	17	1,400	240.4	108.7	25,857
2782 - Blankbooks and looseleaf binders	3	175	(D)	(D)	-
2791 - Typesetting	22	400	16.4	2.3	20,500
Total	807	20,525	1,227.4	426.2	20,493

Source: 1997 Manufacturing STATROM [machine-readable data files]. MStat97. Editorial Code and Data, Inc., Detroit, Michigan, 1997. Primary source: 1992 Economic Census.

★ 34 ★

State Summaries

Kansas: Publishing Summary, 1992

The publishing industry in Kansas represented **1.173%** of all publishing establishments in the U.S. in 1992. The state's population was **0.991%** of the U.S. population. Kansas's reported employment in this sector was **1.375%** of the U.S. sector's employment. And the state's reported shipments were **1.097%** of the U.S. sector's shipments.

Industry	Establish-ments	Employ-ment	Shipments ($ mil.)	Cost of materials ($ mil.)	Payroll per employee ($)
2711 - Newspapers	184	4,100	220.7	37.7	18,585
2721 - Periodicals	35	500	111.2	29.5	29,600
2731 - Book publishing	25	100	9.0	3.3	19,000
2732 - Book printing	3	1,750	(D)	(D)	-
2741 - Miscellaneous publishing	43	2,000	443.3	57.1	25,500
2752 - Commercial printing, lithographic	321	4,800	667.4	314.9	25,708
2759 - Commercial printing, nec	76	1,900	166.3	66.1	23,368
2761 - Manifold business forms	18	1,700	173.5	77.8	25,588
2771 - Greeting cards	3	1,750	(D)	(D)	-
2782 - Blankbooks and looseleaf binders	7	750	(D)	(D)	-
2789 - Bookbinding and related work	10	375	(D)	(D)	-
2791 - Typesetting	23	375	(D)	(D)	-
Total	748	20,100	1,791.4	586.4	23,523

Source: 1997 *Manufacturing STATROM* [machine-readable data files]. MStat97. Editorial Code and Data, Inc., Detroit, Michigan, 1997. Primary source: 1992 *Economic Census.*

★ 35 ★

State Summaries

Kentucky: Publishing Summary, 1992

The publishing industry in Kentucky represented **1.093%** of all publishing establishments in the U.S. in 1992. The state's population was **1.475%** of the U.S. population. Kentucky's reported employment in this sector was **1.492%** of the U.S. sector's employment. And the state's reported shipments were **0.900%** of the U.S. sector's shipments.

Industry	Establish-ments	Employ-ment	Shipments ($ mil.)	Cost of materials ($ mil.)	Payroll per employee ($)
2711 - Newspapers	156	4,400	320.9	62.7	22,682
2721 - Periodicals	45	375	(D)	(D)	-
2731 - Book publishing	20	900	66.9	18.7	11,889
2732 - Book printing	9	1,400	128.7	49.0	28,714
2741 - Miscellaneous publishing	33	800	122.6	13.2	23,875

[Continued]

★ 35 ★

Kentucky: Publishing Summary, 1992
[Continued]

Industry	Establish-ments	Employ-ment	Shipments ($ mil.)	Cost of materials ($ mil.)	Payroll per employee ($)
2752 - Commercial printing, lithographic	286	7,000	725.3	296.1	26,129
2754 - Commercial printing, gravure	5	375	(D)	(D)	-
2759 - Commercial printing, nec	104	1,750	(D)	(D)	-
2761 - Manifold business forms	8	700	105.1	51.1	21,714
2771 - Greeting cards	7	3,750	(D)	(D)	-
2782 - Blankbooks and looseleaf binders	5	175	(D)	(D)	-
2791 - Typesetting	19	175	(D)	(D)	-
Total	697	21,800	1,469.5	490.8	24,204

Source: 1997 *Manufacturing STATROM* [machine-readable data files]. MStat97. Editorial Code and Data, Inc., Detroit, Michigan, 1997. Primary source: 1992 *Economic Census.*

★ 36 ★

State Summaries

Louisiana: Publishing Summary, 1992

The publishing industry in Louisiana represented **0.933**% of all publishing establishments in the U.S. in 1992. The state's population was **1.685**% of the U.S. population. Louisiana's reported employment in this sector was **0.616**% of the U.S. sector's employment. And the state's reported shipments were **0.432**% of the U.S. sector's shipments.

Industry	Establish-ments	Employ-ment	Shipments ($ mil.)	Cost of materials ($ mil.)	Payroll per employee ($)
2711 - Newspapers	107	4,300	342.5	81.4	23,302
2721 - Periodicals	36	200	15.3	5.0	21,500
2731 - Book publishing	15	100	8.4	2.4	23,000
2741 - Miscellaneous publishing	31	200	15.5	4.0	17,500
2752 - Commercial printing, lithographic	273	2,800	196.3	90.0	20,214
2759 - Commercial printing, nec	96	700	59.4	31.1	20,429
2761 - Manifold business forms	12	300	37.0	19.6	21,667
2782 - Blankbooks and looseleaf binders	7	300	25.6	4.1	25,000
2791 - Typesetting	18	100	6.0	1.2	22,000
Total	595	9,000	706.0	238.8	21,933

Source: 1997 *Manufacturing STATROM* [machine-readable data files]. MStat97. Editorial Code and Data, Inc., Detroit, Michigan, 1997. Primary source: 1992 *Economic Census.*

★ 37 ★

State Summaries

Maine: Publishing Summary, 1992

The publishing industry in Maine represented **0.453%** of all publishing establishments in the U.S. in 1992. The state's population was **0.485%** of the U.S. population. Maine's reported employment in this sector was **0.325%** of the U.S. sector's employment. And the state's reported shipments were **0.202%** of the U.S. sector's shipments.

Industry	Establish-ments	Employ-ment	Shipments ($ mil.)	Cost of materials ($ mil.)	Payroll per employee ($)
2711 - Newspapers	68	2,400	140.9	25.7	23,417
2721 - Periodicals	23	200	24.3	7.9	34,500
2731 - Book publishing	14	100	15.9	3.7	32,000
2741 - Miscellaneous publishing	19	200	18.7	2.5	24,500
2752 - Commercial printing, lithographic	124	1,500	130.3	65.1	23,400
2754 - Commercial printing, gravure	2	175	(D)	(D)	-
2759 - Commercial printing, nec	39	175	(D)	(D)	-
Total	289	4,750	330.1	104.9	24,159

Source: 1997 *Manufacturing STATROM* [machine-readable data files]. MStat97. Editorial Code and Data, Inc., Detroit, Michigan, 1997. Primary source: 1992 *Economic Census*.

★ 38 ★

State Summaries

Maryland: Publishing Summary, 1992

The publishing industry in Maryland represented **1.835%** of all publishing establishments in the U.S. in 1992. The state's population was **1.929%** of the U.S. population. Maryland's reported employment in this sector was **1.817%** of the U.S. sector's employment. And the state's reported shipments were **1.546%** of the U.S. sector's shipments.

Industry	Establish-ments	Employ-ment	Shipments ($ mil.)	Cost of materials ($ mil.)	Payroll per employee ($)
2711 - Newspapers	86	4,900	486.6	81.4	30,265
2721 - Periodicals	103	1,600	222.1	58.9	31,688
2731 - Book publishing	64	800	99.3	33.8	29,375
2732 - Book printing	25	1,700	171.1	92.4	31,235
2741 - Miscellaneous publishing	77	1,700	215.3	41.8	30,176
2752 - Commercial printing, lithographic	539	10,300	1,062.1	463.7	31,340
2754 - Commercial printing, gravure	15	375	(D)	(D)	-
2759 - Commercial printing, nec	138	1,750	(D)	(D)	-
2761 - Manifold business forms	9	700	142.2	61.0	26,714
2771 - Greeting cards	5	175	(D)	(D)	-

[Continued]

★ 38 ★

Maryland: Publishing Summary, 1992
[Continued]

Industry	Establish-ments	Employ-ment	Shipments ($ mil.)	Cost of materials ($ mil.)	Payroll per employee ($)
2782 - Blankbooks and looseleaf binders	12	900	73.2	21.5	22,111
2789 - Bookbinding and related work	26	900	52.9	12.7	24,111
2791 - Typesetting	71	750	(D)	(D)	-
Total	1,170	26,550	2,524.8	867.2	30,213

Source: 1997 *Manufacturing STATROM* [machine-readable data files]. MStat97. Editorial Code and Data, Inc., Detroit, Michigan, 1997. Primary source: 1992 *Economic Census.*

★ 39 ★

State Summaries

Massachusetts: Publishing Summary, 1992

The publishing industry in Massachusetts represented **2.732%** of all publishing establishments in the U.S. in 1992. The state's population was **2.357%** of the U.S. population. Massachusetts's reported employment in this sector was **3.350%** of the U.S. sector's employment. And the state's reported shipments were **3.601%** of the U.S. sector's shipments.

Industry	Establish-ments	Employ-ment	Shipments ($ mil.)	Cost of materials ($ mil.)	Payroll per employee ($)
2711 - Newspapers	188	14,800	1,191.2	211.4	29,797
2721 - Periodicals	183	3,600	634.4	178.6	36,417
2731 - Book publishing	103	4,800	1,133.4	416.1	35,958
2732 - Book printing	29	3,100	285.8	114.6	29,903
2741 - Miscellaneous publishing	96	2,500	1,018.1	248.5	30,560
2752 - Commercial printing, lithographic	760	12,000	1,190.0	500.9	29,708
2759 - Commercial printing, nec	231	3,750	(D)	(D)	-
2761 - Manifold business forms	15	800	122.8	38.6	26,625
2771 - Greeting cards	9	300	39.7	8.8	22,667
2782 - Blankbooks and looseleaf binders	13	1,600	170.5	56.6	23,312
2789 - Bookbinding and related work	33	1,000	48.8	9.5	21,200
2791 - Typesetting	82	700	46.8	9.7	26,714
Total	1,742	48,950	5,881.5	1,793.3	30,434

Source: 1997 *Manufacturing STATROM* [machine-readable data files]. MStat97. Editorial Code and Data, Inc., Detroit, Michigan, 1997. Primary source: 1992 *Economic Census.*

Michigan: Publishing Summary, 1992

The publishing industry in Michigan represented **3.228%** of all publishing establishments in the U.S. in 1992. The state's population was **3.708%** of the U.S. population. Michigan's reported employment in this sector was **3.098%** of the U.S. sector's employment. And the state's reported shipments were **3.183%** of the U.S. sector's shipments.

Industry	Establish- ments	Employ- ment	Shipments ($ mil.)	Cost of materials ($ mil.)	Payroll per employee ($)
2711 - Newspapers	230	14,100	1,025.4	235.0	25,638
2721 - Periodicals	106	1,900	181.6	47.2	25,947
2731 - Book publishing	58	1,500	295.3	77.0	26,667
2732 - Book printing	26	2,900	242.1	90.9	23,517
2741 - Miscellaneous publishing	100	3,100	1,112.8	121.6	30,710
2752 - Commercial printing, lithographic	1,033	14,400	1,599.2	705.9	27,181
2754 - Commercial printing, gravure	14	200	23.7	15.7	19,500
2759 - Commercial printing, nec	312	3,500	335.5	153.9	24,943
2761 - Manifold business forms	33	1,500	204.3	98.2	31,600
2782 - Blankbooks and looseleaf binders	18	1,000	121.2	31.7	27,700
2789 - Bookbinding and related work	25	375	(D)	(D)	-
2791 - Typesetting	103	800	57.4	11.2	26,250
Total	2,058	45,275	5,198.5	1,588.3	26,568

Source: 1997 *Manufacturing STATROM* [machine-readable data files]. MStat97. Editorial Code and Data, Inc., Detroit, Michigan, 1997. Primary source: 1992 *Economic Census.*

Minnesota: Publishing Summary, 1992

The publishing industry in Minnesota represented **2.326%** of all publishing establishments in the U.S. in 1992. The state's population was **1.760%** of the U.S. population. Minnesota's reported employment in this sector was **3.093%** of the U.S. sector's employment. And the state's reported shipments were **2.628%** of the U.S. sector's shipments.

Industry	Establish- ments	Employ- ment	Shipments ($ mil.)	Cost of materials ($ mil.)	Payroll per employee ($)
2711 - Newspapers	287	8,500	596.6	112.8	24,600
2721 - Periodicals	109	1,600	294.2	61.1	25,625
2731 - Book publishing	48	6,200	833.9	318.0	29,742
2732 - Book printing	8	300	21.5	5.7	24,000
2741 - Miscellaneous publishing	75	1,000	167.8	39.0	26,100

[Continued]

★ 41 ★

Minnesota: Publishing Summary, 1992
[Continued]

Industry	Establish- ments	Employ- ment	Shipments ($ mil.)	Cost of materials ($ mil.)	Payroll per employee ($)
2752 - Commercial printing, lithographic	675	20,000	2,060.3	868.7	28,150
2759 - Commercial printing, nec	175	3,750	(D)	(D)	-
2761 - Manifold business forms	19	1,200	154.2	67.9	31,500
2782 - Blankbooks and looseleaf binders	14	1,000	99.7	22.2	25,500
2789 - Bookbinding and related work	30	750	(D)	(D)	-
2791 - Typesetting	43	900	65.2	12.1	31,111
Total	1,483	45,200	4,293.4	1,507.5	27,570

Source: 1997 *Manufacturing STATROM* [machine-readable data files]. MStat97. Editorial Code and Data, Inc., Detroit, Michigan, 1997. Primary source: 1992 *Economic Census.*

★ 42 ★

State Summaries

Mississippi: Publishing Summary, 1992

The publishing industry in Mississippi represented **0.516**% of all publishing establishments in the U.S. in 1992. The state's population was **1.027**% of the U.S. population. Mississippi's reported employment in this sector was **0.431**% of the U.S. sector's employment. And the state's reported shipments were **0.209**% of the U.S. sector's shipments.

Industry	Establish- ments	Employ- ment	Shipments ($ mil.)	Cost of materials ($ mil.)	Payroll per employee ($)
2711 - Newspapers	105	2,600	165.7	37.5	18,269
2752 - Commercial printing, lithographic	162	2,000	156.1	68.7	23,300
2754 - Commercial printing, gravure	3	750	(D)	(D)	-
2759 - Commercial printing, nec	47	375	(D)	(D)	-
2761 - Manifold business forms	7	200	19.9	8.6	25,500
2782 - Blankbooks and looseleaf binders	5	375	(D)	(D)	-
Total	329	6,300	341.7	114.8	20,667

Source: 1997 *Manufacturing STATROM* [machine-readable data files]. MStat97. Editorial Code and Data, Inc., Detroit, Michigan, 1997. Primary source: 1992 *Economic Census.*

★ 43 ★

State Summaries

Missouri: Publishing Summary, 1992

The publishing industry in Missouri represented **2.381**% of all publishing establishments in the U.S. in 1992. The state's population was **2.041**% of the U.S. population. Missouri's reported employment in this sector was **2.672**% of the U.S. sector's employment. And the state's reported shipments were **1.416**% of the U.S. sector's shipments.

Industry	Establish-ments	Employ-ment	Shipments ($ mil.)	Cost of materials ($ mil.)	Payroll per employee ($)
2711 - Newspapers	292	8,200	665.3	144.4	23,207
2721 - Periodicals	77	2,400	176.6	46.3	23,833
2731 - Book publishing	53	1,750	(D)	(D)	-
2732 - Book printing	12	1,750	(D)	(D)	-
2741 - Miscellaneous publishing	46	750	(D)	(D)	-
2752 - Commercial printing, lithographic	666	10,600	1,033.7	453.7	28,358
2754 - Commercial printing, gravure	7	375	(D)	(D)	-
2759 - Commercial printing, nec	211	1,750	(D)	(D)	-
2761 - Manifold business forms	27	1,400	289.3	114.7	26,214
2771 - Greeting cards	6	7,500	(D)	(D)	-
2782 - Blankbooks and looseleaf binders	20	1,300	101.1	29.7	22,077
2789 - Bookbinding and related work	34	375	(D)	(D)	-
2791 - Typesetting	67	900	47.7	12.2	25,667
Total	1,518	39,050	2,313.7	801.0	25,669

Source: 1997 *Manufacturing STATROM* [machine-readable data files]. MStat97. Editorial Code and Data, Inc., Detroit, Michigan, 1997. Primary source: 1992 *Economic Census*.

★ 44 ★

State Summaries

Montana: Publishing Summary, 1992

The publishing industry in Montana represented **0.263**% of all publishing establishments in the U.S. in 1992. The state's population was **0.324**% of the U.S. population. Montana's reported employment in this sector was **0.157**% of the U.S. sector's employment. And the state's reported shipments were **0.090**% of the U.S. sector's shipments.

Industry	Establish-ments	Employ-ment	Shipments ($ mil.)	Cost of materials ($ mil.)	Payroll per employee ($)
2711 - Newspapers	76	1,500	94.9	16.2	17,467
2741 - Miscellaneous publishing	13	100	7.7	1.6	16,000
2752 - Commercial printing, lithographic	79	700	43.6	16.4	18,286
Total	168	2,300	146.2	34.2	17,652

Source: 1997 *Manufacturing STATROM* [machine-readable data files]. MStat97. Editorial Code and Data, Inc., Detroit, Michigan, 1997. Primary source: 1992 *Economic Census*.

★ 45 ★

State Summaries

Nebraska: Publishing Summary, 1992

The publishing industry in Nebraska represented **0.720%** of all publishing establishments in the U.S. in 1992. The state's population was **0.631%** of the U.S. population. Nebraska's reported employment in this sector was **0.662%** of the U.S. sector's employment. And the state's reported shipments were **0.426%** of the U.S. sector's shipments.

Industry	Establish-ments	Employ-ment	Shipments ($ mil.)	Cost of materials ($ mil.)	Payroll per employee ($)
2711 - Newspapers	139	3,200	194.2	39.3	17,687
2721 - Periodicals	26	400	49.4	14.7	27,500
2731 - Book publishing	11	175	(D)	(D)	-
2732 - Book printing	4	175	(D)	(D)	-
2741 - Miscellaneous publishing	13	375	(D)	(D)	-
2752 - Commercial printing, lithographic	194	3,400	301.1	146.0	24,441
2759 - Commercial printing, nec	58	1,400	151.6	77.6	24,929
2761 - Manifold business forms	6	375	(D)	(D)	-
2789 - Bookbinding and related work	8	175	(D)	(D)	-
Total	459	9,675	696.3	277.6	22,095

Source: 1997 *Manufacturing STATROM* [machine-readable data files]. MStat97. Editorial Code and Data, Inc., Detroit, Michigan, 1997. Primary source: 1992 *Economic Census.*

★ 46 ★

State Summaries

Nevada: Publishing Summary, 1992

The publishing industry in Nevada represented **0.336%** of all publishing establishments in the U.S. in 1992. The state's population was **0.521%** of the U.S. population. Nevada's reported employment in this sector was **0.257%** of the U.S. sector's employment. And the state's reported shipments were **0.205%** of the U.S. sector's shipments.

Industry	Establish-ments	Employ-ment	Shipments ($ mil.)	Cost of materials ($ mil.)	Payroll per employee ($)
2711 - Newspapers	37	1,600	199.3	35.7	23,125
2721 - Periodicals	18	100	13.5	3.4	31,000
2752 - Commercial printing, lithographic	103	1,100	96.3	38.8	24,636
2754 - Commercial printing, gravure	7	375	(D)	(D)	-
2759 - Commercial printing, nec	41	375	(D)	(D)	-
2761 - Manifold business forms	8	200	25.8	13.5	18,000
Total	214	3,750	334.9	91.4	23,600

Source: 1997 *Manufacturing STATROM* [machine-readable data files]. MStat97. Editorial Code and Data, Inc., Detroit, Michigan, 1997. Primary source: 1992 *Economic Census.*

State Summaries

New Hampshire: Publishing Summary, 1992

The publishing industry in New Hampshire represented **0.560%** of all publishing establishments in the U.S. in 1992. The state's population was **0.437%** of the U.S. population. New Hampshire's reported employment in this sector was **0.500%** of the U.S. sector's employment. And the state's reported shipments were **0.361%** of the U.S. sector's shipments.

Industry	Establish- ments	Employ- ment	Shipments ($ mil.)	Cost of materials ($ mil.)	Payroll per employee ($)
2711 - Newspapers	55	2,100	118.4	20.5	21,143
2721 - Periodicals	33	600	131.9	27.8	34,000
2731 - Book publishing	11	200	21.1	4.2	22,000
2741 - Miscellaneous publishing	23	200	14.9	4.1	18,000
2752 - Commercial printing, lithographic	151	1,800	154.9	66.8	25,111
2759 - Commercial printing, nec	44	600	57.4	22.5	23,833
2761 - Manifold business forms	6	700	90.7	32.4	30,143
2771 - Greeting cards	6	175	(D)	(D)	-
2782 - Blankbooks and looseleaf binders	3	375	(D)	(D)	-
2789 - Bookbinding and related work	9	375	(D)	(D)	-
2791 - Typesetting	16	175	(D)	(D)	-
Total	357	7,300	589.3	178.3	24,742

Source: 1997 *Manufacturing STATROM* [machine-readable data files]. MStat97. Editorial Code and Data, Inc., Detroit, Michigan, 1997. Primary source: 1992 *Economic Census.*

State Summaries

New Jersey: Publishing Summary, 1992

The publishing industry in New Jersey represented **3.720%** of all publishing establishments in the U.S. in 1992. The state's population was **3.061%** of the U.S. population. New Jersey's reported employment in this sector was **3.757%** of the U.S. sector's employment. And the state's reported shipments were **3.965%** of the U.S. sector's shipments.

Industry	Establish- ments	Employ- ment	Shipments ($ mil.)	Cost of materials ($ mil.)	Payroll per employee ($)
2711 - Newspapers	186	11,900	1,134.6	261.9	27,681
2721 - Periodicals	195	4,000	683.4	182.5	38,550
2731 - Book publishing	116	6,300	1,350.9	325.0	32,825
2732 - Book printing	24	700	82.5	19.0	41,000
2741 - Miscellaneous publishing	118	2,500	255.5	54.9	34,680
2752 - Commercial printing, lithographic	1,091	17,500	1,916.8	818.0	32,331

[Continued]

★ 48 ★

New Jersey: Publishing Summary, 1992
[Continued]

Industry	Establish-ments	Employ-ment	Shipments ($ mil.)	Cost of materials ($ mil.)	Payroll per employee ($)
2754 - Commercial printing, gravure	24	400	44.6	13.6	32,000
2759 - Commercial printing, nec	384	4,900	453.0	179.8	27,714
2761 - Manifold business forms	29	1,200	201.8	103.7	31,917
2771 - Greeting cards	5	400	42.4	9.5	26,250
2782 - Blankbooks and looseleaf binders	15	1,400	101.3	23.6	26,786
2789 - Bookbinding and related work	65	2,300	124.8	27.6	24,130
2791 - Typesetting	120	1,400	85.3	14.5	28,571
Total	2,372	54,900	6,476.9	2,033.6	31,002

Source: 1997 *Manufacturing STATROM* [machine-readable data files]. MStat97. Editorial Code and Data, Inc., Detroit, Michigan, 1997. Primary source: 1992 *Economic Census*.

★ 49 ★

State Summaries

New Mexico: Publishing Summary, 1992

The publishing industry in New Mexico represented **0.450**% of all publishing establishments in the U.S. in 1992. The state's population was **0.621**% of the U.S. population. New Mexico's reported employment in this sector was **0.269**% of the U.S. sector's employment. And the state's reported shipments were **0.139**% of the U.S. sector's shipments.

Industry	Establish-ments	Employ-ment	Shipments ($ mil.)	Cost of materials ($ mil.)	Payroll per employee ($)
2711 - Newspapers	57	2,100	140.3	26.0	19,000
2721 - Periodicals	28	100	11.9	4.0	31,000
2731 - Book publishing	24	175	(D)	(D)	-
2741 - Miscellaneous publishing	14	100	4.1	1.0	13,000
2752 - Commercial printing, lithographic	125	1,100	70.3	30.3	19,000
2759 - Commercial printing, nec	37	175	(D)	(D)	-
2761 - Manifold business forms	2	175	(D)	(D)	-
Total	287	3,925	226.6	61.3	19,176

Source: 1997 *Manufacturing STATROM* [machine-readable data files]. MStat97. Editorial Code and Data, Inc., Detroit, Michigan, 1997. Primary source: 1992 *Economic Census*.

★ 50 ★

State Summaries

New York: Publishing Summary, 1992

The publishing industry in New York represented **8.185%** of all publishing establishments in the U.S. in 1992. The state's population was **7.120%** of the U.S. population. New York's reported employment in this sector was **10.230%** of the U.S. sector's employment. And the state's reported shipments were **15.669%** of the U.S. sector's shipments.

Industry	Establish-ments	Employ-ment	Shipments ($ mil.)	Cost of materials ($ mil.)	Payroll per employee ($)
2711 - Newspapers	504	31,600	3,341.4	702.4	35,174
2721 - Periodicals	622	34,000	9,618.1	2,706.6	45,206
2731 - Book publishing	383	20,400	6,272.3	2,089.7	41,098
2732 - Book printing	53	3,200	277.3	107.8	29,719
2741 - Miscellaneous publishing	382	9,000	1,127.7	296.5	28,700
2752 - Commercial printing, lithographic	2,053	30,700	3,168.5	1,291.4	29,492
2754 - Commercial printing, gravure	36	500	74.7	36.2	29,400
2759 - Commercial printing, nec	670	8,500	763.5	305.1	25,906
2761 - Manifold business forms	48	2,100	208.9	86.2	30,952
2771 - Greeting cards	14	300	47.7	10.9	24,333
2782 - Blankbooks and looseleaf binders	54	3,200	316.7	118.9	21,469
2789 - Bookbinding and related work	122	2,700	134.8	29.8	22,148
2791 - Typesetting	278	3,300	243.3	47.6	31,303
Total	5,219	149,500	25,594.9	7,829.1	35,349

Source: 1997 *Manufacturing STATROM* [machine-readable data files]. MStat97. Editorial Code and Data, Inc., Detroit, Michigan, 1997. Primary source: 1992 *Economic Census.*

★ 51 ★

State Summaries

North Carolina: Publishing Summary, 1992

The publishing industry in North Carolina represented **2.246%** of all publishing establishments in the U.S. in 1992. The state's population was **2.689%** of the U.S. population. North Carolina's reported employment in this sector was **1.967%** of the U.S. sector's employment. And the state's reported shipments were **1.295%** of the U.S. sector's shipments.

Industry	Establish-ments	Employ-ment	Shipments ($ mil.)	Cost of materials ($ mil.)	Payroll per employee ($)
2711 - Newspapers	215	9,900	671.9	132.5	21,636
2721 - Periodicals	77	1,100	133.1	44.7	25,909
2731 - Book publishing	46	500	106.3	35.6	26,800
2732 - Book printing	14	1,400	98.1	37.1	23,571

[Continued]

★ 51 ★

North Carolina: Publishing Summary, 1992
[Continued]

Industry	Establish-ments	Employ-ment	Shipments ($ mil.)	Cost of materials ($ mil.)	Payroll per employee ($)
2741 - Miscellaneous publishing	47	750	(D)	(D)	-
2752 - Commercial printing, lithographic	679	9,000	869.3	378.0	23,722
2754 - Commercial printing, gravure	16	1,750	(D)	(D)	-
2759 - Commercial printing, nec	218	1,750	(D)	(D)	-
2761 - Manifold business forms	31	1,200	139.9	67.0	24,000
2782 - Blankbooks and looseleaf binders	11	500	56.0	10.7	27,600
2789 - Bookbinding and related work	27	600	26.2	6.0	18,167
2791 - Typesetting	51	300	13.8	3.1	20,333
Total	1,432	28,750	2,114.6	714.7	22,947

Source: 1997 *Manufacturing STATROM* [machine-readable data files]. MStat97. Editorial Code and Data, Inc., Detroit, Michigan, 1997. Primary source: 1992 *Economic Census.*

★ 52 ★

State Summaries

North Dakota: Publishing Summary, 1992

The publishing industry in North Dakota represented **0.221**% of all publishing establishments in the U.S. in 1992. The state's population was **0.250**% of the U.S. population. North Dakota's reported employment in this sector was **0.174**% of the U.S. sector's employment. And the state's reported shipments were **0.078**% of the U.S. sector's shipments.

Industry	Establish-ments	Employ-ment	Shipments ($ mil.)	Cost of materials ($ mil.)	Payroll per employee ($)
2711 - Newspapers	68	1,500	85.2	14.5	17,400
2741 - Miscellaneous publishing	5	175	(D)	(D)	-
2752 - Commercial printing, lithographic	44	700	42.5	17.1	19,286
2759 - Commercial printing, nec	24	175	(D)	(D)	-
Total	141	2,550	127.7	31.6	18,000

Source: 1997 *Manufacturing STATROM* [machine-readable data files]. MStat97. Editorial Code and Data, Inc., Detroit, Michigan, 1997. Primary source: 1992 *Economic Census.*

State Summaries

Ohio: Publishing Summary, 1992

The publishing industry in Ohio represented **3.907%** of all publishing establishments in the U.S. in 1992. The state's population was **4.329%** of the U.S. population. Ohio's reported employment in this sector was **4.530%** of the U.S. sector's employment. And the state's reported shipments were **3.775%** of the U.S. sector's shipments.

Industry	Establish- ments	Employ- ment	Shipments ($ mil.)	Cost of materials ($ mil.)	Payroll per employee ($)
2711 - Newspapers	286	16,600	1,364.0	272.4	25,458
2721 - Periodicals	120	3,500	476.2	113.0	28,371
2731 - Book publishing	64	3,800	495.6	94.7	35,447
2732 - Book printing	19	2,400	256.5	97.0	27,792
2741 - Miscellaneous publishing	103	1,800	163.3	36.0	21,056
2752 - Commercial printing, lithographic	1,229	21,900	1,984.9	825.6	26,452
2754 - Commercial printing, gravure	15	500	71.9	38.5	33,400
2759 - Commercial printing, nec	450	8,600	875.5	368.2	25,965
2761 - Manifold business forms	36	2,700	337.9	128.7	27,926
2771 - Greeting cards	6	1,750	(D)	(D)	-
2782 - Blankbooks and looseleaf binders	27	1,100	101.1	24.8	26,909
2789 - Bookbinding and related work	38	750	(D)	(D)	-
2791 - Typesetting	98	800	39.7	5.7	21,125
Total	2,491	66,200	6,166.6	2,004.6	26,725

Source: 1997 *Manufacturing STATROM* [machine-readable data files]. MStat97. Editorial Code and Data, Inc., Detroit, Michigan, 1997. Primary source: 1992 *Economic Census.*

State Summaries

Oklahoma: Publishing Summary, 1992

The publishing industry in Oklahoma represented **1.077%** of all publishing establishments in the U.S. in 1992. The state's population was **1.262%** of the U.S. population. Oklahoma's reported employment in this sector was **0.765%** of the U.S. sector's employment. And the state's reported shipments were **0.585%** of the U.S. sector's shipments.

Industry	Establish- ments	Employ- ment	Shipments ($ mil.)	Cost of materials ($ mil.)	Payroll per employee ($)
2711 - Newspapers	175	4,700	337.1	62.9	21,298
2721 - Periodicals	33	400	93.8	16.8	24,500
2731 - Book publishing	22	200	23.1	8.1	18,000
2741 - Miscellaneous publishing	26	300	33.1	9.0	21,000

[Continued]

★ 54 ★

Oklahoma: Publishing Summary, 1992
[Continued]

Industry	Establish-ments	Employ-ment	Shipments ($ mil.)	Cost of materials ($ mil.)	Payroll per employee ($)
2752 - Commercial printing, lithographic	302	3,400	354.1	168.6	22,676
2754 - Commercial printing, gravure	1	175	(D)	(D)	-
2759 - Commercial printing, nec	107	750	(D)	(D)	-
2761 - Manifold business forms	8	700	115.1	59.6	26,857
2782 - Blankbooks and looseleaf binders	4	375	(D)	(D)	-
2789 - Bookbinding and related work	9	175	(D)	(D)	-
Total	687	11,175	956.3	325.0	22,237

Source: 1997 Manufacturing STATROM [machine-readable data files]. MStat97. Editorial Code and Data, Inc., Detroit, Michigan, 1997. Primary source: 1992 Economic Census.

★ 55 ★

State Summaries

Oregon: Publishing Summary, 1992

The publishing industry in Oregon represented **1.390%** of all publishing establishments in the U.S. in 1992. The state's population was **1.170%** of the U.S. population. Oregon's reported employment in this sector was **1.020%** of the U.S. sector's employment. And the state's reported shipments were **0.978%** of the U.S. sector's shipments.

Industry	Establish-ments	Employ-ment	Shipments ($ mil.)	Cost of materials ($ mil.)	Payroll per employee ($)
2711 - Newspapers	121	4,800	370.8	82.6	23,708
2721 - Periodicals	46	500	69.0	21.6	23,400
2731 - Book publishing	53	400	56.8	23.2	25,750
2732 - Book printing	6	300	43.3	14.4	31,000
2741 - Miscellaneous publishing	51	700	127.9	18.6	26,143
2752 - Commercial printing, lithographic	420	5,300	634.3	300.9	28,566
2759 - Commercial printing, nec	106	800	71.8	31.4	24,000
2761 - Manifold business forms	19	1,000	145.6	74.0	30,300
2782 - Blankbooks and looseleaf binders	9	700	52.9	18.1	21,286
2789 - Bookbinding and related work	21	300	18.4	2.6	28,333
2791 - Typesetting	34	100	6.7	1.0	28,000
Total	886	14,900	1,597.5	588.4	26,208

Source: 1997 Manufacturing STATROM [machine-readable data files]. MStat97. Editorial Code and Data, Inc., Detroit, Michigan, 1997. Primary source: 1992 Economic Census.

Pennsylvania: Publishing Summary, 1992

The publishing industry in Pennsylvania represented **3.982%** of all publishing establishments in the U.S. in 1992. The state's population was **4.719%** of the U.S. population. Pennsylvania's reported employment in this sector was **5.755%** of the U.S. sector's employment. And the state's reported shipments were **5.777%** of the U.S. sector's shipments.

Industry	Establish-ments	Employ-ment	Shipments ($ mil.)	Cost of materials ($ mil.)	Payroll per employee ($)
2711 - Newspapers	306	21,900	1,677.1	342.5	26,160
2721 - Periodicals	159	4,700	1,192.4	427.5	32,149
2731 - Book publishing	78	3,300	835.8	232.9	34,848
2732 - Book printing	33	5,200	444.3	156.4	24,692
2741 - Miscellaneous publishing	116	3,900	779.7	189.8	24,128
2752 - Commercial printing, lithographic	1,222	24,300	2,400.4	1,013.5	27,605
2754 - Commercial printing, gravure	13	1,600	285.8	143.5	39,375
2759 - Commercial printing, nec	378	6,100	525.7	220.1	23,443
2761 - Manifold business forms	64	4,500	847.1	444.9	27,133
2771 - Greeting cards	3	750	(D)	(D)	-
2782 - Blankbooks and looseleaf binders	18	2,600	248.4	60.3	23,692
2789 - Bookbinding and related work	44	1,750	(D)	(D)	-
2791 - Typesetting	105	3,500	200.0	26.5	24,714
Total	2,539	84,100	9,436.7	3,257.9	27,065

Source: 1997 *Manufacturing STATROM* [machine-readable data files]. MStat97. Editorial Code and Data, Inc., Detroit, Michigan, 1997. Primary source: 1992 *Economic Census*.

Rhode Island: Publishing Summary, 1992

The publishing industry in Rhode Island represented **0.359%** of all publishing establishments in the U.S. in 1992. The state's population was **0.395%** of the U.S. population. Rhode Island's reported employment in this sector was **0.370%** of the U.S. sector's employment. And the state's reported shipments were **0.222%** of the U.S. sector's shipments.

Industry	Establish-ments	Employ-ment	Shipments ($ mil.)	Cost of materials ($ mil.)	Payroll per employee ($)
2711 - Newspapers	22	2,300	162.4	37.6	31,696
2721 - Periodicals	13	200	21.3	4.4	27,500
2752 - Commercial printing, lithographic	125	1,600	152.2	61.1	31,063
2754 - Commercial printing, gravure	6	175	(D)	(D)	-

[Continued]

★ 57 ★

Rhode Island: Publishing Summary, 1992
[Continued]

Industry	Establish-ments	Employ-ment	Shipments ($ mil.)	Cost of materials ($ mil.)	Payroll per employee ($)
2759 - Commercial printing, nec	56	375	(D)	(D)	-
2761 - Manifold business forms	5	200	26.7	12.8	31,500
2771 - Greeting cards	1	375	(D)	(D)	-
2782 - Blankbooks and looseleaf binders	1	175	(D)	(D)	-
Total	229	5,400	362.6	115.9	31,256

Source: 1997 *Manufacturing STATROM* [machine-readable data files]. MStat97. Editorial Code and Data, Inc., Detroit, Michigan, 1997. Primary source: 1992 *Economic Census*.

★ 58 ★
State Summaries

South Carolina: Publishing Summary, 1992

The publishing industry in South Carolina represented **0.950**% of all publishing establishments in the U.S. in 1992. The state's population was **1.416**% of the U.S. population. South Carolina's reported employment in this sector was **0.739**% of the U.S. sector's employment. And the state's reported shipments were **0.439**% of the U.S. sector's shipments.

Industry	Establish-ments	Employ-ment	Shipments ($ mil.)	Cost of materials ($ mil.)	Payroll per employee ($)
2711 - Newspapers	105	4,500	309.7	60.1	20,556
2721 - Periodicals	35	200	14.6	5.0	16,000
2731 - Book publishing	21	100	7.7	1.9	19,000
2732 - Book printing	5	200	16.1	2.8	23,500
2741 - Miscellaneous publishing	33	200	18.1	4.6	25,000
2752 - Commercial printing, lithographic	304	3,200	217.3	85.7	20,812
2754 - Commercial printing, gravure	3	750	(D)	(D)	-
2759 - Commercial printing, nec	88	750	(D)	(D)	-
2761 - Manifold business forms	8	600	111.1	54.1	28,333
2782 - Blankbooks and looseleaf binders	4	300	22.8	6.1	17,333
Total	606	10,800	717.4	220.3	21,086

Source: 1997 *Manufacturing STATROM* [machine-readable data files]. MStat97. Editorial Code and Data, Inc., Detroit, Michigan, 1997. Primary source: 1992 *Economic Census*.

★ 59 ★

State Summaries

South Dakota: Publishing Summary, 1992

The publishing industry in South Dakota represented **0.284%** of all publishing establishments in the U.S. in 1992. The state's population was **0.279%** of the U.S. population. South Dakota's reported employment in this sector was **0.186%** of the U.S. sector's employment. And the state's reported shipments were **0.050%** of the U.S. sector's shipments.

Industry	Establish-ments	Employ-ment	Shipments ($ mil.)	Cost of materials ($ mil.)	Payroll per employee ($)
2711 - Newspapers	91	1,600	81.5	16.0	15,000
2752 - Commercial printing, lithographic	77	750	(D)	(D)	-
2759 - Commercial printing, nec	13	375	(D)	(D)	-
Total	181	2,725	81.5	16.0	15,000

Source: 1997 *Manufacturing STATROM* [machine-readable data files]. MStat97. Editorial Code and Data, Inc., Detroit, Michigan, 1997. Primary source: 1992 *Economic Census.*

★ 60 ★

State Summaries

Tennessee: Publishing Summary, 1992

The publishing industry in Tennessee represented **1.931%** of all publishing establishments in the U.S. in 1992. The state's population was **1.974%** of the U.S. population. Tennessee's reported employment in this sector was **2.296%** of the U.S. sector's employment. And the state's reported shipments were **1.953%** of the U.S. sector's shipments.

Industry	Establish-ments	Employ-ment	Shipments ($ mil.)	Cost of materials ($ mil.)	Payroll per employee ($)
2711 - Newspapers	167	7,400	489.0	84.5	18,378
2721 - Periodicals	68	2,400	196.4	29.3	27,833
2731 - Book publishing	67	1,500	222.6	90.7	26,067
2732 - Book printing	11	3,900	323.8	113.1	24,205
2741 - Miscellaneous publishing	106	1,300	143.8	57.3	22,692
2752 - Commercial printing, lithographic	547	9,600	861.7	373.0	25,656
2754 - Commercial printing, gravure	15	2,200	458.1	273.2	34,864
2759 - Commercial printing, nec	152	2,000	190.0	85.9	25,750
2761 - Manifold business forms	25	1,100	157.2	66.5	26,273
2771 - Greeting cards	1	175	(D)	(D)	-
2782 - Blankbooks and looseleaf binders	16	1,500	136.4	43.2	26,200
2789 - Bookbinding and related work	23	300	10.7	2.7	15,000
2791 - Typesetting	33	175	(D)	(D)	-
Total	1,231	33,550	3,189.7	1,219.4	24,488

Source: 1997 *Manufacturing STATROM* [machine-readable data files]. MStat97. Editorial Code and Data, Inc., Detroit, Michigan, 1997. Primary source: 1992 *Economic Census.*

Texas: Publishing Summary, 1992

The publishing industry in Texas represented **6.259**% of all publishing establishments in the U.S. in 1992. The state's population was **6.938**% of the U.S. population. Texas's reported employment in this sector was **4.795**% of the U.S. sector's employment. And the state's reported shipments were **3.653**% of the U.S. sector's shipments.

Industry	Establish- ments	Employ- ment	Shipments ($ mil.)	Cost of materials ($ mil.)	Payroll per employee ($)
2711 - Newspapers	634	20,800	1,938.4	480.3	23,212
2721 - Periodicals	204	3,100	301.2	85.7	25,871
2731 - Book publishing	116	3,200	517.4	124.6	26,719
2732 - Book printing	27	2,200	167.0	72.9	25,455
2741 - Miscellaneous publishing	196	2,400	307.5	79.9	26,625
2752 - Commercial printing, lithographic	1,935	20,800	1,903.1	848.5	25,163
2754 - Commercial printing, gravure	19	750	(D)	(D)	-
2759 - Commercial printing, nec	543	7,500	(D)	(D)	-
2761 - Manifold business forms	76	3,400	526.6	262.4	26,676
2771 - Greeting cards	6	175	(D)	(D)	-
2782 - Blankbooks and looseleaf binders	40	2,500	239.2	64.9	22,640
2789 - Bookbinding and related work	51	1,500	66.7	15.1	18,800
2791 - Typesetting	144	1,750	(D)	(D)	-
Total	3,991	70,075	5,967.1	2,034.3	24,496

Source: 1997 *Manufacturing STATROM* [machine-readable data files]. MStat97. Editorial Code and Data, Inc., Detroit, Michigan, 1997. Primary source: 1992 *Economic Census.*

Utah: Publishing Summary, 1992

The publishing industry in Utah represented **0.602**% of all publishing establishments in the U.S. in 1992. The state's population was **0.712**% of the U.S. population. Utah's reported employment in this sector was **0.674**% of the U.S. sector's employment. And the state's reported shipments were **0.463**% of the U.S. sector's shipments.

Industry	Establish- ments	Employ- ment	Shipments ($ mil.)	Cost of materials ($ mil.)	Payroll per employee ($)
2711 - Newspapers	58	2,800	163.6	32.0	17,464
2721 - Periodicals	23	300	36.8	10.5	28,667
2731 - Book publishing	28	100	12.0	4.7	25,000
2732 - Book printing	10	800	79.3	39.7	19,750

[Continued]

★ 62 ★

Utah: Publishing Summary, 1992
[Continued]

Industry	Establish-ments	Employ-ment	Shipments ($ mil.)	Cost of materials ($ mil.)	Payroll per employee ($)
2741 - Miscellaneous publishing	20	1,600	147.3	53.4	24,250
2752 - Commercial printing, lithographic	169	2,300	167.9	60.4	23,043
2759 - Commercial printing, nec	55	750	(D)	(D)	-
2761 - Manifold business forms	9	700	119.3	36.1	27,429
2782 - Blankbooks and looseleaf binders	5	300	19.2	3.7	18,000
2789 - Bookbinding and related work	7	200	10.3	1.6	19,000
Total	384	9,850	755.7	242.1	21,538

Source: 1997 *Manufacturing STATROM* [machine-readable data files]. MStat97. Editorial Code and Data, Inc., Detroit, Michigan, 1997. Primary source: 1992 *Economic Census.*

★ 63 ★
State Summaries

Vermont: Publishing Summary, 1992

The publishing industry in Vermont represented **0.369**% of all publishing establishments in the U.S. in 1992. The state's population was **0.224**% of the U.S. population. Vermont's reported employment in this sector was **0.363**% of the U.S. sector's employment. And the state's reported shipments were **0.239**% of the U.S. sector's shipments.

Industry	Establish-ments	Employ-ment	Shipments ($ mil.)	Cost of materials ($ mil.)	Payroll per employee ($)
2711 - Newspapers	53	1,100	67.9	12.6	19,273
2721 - Periodicals	20	300	44.3	14.2	26,667
2731 - Book publishing	25	375	(D)	(D)	-
2732 - Book printing	4	750	(D)	(D)	-
2741 - Miscellaneous publishing	16	300	10.3	1.9	18,667
2752 - Commercial printing, lithographic	74	1,700	146.0	58.7	26,118
2759 - Commercial printing, nec	29	175	(D)	(D)	-
2761 - Manifold business forms	4	500	115.9	53.5	29,800
2791 - Typesetting	10	100	5.2	0.7	27,000
Total	235	5,300	389.6	141.6	24,200

Source: 1997 *Manufacturing STATROM* [machine-readable data files]. MStat97. Editorial Code and Data, Inc., Detroit, Michigan, 1997. Primary source: 1992 *Economic Census.*

★ 64 ★

State Summaries

Virginia: Publishing Summary, 1992

The publishing industry in Virginia represented **2.127%** of all publishing establishments in the U.S. in 1992. The state's population was **2.506%** of the U.S. population. Virginia's reported employment in this sector was **2.277%** of the U.S. sector's employment. And the state's reported shipments were **1.821%** of the U.S. sector's shipments.

Industry	Establish-ments	Employ-ment	Shipments ($ mil.)	Cost of materials ($ mil.)	Payroll per employee ($)
2711 - Newspapers	174	11,300	1,065.6	236.9	25,088
2721 - Periodicals	133	1,800	194.7	46.2	29,889
2731 - Book publishing	52	1,750	(D)	(D)	-
2732 - Book printing	13	1,750	(D)	(D)	-
2741 - Miscellaneous publishing	86	1,000	109.1	24.0	28,200
2752 - Commercial printing, lithographic	637	11,100	1,012.6	449.6	27,216
2754 - Commercial printing, gravure	15	1,600	308.9	174.8	33,438
2759 - Commercial printing, nec	168	900	76.1	34.5	22,333
2761 - Manifold business forms	17	900	135.0	58.1	20,556
2782 - Blankbooks and looseleaf binders	10	600	51.9	11.7	22,000
2789 - Bookbinding and related work	14	175	(D)	(D)	-
2791 - Typesetting	37	400	20.2	2.5	25,750
Total	1,356	33,275	2,974.1	1,038.3	26,459

Source: 1997 *Manufacturing STATROM* [machine-readable data files]. MStat97. Editorial Code and Data, Inc., Detroit, Michigan, 1997. Primary source: 1992 *Economic Census.*

★ 65 ★

State Summaries

Washington: Publishing Summary, 1992

The publishing industry in Washington represented **1.979%** of all publishing establishments in the U.S. in 1992. The state's population was **2.018%** of the U.S. population. Washington's reported employment in this sector was **1.543%** of the U.S. sector's employment. And the state's reported shipments were **1.111%** of the U.S. sector's shipments.

Industry	Establish-ments	Employ-ment	Shipments ($ mil.)	Cost of materials ($ mil.)	Payroll per employee ($)
2711 - Newspapers	186	10,400	720.1	130.3	24,596
2721 - Periodicals	102	900	76.4	20.9	29,111
2731 - Book publishing	61	375	(D)	(D)	-
2732 - Book printing	8	375	(D)	(D)	-
2741 - Miscellaneous publishing	88	1,000	186.0	42.7	25,700

[Continued]

★ 65 ★

Washington: Publishing Summary, 1992
[Continued]

Industry	Establish-ments	Employ-ment	Shipments ($ mil.)	Cost of materials ($ mil.)	Payroll per employee ($)
2752 - Commercial printing, lithographic	599	6,400	579.9	219.6	26,250
2759 - Commercial printing, nec	140	1,600	133.8	49.9	24,938
2761 - Manifold business forms	15	400	39.6	18.9	27,250
2782 - Blankbooks and looseleaf binders	8	600	52.9	12.2	28,500
2789 - Bookbinding and related work	24	400	16.6	2.0	19,250
2791 - Typesetting	31	100	8.7	1.4	25,000
Total	1,262	22,550	1,814.0	497.9	25,404

Source: 1997 Manufacturing STATROM [machine-readable data files]. MStat97. Editorial Code and Data, Inc., Detroit, Michigan, 1997. Primary source: 1992 Economic Census.

★ 66 ★

State Summaries

West Virginia: Publishing Summary, 1992

The publishing industry in West Virginia represented **0.323**% of all publishing establishments in the U.S. in 1992. The state's population was **0.712**% of the U.S. population. West Virginia's reported employment in this sector was **0.325**% of the U.S. sector's employment. And the state's reported shipments were **0.142**% of the U.S. sector's shipments.

Industry	Establish-ments	Employ-ment	Shipments ($ mil.)	Cost of materials ($ mil.)	Payroll per employee ($)
2711 - Newspapers	80	2,900	151.6	29.8	16,310
2732 - Book printing	2	375	(D)	(D)	-
2752 - Commercial printing, lithographic	94	1,000	72.0	31.3	23,700
2759 - Commercial printing, nec	27	100	8.8	3.6	20,000
2761 - Manifold business forms	3	375	(D)	(D)	-
Total	206	4,750	232.4	64.7	18,250

Source: 1997 Manufacturing STATROM [machine-readable data files]. MStat97. Editorial Code and Data, Inc., Detroit, Michigan, 1997. Primary source: 1992 Economic Census.

State Summaries

Wisconsin: Publishing Summary, 1992

The publishing industry in Wisconsin represented **2.280%** of all publishing establishments in the U.S. in 1992. The state's population was **1.967%** of the U.S. population. Wisconsin's reported employment in this sector was **3.158%** of the U.S. sector's employment. And the state's reported shipments were **2.560%** of the U.S. sector's shipments.

Industry	Establish-ments	Employ-ment	Shipments ($ mil.)	Cost of materials ($ mil.)	Payroll per employee ($)
2711 - Newspapers	235	10,900	624.8	127.8	18,321
2721 - Periodicals	97	2,000	296.3	75.3	23,600
2731 - Book publishing	39	1,100	211.9	193.3	30,455
2732 - Book printing	18	2,400	298.3	154.5	31,875
2741 - Miscellaneous publishing	92	1,600	73.8	21.1	14,375
2752 - Commercial printing, lithographic	678	19,900	1,812.5	706.1	25,930
2754 - Commercial printing, gravure	9	100	12.7	6.2	29,000
2759 - Commercial printing, nec	190	5,300	553.7	205.4	26,943
2761 - Manifold business forms	24	1,000	225.2	96.4	27,100
2782 - Blankbooks and looseleaf binders	9	750	(D)	(D)	-
2789 - Bookbinding and related work	19	600	47.1	14.5	19,667
2791 - Typesetting	44	500	25.2	5.7	20,800
Total	1,454	46,150	4,181.5	1,606.3	24,029

Source: 1997 *Manufacturing STATROM* [machine-readable data files]. MStat97. Editorial Code and Data, Inc., Detroit, Michigan, 1997. Primary source: 1992 *Economic Census.*

State Summaries

Wyoming: Publishing Summary, 1992

The publishing industry in Wyoming represented **0.140%** of all publishing establishments in the U.S. in 1992. The state's population was **0.183%** of the U.S. population. Wyoming's reported employment in this sector was **0.077%** of the U.S. sector's employment. And the state's reported shipments were of the U.S. sector's shipments.

Industry	Establish-ments	Employ-ment	Shipments ($ mil.)	Cost of materials	Payroll per employee
2711 - Newspapers	42	750	(D)	(D)	-
2752 - Commercial printing, lithographic	47	375	(D)	(D)	-
Total	89	1,125	-	-	-

Source: 1997 *Manufacturing STATROM* [machine-readable data files]. MStat97. Editorial Code and Data, Inc., Detroit, Michigan, 1997. Primary source: 1992 *Economic Census.*

Miscellaneous Publishing

★ 69 ★

General Statistics on the Miscellaneous Publishing Industry, 1982-1998

Misc. publishing includes atlases, newsletters, sheet music, race track programs, manuals, directories and yearbooks.

Year	Com-panies	Establishments		Employment			Compensation	
		Total	With 20 or more employees	Total (000)	Production workers (000)	Hours (mil.)	Payroll ($ mil.)	Wages ($ hr.)
1982	1,951	2,057	430	45.3	17.9	29.2	705.9	7.06
1983	NA	NA	NA	44.8	18.4	29.9	712.2	7.08
1984	NA	NA	NA	42.0	16.6	28.2	775.9	7.48
1985	NA	NA	NA	52.0	17.1	29.5	1,047.4	8.11
1986	NA	NA	NA	53.1	18.4	31.3	1,129.1	8.80
1987	2,136	2,369	597	69.4	24.1	44.1	1,513.2	8.28
1988	NA	NA	NA	NA	NA	43.0	1,553.4	NA
1989	NA	2,131	577	62.4	22.1	40.2	1,594.2	9.24
1990	NA	NA	NA	65.2	22.3	40.2	1,707.8	9.40
1991	NA	NA	NA	65.0	22.6	43.4	1,779.7	9.60
1992	3,159	3,390	570	65.4	23.7	43.3	1,732.9	10.80
1993	NA	NA	NA	66.6	22.8	42.6	1,896.8	10.41
1994	NA	NA	NA	71.2	25.3	47.5	1,982.1	10.39
1995	NA	NA	NA	NA	NA	49.0[1]	2,196.3[1]	NA
1996	NA	NA	NA	NA	NA	50.6[1]	2,310.9[1]	NA
1997	NA	NA	NA	NA	NA	52.2[1]	2,425.4[1]	NA
1998	NA	NA	NA	NA	NA	53.8[1]	2,539.9[1]	NA

Source: 1997 *Manufacturing STATROM* [machine-readable data files]. MStat97. Editorial Code and Data, Inc., Detroit, Michigan, 1997. Primary source: 1982, 1987, 1992 *Economic Census*; *Annual Survey of Manufactures*, 1983-1986, 1988-1991, 1993-1994. Establishment counts for non-Census years are from *County Business Patterns*; establishment values for 1983-1984 are extrapolations. Industries reclassified in 1987 will not have data for prior years. *Notes:* NA = Not available. 1. Items are projected by the editors.

★ 70 ★

Miscellaneous Publishing

General Indices of Change in the Miscellaneous Publishing Industries, 1982-1998

Misc. publishing includes atlases, catalogs, newsletters, sheet music, race track programs, manuals, directories and yearbooks.

| Year | Com-panies | Establishments | | Employment | | | Compensation | | Cost of materials | Production ($ million) | | | Capital investment |
		Total	With 20 or more employees	Total (000)	Production workers (000)	Hours (mil.)	Payroll ($ mil.)	Wages ($ hr.)		Value added by manufacture	Value of shipments[1]	
1982	62	61	75	69	76	67	41	65	37	23	26	35
1983	NA	NA	NA	69	78	69	41	66	38	25	27	43
1984	NA	NA	NA	64	70	65	45	69	38	27	29	36
1985	NA	NA	NA	80	72	68	60	75	48	38	40	58
1986	NA	NA	NA	81	78	72	65	81	50	43	45	54
1987	68	70	105	106	102	102	87	77	72	71	71	70
1988	NA	NA	NA	NA	NA	99	90	NA	79	73	74	NA
1989	NA	63	101	95	93	93	92	86	83	71	73	76
1990	NA	NA	NA	100	94	93	99	87	92	78	81	94
1991	NA	NA	NA	99	95	100	103	89	100	86	89	87
1992	100	100	100	100	100	100	100	100	100	100	100	100
1993	NA	NA	NA	102	96	98	109	96	105	108	108	73
1994	NA	NA	NA	109	107	110	114	96	113	112	112	101
1995	NA	NA	NA	NA	NA	113[2]	127[2]	NA	123[2]	121[2]	122[2]	NA
1996	NA	NA	NA	NA	NA	117[2]	133[2]	NA	131[2]	129[2]	130[2]	NA
1997	NA	NA	NA	NA	NA	121[2]	140[2]	NA	139[2]	137[2]	138[2]	NA
1998	NA	NA	NA	NA	NA	124[2]	147[2]	NA	146[2]	145[2]	145[2]	NA

Source: 1997 *Manufacturing STATROM* [machine-readable data files]. MStat97. Editorial Code and Data, Inc., Detroit, Michigan, 1997. Primary source: 1982, 1987, 1992 *Economic Census; Annual Survey of Manufactures*, 1983-1986, 1988-1991, 1993-1994. Establishment counts for non-Census years are from *County Business Patterns*; establishment values for 1983-1984 are extrapolations. Industries reclassified in 1987 will not have data for prior years. Values reflect change from the base year, 1992. Values above 100 mean greater than 1992, values below 100 mean less than 1992, and a value of 100 in the 1982-1991 or 1993-1998 period means same as 1992. *Notes:* NA = Not available. 1. "Industry Shipments" and "Product Shipments" are rarely the same value. 2. Items are projected by the editors.

★ 71 ★

Miscellaneous Publishing

General Production Statistics on the Miscellaneous Publishing Industry, 1982-1998

Misc. publishing includes atlases, catalogs, newsletters, sheet music, race track programs, manuals, directories and yearbooks.

| Year | Production ($ million) | | | |
	Cost of materials	Value added by manufacture	Value of shipments[1]	Capital investment
1982	909.6	1,958.2	2,871.3	67.1
1983	943.4	2,105.4	3,011.7	82.5
1984	949.4	2,321.9	3,222.9	69.1
1985	1,199.5	3,264.6	4,437.0	109.7
1986	1,246.9	3,631.5	4,887.4	102.6
1987	1,791.0	6,022.9	7,809.5	133.0
1988	1,953.8	6,248.1	8,154.4	NA

[Continued]

★ 71 ★

General Production Statistics on the Miscellaneous Publishing Industry, 1982-1998
[Continued]

| Year | Production ($ million) | | | |
	Cost of materials	Value added by manufacture	Value of shipments[1]	Capital investment
1989	2,056.3	6,060.0	8,021.2	144.0
1990	2,266.7	6,656.2	8,874.7	178.6
1991	2,469.8	7,353.6	9,762.0	165.5
1992	2,476.7	8,524.9	10,977.1	190.4
1993	2,592.1	9,218.1	11,806.6	138.5
1994	2,802.6	9,522.7	12,332.4	192.8
1995	3,044.0[2]	10,342.8[2]	13,394.4[2]	NA
1996	3,238.6[2]	11,004.3[2]	14,251.1[2]	NA
1997	3,433.3[2]	11,665.8[2]	15,107.8[2]	NA
1998	3,628.0[2]	12,327.3[2]	15,964.5[2]	NA

Source: 1997 *Manufacturing STATROM* [machine-readable data files]. MStat97. Editorial Code and Data, Inc., Detroit, Michigan, 1997. Primary source: 1982, 1987, 1992 *Economic Census*; *Annual Survey of Manufactures*, 1983-1986, 1988-1991, 1993-1994. Establishment counts for non-Census years are from *County Business Patterns*; establishment values for 1983-1984 are extrapolations. Industries reclassified in 1987 will not have data for prior years. *Notes:* NA = Not available. 1. "Industry Shipments" and "Product Shipments" are rarely the same value. 2. Items are projected by the editors.

★ 72 ★
Miscellaneous Publishing

Materials Consumed by the Miscellaneous Publishing Industries

Misc. publishing includes atlases, catalogs, newsletters, sheet music, race track programs, manuals, directories and yearbooks.

Material	Delivered cost ($ mil.)
Materials, ingredients, containers, and supplies	708.6
Newsprint	43.5
Coated paper	75.2
Uncoated paper	103.8
Printing inks (complete formulations)	4.3
All other materials and components, parts, containers, and supplies	219.6
Materials, ingredients, containers, and supplies, nsk	262.2

Source: 1997 *Manufacturing STATROM* [machine-readable data files]. MStat97. Editorial Code and Data, Inc., Detroit, Michigan, 1997. Primary source: 1992 *Economic Census*. Explanation of symbols used: nsk: Not specified by kind.

Miscellaneous Publishing

Product Share Details in the Miscellaneous Publishing Industries

Misc. publishing includes atlases, catalogs, newsletters, sheet music, race track programs, manuals, directories and yearbooks. Product code refers to the SIC classification.

Product code	Shipments ($ mil.)	% of total	Product name
2741	11,567.1	100.00	MISCELLANEOUS PUBLISHING
27416	4,807.5	41.56	Telephone directory publishing
27417	613.4	5.30	Catalog and directory (except telephone directory)
2741713	492.6	80.31	Directory
2741716	110.4	18.00	Catalog
2741700	10.5	1.71	Catalogs and directories, n.s.k.
27418	897.6	7.76	Business service publication publishing
27419	214.4	1.85	Pattern publishing, including clothing patterns
2741A	990.6	8.56	Shopping news publishing
2741B	2,216.9	19.17	Other miscellaneous publishing
2741B13	810.4	36.56	Card publishing, other than greeting cards
2741B14	23.1	1.04	Sheet music publishing (less than five pages)
2741B15	286.8	12.94	Calendar publishing
2741B17	67.8	3.06	Multimedia kit publishing
2741B18	169.2	7.63	Map, hydrographic chart, and globe cover publishing
2741B20	79.2	3.57	Atlas and gazetteer publishing
2741B23	232.6	10.49	Micropublishing (publishing in microfilm, microfiche formats)
2741B25	59.7	2.69	Travel guide publishing, in brochure or pamphlet form
2741B27	51.3	2.31	Poster publishing
2741B29	78.6	3.55	Yearbook publishing
2741B71	285.1	12.86	Other miscellaneous publication publishing
2741B00	73.2	3.30	Other miscellaneous publishing, n.s.k.
27410	1,826.8	15.79	Miscellaneous publishing, n.s.k.

Source: 1997 *Manufacturing STATROM* [machine-readable data files]. MStat97. Editorial Code and Data, Inc., Detroit, Michigan, 1997. Primary source: 1992 *Economic Census*. The values shown are percent of total shipments in an industry. Values of indented subcategories are summed in the main headings. The abbreviation n.s.k. stands for 'not specified by kind' and nec for 'not elsewhere classified.'

★ 74 ★

Miscellaneous Publishing

Production: Indices of Change in the Miscellaneous Publishing Industry, 1982 -1998

Misc. publishing includes atlases, catalogs, newsletters, sheet music, race track programs, manuals, directories and yearbooks.

Year	Production ($ million)			
	Cost of materials	Value added by manufacture	Value of shipments[1]	Capital investment
1982	37	23	26	35
1983	38	25	27	43
1984	38	27	29	36
1985	48	38	40	58
1986	50	43	45	54
1987	72	71	71	70
1988	79	73	74	NA
1989	83	71	73	76
1990	92	78	81	94
1991	100	86	89	87
1992	100	100	100	100
1993	105	108	108	73
1994	113	112	112	101
1995	123[2]	121[2]	122[2]	NA
1996	131[2]	129[2]	130[2]	NA
1997	139[2]	137[2]	138[2]	NA
1998	146[2]	145[2]	145[2]	NA

Source: 1997 *Manufacturing STATROM* [machine-readable data files]. MStat97. Editorial Code and Data, Inc., Detroit, Michigan, 1997. Primary source: 1982, 1987, 1992 *Economic Census*; *Annual Survey of Manufactures*, 1983-1986, 1988-1991, 1993-1994. Establishment counts for non-Census years are from *County Business Patterns*; establishment values for 1983-1984 are extrapolations. Industries reclassified in 1987 will not have data for prior years. Values reflect change from the base year, 1992. Values above 100 mean greater than 1992, values below 100 mean less than 1992, and a value of 100 in the 1982-1991 or 1993-1998 period means same as 1992. *Notes:* NA = Not available. 1. "Industry Shipments" and "Product Shipments" are rarely the same value. 2. Items are projected by the editors.

★ 75 ★

Miscellaneous Publishing

Occupations Employed by the Miscellaneous Publishing Industries

Misc. publishing includes atlases, catalogs, newsletters, sheet music, race track programs, manuals, directories and yearbooks.

Occupation	% of total 1994	Change to 2005
Sales & related workers, nec	16.1	8.0
Writers & editors, including technical writers	5.8	8.0
General office clerks	4.6	-7.9
General managers & top executives	4.5	2.5
Artists & commercial artists	3.3	9.7
Driver/sales workers	2.7	29.6
Marketing, advertising, & PR managers	2.7	8.0
Clerical supervisors & managers	2.6	10.5
Secretaries, ex legal & medical	2.4	-1.6
Bookkeeping, accounting, & auditing clerks	2.2	-19.0
Proofreaders & copy markers	2.0	-29.8
Data entry keyers, ex composing	2.0	-20.3
Marketing & sales worker supervisors	2.0	8.0
Hand packers & packagers	1.8	-7.4
Receptionists & information clerks	1.7	8.0
Advertising clerks	1.7	18.8
Paste-up workers	1.6	-29.8
Printing press machine setters, operators	1.4	-13.5
Truck drivers light & heavy	1.4	11.4
Typists & word processors	1.4	-46.0
Adjustment clerks	1.3	29.7
Data entry keyers, composing	1.2	-73.1
Offset lithographic press operators	1.2	8.0
Blue collar worker supervisors	1.2	2.8
Order clerks, materials, merchandise, & service	1.2	5.7
Production, planning, & expediting clerks	1.2	7.9
Professional workers, nec	1.2	29.5
Systems analysts	1.1	72.9
Bindery machine operators & set-up operators	1.0	8.0
Managers & administrators, nec	1.0	8.0
Electronic pagination systems workers	1.0	72.8

Source: 1997 *Manufacturing STATROM* [machine-readable data files]. MStat97. Editorial Code and Data, Inc., Detroit, Michigan, 1997. Primary source: *Industry-Occupation Matrix*, Bureau of Labor Statistics. These data relate to one or more 3-digit SIC industry groups rather than to a single 4-digit SIC. The change reported for each occupation to the year 2005 is a percent of growth or decline as estimated by the Bureau of Labor Statistics. The abbreviation nec stands for 'not elsewhere classified.'

★ 76 ★

Miscellaneous Publishing

Selected Ratios for the Miscellaneous Publishing Industries

Misc. publishing includes atlases, catalogs, newsletters, sheet music, race track programs, manuals, directories and yearbooks.

For 1992	Average of all manufacturing	Miscellaneous publishing	Index
Employees per establishment	46	19	42
Payroll per establishment	1,332,320	511,180	38
Payroll per employee	29,181	26,497	91
Production workers per establishment	31	7	22
Wages per establishment	734,496	137,947	19
Wages per production worker	23,390	19,732	84
Hours per production worker	2,025	1,827	90
Wages per hour	11.55	10.80	93
Value added per establishment	3,842,210	2,514,720	65
Value added per employee	84,153	130,350	155
Value added per production worker	122,353	359,700	294
Cost per establishment	4,239,462	730,590	17
Cost per employee	92,853	37,870	41
Cost per production worker	135,003	104,502	77
Shipments per establishment	8,100,800	3,238,083	40
Shipments per employee	177,425	167,846	95
Shipments per production worker	257,966	463,169	180
Investment per establishment	278,244	56,165	20
Investment per employee	6,094	2,911	48
Investment per production worker	8,861	8,034	91

Source: 1997 *Manufacturing STATROM* [machine-readable data files]. MStat97. Editorial Code and Data, Inc., Detroit, Michigan, 1997. Primary source: 1982, 1987, 1992 *Economic Census*; *Annual Survey of Manufactures*, 1983-1986, 1988-1991, 1993-1994. Establishment counts for non-Census years are from *County Business Patterns*; establishment values for 1983-1984 are extrapolations. Industries reclassified in 1987 will not have data for prior years. Values reflect change from the base year, 1992. Values above 100 mean greater than 1992, values below 100 mean less than 1992, and a value of 100 in the 1982-1991 or 1993-1998 period means same as 1992. The 'Average of All Manufacturing' column represents the average of all manufacturing industries reported for the most recent complete year available. The Index shows the relationship between the Average and the Analyzed Industry. For example, 100 means that they are equal; 500 that the Analyzed Industry is five times the average; 50 means that the Analyzed Industry is half the national average.

★ 77 ★

Miscellaneous Publishing

State Level Data for the Miscellaneous Publishing Industries

The states are presented in ranked order by level of shipments. Misc. publishing includes atlases, catalogs, newsletters, sheet music, race track programs, manuals, directories and yearbooks.

State	Establish-ments	Shipments total ($ mil.)	% of U.S.	Per establish-ment	Employ-ment total number	% of U.S.	Per establish-ment	Wages ($/hour)	Cost as % of shipments	Investment per employee ($)
California	473	1,965.2	17.9	4.2	8,500	13.0	18	10.75	18.1	4,424
New York	382	1,127.7	10.3	3.0	9,000	13.8	24	13.40	26.3	1,678
Michigan	100	1,112.8	10.1	11.1	3,100	4.7	31	12.38	10.9	3,355
Massachusetts	96	1,018.1	9.3	10.6	2,500	3.8	26	11.10	24.4	NA
Pennsylvania	116	779.7	7.1	6.7	3,900	6.0	34	8.91	24.3	2,513
Illinois	136	741.5	6.8	5.5	3,500	5.4	26	16.38	47.5	1,514
Colorado	79	533.4	4.9	6.8	3,400	5.2	43	11.91	17.4	6,059
Kansas	43	443.3	4.0	10.3	2,000	3.1	47	9.91	12.9	2,050
Texas	196	307.5	2.8	1.6	2,400	3.7	12	9.85	26.0	1,208
New Jersey	118	255.5	2.3	2.2	2,500	3.8	21	14.33	21.5	1,480
Florida	199	225.6	2.1	1.1	2,900	4.4	15	9.00	24.2	1,517
Maryland	77	215.3	2.0	2.8	1,700	2.6	22	10.00	19.4	1,824
Washington	88	186.0	1.7	2.1	1,000	1.5	11	10.71	23.0	1,400
Minnesota	75	167.8	1.5	2.2	1,000	1.5	13	10.75	23.2	NA
Ohio	103	163.3	1.5	1.6	1,800	2.8	17	8.67	22.0	NA
Utah	20	147.3	1.3	7.4	1,600	2.4	80	7.11	36.3	NA
Tennessee	106	143.8	1.3	1.4	1,300	2.0	12	9.33	39.8	1,462
Oregon	51	127.9	1.2	2.5	700	1.1	14	13.80	14.5	2,714
Kentucky	33	122.6	1.1	3.7	800	1.2	24	9.14	10.8	750
Connecticut	60	112.6	1.0	1.9	1,100	1.7	18	10.87	24.7	1,545
Virginia	86	109.1	1.0	1.3	1,000	1.5	12	9.29	22.0	1,300
Wisconsin	92	73.8	0.7	0.8	1,600	2.4	17	8.75	28.6	875
Iowa	51	73.2	0.7	1.4	1,000	1.5	20	7.50	21.2	600
Indiana	44	54.8	0.5	1.2	600	0.9	14	10.25	23.7	NA
Hawaii	12	41.7	0.4	3.5	200	0.3	17	11.00	28.8	3,000
District of Columbia	26	33.4	0.3	1.3	300	0.5	12	12.00	17.1	2,000
Oklahoma	26	33.1	0.3	1.3	300	0.5	12	5.00	27.2	667
Alabama	25	30.3	0.3	1.2	400	0.6	16	7.80	27.1	2,250
Maine	19	18.7	0.2	1.0	200	0.3	11	10.00	13.4	2,000
South Carolina	33	18.1	0.2	0.5	200	0.3	6	17.00	25.4	1,000
Louisiana	31	15.5	0.1	0.5	200	0.3	6	9.00	25.8	NA
New Hampshire	23	14.9	0.1	0.6	200	0.3	9	10.00	27.5	1,500
Idaho	20	14.1	0.1	0.7	200	0.3	10	8.00	19.1	1,500
Vermont	16	10.3	0.1	0.6	300	0.5	19	7.75	18.4	NA
Montana	13	7.7	0.1	0.6	100	0.2	8	4.00	20.8	NA
New Mexico	14	4.1	0.0	0.3	100	0.2	7	4.00	24.4	NA
Georgia	65	(D)	NA	NA	375[1]	0.6	6	NA	NA	NA
North Carolina	47	(D)	NA	NA	750[1]	1.1	16	NA	NA	NA
Missouri	46	(D)	NA	NA	750[1]	1.1	16	NA	NA	NA
Arizona	41	(D)	NA	NA	750[1]	1.1	18	NA	NA	NA
Arkansas	18	(D)	NA	NA	175[1]	0.3	10	NA	NA	NA
Nebraska	13	(D)	NA	NA	375[1]	0.6	29	NA	NA	NA
North Dakota	5	(D)	NA	NA	175[1]	0.3	35	NA	NA	NA

Source: 1997 *Manufacturing STATROM* [machine-readable data files]. MStat97. Editorial Code and Data, Inc., Detroit, Michigan, 1997. Primary source: 1992 *Economic Census*. The states are in descending order of shipments or establishments (if shipment data are missing for the majority). The symbol (D) appears when data are withheld to prevent disclosure of competitive information. States marked with (D) are sorted by number of establishments. *Notes:* NA = Not available. 1. Indicates the midpoint of a range.

★ 78 ★

Miscellaneous Publishing

Miscellaneous Publishing: States with Most Activity

The industry is shown by segment. This category includes the printing of atlases, maps, calendars, directories, race track programs, technical manuals, and sheet music.

State	Shipments as % of U.S.	Employment as % of U.S.	Payroll as % of U.S.	Cost of Materials as % of U.S.	Investment as % of U.S.
California	19.20	13.00	13.50	17.90	19.20
Michigan	11.70	4.70	4.60	10.10	11.70
New York	9.80	13.80	11.00	10.30	9.80
Massachusetts	9.00	3.80	2.10	9.30	9.00
Pennsylvania	6.90	6.00	8.90	7.10	6.90
Colorado	5.20	5.20	7.20	4.90	5.20
Illinois	4.60	5.40	5.10	6.80	4.60
Kansas	4.50	3.10	2.10	4.00	4.50
Texas	2.60	3.70	3.00	2.80	2.60
New Jersey	2.30	3.80	3.00	2.30	2.30
Maryland	2.00	2.60	1.70	2.00	2.00
Florida	2.00	4.40	4.20	2.10	2.00
Washington	1.60	1.50	1.70	1.70	1.60
Minnesota	1.50	1.50	2.10	1.50	1.50
Ohio	1.50	2.80	3.00	1.50	1.50
Kentucky	1.30	1.20	1.70	1.10	1.30
Oregon	1.20	1.10	1.30	1.20	1.20
Utah	1.20	2.40	1.70	1.30	1.20
Tennessee	1.00	2.00	3.40	1.30	1.00
Virginia	1.00	1.50	1.70	1.00	1.00
Connecticut	1.00	1.70	2.10	1.00	1.00

Source: 1997 *Manufacturing STATROM* [machine-readable data files]. MStat97. Editorial Code and Data, Inc., Detroit, Michigan, 1997. Primary source: *Economic Census for 1992* and earlier years. The *Economic Census* is conducted by the Bureau of the Census, U.S. Department of Commerce, Washington, DC 20233.

Sales and Distribution

★ 79 ★

Publishers Projected Sales, 1995-1996

[In millions]

Segment	1995		1996		% Change	
	Units	Dollars	Units	Dollars	Units	Dollars
Trade	850.9	5,655.2	869.5	5,972.7	2.2	5.6
Adult	486.2	4,302.7	492.4	4,532.3	1.3	5.3
Juvenile	364.7	1,352.5	377.1	1,440.4	3.4	6.5
Mass Market	487.9	1,346.5	489.3	1,384.2	0.3	2.8
Book Clubs	120.8	938.6	121.4	984.8	0.5	4.9
Mail Order	96.7	564.5	93.9	559.1	-2.9	-1.0
Religious	155.4	1,036.2	157.7	1,074.9	1.5	3.7
Professional	165.4	3,869.3	166.8	4,074.4	0.9	5.3
University Press	17.7	339.7	17.8	357.4	0.5	5.2
Elhi	246.6	2,466.2	248.0	2,524.8	0.6	2.4
College	155.0	2,324.8	151.0	2,306.2	-2.6	-0.8
Standard. Tests	-	167.3	-	178.0	-	6.4
Sub. Reference	1.2	670.8	1.2	697.6	0	4.0
Total	2,297.6	19,379.1	2,316.7	20,114.1	0.8	3.8

Source: Milliot, Jim. "BISG Sees Only Modest Sales Gains for 1996." *Publishers Weekly,* 8 July 1996, p. 12. Primary source: *Book Industry Study Group Trends.*

★ 80 ★

Sales and Distribution

Publishers Projected Sales, 1996-1997

[In millions]

Segment	1996		1997		% change	
	Units	Dollars	Units	Dollars	Units	Dollars
Trade	847.3	5,626.0	857.4	5,825.5	1.2	3.5
Adult	458.8	4,146.8	456.1	4,254.6	-0.6	2.6
Juvenile	388.5	1,479.2	401.3	1,570.9	3.3	6.2
Mass Market	516.3	1,533.3	528.2	1,604.7	2.3	4.7
Book Clubs	135.5	1,091.8	141.3	1,184.3	4.3	8.5
Mail Order	96.4	579.5	95.2	575.4	-1.2	-0.7
Religious	164.4	1,104.2	170.2	1,179.4	3.5	6.8
Professional	163.6	3,994.6	166.5	4,227.3	1.8	5.8

[Continued]

★ 80 ★

Publishers Projected Sales, 1996-1997
[Continued]

Segment	1996		1997		% change	
	Units	Dollars	Units	Dollars	Units	Dollars
University Press	17.4	349.3	17.8	317.7	2.4	6.4
Elhi	255.4	2,607.6	268.3	2,774.5	5.0	6.4
College	162.6	2,485.8	167.0	2,659.0	2.7	7.0
Standard. Tests	-	178.7	-	190.3	-	6.5
Sub. Reference	1.2	706.1	1.2	728.7	0	3.2
Total	2360.1	20,256.9	2413.1	21,321.6	2.2	5.3

Source: "BISG Predicts a 5% Gain in Book Sales in 1997." *Publishers Weekly,* 7 July 1997, p. 12.
Primary source: *Book Industry Study Group Trends, 1997.*

★ 81 ★
Sales and Distribution

Publishing End Market Indicators

	Actual value			Annual average	Annual % change		
	Q4/98	Q3/96	Q4/95	1996	1996	1997	1998
Consumer spending[1]							
Nondurables	1,447.4	1,442.2	1,423.2	1,441.7	1.4	2.4	1.6
Books & Maps	20.0	19.1	18.8	19.8	1.8	1.5	0.7
Magazines & Maps	23.8	23.3	23.1	23.3	1.2	0.7	0.5
Publisher's new sales[2]							
Adult Trade	1,171.9	1,226.6	1,084.8	4,146.8	2.1	2.8	0.2
Juvenile Trade	291.4	495.7	308.0	1,479.2	11.5	5.1	4.8
Mass Market	294.3	464.0	267.9	1,533.3	2.3	3.2	1.8
Professional	1,067.1	953.0	1,003.9	3,994.6	3.2	3.7	1.1
ElHi Texts	309.0	1,543.4	263.1	2,607.1	5.7	10.5	4.2
College Texts	595.5	1,395.7	657.7	2,485.8	8.9	4.7	1.2

Source: "Publishing End Market Indicators." *Graphic Arts Monthly* (April 1997), p. 104. *Notes:* 1. Seasonally and inflation adjusted annualized rates; billions of dollars. U.S. Department of Commerce. 2. Millions of dollars, not seasonally adjusted. Association of American Publishers.

Companies

★ 82 ★

Brand Name Marketing by Publishers

Publishers are generating new revenue by marketing products branded with their magazine names. The table shows selected companies ranked by revenue generated from brand name marketing. Items marketed include fishing gear, apparel and toys. The Meredith Corporation markets Better Homes and Gardens.

Magazine	Percentage
Meredith Corporation	67
Playboy	52
Hachette Filipacchi	10
Hearst	5
Times Mirror	5-10

Source: "Extending the Brand Name." *New York Times,* 18 November 1996, p. C1. Primary source: magazine companies.

★ 83 ★

Companies

Harcourt Brace Sales by Segment, 1996

[In millions of dollars]

Segment	1995	1996	% change
Elementary	$190.5	$179.1	-6.0%
Secondary	124.2	140.0	12.7
College	156.6	155.8	-0.5
Testing	117.9	143.5	21.7
STMP	305.2	342.6	12.2
International	140.9	137.6	-2.3
Trade	37.9	38.9	2.9
Intercompany	(55.5)	(44.9)	-
Total	1,017.6	1,092.6	7.4

Source: "Harcourt Sales, Profits UP in 1996." *Publishers Weekly,* 10 March 1997, p. 14.

★ 84 ★
Companies

IPC's Best-Selling Titles

Reed Elsevier recently announced the sale of its UK magazine business IPC. Reed Elsevier is planning a merger with Wolters Kluwer to form the world's largest scientific and professional publisher. The table shows the circulation of IPC's top titles over a six month period.

Magazine	Circulation
What's on TV	1,702,184
TV Times	892,760
Woman	748,827
Woman's Own	712,484
Woman's Weekly	663,384
Chat	497,044
Marie Claire	435,006
Loaded	380,420
Woman & Home	333,621
Essentials	312,996

Source: Ryle, Sarah. "Reed to Sell IPC Magazines." *The Guardian,* 28 October 1997, p. 21. Primary source: Reed Elsevier.

★ 85 ★
Companies

Japan's Top Publishers, 1996

Other - 60.3
Recruit - 11.7
Kodansha - 9.5
Shueisha - 7.9
Shogakukan - 7.5
Gakken - 3.1

The value of books and magazines published grew to $18.1 billion. Market shares are shown in percent.

Company	Share
Recruit	11.7
Kodansha	9.5
Shueisha	7.9
Shogakukan	7.5

[Continued]

★ 85 ★

Japan's Top Publishers, 1996
[Continued]

Company	Share
Gakken	3.1
Other	60.3

Source: "Sector Breakdown Shows Market Shares in Japan." *Nikkei Weekly,* 4 August 1997, p. 4. Primary source: Nihon Keizai Shimbun Inc.

★ 86 ★

Companies

Leading Entertainment Publishers by Sales Growth

Data show growth in sales.

[In percent]

Company	Growth			
	Sales		Earnings per share	
	5-year Average	Latest 12 Months	5-year Average	Latest 12 Months
Publishing:				
Valassis	[1]	9.8	-57.8[5]	8.7
Reader's Digest Assn.	5.4	-2.5	-10	-75.7
Marvel Entertainment	61.3	6.9	[1]	[2]
Scholastic	16.5	19.3	14.1	-31.0
Gannett	3.4	14.0	10.2	71.1
Movies:				
Walt Disney	22.6	54.7	14.0	-24.6
AMC Entertainment	9.8	12.1	42.0[5]	-52.8
Seagram	12.7	50.3	-21.1	-93.2
Handleman	8.6	-1.1	[1]	[2]
Time Warner Companies	-10.6	9.2	[1]	[3]

Source: "49th Annual Report on American Industry" *Forbes,* 13 January 1997, page 92. *Notes:* 1. Not meaningful. 2. Profit to deficit. 3. Deficit to deficit. 4. Deficit. 5. Three year average.

★ 87 ★

Companies

Operating Performance of Publically Held Book Publishers, 1995-1996

[In millions of dollars]

Publisher	1995 Operating data			1996 Operating data		
	Revenue	Op. income	Margin	Revenue	Op. income	Margin
Dove	$11.1	$0.1	1.6	$26.8	($6.4)	-23.8%
Golden Books[9]	306.5	(23.3)	-7.5	204.1	(73.2)	-35.9
Harcourt Brace[9]	1017.6	177.5	17.4	1092.6	197.0	18.0
Harlequin[9]	484.8	$77.0	15.9	$509.3	$81.0	15.9
HarperCollins[1,9]	1096.0	134.0	12.2	932.0	68.0	7.3
Houghton Mifflin	529.0	(13.1)	-2.4	717.9	87.4	12.1
McGraw-Hill Ed.[2,9]	1235.6	162.6	13.1	1277.9	151.9	9.0
Pages	50.2	(6.2)	-12.3	29.9	0.6	2.0
Pearson[3,9]	727.9	65.4	8.9	934.5	99.1	10.6
Reader's Digest[4,9]	2099.8	339.3	16.1	2100.0	322.1	15.3
Scholastic[5]	749.9	67.7	9.0	928.6	57.8	6.2
Simon & Schuster[9]	2171.1	186.3	8.6	2331.7	217.2	9.3
Thomas Nelson[6]	219.8	(0.9)	-0.4	243.4	9.5	3.9
Times Mirror[7,9]	1091.0	(131.4)	-12.0	1031.2	58.7	5.7
Waverly	156.1	5.3	3.4	171.0	6.3	3.7
John Wiley[8]	362.7	33.0	9.1	432.0	34.8	8.0
World Book[9]	157.9	7.4	4.7	119.0	10.3	8.6

Source: "Publishers' Margins Show Surprising Strength in 1996." *Publishers Weekly,* 30 June 1997, p. 10. *Notes:* 1. For fiscal years ended June 30, 1996, 1995. 2. For the M-H Educational and Professional Publishing Group. 3. Combination of Penguin and AWL. 4. For book publishing & video units, fiscal years June 30, 1995. 5. For fiscal years ended May 31, 1996, 1995. 6. For fiscal years ended March 31, 1997, 1996. 7. For Professional Information Group. 8. For fiscal years ended April 30, 1997, 1996. 9. Denotes companies where corporate expenses are not deducted prior to operating income.

★ 88 ★

Companies

Playboy's Revenue

Data show ratio of net profit to loss.

[In percent]

Year	Amount
1990	2.4
1991	3.1
1992	4.1
1993	0.9
1994	-12.4
1995	0.6

[Continued]

★ 88 ★

Playboy's Revenue
[Continued]

Year	Amount
1996	4.3
1997	8.4

Source: "The Case of the Bouncing Bunny." *The Economist,* 26 July 1997, p. 58. Primary source: Gruntal & Co. and company reports.

★ 89 ★

Companies

Poland's Top Publishers

Total publishing sales in Poland reached zl.870 million and are expected to top zl.1 billion in 1997.

Name	Field	Sales (zl. million)	Profits (zl. million)	Titles published
Wydawnictwa Szkolne i Pedagogiczne	Textbooks	152.9	16.5	679
Wydawnictwo Naukowe PWN	Reference books, science	113.3	25.0	350
Swiat Ksiazki	Literature, self-education	61.0	-0.078	205
Muza	Literature	29.0	4.0	252
Polskie Przedsiebiorstwo Wydawnictw Kartograficznych im. E. Romera	Maps, atlases	25.2	4.7	155
Egmont	Children's books	16.9	NA	128
Amber	Literature, self-education	13.0	0.4	311
Arkady	Albums, self-education	11.3	1.7	83
BGW	Non-fiction	10.5	1.3	57
Wiedza Powszechna	Dictionaries popular science	10.5	0.35	79
Bellona	Literature, non-fiction	10.2	0.257	159
Proszynski i S-ka	Literature, popular science	10.0	1.2	178
Panstwowy Instytut Wydawniczy	Literature, essays	9.4	0.375	137
Multico	Albums	9.0	NA	45
Wydawnictwo Dolnoslaskie	Literature, essays	8.5	0.410	158

Source: "Volume Trading." *The Warsaw Voice,* 24 August 1997, p. 12. Primary source: *Rzeczpospolita Daily.*

★ 90 ★

Companies

Publishers Weekly Bestsellers by Corporation, 1995

Company	Hardcover			Paperback		
	# of Bks	# of Wks	Share[1]	# of Bks	# of Wks	Share[1]
Random House Inc.	54	446	29.2	30	227	14.8
Bantam Doubleday Dell	28	197	12.9	43	318	20.8
Simon & Schuster	32	194	12.7	29	231	15.1
HarperCollins	15	160	10.5	8	115	7.5
Time Warner	11	178	11.6	9	93	6.1
Putnam Berkley	15	74	4.9	27	174	11.4
Penguin USA	5	29	1.9	12	89	5.8
Hearst	5	26	1.7	5	17	1.1
St. Martin's	5	48	3.1	5	14	0.9
Hyperion	5	38	2.5	3	19	1.2
Health Communications	-	-	-	2	86	5.6
Workman	-	-	-	3	75	4.9
Running Press	1	45	2.9	-	-	-
New World	1	43	2.8	-	-	-
Andrews & McMeel	1	3	0.2	6	29	1.9

Source: Maryles, Daisy. "Bestsellers 1995 Winning Combinations." *Publishers Weekly,* 1 January 1996, p. 50. *Notes:* 1. This figure represents the publisher's share of the 1,530 hardcover or 1,530 paperback bestseller positions during 1995.

★ 91 ★

Companies

Publishers Weekly's Hardcover Bestsellers, 1996

Figures are based on the publisher's share of the 1,560 hardcover positions of 1996.

Company	Books	Weeks	Share (%)
Random House Inc.	44	319	20.4
Bantam Doubleday Dell	28	251	16.1
Simon & Schuster	24	176	11.3
HarperCollins	16	225	14.4
Time Warner	14	200	12.8
Putnam Berkley	20	136	8.7
Penguin USA	5	65	4.2
Hyperion	6	33	2.1
Hearst	3	8	0.5
St. Martin's	3	11	0.7
Andrews & McMeel	1	5	0.3

Source: Maryles, Daisy. "How the Winners Made It to the Top." *Publishers Weekly,* 6 January 1997, p. 46.

★ 92 ★

Companies

Publishers Weekly's Paperback Bestsellers, 1996

Figures are based on the publishers share of the 1,560 paperback positions in 1996.

Company	Books	Weeks	Share (%)
Random House Inc.	32	348.5	22.3
Bantam Doubleday Dell	38	241	15.4
Simon & Schuster	23	183.5	11.8
HarperCollins	12	59	3.8
Time Warner	16	98	6.3
Putnam Berkley	24	129	8.3
Penguin USA	17	188	12.1
Hyperion	3	16	1.0
Hearst	6	15	1.0
St. Martin's	3	19	1.2
Health Communications	4	97	6.2
Andrews & McMeel	8	75	4.8
Workman	1	33	2.1

Source: Maryles, Daisy. "How the Winners Made It to the Top." *Publishers Weekly,* 6 January 1997, p. 46.

★ 93 ★

Companies

Top 10 Things You Didn't Know About Harlequin Books

1. Harlequin saga is a bodice-ripping good yarn.

2. Harlequin paid one of its former authors $200,000 (U.S.) per year for life *not* to write for the competition.

3. It was Christopher Ondaatje who helped the founding Bonnycastle family shore up its source of supply in the 1970s - the key to Harlequin's market domination.

4. Harlequin's most damaging mistake was ending its U.S. distribution agreement.

5. Japanese readers prefer "unhappy endings in which everybody parts in...tears but having done their duty."

6. According to Margaret Atwood, the genre is not completely antifeminist because the stories dwell on female power to control men.

[Continued]

★ 93 ★

Top 10 Things You Didn't Know About Harlequin Books
[Continued]

7. Retailers stock more copies when the covers reveal more female skin.

8. In the Arab world, 40% of romance-buyers are male.

9. The big profits are in subscriptions, not retail sales.

10. Harlequin's best CEOs were packaged goods pros from Procter & Gamble.

Source: Report on Business Magazine (October 1996), p. 28.

★ 94 ★

Companies

Top Book Publishers Worldwide, 1995

From the source: "The global book market has become increasingly consolidated in the 1990s, with the world's 10 largest book publishing groups controlling 25 percent of a market worth $80 billion at retail last year. Big publishers have steadily increased their global market share during the 1990s. Euromonitor identifies the most highly consolidated markets as Spain, France and Germany, where the three largest publishers command at least 50 percent of total book sales. In the U.S.—the world's largest market, worth $25.49 billion at retail last year—the "big three" accounted for 21 percent of sales, with the 20 largest companies commanding 60 percent. Euromonitor expects the large groups to continue to gain market share in the late 1990s, with total book sales also expected to increase. Retail sales rose 24 percent from 1991 to 1995, and showed 8 percent growth last year, largely because of price increases fuelled by higher paper prices. The global book market is expected to grow 10.6 percent to $90.26 billion at retail in 2000. Central Europe will be the fastest growing region, with sales set to increase 19 percent—to $1.57 billion—by 2000. The Americas will show growth of 15.9 percent to $37 billion over the same period, largely because of a steep increase in Latin American sales. However, Euromonitor warns that book publishers face a tough task in raising profitability, particularly in mass market fiction, where average margins have slipped below 10 percent, against 20 percent for educational non-fiction.

Publisher	Sales ($ bil.)
Bertelsmann	4,766
Warner Books	3,722
Simon & Schuster	2,171
Pearson	1,748

[Continued]

★ 94 ★

Top Book Publishers Worldwide, 1995
[Continued]

Publisher	Sales ($ bil.)
Reader's Digest	1,629
Random House	1,500
Groupe de la Cite	1,480
Planeta	1,364
Hachette Livre	1,251
Reed Books	1,111
Harcourt Brace	900
HarperCollins	711
Putnam Publishing	381
Dorling Kindersley	220
Total	22,954

Source: Rawsthorn, Alice. "World Book Market Faces Further Consolidation." *Financial Times,* 2 October 1996, p. 16. Primary source: Euromonitor estimates.

★ 95 ★

Companies

Top Educational Publishers, 1996

Here is a list of educational publishers, based on sales in the K-12 and college markets. Simon R. Schuster tops the list with sales of $1.259 billion.

Company	Company
Simon & Schuster	Scholastic
McGraw-Hill	Thomson
Pearson	Harcourt
Houghton Mifflin	

Source: From the Internet, http://www.bookwire.com/subtext/publishing.article$2098. Primary source: *Subtext.*

★ 96 ★

Companies

Top Entertainment Publishers, 1996

Company	Sales Latest 12 Months ($ mil.)	Net Income Latest 12 Months ($ mil.)	Profit Margin Latest 12 Months (%)	Debt to Capita Latest (%)
Publishing:				
Valassis	654	22	3.4	340.4
Reader's Digest Assn.	3,012	61	2.0	0.0
Marvel Entertainment	814	-86	[1]	69.9
Scholastic	952	28	2.9	47.4
Gannett	4,456	810	18.2	50.5
Movies:				
Walt Disney	18,739	1,214	6.5	28.9
AMC Entertainment	684	23	3.3	60.1
Seagram	11,232	242	2.2	16.2
Handleman	1,179	-21	[1]	35.5
Time Warner Companies	8,726	-182	[1]	50.7

Source: "49th Annual Report on American Industry" *Forbes*, 13 January 1997, p. 92. *Note:* 1. Deficit.

★ 97 ★

Companies

Top Professional Publishers by Segment Revenue 1995-96

Data show worldwide revenues in millions of dollars.

Company	1995	1996
Thomson[1]	$2,577	$3,386
TCPI Unit:	1,290	1,452
STM (e)[2]	192	209
Reference	308	351
Healthcare	329	360
IP/Automotive	295	333
Regulatory	166	199
TFPPG Unit:	1,287	1,934
West/Legal[1]	652	1,154
Financial Services	635	780

[Continued]

★ 97 ★

Top Professional Publishers by Segment Revenue
1995-96
[Continued]

Company	1995	1996
Reed-Elsevier (e)	2,403	2,644
Scientific[3]	830	863
Professional[3]	1,462	1,657
R.R. Bowker (e)	111	124
Wolters Kluwer[4]	1,256	2,002
Legal/Tax[4]	475	1,142
Business	519	575
Medical/Scientific	262	285
McGraw-Hill (e)	1,345	1,373
Professional Books[5]	197	200
Shepard's[6]	109	57
Financial Services	787	856
Other[7]	252	260
Times Mirror[8]	632	629
Matthew Bender (e)	200	196
Mosby-Year Book (e)	300	285
Jeppesen Sanderson (e)	132	148
Harcourt	390	426
STMP	305	343
International[9]	85	83
IHS	265	290
Wiley[10]	214	236
STM	132	149
Other	82	87
BNA[11]	200	206
Simon & Schuster[12]	148	165
Waverly	156	171
Book Publishing	98	106
Periodical Publishing	52	58

[Continued]

★ 97 ★

Top Professional Publishers by Segment Revenue
1995-96
[Continued]

Company	1995	1996
Electronic Publishing	6	7
Total, 11 companies	$9,586	$11,528

Source: From the Internet, http:// simbanet.com/sources/pprsam.html#chart1, 9 May 1997.
Notes: Note: (e) = estimated. 1. 1996 figure includes six months of West, or an estimated $400 million (total annual revenues for West are estimated at about $870 million for the year ended July 1996; however, the total includes about $70 million to $90 million in educational textbooks). 2. Thomson reported revenues of $851 million in 1996 and $698 million in 1995 in its education/ science line; of the totals, approximately $641.8 million in 1996 and $506 million in 1995 was from school and college textbooks. 3. Translated from pounds sterling at $1.56. 4. 1996 figure includes revenues from legal and tax publisher CCH Inc., which the company acquired in 1996. CCH's 1995 revenues were estimated at about $600 million. Translated from Dutch Guilder at $.57. 5. McGraw-Hill's professional book publishing group had total revenues of $389 million in 1996 vs. $384 million in 1995. However, about $190 million of the total is from continuing education operation and international textbook sales, suggesting professional and business book revenues of about $200 million. 6. McGraw-Hill sold its Shepherd's citations operation in 1996 and its non-citations operation in 1995. 7. Other revenues for McGraw-Hill include Sweet's, F.W. Dodge, newsletters and other operations. 8. Doesn't include revenues from its 50% stake in Shepherd's legal citations business. 9. Harcourt reported $137.6 million in international sales of educational and professional products in 1996; approximately 60% of the total, or $83 million, is professional, the company confirmed. 10. Figures for fiscal year ending April 30. 11. Includes revenues from information publishing (Tax Management, Pike & Fischer and BNA Books)—or 88.7% of company revenues. Doesn't include commercial printing, software and training. 12. 1996 total includes about six months of revenues from Pfeiffer & Company or $4.5 million; doesn't include MacMillan Computer Publishing.

★ 98 ★

Companies

Top Publishing Companies, 1995

Publisher	1995 revenues ($ mil.)	% change vs. 1994	1995 Ad Pages	% change vs. 1994
Time Warner Inc.	2,010.5	11.2	22,412	7.2
Hearst Magazines	901.7	14.1	13,352	5.8
Conde Nast	750.0	12.0	18,737	6.2
Hachette Filipacchi	696.8	11.6	17,202	3.8
Meredith Corp.	562.0	16.3	6,740	-2.6
Parade Publications	515.6	15.2	740	3.3
Ziff-Davis	472.6	22.5	12,526	26.6
Gruner & Jahr	423.7	-1.5	5,806	-4.7
News America	406.9	3.9	3,229	1.6
Newsweek Inc.	331.9	19.0	2,300	10.7
Times Mirror	300.6	11.5	11,665	7.8
New York Times Co.	295.3	7.5	8,721	-1.3

[Continued]

★ 98 ★

Top Publishing Companies, 1995
[Continued]

Publisher	1995 revenues ($ mil.)	% change vs. 1994	1995 Ad Pages	% change vs. 1994
McGraw-Hill	267.6	14.5	3,816	4.8
Reader's Digest	249.3	30.8	3,039	6.0
U.S. News/The Atlantic	240.5	0.6	2,933	-5.6
Gannett	229.6	5.3	695	-4.9
Forbes Inc.	212.4	8.7	4,968	7.8
K-III Communications	188.5	13.8	6,352	7.9
Wenner Media	141.3	21.2	3,399	9.5
Rodale Press	119.0	22.5	3,643	6.1
Petersen Publishing	112.4	-0.8	4,228	-6.3
American Express	91.4	18.1	2,349	9.5
Cahners	90.8	7.2	3,259	2.0
Pace Communications	80.1	23.8	2,386	8.8
Goldhirsh Group	72.4	23.8	1,388	13.7
Lang Communications	67.5	12.0	1,808	4.0
Johnson Publishing	64.6	9.2	1,947	1.8
National Geographic	62.2	7.3	646	2.4
Weider Publications	60.3	5.2	2,735	-2.4
General Media	56.2	-8.9	2,880	-8.1
Walt Disney	47.6	34.6	1,419	13.5
Playboy Enterprises	47.2	3.0	626	-3.6

Source: "Top Publishing Companies." Brandweek, 4 March 1996, p. 27. Primary source: Competitive Media Reporting.

★ 99 ★

Companies

Top U.S. Publishers and Printers

Company	Rev. ($ mil.)	Profits ($ mil.)	Employees
R.R. Donnelley & Sons	6,599	158	38,000
Gannett	4,665	943	33,300
Times Mirror	3,401	206	18,521
Reader's Digest Association	3,098	81	6,300
McGraw-Hill	3,075	496	16,220
Knight-Ridder	2,775	268	20,263
New York Times	2,615	85	12,800
Dow Jones	2,482	190	11,844

[Continued]

★ 99 ★

Top U.S. Publishers and Printers
[Continued]

Company	Rev. ($ mil.)	Profits ($ mil.)	Employees
Tribune	2,406	372	10,700
American Greetings	2,012	115	21,700
Deluxe	1,896	65	19,640
Washington Post	1,853	221	7,300
World Color Press	1,641	47	12,500
E.W. Scripps	1,392	157	6,800
K-III Communications	1,374	8	7,200
Big Flower Press Holdings	1,202	5	6,410
Reynolds & Reynolds	1,100	94	7,544
Banta	1,084	51	6,100
Total	44,670	3,236	263,142

Source: "Fortune 1 Thousand Ranked Within Industries." Fortune, 28 April 1997, p. F59.

★ 100 ★

Companies

Top U.S. Trade Publishers, 1996-97

Firms are ranked by estimated sales in millions of dollars. The source did not provide figures for 1995.

Publisher	1996 ($ mil.)	1997 ($ mil.)	% change over 1995
Random House	1,250	1,250	0.0
Simon & Schuster	911	855	6.5
HarperCollins[1]	737	740	-0.4
Bantam/Doubleday/Dell	670	700	-4.3
Penguin USA[2]	306	312	-1.9
Warner/Little Brown	290	295	-1.7
Putnam	276	280	-1.4
St. Martin's Press	160	162	-1.2
Avon/Morrow	155	160	-3.1
Houghton Mifflin	82	87	-5.7

Source: From the Internet, http://www.bookwire.com/subtext/publishing.article$2,560, 10 September 1997. Notes: 1. Includes Zondervan. 2. Penguin USA sales only.

Costs and Margins

★ 101 ★

Profit Margins for Books and Magazines

Books typically carry a gross profit margin of about 40 percent based on cover prices that are higher—and often significantly higher—than magazine cover prices. The percentage markup is even higher for other items such as greeting cards, mugs with the faces of famous authors, calendars and fancy bookmarks. By contrast, magazines from an independent distributor with a monopoly on many popular titles earn only 20 percent of the cover price. That's not enough profit for some independent stores that decide either to drop magazines entirely or to carry them merely as a customer service—and certainly not to aggressively seek out more.

Source: Freedman, Eric. "Make the Bookstore Connection." *Folio,* 1 June 1996, p. 100.

★ 102 ★

Costs and Margins

Publishers' Manufacturing Expenses Project Average Dollars-Per-Unit Manufactured

Item	1996	1997	1998
Adult trade – hardbound	3.52	3.70	3.89
Plant	0.60	0.63	0.67
Paper, printing & binding	2.92	3.07	3.22
Adult trade – paperbound	2.23	2.37	2.52
Plant	0.29	0.31	0.33
Paper, printing & binding	1.94	2.06	2.19
Juvenile trade – hardbound	1.59	1.66	1.74
Plant	0.16	0.16	0.17
Paper, printing & binding	1.43	1.50	1.57
Juvenile trade – paperbound	1.11	1.18	1.25
Plant	0.10	0.11	0.12
Paper, printing & binding	1.01	1.07	1.13

[Continued]

★ 102 ★

Publishers' Manufacturing Expenses Project Average
Dollars-Per-Unit Manufactured
[Continued]

Item	1996	1997	1998
Mass market paperback (rack-size)	0.62	0.66	0.71
Book clubs – hardbound	2.72	2.76	2.81
Book clubs – paperbound	0.39	0.41	0.43
Mail order publications	1.45	1.51	1.57
Religious – hardbound	4.85	5.08	5.33
Plant	0.38	0.41	0.44
Paper, printing & binding	4.47	4.67	4.89
Religious – paperbound	1.62	1.70	1.79
Plant	0.20	0.23	0.25
Paper, printing & binding	1.42	1.46	1.54
Professional – hardbound	11.02	11.50	12.11
Plant	2.89	3.04	3.22
Paper, printing & binding	8.13	8.46	8.89
Professional – paperbound	2.44	2.54	2.66
Plant	0.37	0.39	0.41
Paper, printing & binding	2.07	2.15	2.25
University press – hardbound	16.49	17.20	18.00
Plant	5.40	5.65	5.93
Paper, printing & binding	11.09	11.55	12.07
University press – paperbound	4.02	4.22	4.44
Plant	0.79	0.82	0.85
Paper, printing & binding	3.23	3.40	3.59
ElHi – hardbound	5.20	5.47	5.77
Plant	1.20	1.28	1.37
Paper, printing & binding	4.00	4.19	4.40

[Continued]

★ 102 ★

Publishers' Manufacturing Expenses Project Average
Dollars-Per-Unit Manufactured
[Continued]

Item	1996	1997	1998
ElHi – paperbound	2.42	2.53	2.66
Plant	0.46	0.49	0.53
Paper, printing & binding	1.96	2.04	2.13
College – hardbound	5.82	6.07	6.35
Plant	1.67	1.75	1.85
Paper, printing & binding	4.15	4.32	4.50
College – paperbound	2.18	2.31	2.47
Plant	0.40	0.43	0.47
Paper, printing & binding	1.78	1.88	2.00
All books total	2.28	2.40	2.53

Source: "Book Industry Forecast: Consumer Spending, Publishers' Manufacturing Expenditure."
High Volume Printing (December 1996), p. 34. Primary source: *Book Industry Trends 1996.*

★ 103 ★
Costs and Margins

What it Costs to Put Together a Book

Putting together a book can cost $10,000 to more than $30,000.

Printing 3,000 copies of a standard 5 1/2-by-8 1/2 inch, 240-page paperback with a four-color cover and black-and-white printing inside typically costs $1.50 to $3.00 per book. A cover price for book like this ranges from $14.95 to $19.95.

A professionally designed cover can range in price from $500 to $7,000.

Source: "Do-It-Yourself Publishing." *Detroit Free Press,* 20 January 1997, p. 7F.

Mergers and Acquisitions

★ 104 ★

Publishing Mergers and Acquisitions, 1996

Buyer	Seller	Property	Price ($ mil.)	% of property
John Wiley & Sons	The Preservation Press	The Preservation Press	NA	100
Quarto Group	Walter Foster Publishing	Walter Foster Publishing	5.0	100
Viacom (Simon & Schuster)	Waite Group	Waite Group	NA	100
Tribune Company	Educational Publishing	Educational Publishing	200.0	100
Tribune Company	NTC Publishing Group	NTC Publishing Group	82.0	100
Pearson	News Corporation	Scott Foresman (Harper Collins Educ. Publishers)	580.0	100
Viacom (Simon & Schuster)	Pfeiffer	Pfeiffer	7.5	100
GP Holding	Western Publishing	Western Publishing (Golden Books Family Entertainment)	65.0	23
Cin Venture Managers	Thomson Corporation	Routledge	43.1	100
John Wiley & Sons	VCH Verlagsgesellch	VCH Verlagsgesellch	100.0	90
McGraw-Hill	Times Mirror	Times Mirror Higher Educ.	250.0	100
Reed Elsevier	United News & Media	Tolley Publishing	153.7	100
Tribune Company	Janson Publications	Janson Publications	4.0	100
Wolters Kluwer	Time Warner	Little, Brown and Company (legal & medical divisions)	NA	100
Harcourt General	Times Mirror	Mosby Doyma Libros	NA	100
Pearson	Seagram (MCA)	Putnam Berkley Group	336.0	100

Source: Milliot, Jim. "Value of Publishing Mergers Tripled in 1996." *Publishers Weekly,* 14 April 1997, p. 12. Primary source: Veronis, Suhler & Associates Communications Industry Transaction Report.

★ 105 ★

Argentina's Publishing Market

The Argentine book market is made up of about 200 publishing firms, 50 percent of which are small companies with revenues of less than $1 million. The rest can be divided as follows: 30 percent with annual sales between $1 and $3 million; 5 percent from $3 to $6 million, and 15 percent are larger companies with a turnover of more than $6 million annually. The publishing sector employs about 7,100 people. Approximately 70 percent are employed in the administrative and publishing areas and the rest in sales. Data are for the first six months of 1996.

Language	Number
Titles	
Spanish	3,621
English	554
French	77
Italian	50
German	47
Portugese	31
Other	68
Total	4,448
Month	
January	594
February	598
March	902
April	898
May	878
June	719
Total	4,589

Source: *National Trade Data Bank: The Export Connection CD-ROM,* STAT-USA, U.S. Department of Commerce, Washington, D.C. 20230, 1 December 1996, p. ISA961201. Primary source: C mara Argentina del Libro, "Listado de Asociados 1996."

★ 106 ★

Foreign Markets

Argentina's Publishing Market by Sector

The Argentine book market is estimated at $500 million. During the 1980s book production averaged 18 million copies. During 1996 the figure has grown to 40 million.

Language	Titles	Number of copies
Media		
Paper	4,413	19,131,928
Diskette	13	4,200
Cassette	11	103,610
CD-ROM	8	25,000
Video	3	2,100
Total	4,448	19,266,838

Source: National Trade Data Bank: The Export Connection CD-ROM, STAT-USA, U.S. Department of Commerce, Washington, D.C. 20280, 1 December 1996, p. ISA961201. Primary source: C mara Argentina del Libro, "Listado de Asociados 1996."

★ 107 ★

Foreign Markets

Canada's Publishing Market

Here are some facts on the Canadian publishing industry (from the source):

- According to the latest available Statistics Canada figures, 37 percent of the 300 Canadian-owned publishing firms lost money in 1992-93, up from 27 percent four years earlier.

- The market is largely dominated by American titles. Also, because of the economics of scale enjoyed by the U.S. publishers (it costs much less, on a per-unit basis, to print 50,000 rather than 5,000 copies of a book), those American books can usually be sold at a lower price than similar Canadian fare.

- 80 percent of books sold in Canada are imports.

- Publishers and authors alike must also deal with the picayune nature of the Canadian writing game. Poetry, even by acclaimed authors, will rarely sell more than 700 copies and almost never makes a profit. A hardcover fiction or nonfiction title that sells 5,000 copies has a good chance of making it on to one of the national best-seller lists. But that same book, priced at $25, will net the author only about $12,000 in royalties.

[Continued]

★ 107 ★

Canada's Publishing Market
[Continued]

- The few books that, by Canadian standards, become runaway best-sellers rarely sell enough copies to bail out a company's losses on the rest of its list. In 1993, McClelland & Stewart, Canada's largest domestically owned, general-interest publishing house, brought out an undisputed blockbuster—Pierre Trudeau's *Memoirs*, with 150,000 sales in in hard cover, and counting. Yet according to company sources, overall M&S still lost money—losses that were in large part underwritten by its owner, Avie Bennett.

- Industry grants, which reward firms for their net sales of Canadian titles, totaled $18.3 million in 1993-1994. Another $7 million came through the Canada Council to offset deficits incurred by "culturally significant" but commercially set unviable books such as first novels and poetry.

- British Columbia's 21 largest publishers had sales of more than $25 million in 1993.

- The average volume published in British Columbia earns a meager $4,500 for its author and about the same for its publisher.

- Federal statistics compiled in 1991 showed that British Columbia residents typically spent almost six hours a week reading books—well above the national average of 4.4 hours.

Source: "Publish and Perish." *Maclean's,* 17 October 1994, pp. 50-53.

★ 108 ★

Foreign Markets

France's Publishing Market

France's publishing sector is highly fragmented as there are about 500 publishing firms having produced at least one book in 1993. However, the market is quite concentrated; four percent of the firms account for more than 52 percent of the total French turnover. Distribution of the market is shown by value and volume of sales.

[In percent]

Segment	By volume	By value
General literature	45.0	36.5
Encyclopedias/dictionaries	8.1	17.3
Art publications	2.9	8.7
Scholarly	6.4	8.5
Practical guidebooks	7.3	8.1
Children/young adult	12.9	6.0
Social/human sciences	5.0	5.5
Adult comics	5.9	3.6
Technical/scientific/medical	2.1	3.4

Source: National Trade Data Bank: The Export Connection CD-ROM, STAT-USA, U.S. Department of Commerce, Washington, D.C. 20230, 27 May 1996, p. ISA9410.

★ 109 ★

Foreign Markets

Russia's Publishing Market

According to a recent market survey conducted by the popular national *Lzvestia*, publishing is now the second largest industry in Russia, in terms of gross sales (vodka sales rank first). The Russia Government's Center of Economic Analysis has reported that the volume of book and magazine production increased 21-29% in the first quarter of 1997. There are now 10,000 registered publishing houses in Russia. It is a highly diverse market, with an increasing focus on niche markets and translations of foreign works. Detective novels are the best-selling types of books, claiming 38% the fiction market. Religion and the occult are the best-selling forms of nonfiction, claiming 26% of the market.

Source: Ivanor, Mikhail. "What is Russia Reading?" *Russian Life,* (July 1997), p. 16.

★ 110 ★

Foreign Markets

Spain: Publisher Direct Sales by Channel

Publishing companies are the primary distributors of books to retailers/end users in Spain. Of the $2.93 billion books sold in 1993, 59% of sales were made by publishers and 41% by distribution companies. Sales are shown in millions of poesetas. Data for door-to-door, mail order, and clubs represent sales directly to individuals.

Channel	Sales (PTA mil.)	Distribution (%)
Door-to-door	74,730	36.0
Bookstores	55,820	26.9
Clubs	20,520	9.9
Mail order	19,370	9.3
Department stores	12,560	6.1
Private companies/ institutions	10,540	5.1
Public institutions	5,450	5.1
Publishers	3,260	1.6
Credit sale companies	2,520	1.2
News stands	570	0.3
Other	2,080	1.0

Source: "Spain - Book Distribution Channels." *National Trade Data Bank:* The Export Connection CD-ROM, STAT-USA, U.S. Department of Commerce, Washington, D.C. 20302, 21 October 1995, p. IMI950921.

★ 111 ★

Foreign Markets

United Kingdom: Top 20 Regional Press Publishers

Publisher	Daily circulation per week (000)	Weekly paid circulation (000)	Weekly free circulation (000)	Total circulation per week (000)
Trinity International Holdings	4,835	1,041	2,763	8,638
Northcliffe Newspapers Group	6,297	327	1,652	8,277
Newsquest Media Group Ltd.	2,878	746	4,084	7,709
United Prov. Newspapers	2,291	303	1,956	4,550
Johnston Press	852	1,023	2,381	4,255
Midland Independent Newspapers	1,865	145	1,648	3,658
Guardian Media Group	1,216	257	1,453	2,927
Eastern Counties Newspapers	1,202	149	1,155	2,506
Midland News Association Ltd.	1,804	43	601	2,448

[Continued]

★ 111 ★

United Kingdom: Top 20 Regional Press Publishers
[Continued]

Publisher	Daily circulation per week (000)	Weekly paid circulation (000)	Weekly free circulation (000)	Total circulation per week (000)
Southern Newspapers	999	244	1,165	2,408
Portsmouth & Sunderland	1,113	91	828	2,032
Caledonia Publishing	1,498	-	-	1,498
Adscene Group pic.	-	204	1,266	1,470
Scotsman Publications Ltd.	987	93	278	1,359
Bristol Evening Post	897	43	340	1,279
Southnews pic	-	214	910	1,123
Home Counties Newspapers	-	141	771	911
DC Thomson & Co. Ltd.	834	-	-	834
Yattendon Investment Trust	378	80	351	809
Independent Newspapers (UK)	-	95	666	761
Total top 20	29,945	5,241	24,265	59,451
All other regional publishers	1,416	1,584	3,869	6,869
Total regional publishers	31,362	6,824	28,133	66,320

Source: Garrett, Alexander. "Local Boy Makes Good." *The Observer,* 21 September 1997, p. 12.

Chapter 3
PUBLISHING: MARKET BY MARKET

This chapter presents statistics in tabular or text format on 19 categories of publishing: Audio Books, Business Books, Calendars, Children's Books, Comic Books, Cookbooks, Detective Novels, Electronic Publishing, Libraries, Maps, Professional Books, Religious Books, Romance Novels, Textbooks, Trading Cards, Translations, University Presses, Yearbooks, and Yellow Pages. Additional markets are treated under separate chapter headings, including *Catalogs*, *Greeting Cards*, *Magazines*, *Music*, and *Newspapers*. More material of interest will be found in the chapter on *Awards, Bestsellers, and Picks*.

Audio Books

★ 112 ★

Audio Book Market

The three largest audiobook clubs, Audio Book Club, The Columbia House Audiobook Club and Audio Books Direct, were all founded in 1994. All three are experiencing growth in membership and titles. Audiobook Club has 215,000 members and Columbia House Audiobook Club has 150,000 members. Sales of audiobooks have grown from $250 million in 1989 to $1.6 billion in 1996, with an annual growth rate of 20 percent. Demand is so high that audiobooks are on the market at the same time as hardcovers. Audio is the highest circulating section of most public libraries in the United States. Self-help titles are the most popular.

Source: "Audiobook Clubs Offer New Markets." *Small Press,* (November/December 1997), p. 64. Primary source: Herrick's Morristown, Audio Publishers Association and *American Bookseller.*

★ 113 ★

Audio Books

Audio Book Sales

More than 54,000 spoken-word titles are now in circulation. Most have been released in the past decade. Prices have been decreasing: a two-pack set that was $20 now costs $10.

Many retail sites offering audio books have begun to appear. Libraries are also beginning to offer a wide range of titles to the public. Some of the Internet sites that sell audio books are: www.audiobooks.com, www.audiobooksource.com, www.audiobookworld.com, www.earful.com/audio, and www.talkingbooks.com

Source: McDaniel, Jobeth. "Listen Up: Don't Drive Your Time Away." *Investor's Business Daily,* 13 January 1997, p. A1.

★ 114 ★

Audio Books

Audio Book Sales by Year

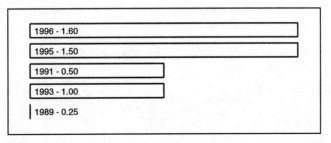

| 1996 - 1.60 |
| 1995 - 1.50 |
| 1991 - 0.50 |
| 1993 - 1.00 |
| 1989 - 0.25 |

The table estimated sales in billions of dollars. The most popular forms are self help, fiction and mystery.

[In dollars]

Year	($ bil.)
1989	0.25
1991	0.50
1993	1.00
1995	1.50
1996	1.60

Source: "More Books Read on Tape", *USA TODAY,* 14 August 1997, p. D1. Primary source: Audio Book Club.

★ 115 ★

Audio Books

Best-Selling Audio Books Among Truckers

Audio books have become so popular among truckers that many truck stops now rent audio cassettes. Books in Motion and Audio Adventures are two clubs that offer audio club memberships.

Title	Author
Iceberg	Clive Cussler
The Intruder	Peter Blauner
Extraordinary Powers	Joseph Finder
Snow Wolf	Glenn Meade
The Mediterranean Caper	Clive Cussler
M is for Malice	Sue Grafton
First Offense	Nancy Rosenberg
The Great Train Robbery	Michael Crichton
Dead Silent	Robert Ferrigno
The Green Mile	Stephen King

Source: Holmstrom, David. "Listening While the Miles Go By." *The Christian Science Monitor,* 27 March 1997, p. B1. Primary source: Audio Adventures Members survey.

★ 116 ★

Audio Books

Top-Selling Audio Books

Data show the year's best selling audio books through the Audio Book Club, the original membership club for books on tape. Figures are as of December 19, 1997, and indicate proportion of sales. For example, for every 10 copies of *Tick Tock* sold, *The Partner* sold 9.7 copies. Table includes title, author, reader.

Title/Author/Reader	Copies
Tick Tock, Dean Kootz, B.D. Wong	10.0
The Partner, John Grisham, Michael Beck	9.7
Ambush at Fort Bragg, Tom Wolfe, Edward Norton	8.9
Unnatural Exposure, Patricia Cornwell, Blair Brown	7.2
Reporter's Life, Walter Cronkite, Walter Cronkite	5.8
Matarese Countdown, Robert Ludlum, Stephen Lang	5.0
Flood Tide, Clive Cussler, Bruce Greenwood	4.2
Special Delivery, Danielle Steel, Richard Poe	2.9
Pretend You Don't See Her, Mary H. Clark, Randy Graff	1.1
Violin, Anne Rice, Maria Tucci	0.8

Source: "USA Snapshots." *USA TODAY,* 24 December 1997, p. D1. Primary source: Audio Book Club.

Business Books

★ 117 ★

Fifty Books Which Made Management

An enormous interest has developed in the field of business and management books. The table shows a list of the most influential books in the field, according to the source.

Title	Author	Year
Corporate Strategy	Igor Ansoff	1965
Organizational Learning	Chris Argyris & Donald Schon	1978
The Functions of the Executive Chester	Barnard	1938
Managing Across Borders	Christopher Barlett & Sumantra Ghoshal	1989
Management Teams	Meredith Belbin	1984
Leaders	Warren Bennis & Burt Nanus	1985
Leadership	James MacGregor Burns	1978
How to Win Friends and Influence People	Dale Carnegie	1937
Reengineering the Corporation	James Champy & Michael Hammer	1933
Strategy and Structure	Alfred Chandler	1962

[Continued]

★ 117 ★

Fifty Books Which Made Management
[Continued]

Title	Author	Year
Out of the Crisis	W. Edwards Deming	1982
The Practice of Management	Peter F. Drucker	1954
The Age of Discontinuity	Peter F. Drucker	1969
General and Industrial Management	Henri Fayol	1916
Dynamic Administration	Mary Parker Follett	1941
My Life and Work	Henry Ford	1923
Corporate-Level Strategy	Michael Goold, Andrew Campbell & Marcus Alexander	1994
Competing for the Future	Gary Hamel & CK Prahalad	1994
The Age of Unreason	Charles Handy	1989
The Motivation to Work	Frederick Herzberg	1959
Planning for Quality	Joseph M. Juran	1988
Change Masters	Rosabeth Moss Kanter	1983
Marketing Management	Philip Kotler	1967
Innovation Marketing	Ted Levitt	1962
The Prince	Nicolo Machiavelli	1500
The Human Side of Enterprise	Douglas McGregor	1960
Motivation and Personality	Abraham Maslow	1954
The Nature of Managerial Work	Henry Mintzberg	1973
The Rise and Fall of Strategic Planning	Henry Mintzberg	1994
The Mind of the Strategist	Kenichi Ohmae	1982
The Borderless World	Kenichi Ohmae	1990
Parkinson's Law	CN Parkinson	1958
The Art of Japanese Management	Richard Pascale & Anthony Athos	1981
Managing on the Edge	Richard Pascale	1990
In Search of Excellence	Tom Peters & Robert Waterman	1982
Liberation Management	Tom Peters	1992
Competitive Strategy	Michael Porter	1980
The Competitive Advantage of Nations	Michael Porter	1990
Organization Culture and Leadership	Edgar Schein	1985
Maverick	Ricardo Semler	1993
The Fifth Discipline	Peter Senge	1990
My Years With General Motors	Alfred P. Sloan	1963
The Wealth of Nations	Adam Smith	1776
The Principles of Scientific Management	Frederick W. Taylor	1911
The Third Wave	Alvin Toffler	1980
Up the Organization	Robert Townsend	1970
Riding the Waves of Culture	Fons Trompenaars	1993

[Continued]

★ 117 ★

Fifty Books Which Made Management

[Continued]

Title	Author	Year
The Art of War	Sun Tzu	500 BC
A Business and its Beliefs	Thomas Watson Jr.	1963
Theory of Social and Economic Organization	Max Weber	1947

Source: "Fads That Speak Volumes." *Financial Times,* 9 December 1996, p. 14.

★ 118 ★

Business Books

United Kingdom: Business/Management Book Publishing

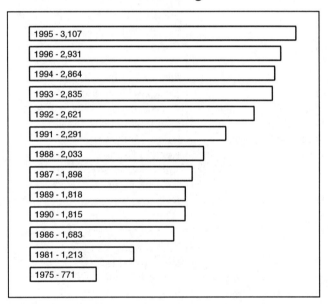

1995 - 3,107
1996 - 2,931
1994 - 2,864
1993 - 2,835
1992 - 2,621
1991 - 2,291
1988 - 2,033
1987 - 1,898
1989 - 1,818
1990 - 1,815
1986 - 1,683
1981 - 1,213
1975 - 771

The business publishing market is valued at 35 million British pounds. While this is a fairly small market, it is expected to be growing at an estimated 20% a year. The market includes everything from training manuals detailing the latest trends to academic tomes.

Year	New titles
1975	771
1981	1,213
1986	1,683
1987	1,898
1988	2,033

[Continued]

★ 118 ★

United Kingdom: Business/Management Book Publishing
[Continued]

Year	New titles
1989	1,818
1990	1,815
1991	2,291
1992	2,621
1993	2,835
1994	2,864
1995	3,107
1996	2,931

Source: Simon, Caulkin. "Are Business Books Hot Stuff? See the Sales Figures - They Speak Volumes." *The Observer,* 16 March 1997, p. 6. Primary source: Whitaker.

Calendars

★ 119 ★

Best-Selling Calendars, 1996

Calendar	Calendar
Angels	Georgia O'Keeffe paintings
Anne Geddes childrens' photos	Goosebumps
Dilbert: Ask Me How My Day Went	Life's Little Instruction Calendar
Disney Days	The Muppets
Gary Larson's "Far Side"	Rottweilers
Friends	Winnie-the-Pooh

Source: "Best-Selling Calendars of 1996: Do You Own One?" *The Christian Science Monitor,* 31 October 1996, p. 2. Primary source: Calendar industry distributors and publishers.

★ 120 ★
Calendars

U.S. Calendar Market

People spend an estimated $4.0 billion each year on calendars in the United States.

Source: Nearman, Barry. "Daze of His Life: Putting Together A Blowout Calendar." *The Wall Street Journal,* 15 December 1997, p. A14.

★ 121 ★

All-Time Best-Selling Children's Books

Book	Hardcover sales ($ 000)
The Poky Little Puppy	14,000
The Tale of Peter Rabbit	9,331
Tootle	8,056
Saggy Baggy Elephant	7,098
Scuffy the Tugboat	7,065
Pat the Bunny	6,147
Green Eggs and Ham	6,065
The Cat in the Hat	5,644
The Littlest Angel	5,425
One Fish Two Fish, Red Fish, Blue Fish	4,822

Source: "All-Time Best-Selling Children's Books." *Business and Society Review,* 1 July 1996, p. 74.

★ 122 ★

Children's Books

Children's Book Market by Unit Sales, 1995-2000

Year	Hardcover (mil.)	Paperback (mil.)	Total
1995	165.6	175.4	341.0
1996	168.0	185.5	353.5
1997	171.5	193.5	365.0
1998	175.0	201.3	376.3
1999	178.2	208.5	386.7
2000	181.0	216.5	397.5
Change 1995-2000 (%)	9.3	23.4	16.6

Source: Milliot, Jim. "Looking Down the Road to 2000." *Publishers Weekly,* 23 September 1996, p. 30. Primary source: *Veronis, Suhler & Associates Communications Forecast.*

★ 123 ★

Children's Books

Children's Book Sales, 1995-2000

Year	Hardcover ($ mil.)	Paperback ($ mil.)	Total
1995	1,286.6	948.5	2,231.1
1996	1,345.6	1,050.1	2,395.7
1997	1,411.9	1,136.8	2,548.7
1998	1,479.9	1,225.5	2,705.4
1999	1,546.8	1,314.0	2,860.8
2000	1,611.7	1,410.6	3,022.3
% change 1995-2000	25.3	48.7	35.5

Source: Milliot, Jim. "Looking Down the Road to 2000." *Publishers Weekly,* 23 September 1996, p. 30. Primary source: *Veronis, Suhler & Associates Communications Forecast.*

★ 124 ★

Children's Books

Children's Book Sales by Channel, 1994

[In percent]

Segment	Share (%)
General retailers	70.2
Libraries and institutions	12.2
School	9.8
Export	3.2
College	1.2
Direct to consumer	0.5
Other	2.9

Source: Publishers Weekly, 21 August 1995, p. 24. Primary source: Book Industry Study Group Trends.

★ 125 ★

Children's Books

Children's Pop-Up Books

Carvajal S.A. is the world's largest producer of children's pop-up books, which are sold in 23 different languages on five continents. That amounts to a 50% share of the total world market.

Source: Thomson, Adam "Most International Trader." *Latin Trade* (January 1997), p. 38.

★ 126 ★

Children's Books

Cost of Books for Kids, 1996

Less than $2.00 - 35	
$3.50-$5.99 - 27	
$2.00-$3.49 - 21	
$6.00 and up - 17	

Data show the prices paid for juvenile books.

Cost	Percentage
Less than $2.00	35
$2.00-$3.49	21
$3.50-$5.99	27
$6.00 and up	17

Source: "USA Snapshots." *USA TODAY,* 15 October 1997, p. D1. Primary source: *1996 Consumer Research Study on Book Purchasing. Note:* Excludes book club and remainder sales.

★ 127 ★

Children's Books

Juvenile Book Sales by Outlet

Outlet	1994 (000)	% of units	1995 (000)	% of units	% change 1994-1995
Total outlets	526,119	100.0	511,807	100.0	-2.7
Total new book stores	81,816	15.6	87,164	17.0	6.5
Chains	54,645	10.4	56,831	11.1	3.6
Independents	27,171	5.2	30,533	6.0	12.4
Total mail	118,620	22.4	114,708	22.4	-3.3
Book clubs	89,589	17.0	91,401	17.9	2.0
Mail order	29,051	5.5	23,307	4.8	-19.8
Total mass market	216,437	41.1	202,900	39.6	-6.3
Food/drug stores	44,733	8.5	39,921	7.38	-10.8
Price clubs	14,950	2.8	14,407	2.8	-3.6
Discount stores	156,754	29.8	148,572	29.0	-5.2

[Continued]

★ 127 ★

Juvenile Book Sales by Outlet
[Continued]

Outlet	1994 (000)	% of units	1995 (000)	% of units	% change 1994-1995
Other outlets	107,035	20.9	109,246	20.8	-2.0
Toy stores	24,290	4.7	27,244	5.2	-10.8
Variety stores	14,881	2.9	16,844	3.2	-11.7
All other outlets	67,864	13.3	65,158	12.4	4.2

Source: Annicelli, Cliff. "Books Blossom in Toy Turf." *Playthings* (May 1997), p. 35. Primary source: American Booksellers Association.

★ 128 ★

Children's Books

Juvenile Book Sales by Type

Juvenile book sales reached 536 million units.

[In percent]

Segment	Share
Fiction	50.0
Coloring/activity	25.0
Nonfiction	10.0
Educational	5.0
Religious	5.0
Book with tape/CDs	2.0
Book with electronic soundpad	2.0
Reference	1.0

Source: "Fiction for Kids." *USA TODAY,* 19 November 1997, p. D1. Primary source: *1996 Consumer Research Study on Book Purchasing.*

★ 129 ★

Children's Books

Top 15 Children's Trade Publishers, 1995

Figures are based on estimated net sales in millions of dollars.

Publisher	1994	1995	% change
Golden Books	290.0	260.0	-10.3
Scholastic	83.0	138.0	66.3
Random House	120.0	125.0	4.2
HarperCollins	93.0	99.5	7.0

[Continued]

★ 129 ★

Top 15 Children's Trade Publishers, 1995
[Continued]

Publisher	1994	1995	% change
Simon & Schuster	90.0	95.0	5.5
Putnam/Grosset	81.0	82.0	1.2
Penguin USA	72.0	75.0	4.2
Disney Juvenile Publishing	45.0	62.0	37.8
Bantam Doubleday Dell	55.0	55.0	0
Hearst (Morrow/Avon)	41.0	43.0	4.9
DK Publishing	26.0	36.0	38.5
Harcourt Brace	20.0	24.1	20.5
Houghton Mifflin	24.0	24.0	0
Little, Brown	20.0	17.5	-12.5
Candlewick	9.5	13.3	40.0
Total	1069.5	1149.4	7.5

Source: Milliot, Jim and Diane Roback. "Top Children's Publishers Post Modest Overall Gains." *Publishers Weekly,* 28 October 1996, p. 34.

★ 130 ★

Children's Books

Who Purchases Children's Books

Data show who purchases books for children. The table compares customers at chain bookstores, general independent booksellers, and stores that sell only children's books and peripheral goods. Figures are based on a survey of 1,500 readers and 341 members of the Association of Booksellers for Children.

[In percent]

Purchaser	Child	Independent	Chain
Mother	41.7	36.5	45.0
Child	6.2	17.2	15.4
Grandparent	8.6	13.4	9.9
Teacher	27.7	12.4	9.6
Father	5.5	9.6	9.4
Friend	4.1	4.1	2.8
Other relative	3.2	3.6	3.8
Unknown	3.2	3.3	4.2

Source: Publishers Weekly, 1 May 1995, p. 36. Primary source: Cahners Publishing.

```
                    Comic Books
```

★ 131 ★

Best-Selling Comics

Data show the best-sellers for the month of August 1996. Kingdom Come is by DC Comics and Spawn is from Image. The rest are all Marvel titles.

Title	Title
Kingdom Come	*Spawn*
Uncanny X-Men	*Generation X*
X-Men	*Wolverine*
Cable	*X-Factor*
Onslaught: Marvel Universe	*X-Man*

Source: Szadkowski, Joseph. "Comics Industry is a Serious Venture." *The Washington Times,* 29 September 1996, p. C1. Primary source: *Comics Retailer.*

★ 132 ★

Comic Books

Comic Book Market by Segment

Category	Share (%)
Comics - black & white, color	72.10
Books - illustrated comics, graphics	7.10
Novels/trade paperbacks miscellaneous	5.90
Cards - sports, non-sports	5.80
Comics/games/sports	4.60
Posters/prints/portfolios/calendars	1.90
Books - sci fi/horror/novels	1.80

Source: "A Comic Is a Many Splendored Thing." *Non-Foods Merchandising* (December 1994), p. 14. Primary source: Diamond Comics Distribution.

★ 133 ★

Comic Books

Comic Books: A Quick Look at the Industry

Here are some facts on the comic industry:

- From 1993 to 1996, the number of comics retailers have fallen from 9,000 owners to 4,500. Industry sales decreased from $1.0 billion to less than $500 million.

[Continued]

★ 133 ★

Comic Books: A Quick Look at the Industry
[Continued]

- In the early 1990's, comic book print runs often averaged in excess of 100,000 copies for key titles.

- The top-selling comic of all time is X-Men No. 1, released October 1991.

Source: Szadkowski, Joseph. 'Comics industry is a Serious Venture." *The Washington Times,* 29 September 1996, p. C1. Primary source: *Comics Retailer.*

★ 134 ★
Comic Books

Growth of the Comic Book Market

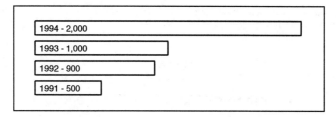

1994 - 2,000
1993 - 1,000
1992 - 900
1991 - 500

The market includes all comic-related merchandise, such as toys, apparel and trading cards.

Year	Value ($ mil.)
1991	500
1992	900
1993	1,000
1994	2,000

Source: "Can't Get Enough of Comic Books." *Non-Foods Merchandising* (December 1994), p. 14. Primary source: *Comic Buyer's Guide 1995 Annual.*

★ 135 ★
Comic Books

Japan's Comic Publishing Market, 1995

Total sales of comic books and magazines reached 586.1 billion yen.

Segment	Share (%)
Comic magazines	28.0
Comic books	11.3
Other books and magazines	60.7

Source: Fulford, Benjamin. "Comics in Japan Not Just Funny Business." *Nikkei Weekly,* 24 February 1997, p. 1. Primary source: Research Institute for Publications.

★ 136 ★
Comic Books

Production of Japanese Comics by Category, 1995

Category	Copies (mil.)
Boys'	662
Young men's	551
Girls'	146
Jokes, games, sex, other subjects	133
Young women's	103

Source: "Indicators." *Far Eastern Economic Review,* 10 October 1996, p. 15. Primary source: *Japanese Book News.*

★ 137 ★
Comic Books

The Cost of a Comic Book

The average comic costs $2.50. The table shows how the cost is divided.

[In dollars]

Segment	Cost
Retailer	1.25
Printer	.50
Publisher	.50
Distributor	.25

Source: Szadkowski, Joseph. "Comics Industry is a Serious Venture." *The Washington Times,* 29 September 1996, p. C1. Primary source: Industry sources.

★ 138 ★

Comic Books

Top Comic Book Producers

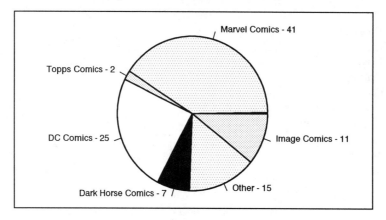

Marvel Comics - 41

Topps Comics - 2

DC Comics - 25

Image Comics - 11

Dark Horse Comics - 7

Other - 15

Market shares are shown for September 1996.

[In percent]

Company	Market share
Marvel Comics	41
DC Comics	25
Image Comics	11
Dark Horse Comics	7
Topps Comics	2
Other	15

Source: Szadkowski, Joseph. "Comics Industry is a Serious Venture." *The Washington Times,* 29 September 1996, p. C1. Primary source: *Comics Retailer.*

★ 139 ★

Comic Books

Top Comic Book Publishers

Shares are based on estimated sales of $650-$725 million in 1994.

[In percent]

Comic Book	Dol. share	Unit share
Marvel	32.70	33.93
DC Comics	19.87	22.30
Image	15.24	16.55
Malibu	5.28	4.90

[Continued]

★ 139 ★

Top Comic Book Publishers
[Continued]

Comic Book	Dol. share	Unit share
Valiant	4.32	4.23
Dark Horse	4.99	3.49
Tekno	1.20	1.46
Wizard Press	2.32	1.24
Topps	1.55	0.80
Viz	1.32	0.71
Others	11.21	10.59

Source: Non-Foods Merchandising (December 1994), p. 14, from Diamond Comics Distribution, Krause Publications.

★ 140 ★

Comic Books

Trade Penetration of Comics

Figures are for 1991-1993.

Location	Rate (%)
Supermarkets	47
Convenience stores	24
Drug stores	18
Discount stores	11

Source: "Statwrap." *Non-Foods Merchandising* (January 1995), p. 8. Primary source: Comic Magazine Association of America, Marvel Entertainment and Curtis Circulation.

★ 141 ★

Comic Books

Where Comic Books Are Sold

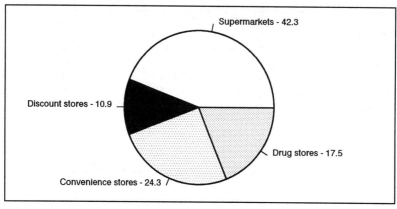

[In percent]

Location	Share (%)
Supermarkets	42.3
Convenience stores	24.3
Drug stores	17.5
Discount stores	10.9

Source: "Statwrap." *Non-Foods Merchandising* (January 1995), p. 8. Primary source: Comic Magazine Association of America.

★ 142 ★

Comic Books

Who Buys Comic Books

- 85% are male.
- 15% are female.
- 50% are pre-teens or teenagers.
- 10-15% are older readers, who account for a disproportionate amount of funds spent.
- 1.5 to 2 million are frequent buyers, readers.
- 10 million are casual buyers, readers.

Source: "All You Need Is Fans." *Non-Foods Merchandising* (December 1994), p. 14. Primary source: *Comic Buyer's Guide 1995 Annual.*

Cookbooks

★ 143 ★

Popular Cookbooks

The table lists the leading cookbooks of 1996, according to *Nations Restaurant News.*

1. *Fish and Shellfish: The Cook's Indispensable Companion*, by James Peterson.

2. *La Cucina Siciliana di Gangivecchio*, by Wanda and Giovanna Tornabene.

3. *The Complete Book of Irish Cooking*, by Darina Allen.

4. *The South, The Beautiful Cookbook*, by Mara Rogers and Jim Auchmutey.

5. *Foods of Sicily*, by Guiliano Bugiali.

6. *Rick Bayless's Mexican Kitchen*, by Rick Bayless.

7. *Patricia Wells At Home in Provence*, by Patricia Wells.

8. *Pedaling Through Burgundy Cookbook*, by Sarah Leah Chase.

9. *Taverna*, by Joyce Goldstein.

10. *The Foods of Thailand*, by Wannaphen Heyman-Sukphan.

Source: "The Year in Review Top 10 Cookbooks" *Nation's Restaurant News,* 23 December 1996, p. 45.

Detective Novels

★ 144 ★

Frequency of Book Purchases by Mystery Readers

Figures are based on a 1990 survey of *Ellery Queen* and *Alfred Hitchcock* readers (circulation approximately 500,000).

Purchases	Subscribers (%)
Purchased any books	75.8
Purchased hardcover books	57.7
Purchased 10+ hardcover books	18.3
Purchased paperback books	66.3
Purchased 10+ paperback books	39.1

Source: "Murder by the Numbers." *Small Press* (July/August 1996), p. 37. Primary source: *Ellery Queen* and *Alfred Hitchcock.*

★ 145 ★

Detective Novels

Number of Books Purchased by Mystery Readers

Category	Average per subscriber
Hardcover	5.7
Paperback	13.3
Total	19.0

Source: "Murder by the Numbers." *Small Press* (July/August 1996), p. 37. Primary source: *Ellery Queen* and *Alfred Hitchcock.*

★ 146 ★

Detective Novels

Number of Books Read by Mystery Readers

Category	Average per subscriber
Hardcover	10.4
Paperbacks	17.7
Total	28.1

Source: "Murder by the Numbers." *Small Press* (July/August 1996), p. 37. Primary source: *Ellery Queen* and *Alfred Hitchcock.*

Electronic Publishing

★ 147 ★

Best-Selling CD-ROM Games

MYST - 3.1

Doom II - 1.7

Microsoft Flight Simulator - 1.7

Doom Shareware - 1.3

Sim City 2000 - 1.0

7th Guest - 0.9

Warcraft II - 0.8

Dark Forces - 0.8

Sim City Classic - 0.8

Ultimate Doom - 0.7

Data show sales for the PC and Mac since 1993.

[In millions]

Game	Units
MYST	3.1
Doom II	1.7
Microsoft Flight Simulator	1.7
Doom Shareware	1.3

[Continued]

★ 147 ★

Best-Selling CD-ROM Games
[Continued]

Game	Units
Sim City 2000	1.0
7th Guest	0.9
Warcraft II	0.8
Dark Forces	0.8
Sim City Classic	0.8
Ultimate Doom	0.7

Source: Schiesel, Seth. "The Games People Play." *New York Times,* 27 October 1997, p. C5. Primary source: PC Data.

★ 148 ★

Electronic Publishing

CD-ROM Title Market by Revenue

Data show the sources of revenue in the consumer CD-ROM market.

Source	Revenue share (%)
Entertainment publishing	35
Entertainment developing	19
Edutainment publishing	12
Distribution	6
Edutainment developing	6
Licensing	5
Online publishing/developing	4
OEM	3
Other	10

Source: Gussin, Lawrence. "The Consumer Title Publishing Business." *Online Inc.,* (January 1997), p. 32.

★ 149 ★

Electronic Publishing

CD-ROM Titles in Print

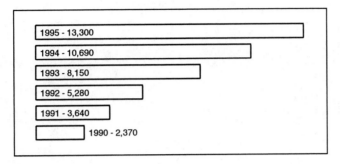

| 1995 - 13,300 |
| 1994 - 10,690 |
| 1993 - 8,150 |
| 1992 - 5,280 |
| 1991 - 3,640 |
| 1990 - 2,370 |

The multimedia market is expected to reach $30 billion in the United States by the year 2000. The source points out that one of the most interesting things about the multimedia market is that it is the general consumer market place that is driving the growth of the market, not the business arena. Recent figures show that CD-ROM software aimed at consumers accounted for 90 percent of unit sales and 76 percent of revenues.

Year	No. of titles
1990	2,370
1991	3,640
1992	5,280
1993	8,150
1994	10,690
1995	13,300

Source: Gill, Penny. "Limitless Possibilities." *HFN: Buyers Guide to Multimedia Computing,* 2 January 1995, p. 5. Primary source: InfoTech.

★ 150 ★

Electronic Publishing

Global CD-ROM Production

United States - 65	
	Germany - 10
	U.K. - 8
	France - 7
	Taiwan - 5
	Other - 5

The world retail value of all electronic publishing products, including audio books, online publications, and CD-ROMs, reached $3.0 billion for the year ended June 1996. The CD-ROM market had sales of over $1.0 billion in the U.S. alone. Sales have been hampered by a small customer base (many computer owners don't own drives), the reluctance of bookstores to promote them and low profit margins due to computer retailers discounts. The table shows production by country.

[In percent]

Country	Market share
United States	65
Germany	10
U.K.	8
France	7
Taiwan	5
Other	5

Source: Rawsthorn, Alice. "A Giant Leap for CD-ROM." *Financial Times,* 7 October 1996, p. 13. Primary source: Euromonitor.

★ 151 ★

Electronic Publishing

Law-Related CD-ROM Publishers

Year	Publishers
1993	107
1994	147
1995	177
1996	182

Source: Schulman, Richard D. "CD-ROM/CD-R in the Legal Labyrinth." *CD-ROM Professional* (November 1996), p. 75. Primary source: InfoSources Publishing.

★ 152 ★

Electronic Publishing

Law-Related CD-ROM Titles Published

Period	Titles
1993	232
1994	415
1995	605
Jan. 1996	850
Mar. 1996	900
Jun. 1996	960

Source: Schulman, Richard D. "CD-ROM/CD-R in the Legal Labyrinth." *CD-ROM Professional* (November 1996), p. 75. Primary source: InfoSources Publishing.

★ 153 ★

Electronic Publishing

Leading Online Magazines

The table shows the readership of Web-only magazines, called E-Zines. Readership is estimated by each Web magazine.

Magazine	Readers
Hotwired (www.hotwired.com)	3,000,000/year
Mr. Showbiz (www.mrshowbiz.com)	23,000/day
Word (www.word.com)	80,000/week
Suck (www.suck.com)	11,000/day
Feed (www.feedmag.com)	25,000/week
Salon (www.salon1999.com)	50,000/month

Source: U.S. News & World Report, 24 June 1996, p. 18.

★ 154 ★

Electronic Publishing

Newspapers Online

Here are some facts about on-line newspapers:

Number of North American dailies on the Internet in 1997: more than 500.

Number of newspapers charging subscriptions for all user access in 1997: 2.

Percentage of on-line publishers who report profits for 1996 or 1997: 36%.

Source: "The State of Small Business 1997." *Inc.,* 20 May 1997, p. 111. Primary source: Newspaper Association of America.

★ 155 ★

Electronic Publishing

Online Minority Publications

Minority publications are increasingly going online. Here is a list of some of the more popular:

Title	Title
www.latinolink.com www.HispanStar.com www.vibe.com	www.blackenterprise www.essence.com www.amagazine.com

Source: Skriloff, Lisa. "A Diverse Netizenry." *Brandweek*, 17 February 1997, p. 17.

★ 156 ★

Electronic Publishing

Online Newspapers by Type

Data are shown based on each periodical's parent company.

Type	Number
Dailies	1,420
Weeklies	648
Publishing groups	119
Business	109
Alternative	72
Specialty papers	68
Online commercial services	37
Dial-ups (BBS)	33
Misc.	96

Source: From the Internet, http://www.mediainfo.elpress.com/ephome/npaper/nphtm/stats. htm, 5 November 1997. Primary source: *Editor & Publisher.*

★ 157 ★

Electronic Publishing

State Data for Sale

Formerly, data collected by state and local governments at taxpayer expense were freely available to the public in paper form. Now that data have been converted to computer tapes, they come with a hefty price tag to businesses such as newspapers. Here are a few examples of public databases recently requested by newspapers for story research and their current prices.

Newspaper	Request	Price ($ mil.)
Houston Chronicle	Motorists arrest records (Texas Department of Public Safety)	60.0
Belleville News Democrat	Driver's license records (State of Ilinois)	37.5
Providence Journal Bulletin	Motor vehicle records (State of Rhode Island)	9.7

Source: Peterson, Iver. "Public Information, Business Rates." *New York Times,* 14 July 1997, p. C1.

★ 158 ★

Electronic Publishing

Top 10 Web Publishers, 1996

Data show revenues generated by advertising on the World Wide Web. Figures are for the first six months of 1996.

Publisher	Revenue ($ mil.)
Netscape	9,664.5
Infoseek	5,785.4
Yahoo!	5,689.1
Lycos	4,123.2
Excite	3,641.0
ZD Net	3,183.1
CNET	3,176.3
ESPNET SportsZone	2,443.3
WebCrawler	2,160.0
NewsPage	2,145.1

Source: "Web Ads Trail Net Radio by Far." *Advertising Age,* 2 September 1996, p. 35. Primary source: *Jupiter Communications' WebTrack AdSpend report. Notes:* Netscape's revenue figures include payments by five search engines to be listed on the company's home page. Jupiter estimates the payments amounted to $6.25 million for the second quarter.

★ 159 ★

Electronic Publishing

Top 15 Web Advertisers, 1996

Company	Spending
Microsoft - 2,905.7	
Netscape - 2,172.9	
IBM - 2,087.2	
Excite - 1,850.2	
Infoseek - 1,772.7	
AT&T - 1,735.7	
CNET - 1,554.7	
Nynex - 1,549.0	
McKinley Group - 1,468.0	
Yahoo! - 1,340.0	
Lycos - 1,294.8	
Digital Equipment - 1,145.7	
Toyota - 868.9	
Individual Inc. - 753.5	
Apple Computer - 716.1	

Data show ad spending on the World Wide Web. Figures are for the first six months of the year.

Company	Spending ($ mil.)
Microsoft	2,905.7
Netscape	2,172.9
IBM	2,087.2
Excite[1]	1,850.2
Infoseek[1]	1,772.7
AT&T	1,735.7
CNET	1,554.7
Nynex	1,549.0
McKinley Group[1]	1,468.0
Yahoo![1]	1,340.0
Lycos[1]	1,294.8
Digital Equipment	1,145.7
Toyota	868.9

[Continued]

★ 159 ★

Top 15 Web Advertisers, 1996

[Continued]

Company	Spending ($ mil.)
Individual Inc.	753.5
Apple Computer	716.1

Source: "Web Ads Trail Net Radio by Far." *Advertising Age,* 2 September 1996, p. 35. Primary source: *Jupiter Communications' WebTrack AdSpend report. Notes:* 1. Jupiter counts as ad spending payments by five search engines to be listed on the Netscape engines to be listed on the Netscape home page. Jupiter estimates the search engines committed an estimated $1.25 million each to the program during the second quarter.

★ 160 ★

Electronic Publishing

Top 20 World Wide Web Sites

Data show the number of "hits", or the number of times each Web site is visited.

Site	No. of daily hits
Netscape	30,000,000
Yahoo!	9,452,579
ESPNet SportsZone	8,500,000
Infoseek Corporation	6,000,000
Pathfinder	4,800,000
Playboy	4,723,957
HotWired	3,000,000
Microsoft	3,000,000
Silicon Graphics	2,640,000
Lycos	2,141,578
The News & Observer Pub.	2,074,958
Penthouse	2,000,000
Internet Shopping Network	1,862,219
Mercury Center	1,626,000
First Virtual	1,452,000
Global Network Navigator	1,211,168
Apple Computer	1,200,000
NewsPage	1,200,000
Electronic Newsstand	1,000,000
Novell	1,000,000

Source: "The Top 20 Sites." *Business Today,* 7 October 1996, p. 39. Primary source: *Traffic Resource.*

★ 161 ★

Electronic Publishing

Top Consumer Sites

The table shows the most popular consumer shopping Web sites, based on a panel of 10,000 households. Sites are ranked by percent of audience.

Site	Purchase	% of audience
Shareware.Com www.shareware.com/	Freeware/shareware	5.9
Columbia House Online www.columbiahouse.com/	Videos, laserdiscs	2.9
ZD Net Software Library www.hotfiles.com/	Freeware/shareware	2.9
CUC International www.cuc.com/	Club sales of products, services	1.8
Amazon.com Books www.amazon.com/	Books	1.6
Surplus Direct www.surplusdirect.com/	Computer hardware, software	1.5
Gateway 2000 www.gw2k.com/	Computer hardware, software	1.4
Jumbo! www.jumbo.com/	Freeware/shareware	1.3
BMG Music Service www.bmgmusicservice.com/	CDs	1.2
Onsale www.onsale.com/	Auction of computer hardware, software consumer electronics	1.1
CDnow www.cdnow.com/	CDs, records, videos, CD-ROMs	1.1

Source: Branwyn, Gareth. "Consumer Shopping Web Sites." *Wired* (March 1997), p. 86. Primary source: PC-Meter, Division of NPD Group Inc.

★ 162 ★

Electronic Publishing

Top Software Publishers, 1996

Sales of PC software grew from $4.1 billion in 1995 to $4.6 billion in 1996. However, the number of new titles fell from 4,146 to 3,972. Data show sales in millions of dollars and estimated market share.

Company	Sales ($ mil.)	Market share
Microsoft	931.3	20.3
CUC	280.9	6.1
Intuit	238.6	5.2
Symantec	191.0	4.2
Broderbund	174.9	3.8
Learning Co.	156.7	3.4
Corel	139.9	3.1
Electronic Arts	121.2	2.6
Adobe	118.2	2.6
GT Interactive	94.0	2.1
Disney	79.0	1.7
Virgin	66.9	1.5
Quarterdeck	61.5	1.3
Lucas Arts	57.3	1.3
Micro Prose	49.4	1.1
Activision	49.2	1.1
Interplay	47.6	1.0
Maxis	43.6	1.0
Mindscape	42.1	0.9
Netscape	39.6	0.9

Source: "Top Software, Top Companies of 1996." *USA TODAY,* 6 February 1997, p. 5D. Primary source: PC Data surveys retailers accounting for 55% of the market and projects industrywide sales totals.

★ 163 ★

Public Library Spending by State

The table shows per capita spending on library collections for 1993. Collection expenditures include books, periodicals, albums, videos and software.

State	Spending ($ per capita)
Ohio	5.57
Indiana	4.95
New York	4.39
New Jersey	4.00
Connecticut	3.88
Massachusetts	3.85
Nevada	3.78
Washington	3.76
District of Columbia	3.76
Illinois	3.65
Kansas	3.58
Maryland	3.54
Missouri	3.51
Alaska	3.48
New Hampshire	3.36
Hawaii	3.29
Minnesota	3.23
Wyoming	3.16
Colorado	3.14
Virginia	3.07
Utah	3.05
Wisconsin	3.04
New Mexico	2.88
Iowa	2.87
Oregon	2.77
Rhode Island	2.77
Nebraska	2.76
South Dakota	2.74
Florida	2.68
Arizona	2.64
Maine	2.61
Michigan	2.43

[Continued]

★ 163 ★

Public Library Spending by State
[Continued]

State	Spending ($ per capita)
Vermont	2.36
North Carolina	2.32
Idaho	2.28
South Carolina	2.12
Delaware	2.09
Oklahoma	2.07
North Dakota	2.00
California	1.99
Louisiana	1.93
Alabama	1.90
Georgia	1.87
Pennsylvania	1.83
Texas	1.71
Kentucky	1.68
Montana	1.55
Tennessee	1.48
West Virginia	1.46
Arkansas	1.37
Mississippi	1.15

Source: "Big Spenders on Books." *The New York Times,* 24 February 1997, p. C9. Primary source: National Center for Education Statistics via American Library Association.

★ 164 ★

Libraries

Who Uses the Library

There are nearly 16,000 public libraries in the United States. In 1994, they had 671,741,000 books on their shelves. With their shrinking budgets, libraries must continually choose between funding book purchasing or high-tech services. Many libraries feature Internet access, CD-ROMs and information databases. The table below shows how libraries are used, based on a survey of 99,088 households.

Library use by household	With children under age 18	Without children
Borrowed books or tapes	53	26
Attended programs, used equipment	26	14
Called for information, book renewal	18	12
Used home computer to link to library	5	3

Source: Grossman, Cathy Lynn. "Libraries are Torn Between Books, Bytes." *USA TODAY,* 17 July 1997, p. D1. Primary source: National Center for Education Statistics American Library Association.

Maps

★ 165 ★

Most Requested Road Maps - 1994

State	Total
Washington, DC	1,429,000
Richmond, VA	1,308,850
New York, NY	1,298,200
Atlanta, GA	1,146,200
Jacksonville, FL	1,137,700

Source: "USA Snapshots." *USA TODAY,* 4 August 1995, p. D1. Primary source: AAA.

★ 166 ★

U.S. Professional Book Exports

The table shows the top markets for exports of technical, scientific and professional books. Figures are in millions of dollars for the first six months of 1997.

Country	Value ($ mil.)
Canada	100.6
Japan	45.3
U.K.	23.7
Australia	14.3
Germany	14.3

Source: From the Internet, http://www.bookwire.com/subtext/International.article $3,487. Primary source: U.S. Department of Commerce.

★ 167 ★

Christian Book Buying by Age

An estimated 21% of adults often or very often shop for Christian/ religious[1] books or Bibles; nearly 60% rarely or never do. Data show percent of these age groups who buy such books.

Age	% who purchase
18-29	35.7
30-39	48.0
40-49	34.8
50-59	43.4
60 and up	50.0

Source: Carey, Anne R. and Marcy E. Mullins. "Age of Religious-Book Buyers." *USA TODAY,* 2 January 1997, p. 1. Primary source: Cahners Research for Zondervan and *Publisher's Weekly.* *Note:* 1. Christian themes or written from Christian perspective.

★ 168 ★

Religious Books

Christian-Themed Book Purchases

Inspirational - 40
Devotion/meditation - 38
Bibles - 35
Christian living - 31
Reference - 21
Study guides - 19
Theology - 18
Fiction - 18

About 42% of people who shop in general bookstores say they brought a Christian/religious book[1] in the past year. Data show types most purchased:

Type	Response (%)
Inspirational	40
Devotion/meditation	38
Bibles	35
Christian living	31
Reference	21
Study guides	19
Theology	18
Fiction	18

Source: Carey, Anne R. and Suzy Parker. "Market for Christian Books." *USA TODAY,* 15 January 1997, p. D1. Primary source: Cahners Research for Zondervan Publishing and *Publishers Weekly. Note:* 1. Christian themes or written from Christian view.

★ 169 ★

Religious Books

Growth in Religious Publishing

Religious and spiritual materials have been the fastest growing segment in adult publishing for the last two years. Some stats.

- Sales of religious publishers have reached $1 billion, with unit sales exceeding 150 million.

- Wal-Mart, Target, Borders, and Barnes & Noble have all expanded their religious inventory. Religious book chains and independents open 20,000 square foot superstores.

[Continued]

★ 169 ★

Growth in Religious Publishing
[Continued]

- Sales at Christian bookstores have apparently tripled to $3 billion since 1980.

- The largest Christian book chain is Family Bookstores, with $135 million in revenues.

- Christian music sales have reached $550 million.

Source: Ferguson, Tim and Josephine Lee. "Spiritual Reality." *Forbes,* 27 January 1997, p. 70.

★ 170 ★

Religious Books

Leading Bible Translations/Versions

Translation/version	Sales (%)
New International	40.0
King James	20.0
New King James	10.0
Living Bible	7.0
New American	5.0
International Children's	4.0
The Message	3.5
New Revised Standard	3.0
All others	7.5

Source: "Gospel According to Market." *USA TODAY,* 24 December 1996, p. D1. Primary source: Zondervan Publishing.

★ 171 ★

Religious Books

Why the Bible is Not Read More

Figures are based on a survey of 1,000 adults.

Reason	Percentage
It's hard to understand	19
It's too long to get through	15
Messages seem to contradict one another	13
It's hard to find parts that relate to your life	12
It's hard to find topics of interest	10
Much of the Bible is boring	8

Source: "The Bible, a Perennial, Runs Into Sales Resistance." *New York Times,* 28 October 1996, p. C10. Primary source: Barna Research via Tyndale House Publishers.

Romance Novels

★ 172 ★

Romance Novel Market

Regular readers spend an average of $1,200 a year on romance novels, usually on paperbacks that cost $6 or $7 each. Sales have risen 8 percent, to $189 million in 1991.

Source: "The Romance Novel Magazine That Has Them Swooning." *New York Times,* 10 December 1996, p. B3.

★ 173 ★

Romance Novels

Romance Then and Now

Ten years ago, there were six major house publishing contemporary category romances: Bantam, Dell, Jove, Harlequin, New American Library and Silhouette. They published 900 titles a year; the average writer earned up to $50,000 a book. Retail price per book: $1.50.

Today, there are three major houses: Bantam, Harlequin (which now owns Silhouette) and Kensington, publishing 800 titles a year. The average writer earns up to $40,000 a book. Price per book: $3.50.

Source: "Romancing the Buck." *Forbes,* 2 June 1997, p. 44. Primary source: Maria Carvainis Agency Inc.

★ 174 ★

Best-Selling Economics Textbooks

Publishers sell about 750,000 new copies of economics textbooks each year, most of them recent editions of perennial favorites. Here are the best-selling introductory economic textbooks, based on industry estimates.

Author(s)	Title, publisher	Editions so far	Estimated yearly sales
Campbell R. McConnell and Stanley L. Brue	*Economics* McGraw-Hill	12 editions since 1962	150,000
William J. Baumol and Alan S. Blinder	*Economics* Harcourt Brace	6 editions since 1979	75,000
Roger LeRoy Miller	*Economics Today* HarperCollins	6 editions since 1973	75,000
Ralph T. Byrns and Gerald W. Stone	*Economics* HarperCollins	6 editions since 1983	75,000
Michael Parkin	*Economics* Addison-Wesley	2 editions since 1990	75,000
Richard G. Lipsey, Paul N. Courant, Douglas D. Purvis and Peter O. Steiner	*Economics* HarperCollins	10 editions since 1965	50,000
Paul A. Samuelson and William D. Nordhaus	*Economics* McGraw-Hill	14 editions since 1948	50,000

Source: "Todays Top Sellers." *New York Times,* 14 March 1995, p. C8. *Notes:* Figures are for full-book equivalents, counting texts that are sold broken up into multiple volumes as a single sale.

★ 175 ★

Textbooks

Leading Social Studies Textbooks

Data show the leading social studies textbooks used in grades 4-12. Figures are shown based on a survey of 572 social studies teachers.

Category and Title	Publisher
Economics: *Economics Today and Tomorrow*	Glencoe (McGraw-Hill)
Geography: *World Geography*	Prentice Hall (Simon & Schuster)
U.S. History: *History of the U.S.*	Houghton Mifflin
World History: *World History: Perspectives On The Past*	D.C. Heath (Houghton Mifflin)

Source: From the Internet, http://www.bookwire.com/subtext/education.article $1,683, 25 June 1997. Primary source: Education Market Research.

★ 176 ★

Textbooks

Leading Social Studies Textbooks by Grade

The table shows the top textbook for each grade based on a survey of 572 social studies teachers.

- 4: Various state history titles

- 5: *The World Around Us: U.S. And It's Neighbors,* McGraw-Hill

- 6: *The World Past and Present,* McGraw-Hill

- 7: *World Geography,* Prentice Hall

- 8: *American Nation,* Prentice Hall

- 9: *World Geography Today,* Holt Rinehart & Winston (Harcourt Brace)

- 10: *World History: Perspectives On The Past,* D.C. Heath

- 11: *The Americans,* McDougal Littell (Houghton Mifflin)

- 12: *Economics Today And Tomorrow,* Glencoe

Source: From the Internet, http://www.bookwire.com/subtext/education.article $1,683, 25 June 1997. Primary source: Education Market Research.

★ 177 ★

Textbooks

Social Studies Text Publishing: Market by Market

From the source: "Most of the newest texts are for grades K-8, with new editions for high school expected in the next couple of years. *Adventures in Time* gained 21 percent of the $46 million social studies market this year, *Educational Marketer,* a Stanford, Conn.- based newsletter covering educational publishing, reported in August. The series cornered 60 percent of the K-6 market in Texas, and sold well in Florida, Indiana, and Virginia. California and North Carolina are expected to adopt new social studies texts next year.

Source: Manzo, Kathleen Kennedy. "Glimmer of History Standards Shows Up in Latest Textbooks." *Education Week,* 8 October 1997, p. 1.

★ 178 ★

Textbooks

Textbooks: The Rising Costs of College Editions

Between 1965 and 1994—the last year for which figures are available—college textbook prices went up by 478 percent. The average physics textbook costs $75; the average literature book costs $45. At two-year institutions in Michigan the average student pays $500 a year for textbooks; at four year institutions, the figure rises to $670 per year. The figures are comparable across the country. The table shows the cost of selected editions.

[In dollars]

Textbook	1975	1985	1997
Accounting (Meigs)	13.95	34.95	61.25
Principles of Physics	14.95	36.95	60.00
Norton Anthology/English Literature	10.95	21.95	39.95

Source: Murray, Diana Dillaber. "Legislature Considers Relief from High Costs." *The Sunday Oakland Press,* 7 December 1997, p. A16. Primary source: *Campus Marketplace,* the newsletter of the National Association of College Stores.

★ 179 ★
Textbooks

The Cost of Textbook Production, 1994-95

Data show the distribution of the textbook dollar.

[In cents]

Segment	Cost
Printing	32.2
Store overhead	20.8
Marketing	13.8
Author income	11.4
Publisher overhead	8.7
Publisher income	7.1
Store income[1]	4.7

Source: Murray, Diana Dillaber. "Throwing the Book at Competition." *The Sunday Oakland Press,* 7 December 1997, p. A1. Primary source: Association of American Publishers and National Association of College Stores. *Notes:* 1. Varies, depending on whether store is owned by school, foundation or private entity.

★ 180 ★
Textbooks

U.S. Textbook Market

According to the source, "Textbook publishing for grades K-12 is big business, with $3.5 billion in sales last year. Five companies—Simon & Schuster, McGraw-Hill, Houghton Mifflin, Harcourt General, and Addison Wesley Longman—make up 70 percent of the market. While in theory the companies produce different texts to accommodate the needs of different states, the presidents of McGraw-Hill, Simon & Schuster, and Addison Wesley Longman told *U.S. News* that, broadly speaking, 80 percent of their texts' content doesn't vary from state to state. Since California, Texas, and Florida account for 25 percent of book purchases, the major publishers regularly develop new texts around these states' needs, then adapt them slightly, at low cost, for others. According to researchers, these texts and the accompanying teachers' guides, along with standardized tests such as the Stanford Achievement Test, have enormous influence over classroom instruction across the country."

Source: Miller, Matthew. "Surprise! National School Standards Exist." *U.S. News & World Report,* 17 November 1997, p. 35.

★ 181 ★

Textbooks

U.S. Textbook Shipments

In terms of dollar value of exports, textbooks are the third largest book category among the nine tracked by the U.S. Department of Commerce. Technical, scientific and professional books topped the list with exports valued at $282.1 million. The table shows the value of exports to the top markets in thousands of dollars.

Country	1996	1997	% change
United Kingdom	29,845	41,456	38.9
Canada	29,642	30,679	3.5
Australia	13,144	11,689	-11.1
Japan	11,227	10,713	-4.6
Mexico	8,244	10,037	21.8
Taiwan	6,153	9,316	51.4
Germany	6,557	6,074	-7.4
Singapore	3,845	3,347	-12.9
Hong Kong	2,093	3,346	59.9
South Korea	4,593	2,771	-39.7
Switzerland	2,327	2,183	-6.2
New Zealand	1,403	2,033	44.9
Peru	749	1,742	132.6
Brazil	391	1,356	246.5
Belgium	1,800	1,249	-30.6
Netherlands	1,377	1,050	-23.7
Top 16 total	123,390	139,041	12.7
World total	140,003	155,770	11.3
Top 16 as % World	88.1	89.3	

Source: From the Internet, http://www.bookwire.com/subtext/international. article $3,395, 1 October 1997. Primary source: *Subtext* and U.S. Department of Commerce. *Note:* Figures for 1997 are for the first six months of the year.

Trading Cards

★ 182 ★

Baseball Card Sales by Year

Baseball card makers have recently tried a variety of gimmicks to jump start the market. The market has suffered from over-production and the players strike of 1994.

[In millions]

Year	Total
1988	250
1989	450
1990	800
1991	1,200
1992	1,100
1993	850
1994	750
1995	700
1996	650[1]
1997	600[1]

Source: *USA TODAY,* 23 October 1997, p. B1 Primary source: *Sports Collectors Digest. Note:* 1. Estimate.

★ 183 ★

Trading Cards

Popular Sports for Trading Cards

An estimated 44% of kids aged 9-13 collect sports trading cards. About one in four of them are girls. The table shows what they collect.

Sport	Response (%)
Basketball	69
Baseball	65
Football	53
Hockey	20
Soccer	6

Source: Hall, Cindy and Suzy Parker. "Top Sports for Trading Cards." *USA TODAY,* 29 November 1996, p. C1. Primary source: *Sports Illustrated for Kids* Omnibus Study.

★ 184 ★

Trading Cards

Sports Card Collecting by Region

Data show the share of boys and girls, ages 3-13, who collect by region. An estimated 62% of boys and 16% of girls collect sports cards.

Area	Share (%)
West North Central	47
East North Central	44
Middle Atlantic	38
New England	41
South Atlantic	45
East South Central	36
West South Central	41
Pacific	41
Mountain	35

Source: "Card-Carrying Sports Fans." *USA TODAY,* 4 August 1997, p. C1. Primary source: NFO Research for Enesco Corp.

★ 185 ★

Trading Cards

Sports/Novelty Card Sales by Year

Data show sales for the year ended March 11, 1995 and March 9, 1996.

Category	Value
52 Weeks ending 3/9/96 - $ Volume (000)	17,916
52 Weeks ending 3/11/95 - $ Volume (000)	29,168
Change in $ Volume - %	-38.6
52 Weeks ending 3/9/96 - Unit Volume (000)	9,425
52 Weeks ending 3/11/95 - Unit Volume (000)	17,745
Change in Unit Volume - %	-46.9

Source: "Trading Cards." *Non-foods Merchandising* (October 1996), p. 36.

★ 186 ★

Foreign Licensing by Poland, 1995

Data show the number of licenses granted to translate foreign works into Polish. After Russian and English, German is the third most widely read foreign language in Eastern Europe.

Language	Licenses
German	454
English	374
Czech	284

Source: From the Internet, http://www.bookwire.com/subtext/International.article $1,911, 9 July 1997. Primary source: Association of the German Book Trade.

★ 187 ★

Translations

The Spanish Language Book Market in the United States

It was the success of *Like Water for Chocolate* in 1994 that really called attention to the U.S. Spanish Language market. The Hispanic population has grown to 30 million people and their buying power has reached $350 billion. Here are some story facts on the Spanish language industry:

- Simon & Schuster launched its Libros en Espanol line in 1995 and now offers 27 titles. Subjects include fiction, nonfiction and translations.

- Vintage manages the Vintage Espanol line. It has 47 titles in cooperation with Grupo Santilana and another 12 titles on its own.

- *Like Water for Chocolate* has sold 113,000 copies as of August 1997.

- Puerto Rico can represent as much as 50% of the Spanish language market for U.S. trade book publishers.

- Circulode Lectures is the only Spanish language book club in the U.S. operating exclusively through mail order. It claims 75,000 members.

Source: Taylor, Sally. "In Search of the Spanish Market." *Publishers Weekly,* 25 August 1997, p. S36.

★ 188 ★

Fast Facts About University Presses

- The first university press books were published at Oxford and Cambridge in the 1580s. Three centuries later, the first university press was established on this side of the Atlantic at Cornell University.

- The oldest continuously operating press in the United States was established at The John Hopkins University in 1878.

- Presses represent an array of universities—large and small, public and private—with some publishing only two or three titles annually vs. ones that issue more than 200 or more books per year.

- Of the approximately 50,000 books published in the United States in 1993, roughly 8,000, or 16 percent, appeared under the imprints of presses that are members of the Association of American Presses.

- AAUP was created as a formal organization in 1937 and established with a central office in New York City since 1959. The association consists of 114 presses.

Source: Brogdon, Ken. "Reinventing the Academic Press." *Small Press,* (May/June 1996), p. 35. Primary source: Association of American University Presses.

★ 189 ★

University Presses

Pennsylvania's University Presses

Sales of university presses reached $385 million in 1995. The number of new titles has grown from 4,500 a decade ago to between 8,000 and 9,000 from 1996. In 1995, more than 85 percent of university book sales came from monographs—narrowly focused, scholarly works. As university budgets shrink, however, publishing houses find themselves receiving less money from the administration. School libraries are receiving less money to purchase books. As a result, university presses are finding they have to compete with large, commercial houses.

University	Established	Staff	Focus	Average new books per year	Average press run	Sales in 1996
Temple University Press	1968	15	Ethnic studies, regional interests	60	2,500 paper 250 hardbound	3 mil.
University of Pennsylvania Press	1890	20	Landscape architecture, anthropology, medieval studies, Asian studies	75	1,000-4,000, depending on audience target	2 mil.
Pennsylvania State University Press	1956	18	Art history, philosophy and religion	70	500-5,000	1.8 mil.

Source: Briggs, Rosland. "Adapting to the Press of Change." *Philadelphia Inquirer,* 23 February 1997, p. D1. Primary source: Temple University Press, University of Pennsylvania Press, Pennsylvania State University Press.

★ 190 ★

University Presses

University Presses

University presses publish about 8,000 books a year, some 15 percent of the 50,000 books published in the United States.

Source: Applebome, Peter. "Publishers' Squeeze Making Tenure Elusive." *New York Times,* 18 November 1996, p. A1.

Yearbooks

★ 191 ★

Yearbook Publishing

Jostens Inc., the nation's biggest yearbook producer, publishes 18,000 yearbooks, 1,000 of them at colleges and universities and the rest at high schools.

Source: Applebome, Peter. "Trends Conspire Against the Yearbook." *New York Times,* 3 December 1996, p. A8.

Yellow Pages

★ 192 ★

Yellow Pages Publishers

Companies are ranked by revenues in millions of dollars.

Publisher	($ mil.)
BellSouth Corp.	1,556.0
GTE Corp.	1,200.0
Bell Atlantic	1,082.0
Pacific Telesis Group	1,003.0
US West	997.0
SBC Communications	946.8
Nynex Corp.	894.4
Ameritech Corp.	795.2
Dun & Bradstreet Corp.	440.1
DonTech	411.7

Source: Advertising Age, 14 August 1995, p. 24, from company reports.

Chapter 4
BOOK PUBLISHING

Book publishing continues to be one of the three major "anchors" of the publishing industry (along with Newspapers and Magazines). This chapter presents data on this industry as a whole. Specific products are covered in the chapter on *Publishing: Market by Market*. Information on awards and bestsellers is presented in the chapter on *Awards, Bestsellers, and Picks*. In this chapter, coverage includes *Industry Statistics*, *Sales and Distribution*, *Retailing*, *Wholesaling*, *Book Fairs*, *Buyers*, *Consumer Spending*, *Production*, and *Foreign Markets*.

★ 193 ★

General Statistics on Book Publishing, 1982-1998

Year	Com-panies	Establishments		Employment			Compensation	
		Total	With 20 or more employees	Total (000)	Production workers (000)	Hours (mil.)	Payroll ($ mil.)	Wages ($ hr.)
1982	2,007	2,130	420	67.1	15.2	30.8	1,327.3	7.70
1983	NA	2,094[1]	427[1]	69.3	17.1	33.0	1,474.9	8.42
1984	NA	2,058[1]	434[1]	69.4	14.9	27.2	1,600.3	9.86
1985	NA	2,023	440	70.9	15.6	28.6	1,672.1	9.78
1986	NA	2,013	449	71.6	14.4	25.6	1,775.6	10.13
1987	2,180	2,298	424	70.1	15.9	28.7	1,859.8	10.67
1988	NA	2,180	428	70.2	16.5	30.4	2,009.8	10.76
1989	NA	2,164	463	73.6	17.1	30.2	2,132.3	11.56
1990	NA	2,144	448	74.4	17.3	31.2	2,299.9	11.68
1991	NA	2,284	451	77.3	17.1	30.0	2,514.1	12.72
1992	2,504	2,644	500	79.6	18.6	35.5	2,675.7	12.49
1993	NA	2,699	473	83.2	18.2	34.5	2,799.2	12.90
1994	NA	2,540[2]	479[2]	87.1	18.7	34.8	2,935.6	13.27
1995	NA	2,588[2]	484[2]	84.1[2]	18.7[2]	33.9[2]	3,022.0[2]	13.96[2]
1996	NA	2,636[2]	489[2]	85.5[2]	19.0[2]	34.4[2]	3,156.2[2]	14.40[2]
1997	NA	2,684[2]	494[2]	86.9[2]	19.3[2]	34.8[2]	3,290.4[2]	14.83[2]
1998	NA	2,732[2]	499[2]	88.3[2]	19.6[2]	35.3[2]	3,424.6[2]	15.27[2]

Source: 1997 Manufacturing STATROM [machine-readable data files]. MStat97. Editorial Code and Data, Inc., Detroit, Michigan, 1997. Primary source: 1982, 1987, 1992 *Economic Census*; *Annual Survey of Manufactures*, 1983-1986, 1988-1991, 1993-1994. Establishment counts for non-Census years are from *County Business Patterns*; establishment values for 1983-1984 are extrapolations. Industries reclassified in 1987 will not have data for prior years. *Notes:* NA = Not available. 1. Interpolations by the editors. 2. Items are projected by the editors.

Industry Statistics

General Indices of Change in the Book Publishing Industry, 1982-1998

Year	Com-panies	Establishments		Employment			Compensation	
		Total	With 20 or more employees	Total (000)	Production workers (000)	Hours (mil.)	Payroll ($ mil.)	Wages ($ hr.)
1982	80	81	84	84	82	87	50	62
1983	NA	79[1]	85[1]	87	92	93	55	67
1984	NA	78[1]	87[1]	87	80	77	60	79
1985	NA	77	88	89	84	81	62	78
1986	NA	76	90	90	77	72	66	81
1987	87	87	85	88	85	81	70	85
1988	NA	82	86	88	89	86	75	86
1989	NA	82	93	92	92	85	80	93
1990	NA	81	90	93	93	88	86	94
1991	NA	86	90	97	92	85	94	102
1992	100	100	100	100	100	100	100	100
1993	NA	102	95	105	98	97	105	103
1994	NA	96[2]	96[2]	109	101	98	110	106
1995	NA	98[2]	97[2]	106[2]	100[2]	96[2]	113[2]	112[2]
1996	NA	100[2]	98[2]	107[2]	102[2]	97[2]	118[2]	115[2]
1997	NA	102[2]	99[2]	109[2]	104[2]	98[2]	123[2]	119[2]
1998	NA	103[2]	100[2]	111[2]	105[2]	99[2]	128[2]	122[2]

Source: 1997 *Manufacturing STATROM* [machine-readable data files]. MStat97. Editorial Code and Data, Inc., Detroit, Michigan, 1997. Primary source: 1982, 1987, 1992 *Economic Census*; *Annual Survey of Manufactures*, 1983-1986, 1988-1991, 1993-1994. Establishment counts for non-Census years are from *County Business Patterns*; establishment values for 1983-1984 are extrapolations. Industries reclassified in 1987 will not have data for prior years. Values reflect change from the base year, 1992. Values above 100 mean greater than 1992, values below 100 mean less than 1992, and a value of 100 in the 1982-1991 or 1993-1998 period means same as 1992. *Notes:* NA = Not available. 1. Interpolations by the editors. 2. Items are projected by the editors.

★ 195 ★

Industry Statistics

General Production Statistics on Book Publishing, 1982-1998

Year	Production ($ million)			
	Cost of materials	Value added by manufacture	Value of shipments[1]	Capital investment
1982	2,420.0	5,291.5	7,740.0	174.1
1983	2,683.2	5,823.8	8,427.4	163.6
1984	2,890.1	6,722.9	9,459.2	199.4
1985	3,021.1	7,395.8	10,196.2	232.1
1986	3,099.8	7,755.9	10,731.5	202.8
1987	3,663.2	9,110.7	12,619.5	239.7
1988	3,988.1	9,851.9	13,570.7	302.4
1989	4,365.5	9,915.5	14,074.2	319.1
1990	4,465.5	10,919.5	15,317.9	329.1
1991	5,001.4	11,683.3	16,596.1	330.5
1992	5,337.7	11,494.4	16,731.1	326.7
1993	5,806.8	12,742.9	18,615.9	282.0
1994	5,826.7	13,681.0	19,418.9	283.0
1995	6,081.0[2]	14,278.1[2]	20,266.5[2]	352.0[2]
1996	6,377.7[2]	14,974.6[2]	21,255.1[2]	365.0[2]
1997	6,674.3[2]	15,671.1[2]	22,243.7[2]	378.1[2]
1998	6,970.9[2]	16,367.6[2]	23,232.3[2]	391.2[2]

Source: 1997 *Manufacturing STATROM* [machine-readable data files]. MStat97. Editorial Code and Data, Inc., Detroit, Michigan, 1997. Primary source: 1982, 1987, 1992 *Economic Census; Annual Survey of Manufactures*, 1983-1986, 1988-1991, 1993-1994. Establishment counts for non-Census years are from *County Business Patterns*; establishment values for 1983-1984 are extrapolations. Industries reclassified in 1987 will not have data for prior years. *Notes:* 1. "Industry Shipments" and "Product Shipments" are rarely the same value.

★ 196 ★

Industry Statistics

Materials Consumed by the Book Publishing Industry

Material	Delivered cost ($ mil.)
Materials, ingredients, containers, and supplies	1,613.7
Newsprint	76.9
Coated paper	192.2
Uncoated paper	305.6

[Continued]

★ 196 ★

Materials Consumed by the Book Publishing Industry

[Continued]

Material	Delivered cost ($ mil.)
Printing inks (complete formulations)	45.9
All other materials and components, parts, containers, and supplies	549.1
Materials, ingredients, containers, and supplies, nsk	444.1

Source: 1997 *Manufacturing STATROM* [machine-readable data files]. MStat97. Editorial Code and Data, Inc., Detroit, Michigan, 1997. Primary source: 1992 *Economic Census*. Explanation of symbols used: nsk: Not specified by kind.

★ 197 ★

Industry Statistics

Product Share Details for the Book Publishing Industry

Product code	Shipments ($ mil.)	% of total	Product name
731	14,785.6	100.00	BOOK PUBLISHING
27311	3,873.7	26.20	Textbook publishing, including teachers' editions
2731111	656.8	16.96	Hardbound elementary school (K-8)
2731112	206.5	5.33	Paperbound elementary school (K-8)
2731113	428.8	11.07	Hardbound high school (9-12)
2731114	178.0	4.60	Paperbound high school (9-12)
2731115	1,117.5	28.85	Hardbound college
2731116	383.0	9.89	Paperbound college
2731121	279.5	7.22	Paperbound elementary school (K-8) workbook
2731123	84.1	2.17	Paperbound high school (9-12) workbook
2731125	141.6	3.66	Paperbound college workbook
2731131	211.0	5.45	Standardized test publishing
2731100	187.1	4.83	Textbooks, including teachers' editions, n.s.k.
27313	2,487.9	16.83	Technical, scientific, and professional book publishing
2731315	837.5	33.66	Hardbound law book publishing
2731317	269.9	10.85	Paperbound law book publishing
2731325	373.3	15.00	Hardbound medical book publishing
2731327	89.2	3.59	Paperbound medical book publishing
2731335	99.6	4.00	Hardbound business book publishing
2731337	179.1	7.20	Paperbound business book publishing
2731345	326.8	13.14	Other hardbound technical, scientific, and professional
2731347	185.6	7.46	Other paperbound technical, scientific, and professional
2731300	126.9	5.10	Technical, scientific, and professional books, n.s.k.
27314	730.2	4.94	Religious book publishing
2731411	82.1	11.24	Hardbound Bible and testament publishing

[Continued]

Product Share Details for the Book Publishing Industry
[Continued]

Product code	Shipments ($ mil.)	% of total	Product name
2731413	18.7	2.56	Paperbound Bible and testament publishing
2731423	22.6	3.10	Hymnal and devotional publishing
2731426	141.7	19.41	Other hardbound religious book publishing
2731428	122.4	16.76	Other paperbound religious book publishing
2731400	342.7	46.93	Religious books, n.s.k.
2731A	916.8	6.20	Mass market rack-size paperbound book publishing
2731111	656.8	16.96	Hardbound elementary school (K-8)
2731112	206.5	5.33	Paperbound elementary school (K-8)
2731113	428.8	11.07	Hardbound high school (9-12)
2731114	178.0	4.60	Paperbound high school (9-12)
2731115	1,117.5	28.85	Hardbound college
2731116	383.0	9.89	Paperbound college
2731121	279.5	7.22	Paperbound elementary school (K-8) workbook
2731123	84.1	2.17	Paperbound high school (9-12) workbook
2731125	141.6	3.66	Paperbound college workbook
2731131	211.0	5.45	Standardized test publishing
2731100	187.1	4.83	Textbooks, including teachers' editions, n.s.k.
27313	2,487.9	16.83	Technical, scientific, and professional book publishing
2731315	837.5	33.66	Hardbound law book publishing
2731317	269.9	10.85	Paperbound law book publishing
2731325	373.3	15.00	Hardbound medical book publishing
2731327	89.2	3.59	Paperbound medical book publishing
2731335	99.6	4.00	Hardbound business book publishing
2731337	179.1	7.20	Paperbound business book publishing
2731345	326.8	13.14	Other hardbound technical, scientific, and professional
2731347	185.6	7.46	Other paperbound technical, scientific, and professional
2731300	126.9	5.10	Technical, scientific, and professional books, n.s.k.
27314	730.2	4.94	Religious book publishing
2731411	82.1	11.24	Hardbound Bible and testament publishing
2731413	18.7	2.56	Paperbound Bible and testament publishing
2731423	22.6	3.10	Hymnal and devotional publishing
2731426	141.7	19.41	Other hardbound religious book publishing
2731428	122.4	16.76	Other paperbound religious book publishing
2731400	342.7	46.93	Religious books, n.s.k.
2731A	916.8	6.20	Mass market rack-size paperbound book publishing
2731B	745.8	5.04	Book club book publishing
2731C	711.2	4.81	Mail order book publishing
2731D	2,647.3	17.90	Adult trade and juvenile book publishing
2731D41	1,202.7	45.43	Hardbound
2731D47	531.8	20.09	Paperbound
2731D51	369.7	13.97	Hardbound juvenile book

[Continued]

★ 197 ★

Product Share Details for the Book Publishing Industry
[Continued]

Product code	Shipments ($ mil.)	% of total	Product name
2731D53	108.6	4.10	Paperbound juvenile book
2731D00	434.5	16.41	Adult trade and juvenile books, n.s.k.
2731E	490.9	3.32	General reference book publishing
2731E21	162.3	33.06	Encyclopedia publishing
2731E41	56.9	11.59	Dictionary and thesaurus publishing
2731E57	239.2	48.73	Other general reference book publishing
2731E00	32.5	6.62	General reference books, n.s.k.
2731F	390.4	2.64	Other book publishing, excluding pamphlets
2731F13	109.5	28.05	Hardbound university press book publishing
2731F15	79.7	20.41	Paperbound university press book publishing, excluding pamphlets
2731F16	94.7	24.26	Music book publishing (hardbound and paperbound), excluding pamphlets
2731F17	58.8	15.06	Other hardboundbook publishing, n.e.c.
2731F19	35.4	9.07	Other paperbound book publishing, n.e.c., excluding pamphlets
2731F00	12.3	3.15	Other books, excluding pamphlets, n.s.k.
2731G	134.8	0.91	Pamphlet publishing (5 through 48 pages)
2731G43	31.3	23.22	Music pamphlet publishing (5 through 48 pages)
2731G59	102.6	76.11	Other pamphlet publishing (5 through 48 pages), including religious and text
2731G00	1.0	0.74	Pamphlets (5 through 48 pages), n.s.k.
2731H	36.1	0.24	Audio book publishing (books recorded on audio cassettes)
2731H00	36.1	100.00	Audio book publishing (books recorded on audio cassettes)
27310	1,620.5	10.96	Book publishing, n.s.k.
2731C	711.2	4.81	Mail order book publishing
2731D	2,647.3	17.90	Adult trade and juvenile book publishing
2731D41	1,202.7	45.43	Hardbound
2731D47	531.8	20.09	Paperbound
2731D51	369.7	13.97	Hardbound juvenile book
2731D53	108.6	4.10	Paperbound juvenile book
2731D00	434.5	16.41	Adult trade and juvenile books , n.s.k.
2731E	490.9	3.32	General reference book publishing
2731E21	162.3	33.06	Encyclopedia publishing
2731E41	56.9	11.59	Dictionary and thesaurus publishing
2731E57	239.2	48.73	Other general reference book publishing
2731E00	32.5	6.62	General reference books, n.s.k.
2731F	390.4	2.64	Other book publishing, excluding pamphlets
2731F13	109.5	28.05	Hardbound university press book publishing
2731F15	79.7	20.41	Paperbound university press book publishing, excluding pamphlets
2731F16	94.7	24.26	Music book publishing (hardbound and paperbound), excluding pamphlets
2731F17	58.8	15.06	Other hardbound book publishing, n.e.c.
2731F19	35.4	9.07	Other paperbound book publishing, n.e.c., excluding pamphlets
2731F00	12.3	3.15	Other books, excluding pamphlets, n.s.k.

[Continued]

★ 197 ★

Product Share Details for the Book Publishing Industry
[Continued]

Product code	Shipments ($ mil.)	% of total	Product name
2731G	134.8	0.91	Pamphlet publishing (5 through 48 pages)
2731G43	31.3	23.22	Music pamphlet publishing (5 through 48 pages)
2731G59	102.6	76.11	Other pamphlet publishing (5 through 48 pages), including religious and text
2731G00	1.0	0.74	Pamphlets (5 through 48 pages), n.s.k.
2731H	36.1	0.24	Audio book publishing (books recorded on audio cassettes)
2731H00	36.1	100.00	Audio book publishing (books recorded on audio cassettes)
27310	1,620.5	10.96	Book publishing, n.s.k.

Source: 1997 *Manufacturing STATROM* [machine-readable data files]. Mstat97. Editorial Code and Data, Inc., Detroit, Michigan, 1997. Primary source: 1992 *Economic Census.* The values shown are percent of total shipments in an industry. Values of indented subcategories are summed in the main headings. The abbreviation n.s.k. stands for 'not specified by kind' and n.e.c. for 'not elsewhere classified'.

★ 198 ★

Industry Statistics

Production: Indices of Change in the Book Publishing Industry, 1982-1998

Year	Production ($ million)			
	Cost of materials	Value added by manufacture	Value of shipments[1]	Capital investment
1982	45	46	46	53
1983	50	51	50	50
1984	54	58	57	61
1985	57	64	61	71
1986	58	67	64	62
1987	69	79	75	73
1988	75	86	81	93
1989	82	86	84	98
1990	84	95	92	101
1991	94	102	99	101
1992	100	100	100	100
1993	109	111	111	86
1994	109	119	116	87
1995	114[2]	124[2]	121[2]	108[2]
1996	119[2]	130[2]	127[2]	112[2]

[Continued]

★ 198 ★

Production: Indices of Change in the Book Publishing Industry, 1982-1998

[Continued]

Year	Production ($ million)			
	Cost of materials	Value added by manufacture	Value of shipments[1]	Capital investment
1997	125[2]	136[2]	133[2]	116[2]
1998	131[2]	142[2]	139[2]	120[2]

Source: 1997 *Manufacturing STATROM* [machine-readable data files]. MStat97. Editorial Code and Data, Inc., Detroit, Michigan, 1997. Primary source: 1982, 1987, 1992 *Economic Census*; *Annual Survey of Manufactures*, 1983-1986, 1988-1991, 1993-1994. Establishment counts for non-Census years are from *County Business Patterns*; establishment values for 1983-1984 are extrapolations. Industries reclassified in 1987 will not have data for prior years. Values reflect change from the base year, 1992. Values above 100 mean greater than 1992, values below 100 mean less than 1992, and a value of 100 in the 1982-1991 or 1993-1998 period means same as 1992. *Notes:* 1. "Industry Shipments" and "Product Shipments" are rarely the same value. 2. Items are projected by the editors.

★ 199 ★

Industry Statistics

Occupations Employed by the Book Manufacturing Industries

Occupation	% of total 1994	Change to 2005
Writers & editors, including technical writers	7.7	14.5
Sales & related workers, nec	5.8	14.5
Bindery machine operators & set-up operators	5.3	14.5
Secretaries, ex legal & medical	3.2	4.3
Machine feeders & offbearers	3.1	3.1
General office clerks	3.1	-2.3
General managers & top executives	3.0	8.7
Offset lithographic press operators	2.7	37.5
Professional workers, nec	2.5	37.5
Adjustment clerks	2.4	37.5
Hand packers & packagers	2.3	-1.8
Helpers, laborers, & material movers, nec	2.2	14.5
Strippers, printing	2.1	2.1
Clerical supervisors & managers	2.0	17.2
Clerical support workers nec	2.0	-8.4
Freight, stock, & material movers, hand	2.0	-8.4
Bookkeeping, accounting, & auditing clerks	2.0	-14.1
Blue collar worker supervisors	2.0	5.5

[Continued]

★ 199 ★

Occupations Employed by the Book Manufacturing Industries
[Continued]

Occupation	% of total 1994	Change to 2005
Marketing, advertising, & PR managers	1.9	14.5
Printing press machine setters, operators	1.9	14.5
Order clerks, materials, merchandise, & service	1.8	12.1
Traffic, shipping, & receiving clerks	1.7	10.2
Assemblers, fabricators, & hand workers, nec	1.6	14.6
Managers & administrators, nec	1.5	14.5
Proofreaders & copy markers	1.4	-25.5
Artists & commercial artists	1.4	16.4
Printing, binding, & related workers, nec	1.2	14.5
Systems analysts	1.2	83.2
Production, planning, & expediting clerks	1.1	37.4
Computer programmers	1.1	-7.2
Management support workers, nec	1.0	14.6

Source: 1997 *Manufacturing STATROM* [machine-readable data files]. MStat97. Editorial Code and Data, Inc., Detroit, Michigan, 1997. Primary source: *Industry-Occupation Matrix*, Bureau of Labor Statistics. These data relate to one or more 3-digit SIC industry groups rather than to a single 4-digit SIC. The change reported for each occupation to the year 2005 is a percent of growth or decline as estimated by the Bureau of Labor Statistics. The abbreviation nec stands for 'not elsewhere classified.'

★ 200 ★

Industry Statistics

Selected Ratios for the Book Publishing Industries

For 1992	Average of all manufacturing	Book publishing	Index
Employees per establishment	46	30	66
Payroll per establishment	1,332,320	1,011,989	76
Payroll per employee	29,181	33,614	115
Production workers per establishment	31	7	22
Wages per establishment	734,496	167,699	23
Wages per production worker	23,390	23,838	102
Hours per production worker	2,025	1,909	94
Wages per hour	11.55	12.49	108
Value added per establishment	3,842,210	4,347,352	113
Value added per employee	84,153	144,402	172
Value added per production worker	122,353	617,978	505

[Continued]

★ 200 ★

Selected Ratios for the Book Publishing Industries

[Continued]

For 1992	Average of all manufacturing	Book publishing	Index
Cost per establishment	4,239,462	2,018,797	48
Cost per employee	92,853	67,057	72
Cost per production worker	135,003	286,973	213
Shipments per establishment	8,100,800	6,327,950	78
Shipments per employee	177,425	210,190	118
Shipments per production worker	257,966	899,522	349
Investment per establishment	278,244	123,563	44
Investment per employee	6,094	4,104	67
Investment per production worker	8,861	17,565	198

Source: 1997 *Manufacturing STATROM* [machine-readable data files]. MStat97. Editorial Code and Data, Inc., Detroit, Michigan, 1997. Primary source: 1982, 1987, 1992 *Economic Census; Annual Survey of Manufactures*, 1983-1986, 1988-1991, 1993-1994. Establishment counts for non-Census years are from *County Business Patterns*; establishment values for 1983-1984 are extrapolations. Industries reclassified in 1987 will not have data for prior years. Values reflect change from the base year, 1992. Values above 100 mean greater than 1992, values below 100 mean less than 1992, and a value of 100 in the 1982-1991 or 1993-1998 period means same as 1992. The 'Average of All Manufacturing' column represents the average of all manufacturing industries reported for the most recent complete year available. The Index shows the relationship between the Average and the Analyzed Industry. For example, 100 means that they are equal; 500 that the Analyzed Industry is five times the average; 50 means that the Analyzed Industry is half the national average.

★ 201 ★

Industry Statistics

State Level Data for the Book Publishing Industry

The states are presented in ranked order by level of shipments.

State	Establish-ments	Shipments total ($ mil.)	% of U.S.	Per establish-ment	Employ-ment total number	% of U.S.	Per establish-ment	Wages ($/hour)	Cost as % of shipments	Investment per employee ($)
New York	383	6,272.3	37.5	16.4	20,400	25.6	53	12.63	33.3	4,711
New Jersey	116	1,350.9	8.1	11.6	6,300	7.9	54	14.19	24.1	2,968
California	405	1,194.9	7.1	3.0	6,800	8.5	17	12.31	27.5	2,794
Massachusetts	103	1,133.4	6.8	11.0	4,800	6.0	47	12.75	36.7	2,396
Illinois	157	1,028.2	6.1	6.5	5,500	6.9	35	11.71	31.1	1,673
Pennsylvania	78	835.8	5.0	10.7	3,300	4.1	42	15.91	27.9	2,242
Minnesota	48	833.9	5.0	17.4	6,200	7.8	129	10.95	38.1	NA
Texas	116	517.4	3.1	4.5	3,200	4.0	28	8.00	24.1	2,531
Ohio	64	495.6	3.0	7.7	3,800	4.8	59	16.95	19.1	NA
Michigan	58	295.3	1.8	5.1	1,500	1.9	26	12.57	26.1	2,467
Connecticut	63	241.5	1.4	3.8	1,300	1.6	21	16.50	30.8	NA
Florida	90	226.2	1.4	2.5	1,400	1.8	16	11.71	18.8	1,143
Tennessee	67	222.6	1.3	3.3	1,500	1.9	22	10.67	40.7	2,400
Wisconsin	39	211.9	1.3	5.4	1,100	1.4	28	16.43	91.2	2,273

[Continued]

★ 201 ★

State Level Data for the Book Publishing Industry
[Continued]

State	Establish-ments	Shipments total ($ mil.)	% of U.S.	Per establish-ment	Employ-ment total number	% of U.S.	Per establish-ment	Wages ($/hour)	Cost as % of shipments	Investment per employee ($)
Colorado	60	137.0	0.8	2.3	1,300	1.6	22	14.90	12.6	2,692
North Carolina	46	106.3	0.6	2.3	500	0.6	11	7.00	33.5	2,000
Maryland	64	99.3	0.6	1.6	800	1.0	13	9.50	34.0	3,375
Kentucky	20	66.9	0.4	3.3	900	1.1	45	9.60	28.0	778
Oregon	53	56.8	0.3	1.1	400	0.5	8	12.00	40.8	1,750
Georgia	30	32.2	0.2	1.1	300	0.4	10	12.50	24.5	1,333
Oklahoma	22	23.1	0.1	1.0	200	0.3	9	5.00	35.1	NA
New Hampshire	11	21.1	0.1	1.9	200	0.3	18	7.00	19.9	NA
Maine	14	15.9	0.1	1.1	100	0.1	7	7.00	23.3	NA
Utah	28	12.0	0.1	0.4	100[1]	0.1	4	NA	39.2	4,000
Kansas	25	9.0	0.1	0.4	100[1]	0.1	4	NA	36.7	NA
Louisiana	15	8.4	0.1	0.6	100	0.1	7	5.00	28.6	NA
South Carolina	21	7.7	0.0	0.4	100	0.1	5	8.00	24.7	NA
Washington	61	(D)	NA	NA	375[1]	0.5	6	NA	NA	NA
Missouri	53	(D)	NA	NA	1,750[1]	2.2	33	NA	NA	3,714
Virginia	52	(D)	NA	NA	1,750[1]	2.2	34	NA	NA	NA
Arizona	44	(D)	NA	NA	375[1]	0.5	9	NA	NA	NA
Indiana	36	(D)	NA	NA	750[1]	0.9	21	NA	NA	NA
Alabama	27	(D)	NA	NA	375[1]	0.5	14	NA	NA	NA
Vermont	25	(D)	NA	NA	375[1]	0.5	15	NA	NA	NA
New Mexico	24	(D)	NA	NA	175[1]	0.2	7	NA	NA	NA
Iowa	18	(D)	NA	NA	750[1]	0.9	42	NA	NA	NA
Nebraska	11	(D)	NA	NA	175[1]	0.2	16	NA	NA	NA
Arkansas	10	(D)	NA	NA	375[1]	0.5	38	NA	NA	NA

Source: 1997 *Manufacturing STATROM* [machine-readable data files]. MStat97. Editorial Code and Data, Inc., Detroit, Michigan, 1997. Primary source: 1992 *Economic Census*. The states are in descending order of shipments or establishments (if shipment data are missing for the majority). The symbol (D) appears when data are withheld to prevent disclosure of competitive information. States marked with (D) are sorted by number of establishments. *Notes:* NA = Not available. 1. Indicates the midpoint of a range.

★ 202 ★

Industry Statistics

Book Publishing: States with Most Activity

The industry is shown by segment.

State	Shipments as % of U.S.	Employment as % of U.S.	Payroll as % of U.S.	Cost of Materials as % of U.S.	Investment as % of U.S.
New York	36.90	25.60	16.70	37.50	36.90
New Jersey	8.90	7.90	4.80	8.10	8.90
California	7.70	8.50	8.60	7.10	7.70
Massachusetts	6.40	6.00	3.20	6.80	6.40
Illinois	6.10	6.90	4.80	6.10	6.10

[Continued]

★ 202 ★

Book Publishing: States with Most Activity
[Continued]

State	Shipments as % of U.S.	Employment as % of U.S.	Payroll as % of U.S.	Cost of Materials as % of U.S.	Investment as % of U.S.
Pennsylvania	5.30	4.10	3.20	5.00	5.30
Minnesota	4.50	7.80	15.60	5.00	4.50
Ohio	3.50	4.80	9.70	3.00	3.50
Texas	3.30	4.00	2.70	3.10	3.30
Michigan	2.00	1.90	2.20	1.80	2.00
Florida	1.50	1.80	2.20	1.40	1.50
Connecticut	1.50	1.60	1.10	1.40	1.50
Tennessee	1.10	1.90	1.60	1.30	1.10
Colorado	1.10	1.60	3.20	0.80	1.10
North Carolina	0.60	0.60	1.10	0.60	0.60
Maryland	0.60	1.00	1.10	0.60	0.60
Kentucky	0.40	1.10	3.20	0.40	0.40
Oregon	0.30	0.50	0.50	0.30	0.30
Wisconsin	0.20	1.40	3.80	1.30	0.20
Georgia	0.20	0.40	0.50	0.20	0.20

Source: 1997 *Manufacturing STATROM* [machine-readable data files]. MStat97. Editorial Code and Data, Inc., Detroit, Michigan, 1997. Primary source: *Economic Census for 1992* and earlier years. The *Economic Census* is conducted by the Bureau of the Census, U.S. Department of Commerce, Washington, DC 20233.

Sales and Distribution

★ 203 ★

Book Sales by Region

Distribution of sales is shown in percent. Data exclude children's books.

Region	Share (%)
Pacific	20
South Atlantic	18
Mid-Atlantic	17
East North Central	14
West South Central	10
Mountain	6
New England	6

[Continued]

★ 203 ★

Book Sales by Region

[Continued]

Region	Share (%)
West North Central	5
East South Central	4

Source: "USA Snapshots." *USA TODAY,* 31 December 1997, p. D1. Primary source: Book Industry Study Group.

★ 204 ★

Sales and Distribution

Book Sales by Year

Data are in billions of units. Figures for 1997 is estimated.

Year	Books
1991	2.04
1992	2.05
1993	2.08
1994	2.13
1995	2.18
1996	2.21
1997	2.27

Source: "Book Report." *The Christian Science Monitor,* 9 December 1997, p. 10. Primary source: Book Industry Study Group.

★ 205 ★

Sales and Distribution

Book Spending: Compound Annual Growth Rates

The future of consumer book publishing still appears promising. There has been an increase in the average number of books purchased by adults, new media has not cut into adult reading time, and there is expected to be a 17% increase in the largest group of readers over the next five years. Data show compound annual growth rates.

[In percent]

Segment	1991-1996	1996-2001
Sub. reference	5.1	5.0
University press	4.9	5.0
Book clubs	3.7	4.5
Mass market	3.1	4.5
Adult trade	5.0	4.4

[Continued]

★ 205 ★

Book Spending: Compound Annual Growth Rates

[Continued]

Segment	1991-1996	1996-2001
Juvenile trade	2.2	3.9
Religious	2.6	3.1
Mail order	2.3	2.4
Consumer total	5.0	5.5

Source: Milliot, Jim. "VS&A Sees Moderate Growth for Consumer Book Spending." *Publishers Weekly,* 28 July 1997, p. 11. Primary source: Veronis, Suhler & Associates Communications Industry Forecast.

★ 206 ★

Sales and Distribution

Discount Book Sales

Sales of books to adults at discount stores rose 21.6% in 1996 to 9% of all sales. The table shows what persuaded buyers to make a purchase.

[In percent]

Reason	Share (%)
Subject/topic	37
Author reputation	31
Price	6
In-store display	6
Cover art/endorsements	6
Book was recommended	3

Source: "The Word on Discount Books." *USA TODAY,* 9 October 1997, p. D1. Primary source: *1996 Consumer Research Study on Book Purchasing.*

★ 207 ★

Sales and Distribution

Fiction Sales by Type

| General fiction - 49.0 |
| Children/youth - 20.0 |
| Horror - 9.0 |
| Mystery - 8.0 |
| Romance - 8.0 |
| Sci-fi/fantasy - 6.0 |

Fiction accounts for about two-thirds of book sales. Data show sales by type.

[In percent]

Segment	Share
General fiction	49.0
Children/youth	20.0
Horror	9.0
Mystery	8.0
Romance	8.0
Sci-fi/fantasy	6.0

Source: "Fiction's Story." *USA TODAY,* 24 December 1996, p. 4D.

Sales and Distribution

Publishers Sales by Category, 1995

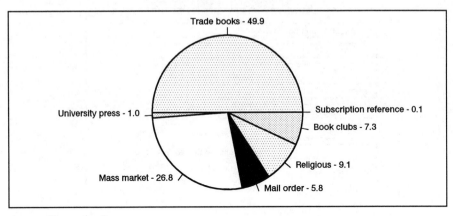

Trade books - 49.9

University press - 1.0

Subscription reference - 0.1

Book clubs - 7.3

Religious - 9.1

Mass market - 26.8

Mail order - 5.8

[In percent]

Segment	Share (%)
Trade books	49.9
Mass market	26.8
Religious	9.1
Book clubs	7.3
Mail order	5.8
University press	1.0
Subscription reference	0.1

Source: "Book Report." *The Christian Science Monitor,* 9 December 1997, p. 10.

★ 209 ★

Sales and Distribution

Top U.S. Publishing Markets

| Los Angeles-Long Beach, CA - 454 |
| Chicago - 366 |
| New York - 363 |
| Washington - 296 |
| Philadelphia - 268 |
| Boston - 249 |
| Seattle-Bellevue-Everett, WA - 176 |
| San Diego - 175 |
| San Francisco - 167 |
| San Jose, CA - 99 |

Chart shows data from column 1.

Data show the top metro areas ranked by book sales and the number of retail bookstores.

Area	Retail bookstores	Sales ($ 000)
Los Angeles-Long Beach, CA	454	$383,902
New York	363	359,716
Chicago	366	271,867
Boston	249	238,116
Washington	296	234,589
Philadelphia	268	161,735
San Francisco	167	138,875
Seattle-Bellevue-Everett, WA	176	131,679
San Jose, CA	99	125,015
San Diego	175	115,419

Source: "Book Report." *The Christian Science Monitor,* 9 December 1997, p. 10.

★ 210 ★

Sales and Distribution

U.S. Book Buying by Year

Sales are shown in billions of dollars.

[In dollars]

Year	Amount
1992	21.00
1993	23.00
1994	24.00
1995	25.00[1]
1996	26.00[1]

Source: "U.S. Book Buying Growth." *USA TODAY,* 6 September 1995, p. D1. Book Industry Trends. *Note:* 1. Projected.

★ 211 ★

Sales and Distribution

U.S. Book Exports

[In millions of dollars]

Country	1995	1996	% change
Canada	$354.3	$336.5	-5.0
United Kingdom	97.0	101.3	4.5
Japan	58.6	74.3	26.8
Australia	58.1	56.5	-2.7
Germany	22.5	21.7	-3.6
Mexico	19.8	24.9	25.5
Singapore	22.0	16.1	-26.7
South Korea	13.1	16.8	27.5
Netherlands	14.7	14.6	-1.0
Taiwan	12.5	14.2	13.2
Total top 10	672.6	676.9	0.6
Total world	829.7	842.1	1.5

Source: "U.S. Book Exports Edge Up 1.5%." *Publishers Weekly,* 9 September 1996, p. 26. Primary source: U.S. Department of Commerce.

★ 212 ★

African-American Owned Bookstores in the United States

There are an estimated 300 African-American owned bookstores nationwide.

Store	City
Afrocentric Books	Chicago, IL
Black Images Book Bazaar	Dallas, TX
Black Books Plus	New York, NY
Karibu Books	Hyattsville, MD
Esowan Books	Los Angeles, CA
Hue-Man Experience	Denver, CO
Apple Book Center	Detroit, MI
Phenix Information Center	San Bernardino, CA

Source: Adelson, Andrea. "Black-Owned Bookstores Defend Niche." *New York Times,* 6 October 1997, p. C9.

★ 213 ★

Retailing

Amazon.Com: A Profile

Amazon.Com is the largest online retailer of books. It began selling books in the summer of 1995. Here is a look at its operating results.

Operations data	1995	1996
Net sales	$511	$15,746
Cost of sales	409	12,287
Gross profit	102	3,459
Operating expenses		
Marketing & sales	200	6,090
Product development	171	2,313
General & administrative	35	1,035
Total operating expenses	406	9,438
Loss from operations	304	5,979
Interest income	1	202
Net loss	303	5,777

Source: Milliot, Jim. "Amazon.com Expects to Generate $34 Million from IPO." *Publishers Weekly,* 31 March 1997, p. 11.

★ 214 ★

Retailing

Book Chains: Average Number of Titles

The table shows the number of titles carried at a typical outlet. As competition increases in the $12 billion U.S. book retailing industry, expect chains to offer everything from cappuccino and CDs to discounts on popular titles.

Chains	Number of titles
Barnes & Noble	150,000
Borders	150,000
Crown Books	85,000

Source: Moukheiber, Zina. "The Price is Right." *Forbes,* 16 December 1996, p. 52.

★ 215 ★

Retailing

Book Club Sales by Year

Book club sales are shown in millions of dollars. Figures for 1997 are estimated.

Year	Sales ($ mil.)	% change
1992	742.3	-1.0
1993	804.7	+8.4
1994	873.9	+8.6
1995	976.1	+11.7
1996	1,091.8	+11.9
1997[1]	1,184.3	+8.5

Source: "Book Club Sales Grow." *USA TODAY,* 26 November 1997, p. D1. Primary source: Book Industry Study Group. *Note:* 1. Estimate.

★ 216 ★

Retailing

Bookstore Chains Operating Performance, 1995-1996

Chain	1995	1996
Barnes & Noble		
Revenue	$1,976.9	$2,448.1
Operating income (loss)	(35.2)	119.7
Operating margin	-1.8%	4.9%

[Continued]

★ 216 ★

Bookstore Chains Operating Performance, 1995-1996
[Continued]

Chain	1995	1996
Borders Group		
Revenue	$1,749.0	$1,958.8
Operating income (loss)	(200.4)	103.1
Operating margin	-11.5%	5.3%
Books-A-Million		
Revenue	$229.8	$278.6
Operating income (loss)	12.3	12.2
Operating margin	5.3%	4.4%
Crown Books		
Revenue	$283.5	$287.7
Operating income (loss)	5.7	(1.4)
Operating margin	2.0%	-0.5%
Total		
Revenue	$4,240.3	$4.973.2
Operating income (loss)	(217.5)	233.6
Operating margin	-5.1%	4.7

Source: Milliot, Jim. "Chains Earned Profits of $233 Million in Fiscal 1997." *Publishers Weekly,* 26 May 1997, p. 12.

★ 217 ★

Retailing

Bookstore Closings

The American Booksellers Association reports that in fiscal year 1994-95, nearly 200 independent bookstores in the US closed shop, up 21.6 percent from a year earlier. And the market share of bookselling by independents has dropped from 32 percent in 1991 to 18 percent in 1996.

Source: The Christian Science Monitor, 7 October 1997, p. 9.

★ 218 ★

Retailing

Canada: Superstores

Item	Value
Chapters superstores	11
Canadian independent superstores	5
Superstores in the United States	680
Barnes & Noble superstores in the United States	440
Size of Canadian book market	$1.85 billion[1]
Size of Chapters' new flagship store on Bloor St. W.	40,000 square feet
Cost of opening each superstore	$2.2 million
Titles carried by superstores	75,000 to 150,000
Titles in average bookstore	15,000
Number of books published in the United States in 1995	62,039
Number of Canadian books (excluding textbooks) published	5,780 ('93-'94, latest available)
Percentage of book sales in Canada not through book stores	40% (est.)
Chapters chain's share of Canadian book market	20% (est.)
Most profitable superstore in the chain	World's Biggest Bookstore, Toronto

Source: Deverell, John. "Chapters' Big Bookstores Try to Beat Rivals to Punch." *Toronto Star,* 8 February 1997, p. 1E. *Note:* 1. Wholesale, including textbooks.

★ 219 ★

Retailing

Chain Stores vs Independents: Store Sales in 1995-96

Figures show sales in millions of dollars from February-July 1996.

Segment	1995 Sales/share	1996 Sales/share	% change sales
Total	$4,116/100.0	$4,257/100.0	3.4
Chains	1,760/42.8	2,097/49.3	19.1
Others	2,356/57.2	2,160/50.7	-8.3

Source: "Scrooge on the Way for Booksellers This Christmas?" *Publishers Weekly,* 21 October 1996, p. 11.

★ 220 ★

Retailing

Largest Bookstores in Singapore

From the source: "The total market size for the book industry in Singapore for 1994 was about US $339.6 million. In Singapore, certain categories of books have potential for growth. These are children's books, reference or intellectual books and light reading materials such as horror or ghost stories, romance and comics in paperbacks. However, the book market is becoming increasingly competitive due to the entry of a growing number of market players. Numerous similar titles have flooded the market, especially for children's books and trade books. Some of the major factors driving the growth of the book market are the high literacy rate, the government's effort in encouraging reading habits, growing affluence of Singaporeans and the desire of parents to instill reading habits in their children. Most Singaporeans go for light reading materials such as romance novels, horror and ghost stories and comics. The more popular titles are usually the international best-selling paperbacks and books that have won major awards. Romance of local flavour has become increasingly popular and publishers are publishing more of such novels and short stories. Novel classics also sell very well in Singapore every year, with more than half of them going to high schools and college bookstores."

Chain	Outlets
Times the Bookshop	22
Popular Book Co.	13
MPH Bookstores	8
Kinokuniya	5

Source: National Trade Data Bank: The Export Connection CD-ROM, STAT-USA, U.S. Department of Commerce, Washington, D.C., 20230, 8 August 1996, p. ISA950801.

★ 221 ★

Retailing

Leading Bookstore Chains

[In millions of dollars]

Chain	Full year		% change
	1997[1]	1996[2]	
Barnes & Noble	$2,448.0	$1,977.0	23.8%
Borders Group	1,958.8	1,749.0	12.0
Crown Books	287.8	283.5	1.5
Books-A-Million	278.6	229.8	21.2
Total	$4,973.2	$4,239.3	17.3%

Source: "Sales Near $5 Billion at Top Bookstore Chains." *Publishers Weekly,* 31 March 1997, p. 12. *Notes:* 1. For the year that closed at the end of January, 1997. 2. For the year that closed at the end of January, 1996.

★ 222 ★

Retailing

Paperback Sales by Outlet

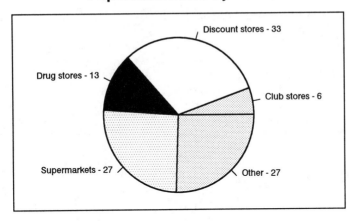

Location	Percentage
Discount stores	33
Supermarkets	27
Drug stores	13
Club stores	6
Other	27

Source: "Statwrap." *Non-Foods Merchandising* (January 1995), p. 8. Primary source: Book Industry Study Group Magazine and Paperback Marketing Institute.

★ 223 ★

Retailing

Retail Sales Growth, 1991-1995

From the source: "1995 consumer book sales were up 32% over 1991 to about one billion. Bookstores selling new books sold about 45% of the total, but sales at other types of sellers are growing faster."

Outlet	Growth (%)
Membership discount stores	208
Bookstores/used	96
Mail order, clubs	49
Discount stores	37
Grocery, drug stores	14
Bookstores/new	11
Other outlets[1]	69

Source: "Buying the Book." *USA TODAY,* 4 September 1996, p. D1. Primary source: American Booksellers Association. *Note:* 1. Includes department stores, cards and gift stores, etc.

★ 224 ★

Retailing

Retail Sales in Book Stores, 1996-1997

Data show unadjusted monthly figures.

[In millions of dollars]

Month	Book store sales	Retail trade total	Durable goods total	Book store sales as a percentage of total durable goods
1996				
January	1,339	173,264	68,706	1.95
February	740	180,251	73,420	1.01
March	726	199,413	82,506	0.88
April	732	198,610	82,958	0.88
May	833	213,754	90,210	0.92
June	817	204,705	85,962	0.95
July	765	204,817	86,024	0.89
August	1,322	212,247	87,258	1.52
September	1,006	195,749	80,509	1.25
October	866	207,531	84,794	1.02
November	870	210,236	80,826	1.08
December	1,531	244,719	90,163	1.70
Total	11,547	2,445,296	993,336	1.16
1997				
January	1,484	186,064	74,051	2.00
February	744	183,530	75,424	1.03
March	759	209,973	86,718	0.88
April	750	204,927	86,686	0.87
May	829	219,101	91,155	0.91
June	810	212,251	90,015	0.90
July	765	216,161	91,355	0.84
August[1]	1,185	220,625	91,054	1.30

Source: Monthly Retail Trade Survey, Services Division, Bureau of the Census, Washington, DC 20233. *Note:* 1. Preliminary figures.

★ 225 ★

Retailing

Superstore Sales and Outlets

[In millions of dollars]

Company	1995		1996		% change	
	Sales	Stores	Sales	Stores	Sales	Stores
Barnes & Noble	$1,350.0	358	$1,861.0	431	37.8%	20.4%
Borders	683.5	116	958.1	157	40.2	35.3
Books-A-Million[1]	180.0	66	228.0	91	26.7	37.9
Crown Books	190.0	84	225.5	109	18.7	29.7
Total	$2,403.5	624	3,272.6	788	36.1	26.3

Source: "Super Store Sales Rise 36% to More Than $3 Billion." *Publishers Weekly,* 19 May 1997, p. 10. *Note:* 1. Sales are estimates.

★ 226 ★

Retailing

The Growth of Superstores

Year	Stores	Sales ($ mil.)
1991	97	280
1992	210	546
1993	334	1,009
1994	469	1,655
1995	624	2,403
1996	788	3,273

Source: "Book Report." *The Christian Science Monitor,* 9 December 1997, p. 10. Primary source: Company reports and *Publishers Weekly.*

★ 227 ★

Retailing

U.K. Book Market, 1995-96

Distribution of sales is shown in percent.

Outlet	Share
WH Smith	16
Walterstone's	10
Dillons	7
Woolworths	3

[Continued]

★ 227 ★

U.K. Book Market, 1995-96
[Continued]

Outlet	Share
Other specialist bookshops	24
Book clubs/mail order	16
Newsagents/gas stations/department stores/record shops	10
John Menzies/other goods stores	8
Supermarkets	6

Source: "On the Shelf." *The Guardian,* 2 June 1997, p. 21. Primary source: Corporate Intelligence on Retailing.

★ 228 ★

Retailing

Where Adults Purchase Books

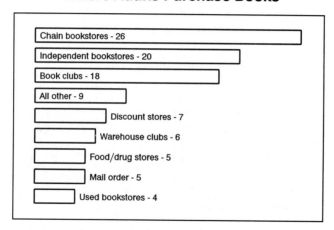

Segment	Percentage
Chain bookstores	26
Independent bookstores	20
Book clubs	18
All other	9
Discount stores	7
Warehouse clubs	6
Food/drug stores	5
Mail order	5
Used bookstores	4

Source: Mutter, John and Elizabeth Bernstein. "Books Wherever You Look: The Mall as Market Microcosm." *Publishers Weekly,* 16 September 1996, p. 24. Primary source: *Consumer Research Study on Book Publishing.*

★ 229 ★

Retailing

Where Canadians Get Their Books

Book buyers in Canada are generally women and relatively young, with 39% of readers falling into the 25-to-39 age bracket. They also prefer paperbacks to hardcovers.

Source	Distribution (%)
Bought by the respondent	49
Borrowed from someone	17
Lent by school or public library	17
Received as a gift	11
Swapped or traded	4
Lent by another institution or organization	2

Source: Milliot, Jim. "Study Finds 69% of Canadians Bought a Book in 6-Mo. Period." *Publishers Weekly,* 1 January 1996, p. 24. Primary source: *Who Buys Books?*

Wholesaling

★ 230 ★

Book Wholesaling

More than 90% of the nation's 15,000 public libraries order their books through Baker & Taylor and spend more than $444 million on books annually.

Source: O'Brien, Timothy L. "Justice Department Joins Lawsuit Against Leading Book Wholesaler." *The Wall Street Journal,* 4 February 1997, p. B5.

Book Fairs

★ 231 ★

Book Fair Sales

Book fair sales rose 20% in 1996, to $125 million, due to an increase in the number of fairs, to 60,000, as well as to an increase in the average revenue generated per fair.

Source: Milliot, Jim. "Retail Sales, Media Vetures Spur Growth at Scholastic." *Publishers Weekly,* 23 September 1996, p. 11.

★ 232 ★

Book Fairs

Popular Book Fairs

Data show the estimated number of annual visitors at selected book fairs. Book fairs have certainly kept up with technological achievements; such events regularly have CD-ROM and on-line demonstrations. However, perhaps the most surprising thing is their growing frequency. Numerous cities across the United States (and abroad) sponsor their own fairs. All events shown take place between September - November.

Event	Visitors
Miami Book Fair International	300,000
New York is Book Country	250,000
Baltimore Book Festival	35,000
Rocky Mountain Book Festival	30,000
Southern Festival of Books	30,000
Northwest Bookfest	23,000
New Jersey Book Festival	20,000
San Francisco Bay Area Book Festival	20,000
Texas Book Festival	10,000

Source: Engelson, Andy. "Book Festivals of Many Flavors." *Publishers Weekly,* 11 August 1997, p. 246.

Buyers

★ 233 ★

Education Level of Book Buyers

Education level	Distribution (%)
Graduate studies	19
College graduate	18
High school graduate	56
Did not complete high school	7

Source: Gabriel, Trip. "Women Buy Fiction in Bulk and Publishers Take Notice." *The New York Times,* 17 March 1997, p. C1. Primary source: The NPD Group; Bureau of the Census.

★ 234 ★

Buyers

Favorite Books to Receive as Holiday Gifts

The table shows the results of a survey.

Type	Response (%)
Mystery/suspense	18
Current fiction	18
Biography	11
Cooking/wine	11
Sci-fi/fantasy	8
Religion/New Age	7
Psychology/self-help	6
Classic/modern literature	6
History	2
Don't know	1
Others	12

Source: Hall, Cindy and Marcia Staimer. "Curling Up with a Gift Book." *USA TODAY,* 12 December 1996, p. D1. Primary source: Gallup for American Booksellers Association.

★ 235 ★

Buyers

Household Income of Book Buyers

Household income	Distribution (%)
More than $75,000	26
$60,000-$74,999	8
$50,000-$59,999	9
$30,000-$49,999	25
Less than $30,000	32

Source: Gabriel, Trip. "Women Buy Fiction in Bulk and Publishers Take Notice." *New York Times,* 17 March 1997, p. C1. Primary source: The NPD Group; Bureau of the Census.

★ 236 ★

Buyers

Popular Types of Books, 1996

Fiction - 50.9

Cooking/crafts - 10.4

Non-fiction - 10.2

Religious - 7.4

Psychology/recovery - 6.2

Technical/science/education - 5.6

Art/literature/poetry - 4.0

Other - 2.8

Reference - 2.3

Travel/regional - 1.4

The table shows the best-selling types of books.

[In percent]

Segment	Share (%)
Fiction	50.9
Cooking/crafts	10.4
Non-fiction	10.2
Religious	7.4
Psychology/recovery	6.2
Technical/science/education	5.6
Art/literature/poetry	4.0
Reference	2.3
Travel/regional	1.4
Other	2.8

Source: "Book Report." *The Christian Science Monitor,* 9 December 1997, p. 10.

★ 237 ★

Buyers

What Teens Want to Read

Data show the favorite types of books of teenagers aged 12-17.

[In percent]

Segment	Boys	Girls
Mystery/crime/suspense	23	30
Horror/scary	26	26
Romance	1	16
Humor	15	10
History/biography	2	6
Science fiction/fantasy	21	5
Don't read	3	3
Other	9	4

Source: "What Teens Want to Read." *USA TODAY,* 10 December 1997, p. D1.

Consumer Spending

★ 238 ★

Black Book Spending

From 1993 to 1996, the amount black households spent on books rose sharply, to $261 million from $178 million, according to Target Market News, a Chicago research firm specializing in the African American market. Meanwhile, the amount these households spent on books in bookstores almost doubled to $229 million from $124 million. The attractiveness of this market for publishers and mainstream booksellers has surged proportionately.

Source: Angel, Karen. "Black Booksellers Aim to Get Their Groove Market." *Publishers Weekly,* 15 September 1997, p. 20.

★ 239 ★

Consumer Spending

Consumer Book Spending, 1991-2001

Data show projected spending in billions of dollars.

Segment	1991 ($ bil.)	2001 ($ bil.)
General retailers	9.1	15.2
College	3.4	5.8
Direct to consumer	2.9	4.8
School	2.4	3.9
Libraries/institutions	1.6	2.7

Source: From the Internet, http://www.bookwire.com/bisg/1997~study.html, (November 1997). Primary source: Book Industry Study Group.

★ 240 ★

Consumer Spending

Consumer Spending on Books

Data are in billions of dollars. Figure for 2001 is estimated.

Year	($ bil.)
1991	20.1
1996	26.1
2001	33.0

Source: "Book Report." *The Christian Science Monitor,* 9 December 1997, p. 10.

★ 241 ★

Consumer Spending

Domestic Spending on Books, 1996-1998

Data are estimated.

Category	1996 ($ mil.)	1997 ($ mil.)	1998 ($ mil.)
Paperbound	10,230.7	10,752.4	11,295.8
Hardbound	14,664.6	15,389.4	16,109.7
Total	24,895.3	26,141.8	27,405.5

Source: "Book Industry Forecast: Consumer Spending, Publishers' Manufacturing Expenditures." *High Volume Printing* (December 1996), p. 34.

Production

★ 242 ★

Book Production

The major publishers turn out 1,000 books a week, many of which have literary merit and most of which lose money.

Source: "Hyping Type." *New York,* 17 June 1996, p. 21.

Foreign Markets

★ 243 ★

Australia's Market Size for Books

Australians are big readers. In a survey in 1994, nearly half the respondents were reading a book. The average weekly expenditure on books was $2.50. The publishing industry contains approximately 1,000 firms. The Australian Government Publishing Service is the largest publisher in the country, producing some 4,000 titles annually. There are 1,800 booksellers in Australia. Angus & Robertson is the largest bookseller, holding 25% of the retail market. There were 13,750 titles published in 1994. Figures are shown in millions of dollars.

Segment	Last year 1995	Current year 1996	Next year 1997	Projected average annual growth rate for following 2 years
Import market	379.2	408.3	424.6	4
Local production	645.6	695.1	722.9	4
Exports	36.0	40.9	41.0	-
Total market	1,024.8	1,103.4	1,147.5	4
Imports from U.S.	144.1	148.9	154.9	4
Exchange rates	1.35	1.27	1.27	-
Estimated future inflation rate	3.4			

Source: National Trade Data Bank: The Export Connection CD-ROM, STAT-USA, U.S. Department of Commerce, Washington, D.C. 20302, 1 February 1997, p. ISA970201.

★ 244 ★

Foreign Markets

Book Production in Germany, 1994

Production is shown in percent.

Segment	Share
Academic	14.3
Children/young adult	6.8
Business	5.4
Medicine	5.2
Law	5.2
Atlases, reference	4.8
Religion	4.8
Geography/travel	3.8
Other	49.7

Source: "Folder for Bookworms." *Press und Sprache* (March 1996), p. 5.

★ 245 ★

Foreign Markets

Book Publishing in Latin America

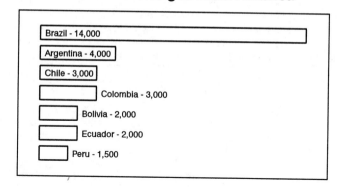

Data show the number of titles published in 1995.

Country	Titles
Brazil	14,000
Argentina	4,000
Chile	3,000
Colombia	3,000
Bolivia	2,000
Ecuador	2,000
Peru	1,500

Source: Latin American Press, 16 May 1996, p. 7. Primary source: *El Comercio.*

★ 246 ★

Foreign Markets

Canada: Book Publishing by Segment

Based on the data provided by respondents, 19 of the companies interviewed represent approximately 67% of the total marketplace (excludes 2 participating publishers who did not share revenue figures).

[In percent]

Area	Share (%)
Law	45
Medical	25
Business	14
General Reference	10
Comp. Science	3
English and Architecture	2
Science	2

Source: From the Internet, http://.pubcouncil.ca/prof-ref-rev.html, (August 1996). Primary source: Canadian Publishers Council.

★ 247 ★

Foreign Markets

Global Book Sales by Region, 1995

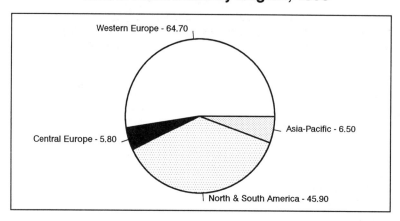

Data show per capita sales by region.

[In dollars]

Region	Sales
Western Europe	64.70
North & South America	45.90
Asia-Pacific	6.50
Central Europe	5.80

Source: "New Study Puts Global Book Market at $80 Billion." *Publishers Weekly,* 14 October 1996, p. 10. *Notes:* Primary source: Euromonitor.

★ 248 ★

Foreign Markets

Latin America: Book Sales by Country

Latin America has a growing book market. Material circulates freely and, with the exception of Chile, no country places any tariff on books. The largest and fastest growing segment is the market for textbooks. Figures are in millions of dollars for 1995.

[In millions]

Country	Amount	% increase over 1994
Brazil	2,526	46.7
Mexico	822	15.6
Argentina	614	4.4
Chile	131	4.8

[Continued]

★ 248 ★

Latin America: Book Sales by Country
[Continued]

Country	Amount	% increase over 1994
Venezuela	90	16.9
Peru	72	1.4
Colombia	63	3.3

Source: "Volumes of Money." Latin Trade, (October 1997), p. 30. Primary source: Euromonitor.

★ 249 ★

Foreign Markets

Leading Book Buying Countries

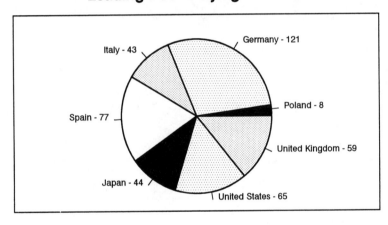

Data show selected countries ranked by per capita spending.

[In dollars]

Country	Amount
Germany	121
Spain	77
United States	65
United Kingdom	59
Japan	44
Italy	43
Poland	8

Source: "Volume Trading." The Warsaw Voice, 24 August 1997, p. 12. Primary source: Rzeczpospolita daily, based on Euromonitor Market Direction, 1996.

★ 250 ★

Foreign Markets

Mexico: Book Publishing by Subject, 1994

Subject	Titles		Issues	
	Number	%	(mil.)	%
Textbooks	2,243	18	43.4	47
Practical books	1,896	15	10.9	12
Encyclopedias & dictionaries	240	2	8.1	9
Children & juvenile books	986	8	7.5	8
Technical & scientific books	2,428	20	7.5	8
Literature	1,781	14	6.0	7
Humanities & social sciences	2,067	17	5.8	6
Religion	616	5	2.6	3
Art books	67	0	0.2	0
Others	145	1	0.3	0

Source: "Mexico - Educational Equipment and Supplies." *National Trade Data Bank:* The Export Connection CD-ROM, STAT-USA, U.S. Department of Commerce, Washington, D.C. 20302, 26 August 1996, p. ISA960301.

★ 251 ★

Foreign Markets

North America's Book Sales

Data compare per capita book sales.

[In dollars]

Country	Per capita
Canada	59
United States	106

Source: "Chapter's New Verse." *Macleans,* 8 July 1996, p. 30.

★ 252 ★

Foreign Markets

Popular Types of Books in Poland

| Action/adventure - 32 |
| Historical - 31 |
| Romance - 29 |
| Classics - 21 |
| Psychology - 18 |
| Popular science - 14 |
| Education - 13 |
| Professional literature - 12 |
| Fantasy - 11 |
| Biography - 7 |
| Horror - 7 |
| Poetry - 5 |
| Military - 5 |
| General non-fiction - 5 |
| Guidebooks - 4 |
| Essays - 4 |
| Erotica - 3 |

About 85 million books were published in Poland in 1996, with the average book costing zl.15-20.

[In percent]

Type of book	Share
Action/adventure	32
Historical	31
Romance	29
Classics	21
Psychology	18
Popular science	14
Education	13
Professional literature	12
Fantasy	11
Biography	7
Horror	7

[Continued]

★ 252 ★

Popular Types of Books in Poland
[Continued]

Type of book	Share
Poetry	5
Military	5
General non-fiction	5
Guidebooks	4
Essays	4
Erotica	3

Source: "Volume Trading." *The Warsaw Voice,* 24 August 1997, p. 12. Primary source: CBOS, 1996.

★ 253 ★

Foreign Markets

Russia: Publishing and Distribution

The table shows some facts on Russia's publishing industry.

The former Soviet textbook firm Prosveshcheniye published 44 million books in 1996, which is an estimated one in ten of all books published in Russia.

EKSMO began publishing four years ago and now launches 100 titles a month, concentrating on Russian-language thrillers and using private distributors to reach readers in remote corners of Russia.

There is a shortage of large bookshops. There are approximately 30 in Moscow, with other large cities having only two or three. As a result most books are sold by one of hundreds of small stalls found in metro stations or underpasses. Because distribution is so hampered, publishers stick to popular, best-selling topics such as Stalin or astrology. Some publishers have created "series," well-known branded titles.

Source: "From Marx to Mills and Boon." *The Economist,* 25 October 1997, p. 68.

★ 254 ★

Foreign Markets

Thailand: Book Market by Category, 1995

Category	Share (%)	Volume ($ mil.)
Textbooks	42	47
Paperback pocket books	26	28
Comics, children and juvenile books	25	27
Technical and how-to books	7	9

Source: "Thailand - Book Publishing Industry." *National Trade Data Bank:* The Export Connection CD-ROM, STAT-USA, U.S. Department of Commerce, Washington, D.C. 20302, 30 October 1996, p. ISA960901.

★ 255 ★

Foreign Markets

Top 10 Publishing: Market by Market Worldwide, 1995

U.S. - 25.49
Japan - 10.47
Germany - 9.96
Great Britain - 3.60
France - 3.38
Spain - 2.99
South Korea - 2.80
Brazil - 2.53
Italy - 2.25
China - 1.76

Global retail sales topped $80.1 billion last year, up 8 percent over 1994. Sales are shown in billions of dollars.

[In dollars]

Country	Total
U.S.	25.49
Japan	10.47
Germany	9.96
Great Britain	3.60
France	3.38

[Continued]

★ 255 ★

Top 10 Publishing: Market by Market Worldwide, 1995
[Continued]

Country	Total
Spain	2.99
South Korea	2.80
Brazil	2.53
Italy	2.25
China	1.76

Source: "Where the Readers Are." *The Christian Science Monitor,* 28 October 1996, p. 2. Primary source: Euromonitor.

★ 256 ★

Foreign Markets

Top Book Buying Nations, 1995

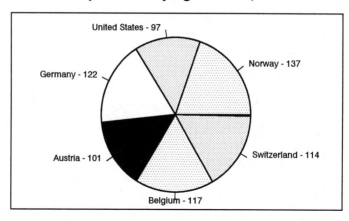

The average American spent almost $97 on books last year—up from about $80 in 1991. Data show the world's top book-buying countries[1] in spending per person (U.S. dollars).

[In dollars]

Country	Spending
Norway	137
Germany	122
Belgium	117
Switzerland	114
Austria	101
United States	97

Source: "World-Class Book Buyers." *USA TODAY,* 27 November 1996, p. D1. Primary source: Euromonitor. *Notes:* 1. Includes all books distributed by retail, institutional, direct mail and mail order outlets in 51 countries.

★ 257 ★

Foreign Markets

U.S./Latin American Book Market

According to the source: "Marquez, Borges, Neruda, Esquivel and Allende top the list for fiction from Latin America. While the U.S. market remains elusive, divided as it is both culturally and geographically, more distributors are bringing in more books from Latin America than ever before. Mexico remains the number one source for books, sending us $48 million worth in 1995, against Spain's $34 million. Both showed substantial increases over 1994, though both declined slightly in the first half of 1995. Spain remains the most reliable supplier in terms of shipments, and their books are often better made and cheaper than those from Argentina, for example. Still, Mexico has been the fastest growing source of books from any Spanish-speaking country. And the U.S. publishers now producing books in Spanish have created a whole new supply line for books—and more than a few headaches, as various editions of the same book compete for the open U.S. market."

Source: "Getting Into the American Market." Publishers Weekly, 23 September 1996, pp. 22-24.

Chapter 5
THE CATALOG INDUSTRY

This chapter presents selected data on the Catalog industry, a significant producer of printed products that are intended to be used in product selection and acquisition by distant buyers. Topics covered include *Sales and Distribution*, *Companies*, *Catalog Users*, and *Foreign Markets*. Electronic dissemination of this type of material is covered under the topic of *Electronic Publishing* in Chapter 3 and, in much more detail, in Gale's *By-the-Numbers: Electronic and Online Publishing*.

Sales and Distribution

★ 258 ★

Catalog Distribution by Region

West - 91.6

Northeast - 90.8

North Central - 87.4

Southeast - 83.2

South Central - 82.4

Data show the percent of U.S. households that receive catalogs.

[In percent]

Region	Share (%)
West	91.6
Northeast	90.8
North Central	87.4
Southeast	83.2
South Central	82.4

Source: Christiana-Beaudry, Laura. "Who Buys Why?" *Catalog Age* (July 1996), p. 183. Primary source: Talmey-Drake Research of Strategy Inc. Figures are based on 643 random telephone interviews.

★ 259 ★

Sales and Distribution

Catalog Sales by Year

Sales are shown in billions of dollars.

Year	Sales ($ bil.)
1992	53.4
1997	78.6[1]
2002	106.8[1]

Source: "Shopping by Mail." *USA TODAY*, 19 November 1997, p. 26A. Primary source: Direct Marketing Association. *Note:* 1. Estimate.

★ 260 ★

Sales and Distribution

Retail Sales in Catalog and Mail Order Houses, 1996-1997

[In millions of dollars]

Month	Total catalog and mail order house sales	Retail trade total	Total except automotive group	Durable goods total	Catalog sales as a percentage of durable goods sales
1996					
January	3,730	197,714	149,641	79,640	4.68
February	3,400	201,085	151,137	81,931	4.15
March	3,763	201,685	151,765	82,641	4.55
April	3,645	202,496	154,039	81,603	4.47
May	3,582	204,177	154,699	83,239	4.30
June	3,296	202,698	154,033	82,315	4.00
July	3,440	203,090	154,338	82,383	4.18
August	3,508	203,087	154,172	82,386	4.26
September	3,731	204,880	155,089	83,108	4.49
October	4,491	206,277	156,163	83,871	5.35
November	5,223	205,789	156,269	83,485	6.26
December	6,203	206,894	156,850	83,785	7.40
Total	48,012	2,439,872	1,848,195	990,387	4.85
1997					
January	3,804	210,233	159,190	85,344	4.46
February	3,432	213,022	160,483	87,786	3.91
March	4,215	212,342	160,484	87,042	4.84
April	4,152	209,934	159,486	85,472	4.86
May	3,975	209,370	159,445	84,759	4.69
June	3,893	210,940	160,192	85,762	4.54
July	3,877	213,549	161,656	87,228	4.44
August	3,944	214,888	161,999	88,194	4.47

Source: Monthly Retail Trade Survey, Services Division, Bureau of the Census, Washington, DC 20233.
Note: 1. Preliminary figures.

★ 261 ★

Sales and Distribution

U.K. Mail Order Market, 1995

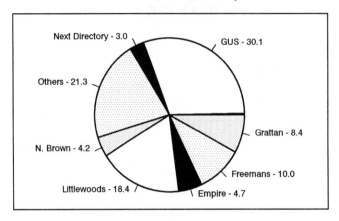

Market shares are shown in percent.

[In percent]

Company	Share (%)
GUS	30.1
Littlewoods	18.4
Freemans	10.0
Grattan	8.4
Empire	4.7
N. Brown	4.2
Next Directory	3.0
Others	21.3

Source: "Lex Comment." *Financial Times,* 19 November 1997, p. 21. Primary source: Corporate Intelligence on Retailing.

★ 262 ★
Sales and Distribution

U.S. Consumer Catalogs by Year

Data show the number of catalogs by year. An estimated 85% of all catalogs are from the consumer market.

[In percent]

Year	Number
1981	4,029
1991	7,427
1992	7,383
1993	7,001
1994	7,091
1995	7,464

Source: Christiana-Beaudry, Laura. "Who Buys Why?" *Catalog Age* (July 1996), p. 183. Primary source: Grey House Publishing.

Companies

★ 263 ★

Land's End: A Profile

Here are some statistics on one of the leading mail order companies:

Item	Value
Packages shipped annually	13 million
Most orders shipped in a day, 1996	154,000
Calls received in a year	14 million
Increase in red ribbon during the holidays	300%
Length of red ribbon ordered for holiday packages	142 miles
Gift-boxing record in a day	8,092
Daily e-mail messages to Web site	500

Source: Woodyard, Chris. "Wisconsin Cataloger Plows Through Storm." *USA TODAY,* 15 December 1997, p. 10B.

★ 264 ★

Companies

Leading U.S. Mail Order Parent Companies

Firms are ranked by worldwide sales in millions of dollars.

Company	Sales ($ mil.)	Sales segment
United Services Automobile Association	6,634.0	Insurance, general merchandise, financial services
Time Warner	5,595.6	Audio-video, books, cable TV, general merchandise, gifts, magazine/periodical subscriptions
Tele Communications	4,464.5	Cable TV
J.C. Penney	4,216.0	General merchandise, insurance
Dell Computer Corp.	4,042.0	Business supplies
American Association of Retired Persons	3,936.1	Health, insurance
Gateway 2000	3,500.0	Business supplies
Berkshire Hathaway	2,915.4	Books, insurance
Comcast Cable	2,631.3	Cable TV, general merchandise
Reader's Digest	2,612.7	Books, collectibles, general merchandise magazine/periodical subscriptions
AT&T	2,025.0	Business services industrial
Fingerhut	1,826.4	Food, general merchandise
Spiegel (Otto Versand)	1,751.5	Apparel, general merchandise, sporting goods
Micro Warehouse	1,670.5	Business supplies, consumer electronics
Hewlett-Packard	1,575.0	Business supplies
Comp-U-Card International	1,555.0	General merchandise
Providian	1,474.7	Financial services, insurance
MCI	1,470.0	Business services
U.S. Government	1,460.9	Business supplies, business services, collectibles, educational services, health
Digital Equipment Corporation	1,350.0	Business supplies
Federated Stores	1,205.3	General merchandise
W.W. Grainger	1,120.0	Industrial
Cox Enterprises	1,074.0	Cable TV
Continental Cablevision	1,052.2	Cable TV
Silver King Communications	1,021.9	General merchandise, apparel

Source: "Mail Order." *Direct Marketing* (August 1996), p. 50.

★ 265 ★

Companies

Mail Order: Top Companies in Japan, 1995

| Cecile - 195,261 |
| Senshukai - 165,828 |
| Benesse - 161,401 |
| Nissen - 131,317 |
| Mutow - 71,990 |
| Dinos - 58,772 |
| Felissimo - 52,000 |
| Takashimaya - 46,507 |
| Mitsukoshi - 45,165 |
| Belluna - 42,610 |

Chart shows data from column 1.

Sales are shown in millions of yen.

Company	FY 1994	FY 1995
Cecile	195,261	194,639
Benesse	161,401	172,696
Senshukai	165,828	168,206
Nissen	131,317	161,636
Mutow	71,990	67,727
Felissimo	52,000	63,000
Dinos	58,772	61,800
Takashimaya	46,507	46,270
Belluna	42,610	45,550
Mitsukoshi	45,165	43,458

Source: "Japan - Large Mail Order Companies." *National Trade Data Bank:* The Export Connection CD-ROM, STAT-USA, U.S. Department of Commerce, Washington, D.C. 20302, 19 December 1996, p. IMI961219. Primary source: *Tsuuhan Shinbun*.

★ 266 ★

Companies

Top Catalogers, 1994

Companies are ranked by sales in millions of dollars.

Company	1994 Sales (mil.)	Type of business
JC Penney	3,817	General merchandise
Dell Computer	3,420	Computer hardware
Gateway 2000	2,600	Computer hardware
DECDirect	2,000	Computer hardware
Spiegel	1,742	General merchandise
Fingerhut	1,719	General merchandise
Land's End	990[1]	Apparel
IBM Direct	950[1]	Computer hardware
L.L. Bean	848	Apparel
Micro Warehouse	776.4	Computer software

Source: "Wired Top 10." Wired (February 1996), p. 4. Primary source: *Catalog Age Online,* (http://www.mediacentral.com/). *Note:* 1. Denotes estimate.

★ 267 ★

Companies

Top Catalogers, 1995-1996

Firms are ranked by sales in millions of dollars.

Company	1995 sales ($ mil.)	1996 sales ($ mil.)	Market segment	Notes
Dell Computer Corp. Austin, TX 512-338-4400	5,144	7,554	Computer hardware	U.S. corporate accounts gain
Gateway 2000 N. Sioux City, SD 605-232-2000	3,676	5,035	Computer hardware	Revenue tops $5 billion for first time
J.C. Penney Plane, TX 972-431-1000	3,378	3,772	General merchandise	
Digital Equipment Merrimack, NH 603-884-5111	3,000	3,300	Computer hardware	
Micro Warehouse Norwalk, CT 203-899-4000	1,308	1,916	Computer hardware, software & peripherals	Restated 1992-95 financials

[Continued]

★ 267 ★

Top Catalogers, 1995-1996
[Continued]

Company	1995 sales ($ mil.)	1996 sales ($ mil.)	Market segment	Notes
Spiegel Downers Grove, IL 630-986-8800	1,760	1,681	General merchandise	Lower productivity from catalogs
Fingerhut Winnetonka, MN 612-932-3100	1,782	1,638	General merchandise	Cut catalog mailings to existing customers
Viking Office Products Los Angeles, CA 213-321-4493	921	1,182	Office supplies	Earnings up 31.2% over 1995
Lands' End Dodgeville, WI 608-935-9341	1,030	1,112	Apparel	Growth in specialty and int'l businesses
Computer Discount Warehouse (CDW) Buffalo Grove, IL 708-465-6000	634.5	928	Computer hardware, software & peripherals	Income soars 71.5% over 1995

Source: *Catalog Age* (August 1997), p. 60.

Catalog Users

★ 268 ★

Catalog Readership

Nearly 100 catalogs a year are stuffed into the mailbox of the average American household, but only 54% of the households actually read the words.

Source: Bird, Laura. "Beyond Mail Order: Catalogs Now Sell Image, Advice." *The Wall Street Journal,* 29 July 1997, p. B1. Primary source: Direct Marketing Association.

★ 269 ★

Catalog Users

Catalog Shopping by Metro Area, 1996

Metro areas are ranked by the greatest number of residents who made purchases from a catalog.

Metro Area	Rank
Boulder-Longmont, CO	1
Middlesex-Somerset-Hunterdon, NJ	2
Ann Arbor, MI	3
Nassau-Suffolk, NY	4
Santa Cruz-Watsonville, CA	5
Santa Fe, NM	6
San Jose, CA	7
Iowa City, IA	8
Dutchess County, NY	9
Madison, WI	10

Source: "At Home Shoppers." *The Wall Street Journal*, 5 December 1997, p. B16. Primary source: National Decision Systems.

★ 270 ★

Catalog Users

Profile of Direct Mail Catalog Buyers

Characteristic	Response (%)
Age 25-64	73
Married	73
No kids at home	56
Owns a dog	35
Has home workshop	30
Professional/technical job	26

Source: Carey, Anne R. and Gary Visgaitis. "Who Shops from Catalogs?" *USA TODAY*, 3 February 1997, p. D1. Primary source: Polk.

★ 271 ★

Catalog Users

Who Receives Catalogs, by Age

[In percent]

Age	Share (%)
18-24	10
25-34	20
35-44	21
45-54	18
55-64	12
65+	14

Source: Christiana-Beaudry, Laura. "Who Buys Why?" *Catalog Age* (July 1996), p. 183. Primary source: Talmey-Drake Research & Strategy Inc. Figures are based on 643 telephone interviews.

★ 272 ★

Catalog Users

Why Men Shop from Catalogs

Reason	% of men
Convenience	40
Variety	19
Price	14
Service	3
Don't know	2
Don't buy	22

Source: "USA Snapshots." *USA TODAY,* 17 December 1997, p. B1. Primary source: Bruskin-Goldring for Direct Marketing Association.

★ 273 ★

Catalog Users

Why Women Shop from Catalogs

Reason	% of women
Convenience	50
Variety	20
Price	9
Service	3

[Continued]

★ 273 ★

Why Women Shop from Catalogs
[Continued]

Reason	% of women
Don't know	1
Don't buy	17

Source: "USA Snapshots." USA TODAY, 17 December 1997, p. B1. Primary source: Bruskin-Goldring for Direct Marketing Association.

Foreign Markets

★ 274 ★

Italy: Best-Selling Catalog Items, 1993

Apparel - 35
Books and records - 22
Houseware items - 16
Home fabrics - 9
Leisure and sport items - 6
Business to business - 6
Food and wines - 3
All others - 3

Type of goods	Share (%)
Apparel	35
Books and records	22
Houseware items	16
Home fabrics	9
Leisure and sport items	6
Business to business	6
Food and wines	3
All others	3

Source: "Italy - Catalog Retail Distribution." National Trade Data Bank: The Export Connection CD-ROM.STAT-USA, U.S. Department of Commerce, Washington, D.C. 20302, 10 May 1995, p. IMI950508.

★ 275 ★

Foreign Markets

Italy's Catalog Sales by Type, 1993-94

Type	1993 Sales ($ mil.)	1993 Share (%)	1994 Sales ($ mil.)	1994 Share (%)
General catalogs	525	63	531	62
Books and records	181	22	193	22
Specialized catalogs	76	9	82	10
Business to business	46	6	52	6

Source: "Italy - Catalog Retail Distribution." *National Trade Data Bank:* The Export Connection CD-ROM, STAT-USA, U.S. Department of Commerce, Washington, D.C. 20302, 10 May 1995, p. IMI950508.

★ 276 ★

Foreign Markets

Mail Order Sales in Europe, 1996

The table shows the countries with the greatest per capita mail order sales. Sales have been converted to dollars from German marks. The table includes mail order's share or retail sales.

Country	Per Capita Sales	% of Retail Sales
Germany	278	5.8
Switzerland	179	2.4
Austria	159	3.9
Japan	141	1.5
Great Britain	140	3.7
France	134	2.4
Denmark	131	NA
Norway	122	NA
Sweden	103	1.9
Finland	101	NA

Source: Rohwedder, Cacilie." *The Wall Street Journal,* 6 January 1998, p. A15. Primary source: German Mail Order Federation. *Note:* NA = not available.

Chapter 6
THE GREETING CARDS INDUSTRY

A highly specialized and distinct segment of publishing is the Greeting Cards industry, profiled in this chapter under the topics of *Industry Statistics* and *Sales Statistics*—the first covering information as reported by the Federal government and the second data published on the industry in other sources.

★ 277 ★

General Statistics on the Greeting Card Industry, 1982-1998

Year	Com-panies	Establishments		Employment			Compensation	
		Total	With 20 or more employees	Total (000)	Production workers (000)	Hours (mil.)	Payroll ($ mil.)	Wages ($ hr.)
1982	139	154	54	20.8	11.7	20.2	344.2	7.68
1983	NA	NA	NA	22.5	13.5	21.0	381.6	8.10
1984	NA	NA	NA	19.8	10.8	18.4	386.2	9.20
1985	NA	NA	NA	19.9	10.8	17.7	397.5	9.43
1986	NA	NA	NA	20.0	10.8	19.3	407.4	9.02
1987	147	162	64	21.5	11.9	21.7	471.1	9.54
1988	NA	NA	NA	NA	NA	19.0	474.1	NA
1989	NA	144	57	20.8	11.2	20.8	537.3	10.15
1990	NA	NA	NA	24.6	12.3	23.7	625.2	10.10
1991	NA	NA	NA	23.9	12.5	22.8	609.1	10.46
1992	157	173	62	22.8	11.8	21.1	585.1	10.76
1993	NA	NA	NA	22.2	12.2	20.5	610.4	11.51
1994	NA	NA	NA	23.2	13.0	22.2	627.5	11.37
1995	NA	NA	NA	NA	NA	22.3[1]	680.4[1]	NA
1996	NA	NA	NA	NA	NA	22.6[1]	706.6[1]	NA
1997	NA	NA	NA	NA	NA	22.8[1]	732.8[1]	NA
1998	NA	NA	NA	NA	NA	23.0[1]	759.1[1]	NA

Source: 1997 *Manufacturing STATROM* [machine-readable data files]. MStat97. Editorial Code and Data, Inc., Detroit, Michigan, 1997. Primary source: 1982, 1987, 1992 *Economic Census*; *Annual Survey of Manufactures*, 1983-1986, 1988-1991, 1993-1994. Establishment counts for non-Census years are from *County Business Patterns*; establishment values for 1983-1984 are extrapolations. Industries reclassified in 1987 will not have data for prior years. *Notes:* NA = Not available. 1. Items are projected by the editors.

★ 278 ★

Industry Statistics

General Indices of Change in the Greeting Card Industry, 1982-1998

Year	Com-panies	Establishments		Employment			Compensation	
		Total	With 20 or more employees	Total (000)	Production workers (000)	Hours (mil.)	Payroll ($ mil.)	Wages ($ hr.)
1982	89	89	87	91	99	96	59	71
1983	NA	NA	NA	99	114	100	65	75
1984	NA	NA	NA	87	92	87	66	86
1985	NA	NA	NA	87	92	84	68	88
1986	NA	NA	NA	88	92	91	70	84
1987	94	94	103	94	101	103	81	89
1988	NA	NA	NA	NA	NA	90	81	NA
1989	NA	83	92	91	95	99	92	94
1990	NA	NA	NA	108	104	112	107	94
1991	NA	NA	NA	105	106	108	104	97
1992	100	100	100	100	100	100	100	100
1993	NA	NA	NA	97	103	97	104	107
1994	NA	NA	NA	102	110	105	107	106
1995	NA	NA	NA	NA	NA	106[1]	116[1]	NA
1996	NA	NA	NA	NA	NA	107[1]	121[1]	NA
1997	NA	NA	NA	NA	NA	108[1]	125[1]	NA
1998	NA	NA	NA	NA	NA	109[1]	130[1]	NA

Source: 1997 *Manufacturing STATROM* [machine-readable data files]. MStat97. Editorial Code and Data, Inc., Detroit, Michigan, 1997. Primary source: 1982, 1987, 1992 *Economic Census; Annual Survey of Manufactures,* 1983-1986, 1988-1991, 1993-1994. Establishment counts for non-Census years are from *County Business Patterns;* establishment values for 1983-1984 are extrapolations. Industries reclassified in 1987 will not have data for prior years. Values reflect change from the base year, 1992. Values above 100 mean greater than 1992, values below 100 mean less than 1992, and a value of 100 in the 1982-1991 or 1993-1998 period means same as 1992. *Notes:* NA = Not available. 1. Items are projected by the editors.

★ 279 ★

Industry Statistics

General Production Statistics on the Greeting Card Industry, 1982-1998

Year	Production ($ million)			
	Cost of materials	Value added by manufacture	Value of shipments[1]	Capital investment
1982	554.6	1,348.8	1,893.6	37.2
1983	666.4	1,611.2	2,250.6	51.1
1984	748.8	1,667.0	2,394.2	91.0
1985	672.9	1,894.8	2,598.0	46.5
1986	620.2	2,036.2	2,681.4	48.4
1987	773.9	2,203.9	2,911.1	65.6
1988	810.7	2,279.2	3,081.7	NA
1989	906.6	2,553.7	3,449.2	107.1
1990	938.3	2,827.5	3,720.7	132.0
1991	870.2	2,925.4	3,809.9	94.1
1992	743.0	3,393.5	4,195.6	85.7
1993	825.8	3,481.6	4,274.5	53.8
1994	915.0	3,660.0	4,507.2	71.0
1995	958.8[2]	3,835.1[2]	4,722.9[2]	NA
1996	1,002.6[2]	4,010.3[2]	4,938.6[2]	NA
1997	1,046.4[2]	4,185.5[2]	5,154.3[2]	NA
1998	1,090.2[2]	4,360.6[2]	5,370.0[2]	NA

Source: 1997 *Manufacturing STATROM* [machine-readable data files]. MStat97. Editorial Code and Data, Inc., Detroit, Michigan, 1997. Primary source: 1982, 1987, 1992 *Economic Census; Annual Survey of Manufactures*, 1983-1986, 1988-1991, 1993-1994. Establishment counts for non-Census years are from *County Business Patterns*; establishment values for 1983-1984 are extrapolations. Industries reclassified in 1987 will not have data for prior years. *Notes:* NA = Not available. 1. "Industry Shipments" and "Product Shipments" are rarely the same value. 2. Items are projected by the editors.

★ 280 ★

Industry Statistics

Materials Consumed by the Greeting Card Industry

Material	Delivered cost ($ mil.)
Materials, ingredients, containers, and supplies	473.2
Coated paper	74.4
Uncoated paper	92.6
Printing inks (complete formulations)	4.7
Paperboard containers, boxes, and corrugated paperboard	17.1
Purchased envelopes	15.9
All other materials and components, parts, containers, and supplies	200.9
Materials, ingredients, containers, and supplies, n.s.k.	67.7

Source: 1997 *Manufacturing STATROM* [machine-readable data files]. MStat97. Editorial Code and Data, Inc., Detroit, Michigan, 1997. Primary source: 1992 *Economic Census*. Explanation of symbols used: n.s.k: Not specified by kind.

★ 281 ★

Industry Statistics

Product Share Details in the Greeting Card Industry

Product code	Shipments ($ mil.)	% of total	Product name
2771	3,078.3	100.00	GREETING CARDS
27711	2,726.3	88.57	Greeting cards (publishers' sales)
2771113	217.5	7.98	Christmas counter greeting cards
2771115	254.6	9.34	Packaged Christmas greeting cards
2771122	186.2	6.83	Valentine counter greeting cards
2771124	23.4	0.86	Packaged Valentine greeting cards
2771126	147.9	5.42	Mother's Day greeting cards
2771127	104.7	3.84	Easter greeting cards
2771129	180.5	6.62	Seasonal greeting cards
2771133	1,451.8	53.25	Everyday counter greeting cards
2771135	60.9	2.23	Packaged everyday greeting cards
2771100	98.7	3.62	Greeting cards, publishers' sales, n.s.k.
27712	88.8	2.88	Greeting cards, printed for publication by others
27710	263.1	8.55	Greeting cards, n.s.k.

Source: 1997 *Manufacturing STATOM* [machine-readable data files]. MStat97. Editorial Code and Data, Inc., Detroit, Michigan, 1997. Primary source: 1992 *Economic Census*. The values shown are percent of total shipments in an industry. Values of indented subcategories are summed in the main headings. The abbreviationn.s.k. stands for 'not specified by kind.'

★ 282 ★

Industry Statistics

Production: Indices of Change in the Greeting Card Industry, 1982 -1998

Year	Production ($ million)			
	Cost of materials	Value added by manufacture	Value of shipments[1]	Capital investment
1982	75	40	45	43
1983	90	47	54	60
1984	101	49	57	106
1985	91	56	62	54
1986	83	60	64	56
1987	104	65	69	77
1988	109	67	73	NA
1989	122	75	82	125
1990	126	83	89	154
1991	117	86	91	110
1992	100	100	100	100
1993	111	103	102	63
1994	123	108	107	83
1995	129[2]	113[2]	113[2]	NA
1996	135[2]	118[2]	118[2]	NA
1997	141[2]	123[2]	123[2]	NA
1998	147[2]	128[2]	128[2]	NA

Source: 1997 *Manufacturing STATROM* [machine-readable data files]. MStat97. Editorial Code and Data, Inc., Detroit, Michigan, 1997. Primary source: 1982, 1987, 1992 *Economic Census*; *Annual Survey of Manufactures*, 1983-1986, 1988-1991, 1993-1994. Establishment counts for non-Census years are from *County Business Patterns*; establishment values for 1983-1984 are extrapolations. Industries reclassified in 1987 will not have data for prior years. Values reflect change from the base year, 1992. Values above 100 mean greater than 1992, values below 100 mean less than 1992, and a value of 100 in the 1982-1991 or 1993-1998 period means same as 1992. *Notes:* NA = Not available. 1. "Industry Shipments" and "Product Shipments" are rarely the same value. 2. Items are projected by the editors.

★ 283 ★

Industry Statistics

Occupations Employed by the Printing Trades Services, including Greeting Card Manufacturers

Occupation	% of total 1994	Change to 2005
Strippers, printing	7.2	-8.6
Sales & related workers nec	5.4	6.3
Electronic pagination systems workers	4.2	63.7
Typesetting & composing machine operators	4.2	-74.3
Printing workers, precision nec	3.8	37.9
General managers & top executives	3.8	-1.5
Hand packers & packagers	3.7	3.0
Artists & commercial artists	2.6	10.7
Proofreaders & copy markers	2.4	-33.2
Production, planning, & expediting clerks	2.3	22.2
Photoengravers	2.3	-28.4
Camera operators	2.1	-18.1
Bookkeeping, accounting, & auditing clerks	2.0	-21.2
Paste-up workers	1.9	-33.3
Machine feeders & offbearers	1.8	7.5
Printing press machine setters, operators	1.7	-9.0
Adjustment clerks	1.6	34.4
Data entry keyers, composing	1.6	-74.3
Secretaries, ex legal & medical	1.6	0.1
General office clerks	1.6	-8.4
Freight, stock, & material movers, hand	1.5	-4.4
Assemblers, fabricators, & hand workers nec	1.4	15.4
Messengers	1.4	-20.6
Clerical supervisors & managers	1.4	10.7
Management support workers nec	1.4	19.5
Platemakers	1.3	-27.7
Offset lithographic press operators	1.3	1.4
Printing, binding, & related workers nec	1.3	14.9
Traffic, shipping, & receiving clerks	1.2	7.2
Industrial production managers	1.2	5.4
Bindery machine operators & set-up operators	1.2	9.9
Data entry keyers, ex composing	1.1	-16.6

Source: Industry-Occupation Matrix, Bureau of Labor Statistics. These data relate to one or more 3-digit SIC industry groups rather than to a single 4-digit SIC. The change reported for each occupation to the year 2005 is a percent of growth or decline as estimated by the Bureau of Labor Statistics. The abbreviation nec stands for 'not elsewhere classified'.

Industry Statistics

Selected Ratios for the Greeting Card Industry

For 1992	Average of all manufacturing	Greeting card publishing	Index
Employees per establishment	46	132	289
Payroll per establishment	1,332,320	3,382,081	254
Payroll per employee	29,181	25,662	88
Production workers per establishment	31	68	217
Wages per establishment	734,496	1,312,347	179
Wages per production worker	23,390	19,240	82
Hours per production worker	2,025	1,788	88
Wages per hour	11.55	10.76	93
Value added per establishment	3,842,210	19,615,607	511
Value added per employee	84,153	148,838	177
Value added per production worker	122,353	287,585	235
Cost per establishment	4,239,462	4,294,798	101
Cost per employee	92,853	32,588	35
Cost per production worker	135,003	62,966	47
Shipments per establishment	8,100,800	24,252,023	299
Shipments per employee	177,425	184,018	104
Shipments per production worker	257,966	355,559	138
Investment per establishment	278,244	495,376	178
Investment per employee	6,094	3,759	62
Investment per production worker	8,861	7,263	82

Source: 1997 *Manufacturing STATROM* [machine-readable data files]. MStat97. Editorial Code and Data, Inc., Detroit, Michigan, 1997. Primary source: 1982, 1987, 1992 *Economic Census*; *Annual Survey of Manufactures*, 1983-1986, 1988-1991, 1993-1994. Establishment counts for non-Census years are from *County Business Patterns*; establishment values for 1983-1984 are extrapolations. Industries reclassified in 1987 will not have data for prior years. Values reflect change from the base year, 1992. Values above 100 mean greater than 1992, values below 100 mean less than 1992, and a value of 100 in the 1982-1991 or 1993-1998 period means same as 1992. The 'Average of All Manufacturing' column represents the average of all manufacturing industries reported for the most recent complete year available. The Index shows the relationship between the Average and the Analyzed Industry. For example, 100 means that they are equal; 500 that the Analyzed Industry is five times the average; 50 means that the Analyzed Industry is half the national average.

★ 285 ★

Industry Statistics

State Level Data for the Greeting Card Industry

The states are presented in ranked order by level of shipments.

State	Establish-ments	Shipments total ($ mil.)	% of U.S.	Per establish-ment	Employ-ment total number	% of U.S.	Per establish-ment	Wages ($/hour)	Cost as % of shipments	Investment per employee ($)
Colorado	8	159.9	3.8	20.0	1,600	7.0	200	8.82	23.2	NA
Illinois	9	157.7	3.8	17.5	1,500	6.6	167	8.45	27.6	2,400
New York	14	47.7	1.1	3.4	300	1.3	21	8.00	22.9	4,000
New Jersey	5	42.4	1.0	8.5	400	1.8	80	11.25	22.4	1,250
Massachusetts	9	39.7	0.9	4.4	300	1.3	33	7.75	22.2	NA
California	29	35.7	0.9	1.2	300	1.3	10	6.50	35.3	2,667
Kentucky	7	(D)	NA	NA	3,750[1]	16.4	536	NA	NA	NA
Missouri	6	(D)	NA	NA	7,500[1]	32.9	1,250	NA	NA	NA
New Hampshire	6	(D)	NA	NA	175[1]	0.8	29	NA	NA	1,143
Ohio	6	(D)	NA	NA	1,750[1]	7.7	292	NA	NA	NA
Texas	6	(D)	NA	NA	175[1]	0.8	29	NA	NA	NA
Maryland	5	(D)	NA	NA	175[1]	0.8	35	NA	NA	NA
Arkansas	3	(D)	NA	NA	3,750[1]	16.4	1,250	NA	NA	NA
Indiana	3	(D)	NA	NA	750[1]	3.3	250	NA	NA	NA
Kansas	3	(D)	NA	NA	1,750[1]	7.7	583	NA	NA	NA
Pennsylvania	3	(D)	NA	NA	750[1]	3.3	250	NA	NA	NA
Georgia	1	(D)	NA	NA	375[1]	1.6	375	NA	NA	NA
Rhode Island	1	(D)	NA	NA	375[1]	1.6	375	NA	NA	NA
Tennessee	1	(D)	NA	NA	175[1]	0.8	175	NA	NA	NA

Source: 1997 *Manufacturing STATROM* [machine-readable data files]. MStat97. Editorial Code and Data, Inc., Detroit, Michigan, 1997. Primary source: 1992 *Economic Census*. The states are in descending order of shipments or establishments (if shipment data are missing for the majority). The symbol (D) appears when data are withheld to prevent disclosure of competitive information. States marked with (D) are sorted by number *Notes:* NA = Not available. 1. Indicates the midpoint of a range.

★ 286 ★

Greeting Card Consumption by Age

The share of adults who bought any greeting card in the past six months declined from 74 percent in 1991 to 65 percent in 1996, according to Mediamark Research, Inc. The table shows the per capita number of cards purchased each year.

Age	Number
Under 19	2
19 to 24	9
25 to 34	36
35 to 44	36
45 to 54	47
55 to 64	57
65 and older	52

Source: "Greetings America." *American Demographics* (February 1997), p. 4.

★ 287 ★

Sales Statistics

Greeting Card Publishing by State

Data show the industry by segment.

State	Shipments as % of U.S.	Employment as % of U.S.	Payroll as % of U.S.	Cost of Materials as % of U.S.	Investment as % of U.S.
Colorado	3.40	7.00	5.10	3.80	3.40
Illinois	3.30	6.60	7.60	3.80	3.30
New York	1.10	1.30	1.70	1.10	1.10
New Jersey	1.00	1.80	1.70	1.00	1.00
Massachusetts	0.90	1.30	1.70	0.90	0.90
California	0.70	1.30	1.70	0.90	0.70

Source: 1997 *Manufacturing STATROM* [machine-readable data files]. MStat97. Editorial Code and Data, Inc., Detroit, Michigan, 1997. Primary source: *Economic Census for 1992* and earlier years. *The Economic Census* is conducted by the Bureau of the Census, U.S. Department of Commerce, Washington, DC 20233.

★ 288 ★

Sales Statistics

Greeting Card Sales by Year

In 1996, a total of 7.4 billion greeting cards are expected to be purchased in the United States. Total retail sales reached $6.85 billion. The average person receives 30 cards per year, eight of which are birthday cards. There are more than 1,500 greeting card publishers in America ranging from major corporations to small family organizations. The table shows sales in billions of dollars.

Year	Sales ($ bil.)
1996	$6.85
1995	6.30
1994	5.90
1993	5.60
1992	5.30
1991	5.00
1990	4.60
1989	4.20
1988	3.90
1987	3.80
1986	3.70
1985	3.50
1984	3.20
1983	2.70
1982	2.50
1981	2.35
1980	2.10

Source: From the Internet, http://www.greetingcard.org/gca/facts.htm.

★ 289 ★
Sales Statistics

Top Holidays for Greeting Cards, 1997

| Christmas - 2,600 |
| Valentine's Day - 900 |
| Mother's Day - 150 |
| Easter - 120 |
| Father's Day - 95 |
| Graduation - 60 |
| Thanksgiving - 30 |
| Halloween - 25 |
| St. Patrick's Day - 15 |
| Jewish New Year - 10 |

The greeting card industry is valued at $7.1 billion. Data show the best-selling occasions.

[In millions]

Season	Cards
Christmas	2,600
Valentine's Day	900
Mother's Day	150
Easter	120
Father's Day	95
Graduation	60
Thanksgiving	30
Halloween	25
St. Patrick's Day	15
Jewish New Year	10

Source: Woodyard, Chris. "Father's Day Cards Evolve With Times." *USA TODAY,* 12 June 1997, p. B1. Primary source: Greeting Card Association.

★ 290 ★

Sales Statistics

U.S. Greeting Cards Market

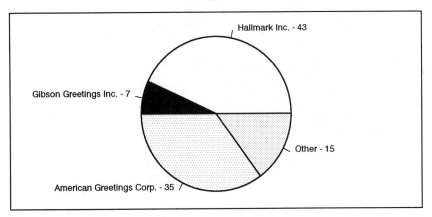

Hallmark Inc. - 43

Gibson Greetings Inc. - 7

Other - 15

American Greetings Corp. - 35

Data show market shares.

Company	Share (%)
Hallmark Inc.	43
American Greetings Corp.	35
Gibson Greetings Inc.	7
Other	15

Source: Coleman, Calmetta Y. "Gibson Greetings Makes Headway in Turnaround Bid." *The Wall Street Journal,* 18 December 1997, p. B4. Gibson Greetings and Baseline.

★ 291 ★

Sales Statistics

Valentine's Day Card Sales

More than 1 billion Valentine's Day greeting cards were sold last year.

Source: "Valentine's Day Rings Up Big Sales for Retailers." *Christian Science Monitor,* 13 February 1997, p. 2. Primary source: National Retail Federation.

★ 292 ★

Sales Statistics

Where Greeting Cards Are Sold, 1995

| Card/gifts - 31 |
| Drug stores - 22 |
| Mass merchandiser - 20 |
| Supermarket - 17 |
| Other - 7 |
| Variety - 2 |
| Department - 1 |

Data show where people purchase greeting cards.

Channel	Share (%)
Card/gifts	31
Drug stores	22
Mass merchandiser	20
Supermarket	17
Variety	2
Department	1
Other	7

Source: DM (September 1996), p. 32. Primary source: American Greetings.

Chapter 7
MAGAZINE PUBLISHING

This chapter presents data on all periodicals except newspapers and serial reference publications. The popular magazine categories are included along with academic journals, business and computer magazines, and other periodicals. Coverage of online magazines is incidental. For a full treatment of that subject, please see Gale's *By-the-Numbers: Electronic and Online Publishing*. Topics include *Industry Statistics*, *Sales and Distribution*, *Publishers*, *Magazine Categories*, *Academic Publishing*, *Advertising*, *Business Magazines*, *Computer Magazines*, *Consumer Magazines*, and *Foreign Markets*.

★ 293 ★

General Statistics on the Periodicals Industry, 1982-1998

| Year | Com-panies | Establishments | | Employment | | | Compensation | |
		Total	With 20 or more employees	Total (000)	Production workers (000)	Hours (mil.)	Payroll ($ mil.)	Wages ($ hr.)
1982	3,144	3,328	690	94.0	17.4	31.9	1,986.1	7.62
1983	NA	NA	NA	93.4	17.3	31.9	2,073.7	8.03
1984	NA	NA	NA	93.5	16.2	28.8	2,231.7	8.71
1985	NA	NA	NA	95.8	16.2	28.4	2,554.5	9.59
1986	NA	NA	NA	98.1	14.2	24.9	2,710.9	11.60
1987	3,757	4,020	876	110.0	18.3	32.4	2,982.7	11.06
1988	NA	NA	NA	111.4	19.1	33.8	3,152.1	11.99
1989	NA	4,101	872	115.9	20.7	32.6	3,422.8	12.45
1990	NA	NA	NA	115.2	21.6	35.4	3,658.5	13.09
1991	NA	NA	NA	110.6	20.7	35.4	3,661.0	13.21
1992	4,390	4,699	991	116.2	20.1	39.0	4,074.5	13.40
1993	NA	NA	NA	117.1	19.7	37.4	4,305.3	12.51
1994	NA	NA	NA	116.4	18.3	34.5	4,273.9	12.97
1995	NA	NA	NA	123.2[1]	20.9[1]	37.7[1]	4,618.7[1]	14.65[1]
1996	NA	NA	NA	125.6[1]	21.2[1]	38.3[1]	4,827.0[1]	15.14[1]
1997	NA	NA	NA	127.9[1]	21.6[1]	39.0[1]	5,035.3[1]	15.62[1]
1998	NA	NA	NA	130.3[1]	21.9[1]	39.7[1]	5,243.6[1]	16.11[1]

Source: 1997 *Manufacturing STATROM* [machine-readable data files]. MStat97. Editorial Code and Data, Inc., Detroit, Michigan, 1997. Primary source: 1982, 1987, 1992 *Economic Census; Annual Survey of Manufactures,* 1983-1986, 1988-1991, 1993-1994. Establishment counts for non-Census years are from *County Business Patterns;* establishment values for 1983-1984 are extrapolations. Industries reclassified in 1987 will not have data for prior years. *Notes:* NA = Not available. 1. Items are projected by the editors.

★ 294 ★

Industry Statistics

General Indices of Change in the Periodicals Industry, 1982-1998

Year	Com-panies	Establishments		Employment			Compensation	
		Total	With 20 or more employees	Total (000)	Production workers (000)	Hours (mil.)	Payroll ($ mil.)	Wages ($ hr.)
1982	72	71	70	81	87	82	49	57
1983	NA	NA	NA	80	86	82	51	60
1984	NA	NA	NA	80	81	74	55	65
1985	NA	NA	NA	82	81	73	63	72
1986	NA	NA	NA	84	71	64	67	87
1987	86	86	88	95	91	83	73	83
1988	NA	NA	NA	96	95	87	77	89
1989	NA	87	88	100	103	84	84	93
1990	NA	NA	NA	99	107	91	90	98
1991	NA	NA	NA	95	103	91	90	99
1992	100	100	100	100	100	100	100	100
1993	NA	NA	NA	101	98	96	106	93
1994	NA	NA	NA	100	91	88	105	97
1995	NA	NA	NA	106[1]	104[1]	97[1]	113[1]	109[1]
1996	NA	NA	NA	108[1]	106[1]	98[1]	118[1]	113[1]
1997	NA	NA	NA	110[1]	107[1]	100[1]	124[1]	117[1]
1998	NA	NA	NA	112[1]	109[1]	102[1]	129[1]	120[1]

Source: 1997 *Manufacturing STATROM* [machine-readable data files]. MStat97. Editorial Code and Data, Inc., Detroit, Michigan, 1997. Primary source: 1982, 1987, 1992 *Economic Census*; *Annual Survey of Manufactures*, 1983-1986, 1988-1991, 1993-1994. Establishment counts for non-Census years are from *County Business Patterns*; establishment values for 1983-1984 are extrapolations. Industries reclassified in 1987 will not have data for prior years. Values reflect change from the base year, 1992. Values above 100 mean greater than 1992, values below 100 mean less than 1992, and a value of 100 in the 1982-1991 or 1993-1998 period means same as 1992. *Notes:* NA = Not available. 1. Items are projected by the editors.

★ 295 ★

Industry Statistics

General Production Statistics on the Periodicals Industry, 1982-1998

Year	Production ($ million)			
	Cost of materials	Value added by manufacture	Value of shipments[1]	Capital investment
1982	4,568.1	6,910.9	11,478.0	194.8
1983	4,603.6	7,868.9	12,436.7	251.7
1984	5,117.6	8,943.9	14,052.6	267.4
1985	5,579.8	9,678.1	15,246.4	339.7
1986	5,558.1	10,196.0	15,719.4	274.1
1987	5,872.7	11,452.1	17,329.2	246.4
1988	6,201.9	12,439.6	18,611.8	246.1
1989	6,581.0	13,248.4	19,787.2	272.2
1990	6,579.6	13,847.7	20,396.7	274.8
1991	6,459.0	13,794.4	20,345.1	223.0
1992	6,200.9	15,833.0	22,033.9	234.4
1993	6,391.2	16,271.9	22,652.5	289.5
1994	5,903.1	15,821.4	21,723.3	306.6
1995	6,638.9[2]	17,793.6[2]	24,431.2[2]	278.7[2]
1996	6,895.1[2]	18,480.2[2]	25,373.9[2]	280.9[2]
1997	7,151.3[2]	19,166.8[2]	26,316.7[2]	283.2[2]
1998	7,407.5[2]	19,853.5[2]	27,259.5[2]	285.4[2]

Source: 1997 *Manufacturing STATROM* [machine-readable data files]. MStat97. Editorial Code and Data, Inc., Detroit, Michigan, 1997. Primary source: 1982, 1987, 1992 *Economic Census*; *Annual Survey of Manufactures*, 1983-1986, 1988-1991, 1993-1994. Establishment counts for non-Census years are from *County Business Patterns*; establishment values for 1983-1984 are extrapolations. Industries reclassified in 1987 will not have data for prior years. *Notes:* 1. "Industry Shipments" and "Product Shipments" are rarely the same value. 2. Items are projected by the editors.

★ 296 ★

Industry Statistics

Materials Consumed by the Periodicals Industry

Material	Delivered cost ($ mil.)
Materials, ingredients, containers, and supplies	2,417.1
Newsprint	66.3
Coated paper	986.1
Uncoated paper	185.2
Printing inks (complete formulations)	220.8
All other materials and components, parts, containers, and supplies	165.9
Materials, ingredients, containers, and supplies, nsk	792.8

Source: 1997 *Manufacturing STATROM* [machine-readable data files]. MStat97. Editorial Code and Data, Inc., Detroit, Michigan, 1997. Primary source: 1992 *Economic Census.* Explanation of symbols used: nsk: Not specified by kind.

★ 297 ★

Industry Statistics

Product Share Details in the Periodicals Industry

Product code	Shipments ($ mil.)	% of total	Product name
2721	20,890.3	100.00	PERIODICAL PUBLISHING
27211	199.9	0.96	Farm periodicals (all receipts)
2721112	54.6	27.31	Farm periodicals (subscriptions, sales)
2721114	145.3	72.69	Farm periodicals (advertising)
27213	2,527.3	12.10	Specialized business, professional periodicals (subscriptions and sales)
2721324	31.0	1.23	Manufacturing
2721325	59.6	2.36	Wholesale and retail trade
2721327	247.4	9.79	Medical and health care business
2721328	66.8	2.64	Electronics/data management business publications
2721330	416.4	16.48	Service (excluding data management)
2721332	894.2	35.38	Other business publications, n.e.c.
2721334	28.3	1.12	Manufacturing (controlled circulation)
2721335	6.1	0.24	Wholesale and retail trade (controlled circulation)
2721337	40.6	1.61	Medical and health care (controlled circulation)
2721338	5.5	0.22	Electronics/data management (controlled circulation)
2721340	7.1	0.28	Service (controlled circulation)

[Continued]

★ 297 ★

Product Share Details in the Periodicals Industry
[Continued]

Product code	Shipments ($ mil.)	% of total	Product name
2721342	54.0	2.14	Other business publications, n.e.c. (controlled circulation)
2721344	183.6	7.26	Scholarly journals
2721346	336.5	13.31	Other professional journals
2721300	150.3	5.95	Specialized business and professional periodicals, n.s.k.
27214	3,717.4	17.79	Specialized business and professional periodicals (advertising)
2721424	16.9	0.45	Manufacturing
2721425	159.5	4.29	Wholesale and retail trade
2721427	104.7	2.82	Medical and health care
2721428	187.8	5.05	Electronics/data management
2721430	64.8	1.74	Service
2721432	772.0	20.77	Other business publications, n.e.c.
2721434	126.0	3.39	Manufacturing (controlled circulation)
2721435	195.5	5.26	Wholesale and retail trade (controlled circulation)
2721437	268.0	7.21	Medical and health care (controlled circulation)
2721438	72.7	1.96	Electronics/data management (controlled circulation)
2721440	119.6	3.22	Service (controlled circulation)
2721442	864.5	23.26	Other business publications, n.e.c. (controlled circulation)
2721444	57.3	1.54	Scholarly journals (advertising receipts)
2721446	64.6	1.74	Other professional journals (advertising receipts)
2721400	643.3	17.31	Specialized business and professional periodicals, n.s.k.
2721A	3,621.0	17.33	General and consumer periodicals (receipts from subscriptions)
2721A20	620.5	17.14	Women's, home, and fashion periodicals
2721A50	414.6	11.45	General news periodicals
2721A60	166.2	4.59	Business news periodicals
2721A70	73.1	2.02	Regional, metropolitan, and city magazines
2721A80	1,239.3	34.23	Special interest (hobby, sports, etc.) periodicals
2721A90	977.7	27.00	General interest periodicals
2721A00	129.5	3.58	General and consumer periodicals, n.s.k.
2721B	1,860.5	8.91	General and consumer periodicals (receipts from single copy sales)
2721B10	213.3	11.46	Comics
2721B20	384.8	20.68	Women's, home, and fashion periodicals
2721B50	122.5	6.58	General news periodicals
2721B60	18.6	1.00	Business news periodicals
2721B70	6.8	0.37	Regional, metropolitan, and city magazines
2721B80	688.5	37.01	Special interest (hobby, sports, etc.) periodicals
2721B90	316.4	17.01	General interest periodicals

[Continued]

★ 297 ★

Product Share Details in the Periodicals Industry
[Continued]

Product code	Shipments ($ mil.)	% of total	Product name
2721B00	109.6	5.89	General and consumer periodicals, n.s.k.
2721C	5,133.5	24.57	General and consumer periodicals (advertising)
2721C10	7.6	0.15	Comics (advertising)
2721C20	1,472.4	28.68	Women's, home, and fashion periodicals, etc. (advertising)
2721C50	626.6	12.21	General news periodicals (advertising)
2721C60	408.2	7.95	Business news periodicals (advertising)
2721C70	126.2	2.46	Regional, metropolitan, and city magazines (advertising)
2721C80	1,511.3	29.44	Special interest (hobby, sports, etc.) periodicals (advertising)
2721C90	732.2	14.26	General interest periodicals (advertising)
2721C00	249.1	4.85	General and consumer periodicals (advertising), n.s.k.
2721D	689.1	3.30	Other periodicals, catalogs, or directories, n.e.c.
2721D10	242.2	35.15	Religious periodicals (subscriptions and sales)
2721D15	51.1	7.42	Religious periodicals (advertising)
2721D24	1.6	0.23	Magazine, comic supplements, Sunday papers (sales and advertising)
2721D31	169.8	24.64	Other periodicals, n.e.c. (subscriptions)
2721D33	37.0	5.37	Other periodicals, n.e.c. (single copy sales)
2721D35	108.3	15.72	Other periodicals, n.e.c. (advertising)
2721D00	79.0	11.46	Other periodicals, except shopping news, catalogs, or directories, n.e.c., n.s.k.
27210	3,141.8	15.04	Periodical publishing, n.s.k.

Source: 1997 *Manufacturing STATROM* [machine-readable data files]. MStat97. Editorial Code and Data, Inc., Detroit, Michigan, 1997. Primary source: 1992 *Economic Census.* The values shown are percent of total shipments in an industry. Values of indented subcategories are summed in the main headings. The abbreviation n.s.k. stands for 'not specified by kind' and n.e.c. for 'not elsewhere classified'.

★ 298 ★

Industry Statistics

Production: Indices of Change in the Periodicals Industry, 1982 -1998

Year	Production ($ million)			
	Cost of materials	Value added by manufacture	Value of shipments[1]	Capital investment
1982	74	44	52	83
1983	74	50	56	107
1984	83	56	64	114
1985	90	61	69	145

[Continued]

★ 298 ★

Production: Indices of Change in the Periodicals Industry, 1982 -1998
[Continued]

Year	Production ($ million)			
	Cost of materials	Value added by manufacture	Value of shipments[1]	Capital investment
1986	90	64	71	117
1987	95	72	79	105
1988	100	79	84	105
1989	106	84	90	116
1990	106	87	93	117
1991	104	87	92	95
1992	100	100	100	100
1993	103	103	103	124
1994	95	100	99	131
1995	107[2]	112[2]	111[2]	119[2]
1996	111[2]	117[2]	115[2]	120[2]
1997	115[2]	121[2]	119[2]	121[2]
1998	119[2]	125[2]	124[2]	122[2]

Source: 1997 *Manufacturing STATROM* [machine-readable data files]. MStat97. Editorial Code and Data, Inc., Detroit, Michigan, 1997. Primary source: 1982, 1987, 1992 *Economic Census; Annual Survey of Manufactures,* 1983-1986, 1988-1991, 1993-1994. Establishment counts for non-Census years are from *County Business Patterns;* establishment values for 1983-1984 are extrapolations. Industries reclassified in 1987 will not have data for prior years. Values reflect change from the base year, 1992. Values above 100 mean greater than 1992, values below 100 mean less than 1992, and a value of 100 in the 1982-1991 or 1993-1998 period means same as 1992. *Notes:* 1. "Industry Shipments" and "Product Shipments" are rarely the same value. 2. Items are projected by the editors.

★ 299 ★

Industry Statistics

Occupations Employed by the Periodicals Industries

Occupation	% of total 1994	Change to 2005
Writers & editors, including technical writers	15.0	28.7
Sales & related workers, nec	10.8	28.7
Secretaries, ex legal & medical	5.1	17.2
General managers & top executives	5.0	22.1
Artists & commercial artists	3.7	60.4
Marketing, advertising, & PR managers	3.3	28.7
General office clerks	3.3	9.7

[Continued]

★ 299 ★

Occupations Employed by the Periodicals Industries
[Continued]

Occupation	% of total 1994	Change to 2005
Bookkeeping, accounting, & auditing clerks	2.9	-3.5
Clerical supervisors & managers	2.4	31.6
Proofreaders & copy markers	2.3	-16.3
Managers & administrators, nec	2.2	28.6
Machine feeders & offbearers	1.8	15.8
Reporters & correspondents	1.7	3.0
Marketing & sales worker supervisors	1.7	28.7
Typists & word processors	1.6	-35.7
Management support workers, nec	1.5	28.6
Professional workers nec	1.4	54.4
Order clerks, materials, merchandise, & service	1.3	26.0
Advertising clerks	1.3	41.6
Computer programmers	1.2	4.2
Data entry keyers, ex composing	1.2	-5.0
Clerical support workers, nec	1.2	2.9
Production, planning, & expediting clerks	1.1	28.6
Offset lithographic press operators	1.1	3.0
Adjustment clerks	1.1	54.4
Mail clerks, ex machine operators, postal service	1.1	-7.3

Source: 1997 *Manufacturing STATROM* [machine-readable data files]. MStat97. Editorial Code and Data, Inc., Detroit, Michigan, 1997. Primary source: *Industry-Occupation Matrix*, Bureau of Labor Statistics. These data relate to one or more 3-digit SIC industry groups rather than to a single 4-digit SIC. The change reported for each occupation to the year 2005 is a percent of growth or decline as estimated by the Bureau of Labor Statistics. The abbreviation nec stands for 'not elsewhere classified.'

★ 300 ★

Industry Statistics

Selected Ratios for the Periodicals Industry

For 1992	Average of all manufacturing	Periodicals industry	Index
Employees per establishment	46	25	54
Payroll per establishment	1,332,320	867,099	65
Payroll per employee	29,181	35,065	120
Production workers per establishment	31	4	14
Wages per establishment	734,496	111,215	15

[Continued]

★ 300 ★

Selected Ratios for the Periodicals Industry

[Continued]

For 1992	Average of all manufacturing	Periodicals industry	Index
Wages per production worker	23,390	26,000	111
Hours per production worker	2,025	1,940	96
Wages per hour	11.55	13.40	116
Value added per establishment	3,842,210	3,369,440	88
Value added per employee	84,153	136,256	162
Value added per production worker	122,353	787,711	644
Cost per establishment	4,239,462	1,319,621	31
Cost per employee	92,853	53,364	57
Cost per production worker	135,003	308,502	229
Shipments per establishment	8,100,800	4,689,062	58
Shipments per employee	177,425	189,620	107
Shipments per production worker	257,966	1,096,214	425
Investment per establishment	278,244	49,883	18
Investment per employee	6,094	2,017	33
Investment per production worker	8,861	11,662	132

Source: 1997 Manufacturing STATROM [machine-readable data files]. MStat97. Editorial Code and Data, Inc., Detroit, Michigan, 1997. Primary source: 1982, 1987, 1992 *Economic Census*; *Annual Survey of Manufactures*, 1983-1986, 1988-1991, 1993-1994. Establishment counts for non-Census years are from *County Business Patterns*; establishment values for 1983-1984 are extrapolations. Industries reclassified in 1987 will not have data for prior years. Values reflect change from the base year, 1992. Values above 100 mean greater than 1992, values below 100 mean less than 1992, and a value of 100 in the 1982-1991 or 1993-1998 period means same as 1992. The 'Average of All Manufacturing' column represents the average of all manufacturing industries reported for the most recent complete year available. The Index shows the relationship between the Average and the Analyzed Industry. For example, 100 means that they are equal; 500 that the Analyzed Industry is five times the average; 50 means that the Analyzed Industry is half the national average.

★ 301 ★

Industry Statistics

State Level Data for the Periodicals Industry

The states are presented in ranked order by level of shipments.

State	Establish-ments	Shipments total ($ mil.)	% of U.S.	Per establish-ment	Employ-ment total number	% of U.S.	Per establish-ment	Wages ($/hour)	Cost as % of shipments	Investment per employee ($)
New York	622	9,618.1	43.7	15.5	34,000	29.3	55	21.74	28.1	2,876
California	646	1,923.9	8.7	3.0	11,100	9.6	17	10.72	26.6	1,559
Illinois	249	1,451.1	6.6	5.8	11,900	10.2	48	13.33	28.6	1,370
Pennsylvania	159	1,192.4	5.4	7.5	4,700	4.0	30	12.56	35.9	1,340
District of Columbia	84	956.0	4.3	11.4	4,600	4.0	55	14.75	25.8	3,391
New Jersey	195	683.4	3.1	3.5	4,000	3.4	21	11.76	26.7	2,300
Massachusetts	183	634.4	2.9	3.5	3,600	3.1	20	12.10	28.2	1,750
Ohio	120	476.2	2.2	4.0	3,500	3.0	29	10.64	23.7	1,771

[Continued]

★ 301 ★

State Level Data for the Periodicals Industry
[Continued]

State	Establish-ments	Shipments total ($ mil.)	% of U.S.	Per establish-ment	Employ-ment total number	% of U.S.	Per establish-ment	Wages ($/hour)	Cost as % of shipments	Investment per employee ($)
Connecticut	108	463.5	2.1	4.3	2,600	2.2	24	12.91	27.4	1,769
Florida	281	368.7	1.7	1.3	3,400	2.9	12	9.77	31.8	1,235
Georgia	108	319.5	1.5	3.0	2,400	2.1	22	12.31	28.6	1,708
Texas	204	301.2	1.4	1.5	3,100	2.7	15	8.65	28.5	NA
Wisconsin	97	296.3	1.3	3.1	2,000	1.7	21	8.70	25.4	3,150
Minnesota	109	294.2	1.3	2.7	1,600	1.4	15	10.60	20.8	NA
Maryland	103	222.1	1.0	2.2	1,600	1.4	16	14.57	26.5	2,750
Alabama	42	212.0	1.0	5.0	1,000	0.9	24	8.33	23.4	1,200
Tennessee	68	196.4	0.9	2.9	2,400	2.1	35	11.12	14.9	NA
Virginia	133	194.7	0.9	1.5	1,800	1.5	14	10.14	23.7	1,000
Michigan	106	181.6	0.8	1.7	1,900	1.6	18	11.71	26.0	1,263
Missouri	77	176.6	0.8	2.3	2,400	2.1	31	10.25	26.2	1,167
Colorado	99	140.9	0.6	1.4	1,100	0.9	11	12.50	26.3	1,818
North Carolina	77	133.1	0.6	1.7	1,100	0.9	14	11.00	33.6	1,727
New Hampshire	33	131.9	0.6	4.0	600	0.5	18	12.00	21.1	1,000
Indiana	65	131.3	0.6	2.0	1,100	0.9	17	10.00	31.0	1,000
Kansas	35	111.2	0.5	3.2	500	0.4	14	6.00	26.5	3,600
Oklahoma	33	93.8	0.4	2.8	400	0.3	12	7.00	17.9	NA
Washington	102	76.4	0.3	0.7	900	0.8	9	15.50	27.4	1,222
Oregon	46	69.0	0.3	1.5	500	0.4	11	11.67	31.3	1,800
Arizona	72	59.4	0.3	0.8	600	0.5	8	7.33	34.5	NA
Nebraska	26	49.4	0.2	1.9	400	0.3	15	12.00	29.8	NA
Vermont	20	44.3	0.2	2.2	300	0.3	15	13.00	32.1	1,000
Utah	23	36.8	0.2	1.6	300	0.3	13	10.00	28.5	2,333
Idaho	21	29.8	0.1	1.4	300	0.3	14	13.50	27.5	1,000
Hawaii	28	28.1	0.1	1.0	200	0.2	7	9.00	28.1	NA
Maine	23	24.3	0.1	1.1	200	0.2	9	6.00	32.5	1,500
Rhode Island	13	21.3	0.1	1.6	200	0.2	15	8.00	20.7	NA
Louisiana	36	15.3	0.1	0.4	200	0.2	6	6.00	32.7	500
South Carolina	35	14.6	0.1	0.4	200	0.2	6	5.00	34.2	NA
Nevada	18	13.5	0.1	0.8	100	0.1	6	12.00	25.2	NA
New Mexico	28	11.9	0.1	0.4	100[1]	0.1	4	NA	33.6	1,000
Kentucky	45	(D)	NA	NA	375[1]	0.3	8	NA	NA	1,867
Iowa	40	(D)	NA	NA	1,750[1]	1.5	44	NA	NA	NA
Arkansas	18	(D)	NA	NA	175[1]	0.2	10	NA	NA	NA

Source: 1997 *Manufacturing STATROM* [machine-readable data files]. MStat97. Editorial Code and Data, Inc., Detroit, Michigan, 1997. Primary source: 1992 *Economic Census.* The states are in descending order of shipments or establishments (if shipment data are missing for the majority). The symbol (D) appears when data are withheld to prevent disclosure of competitive information. States marked with (D) are sorted by number of establishments. *Notes:* NA = Not available. 1. Indicates the midpoint of a range.

★ 302 ★

Industry Statistics

Periodical Industry: States with Most Activity

Data show the periodical industry by sector.

State	Shipments as % of U.S.	Employment as % of U.S.	Payroll as % of U.S.	Cost of Materials as % of U.S.	Investment as % of U.S.
New York	43.70	29.30	19.90	43.70	43.70
California	8.90	9.60	11.40	8.70	8.90
Illinois	6.50	10.20	10.90	6.60	6.50
Pennsylvania	4.80	4.00	2.50	5.40	4.80
D.C.	4.60	4.00	2.00	4.30	4.60
New Jersey	3.10	3.40	4.50	3.10	3.10
Massachusetts	2.90	3.10	2.50	2.90	2.90
Ohio	2.30	3.00	3.50	2.20	2.30
Connecticut	2.10	2.20	2.50	2.10	2.10
Florida	1.60	2.90	3.00	1.70	1.60
Minnesota	1.50	1.40	1.50	1.30	1.50
Georgia	1.40	2.10	4.50	1.50	1.40
Texas	1.40	2.70	4.00	1.40	1.40
Wisconsin	1.40	1.70	2.50	1.30	1.40
Tennessee	1.10	2.10	2.50	0.90	1.10
Alabama	1.00	0.90	1.00	1.00	1.00
Maryland	1.00	1.40	1.50	1.00	1.00
Virginia	0.90	1.50	2.00	0.90	0.90
Michigan	0.80	1.60	2.00	0.80	0.80
Missouri	0.80	2.10	3.00	0.80	0.80

Source: 1997 *Manufacturing STATROM* [machine-readable data files]. MStat97. Editorial Code and Data, Inc., Detroit, Michigan, 1997. Primary source: *Economic Census for 1992* and earlier years. The *Economic Census* is conducted by the Bureau of the Census, U.S. Department of Commerce, Washington, DC 20233.

Sales and Distribution

★ 303 ★

Cross-Gender Readership

Editors acknowledge that gender-specific magazines do have readers of the opposite sex. The most recent MRI audit indicates that of *Playboy's* total audience of 10 million, 1.4 million are women. Of *Cosmopolitan's* total audience of 15 million, 2.7 million are men. Many subscribe under their own name.

Source: Garigliano, Jeff. *"Notorious* Lives Up to its Name." *Folio,* 1 October 1997, p. 20.

★ 304 ★

Sales and Distribution

Magazine Sales by Outlet, 1995

| Supermarkets - 41.24 |
| Miscellaneous - 16.59 |
| Discount stores - 11.92 |
| Drugstores - 9.60 |
| Convenience stores - 9.39 |
| Newsstands - 4.11 |
| Bookstores - 4.06 |
| Terminals - 3.10 |

Chart shows data from column 1.

The magazine distribution market has recently experienced a string of consolidations. While supermarkets, who lead the market, have experienced greater efficiency, there are still problems. Wholesalers must now make deliveries in a broader area. If deliveries are late, weeklies can lose 10% to 20% of sales every day they are late.

Outlet	Share (%)	Volume ($ mil.)	% change over 1994
Supermarkets	41.24	1,600	3.35
Miscellaneous	16.59	674	83.5
Discount stores	11.92	484	15.84
Drugstores	9.60	390	26.34
Convenience stores	9.39	381	-36.20
Newsstands	4.11	167	-7.00
Bookstores	4.06	164	-26.00
Terminals	3.10	126	-34.11

Source: Liebeskind, Ken. "Consolidation Hits a Few Bumps." *Non-foods Merchandising* (September 1996), p. 27. Primary source: Council for Periodical Distributors of the Americas.

★ 305 ★

Sales and Distribution

Magazine Sales by Segment

Tabloids - 24.8

Family & Home - 22.5

TV & Movie - 21.9

Lifestyles - 16.0

Women's Fashion - 5.6

Social/Literary - 3.0

Health/Fitness - 1.8

Special Interest - 1.7

Other - 1.6

News - 1.1

Magazine	Percentage
Tabloids	24.8
Family & Home	22.5
TV & Movie	21.9
Lifestyles	16.0
Women's Fashion	5.6
Social/Literary	3.0
Health/Fitness	1.8
Special Interest	1.7
News	1.1
Other	1.6

Source: "Magazine Sales by Segment." *Supermarket Business* (February 1997), p. 74. Primary source: Audit Bureau of Circulation.

★ 306 ★

Sales and Distribution

Magazines and Niche Markets

From the source: "During the 1950's, when Americans were seemingly of a common mind, general-interest magazines like Life, Look and The Saturday Evening Post thrived. But over the years, readers have found niches and in them magazines. Here is a look at how magazines have narrowed the focus of ones that preceded them. Shown with the title is the year each publication was founded and how much paid circulation the publisher promised the advertisers in December 1996, also known as rate base circulation."

Title	Year	Circulation
Saturday Evening Post	1728	450,000
McCall's	1876	4.2 mil.
Field & Stream	1895	1.75 mil.
Time	1923	4.1 mil.
Fortune	1930	740,000
Sports Illustrated	1954	3.3 mil.
People	1974	3.2 mil.
Outside	1977	500,000
Self	1979	1.1 mil.
Elle	1985	875,000
Child	1986	775,000
Entertainment Weekly	1990	1.3 mil.
Whitetail Hunting Strategies	1991	67,000
Allure	1991	700,000
Smart Money	1992	600,000
Fit Pregnancy	1993	200,000
Family Life	1993	400,000
Marie Claire	1994	525,000
In Style	1994	700,000
American Cheerleader	1995	125,000
Modern Dad	1995	100,000
Snowboard Life	1996	85,000
Tactical Bowhunting	1996	52,000

Source: "From Similar Roots, but Bearing New Fruit." *New York Times,* 2 January 1997, p. C16. Primary source: Audit Bureau of Circulation.

★ 307 ★

Sales and Distribution

Where Magazines Are Sold

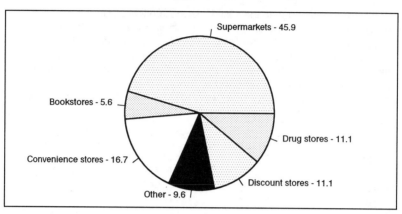

Supermarkets - 45.9

Bookstores - 5.6

Drug stores - 11.1

Convenience stores - 16.7

Discount stores - 11.1

Other - 9.6

[In percent]

Location	Share (%)
Supermarkets	45.9
Convenience stores	16.7
Discount stores	11.1
Drug stores	11.1
Bookstores	5.6
Other	9.6

Source: "Statwrap." *Non-Foods Merchandising* (January 1995), p. 8. Primary source: Magazine and Paperback Marketing Institute.

Publishers

★ 308 ★

Leading Magazine Publishers, 1996

Companies are ranked by revenues in millions of dollars.

Company	1996 revenues ($ mil.)	% change vs. 1995	1996 ad pages	% change vs. 1995
Time Inc.	2,397.4	18.4	24,955	9.0
Conde Nast	860.4	14.7	19,957	6.5
Hearst Magazines	833.7	-7.5	12,343	-7.5
Hachette Filipacchi	812.7	10.6	19,371	-0.3

[Continued]

★ 308 ★
Leading Magazine Publishers, 1996
[Continued]

Company	1996 revenues ($ mil.)	% change vs. 1995	1996 ad pages	% change vs. 1995
Meredith Corp.	636.3	13.2	7,117	5.6
Parade Publications	494.0	-4.2	650	-12.2
Ziff-Davis	465.1	-1.6	11,513	-8.1
Gruner & Jahr	459.7	8.5	5,933	2.2
News America	403.0	-1.0	3,039	-5.9
Newsweek Inc.	383.8	15.6	2,533	10.2
New York Times Co.	333.5	12.9	8,590	-1.5
K-III Communications	305.4	9.3	9,770	1.7
McGraw-Hill	298.8	11.6	3,885	1.8
Times Mirror	287.7	-4.3	10,232	-12.3
Reader's Digest	254.0	8.4	2,577	1.5
U.S. News/The Atlantic	245.0	1.9	2,735	-6.8
Forbes Inc.	231.1	9.0	5,053	2.1
Gannett	228.6	-0.4	602	-13.4
Wenner Media	161.0	14.0	3,357	-1.2
Rodale Press	145.7	22.5	3,850	5.9
Petersen Publishing	119.1	6.0	4,058	-4.0
Pace Communications	116.9	23.9	3,114	3.3
CMP	114.2	8.1	5,712	-8.2
American Express	111.8	22.4	2,556	8.8
New Yorker Magazine	84.7	6.9	2,038	-4.4
Goldhirsh Group	77.7	7.3	1,380	-0.6
National Geographic	70.7	13.8	647	0.1
Weider Publications	68.9	14.3	2,896	5.9
Johnson Publishing	64.6	-0.0	1,859	-4.5
Fairchild Publications	63.3	42.8	1,586	14.0
AARP	59.5	-6.0	239	-7.4
Walt Disney	58.3	22.5	1,396	-1.6
American Airlines Mag. Pub.	50.2	15.9	3,094	2.3
Essence Communications	48.7	11.5	1,811	-3.5
Playboy Enterprises	47.9	1.5	590	-5.8

Source: "Top Magazine Publishing Companies." *Adweek*, 3 March 1997, p. 26. Primary source: Competitive Media Reporting.

★ 309 ★

Publishers

Self-Publishing of Magazines

The firms and companies below are some of those that have recently been active in magazine acquisitions and start-ups.

Publisher	Publisher
Advanstar Holdings, Inc. 575 Boylston Street Boston, MA 02116 617-267-6500 Robert Krakoff, Chairman/CEO	Lehman Brothers, Inc. 3 World Financial Center New York,NY 10285 212-526-3484 Chris Cosentino, Vice President
Boston Ventures Management Inc. 21 Custom House Street Boston, MA 02110 617-737-3700 John Hunt	M/C Partners 75 State Street, Suite 2500 Boston, MA 02109 617-345-7217 Christopher S. Gaffney, General Partner
Concord Ventures, Inc. P.O. Box 10 Concord, MA 01742 508-371-0995 H. Mason Fackert III Managing Director and CEO	Signet Bank Media Communications Group 7799 Leesburg Pike, Suite 500 Falls Church, VA 22043 703-714-5016 John Slabaugh, Vice President
Freedom Magazines, Inc. 17666 Fitch Irvine, CA 92614 714-553-9292 Sam Wolgemuth, President	State Street Bank and Trust Company 225 Franklin Street Boston, MA 02110 617-654-3616 David M. Gaffney, Senior Vice President, Specialized Lending
Hachette Filipacchi Magazines, Inc. 1633 Broadway New York, NY 10019 212-767-6000 David J. Pecker, President, CEO	VS&A Communications Partners LP 350 Park Avenue New York, NY 10022 212-935-4990 Jeffrey T. Stevenson, General Partner and President
Hearst Magazine Enterprises 959 8th Avenue New York, NY 10019 212-649-2282 John Mack Carter, President	

Source: Folio, 1 October 1996, p. 30.

★310★

Fastest-Growing Magazine Categories, 1996

Revenues are shown in billions of dollars.

Type	Revenue	Percent change
Home service & home	1.6	11.4
Newsweeklies	4.7	8.8
Business & finance	1.5	8.7
Women's	3.2	5.2
Sports	0.6	5.1
Men's	0.8	2.4

Source: "USA Snapshots." *USA TODAY,* 4 September 1997, p. B1. Primary source: *Advertising Age.*

★ 311 ★
Magazine Categories

Top Categories for New Magazines

Sports - 111
Epicurean - 58
Special interest - 57
Computers - 53
Sex - 51
Crafts, games, hobbies and models - 42
Home - 39
Media personalities - 33
Metropolitan/regional/state - 31
Comics and comic techniques - 31

There were a total of 933 new magazines launched in 1996, an 11 percent increase over 1995. Through the first few months of 1997, new magazine launchings are averages 100 a month. A new launch on average costs $4.57 and has 88 pages.

Category	Total
Sports	111
Epicurean	58
Special interest	57
Computers	53
Sex	51
Crafts, games, hobbies and models	42
Home	39
Media personalities	33
Metropolitan/regional/state	31
Comics and comic techniques	31

Source: "New Magazine Launches." *American Demographics* (August 1997), p. 33. Primary source: Samir Husni, University of Mississippi.

★ 312 ★

Magazine Categories

Top Categories for New Magazines - Percent

Data from the previous table are shown, here, expressed as percent share of all new categories—the manner in which this source chose to display the original data.

[In percent]

Segment	Share
Sports	22.0
Epicurean	11.5
Special interest	11.5
Computers	10.5
Sex	10.1
Crafts/games	8.3
Home	7.8
Media	6.5
Metro/regional	6.2
Comics	5.7

Source: "A Look at What's New." *New York Times,* 20 October 1997, p. 12. Primary source: Samir Husni.

Academic Publishing

★ 313 ★

World Scientific Journals: Types of Articles by Field, 1993

A total of 4,681 natural science and engineering journals are covered by the Institute of Scientific Information's (ISI) Science Citation Index (SCI). SCI covers major referred scientific and technical journals from across the world. The table shows the types of articles by field.

Field	Share
Clinical medicine	31.0
Biomedical	17.0
Physics	16.0
Chemistry	14.0
Biology	8.0
Engineering/technology	7.0
Earth/space	5.0
Mathematics	2.0

Source: From the Internet, *Science and Engineering Indicators,* at http://www.nsf.gov/, 19 September 1996.

★ 314 ★

Academic Publishing

World Scientific Journals: Types of Articles by Region, 1993

A total of 4,681 natural science and engineering journals are covered by the Institute of Scientific Information's (ISI) Science Citation Index (SCI). SCI covers major referred scientific and technical journals from across the world. It classifies journals, and the articles appearing in them, into 99 subfields under 8 broad fields: biological sciences, biomedical sciences, clinical medicine, chemistry, physics, earth and space sciences, mathematics and engineering technologies. Distribution is shown in percent.

Country	Share
North America	38.0
Western Europe	27.0
East/Southeast Asia	12.0
Former Soviet Union	6.0
Northern Europe	4.0
Pacific Ocean states	3.0
Southern Europe	3.0
Former Soviet Block	2.0
South, Central America	2.0
Other Asian nations	2.0
Africa	1.0
Middle East	1.0

Source: From the Internet, *Science and Engineering Indicators,* at http://www.nsf.gov/, 19 September 1996.

Advertising

★ 315 ★

Ad Spending in Minority Publications

The table shows the increase in ad revenues for minority publications. Figures are in millions of dollars. Percent increase is from 1995-96.

Segment	($ mil.)	% Increase
Gay/lesbian press	73.7	19.6
Hispanic press	186.5	11.0
African American press	860.0	3.0

Source: Wilke, Michael. "Gay Press Sets Pace with 19.6% Ad Increase." *Advertising Age,* 9 September 1996, p. S4. Primary source: *Hispanic Business, Gay Press Report, Target Market News.*

★ 316 ★

Advertising

Magazine Ad Page Leaders, 1996

Data are for the first six months of the year.

Magazine	Pages	% change	Dollars	% change
PC Magazine	2,924.36	-5.5	149,039,539	2.6
Forbes	1,770.74	-3.6	89,430,937	2.5
People	1,745.66	15.4	245,484,790	26.3
Business Week	1,711.95	-3.2	132,195,575	7.9
Bride's	1,651.28	3.8	40,928,775	5.4
TV Guide	1,532.04	-6.3	203,115,250	-5.2
Modern Bride	1,482.41	-1.3	33,910,699	3.5
Economist	1,451.63	-2.0	21,894,922	5.9
Fortune	1,429.86	7.6	85,475,229	11.9
Windows Magazine	1,344.43	-16.3	31,317,246	12.0
Sports Illustrated	1,330.36	8.8	241,684,624	21.1
PC Computing	1,193.30	-0.7	43,963,736	8.9
New York Magazine	1,175.57	2.0	23,332,012	3.6
Newsweek	1,170.68	12.2	172,509,010	15.7
Time	1,088.58	1.0	196,514,810	4.7
Vogue	1,071.31	-6.6	57,558,921	6.0
American Way	1,005.82	-2.8	17,628,630	14.3
Bridal Guide	994.94	-11.8	13,606,072	0.7
U.S. News & World Report	953.07	0.9	101,695,448	5.3
Entrepeneur	948.83	2.7	18,756,371	18.8
The New Yorker	948.24	-4.4	38,107,719	4.1
Boating	919.42	-8.6	19,167,434	5.7
Better Homes & Gardens	908.06	14.3	169,087,832	30.0
Golf World	890.28	-14.2	12,557,670	-0.1
Popular Photography	833.36	8.6	22,397,062	10.7

Source: Kelly, Keith J. "1st Half Deliver Bad News for Most Consumer Titles." *Advertising Age,* 22 July 1996, p. 38. Primary source: Publishers Information Bureau. *Note:* Percent change compares the same period a year earlier.

★ 317 ★

Advertising

Top 50 Magazines in Ad Revenue, 1995

Data include Sunday newspaper magazines.

Magazine	1995 revenues ($ mil.)	$ change vs. 1994
Parade	515.6	15.2
People Weekly	437.7	7.9
Sports Illustrated	435.7	13.1
TV Guide	406.9	3.9
Time	404.5	8.7
Newsweek	331.9	19.0
PC Magazine	331.1	11.8
Better Homes & Gardens	274.4	24.2
Business Week	267.6	14.5
Good Housekeeping	238.7	9.2
USA Weekend	229.6	5.3
U.S. News & World Report	222.4	0.5
Forbes	205.7	8.7
Woman's Day	197.5	18.1
Reader's Digest	186.6	38.9
Fortune	179.5	9.7
Family Circle	164.0	-8.3
Cosmopolitan	159.7	7.9
Ladies' Home Journal	158.5	14.2
New York Times Magazine	119.3	7.8
Vogue	116.4	4.9
Redbook	112.5	12.1
Money	105.3	1.1
McCall's	104.1	-9.0
Glamour	103.7	5.5
PC Computing	101.3	25.5
Southern Living	100.4	4.1
Rolling Stone	97.8	17.5
Golf Digest	94.3	13.9
Entertainment Weekly	88.9	27.1
Country Living	86.1	27.0
Car and Driver	84.9	3.1
New Yorker	79.2	2.2
Parents	74.5	19.3
Inc.	72.4	23.8
Bride's	71.3	2.2

[Continued]

★ 317 ★

Top 50 Magazines in Ad Revenue, 1995
[Continued]

Magazine	1995 revenues ($ mil.)	$ change vs. 1994
Vanity Fair	70.9	32.4
Elle	70.7	17.6
Harper's Bazaar	65.6	19.9
Golf	65.3	18.5
Modern Maturity	63.3	18.9
Modern Bride	59.5	11.4
Road & Track	57.3	5.8
House Beautiful	55.4	15.1
Travel & Leisure	53.8	11.1
Self	53.4	5.9
National Geographic	52.3	9.6
Seventeen	51.6	7.8
Sunset	51.4	4.0
GQ	50.3	1.7

Source: "The Big Books." *Adweek-Midwest Edition,* 4 March 1996, p. 26. Primary source: Competitive Media Reporting.

★ 318 ★

Advertising

Top Advertising Categories, 1995

Categories	Spending ($ mil.)	% change vs. 1994	1994 rank
Automotive	1,380.3	10.1	2
Direct Response Companies	1,319.7	1.0	1
Toiletries & Cosmetics	898.2	2.2	3
Computers, Office Equipment	892.4	26.6	5
Business & Consumer Services	835.9	17.9	4
Foods & Food Products	725.7	30.0	7
Apparel, Footwear & Accessories	622.2	8.5	6
Drugs & Remedies	592.6	17.2	8
Travel, Hotels & Resorts	497.5	4.4	9
Cigarettes, Tobacco	327.9	7.0	10
Retail	325.6	14.7	11
Publishing & Media	297.2	11.7	12
Sporting Goods, Toys & Games	255.4	23.5	13
Jewelry, Opticals & Cameras	243.1	26.9	14

[Continued]

★ 318 ★

Top Advertising Categories, 1995
[Continued]

Categories	Spending ($ mil.)	% change vs. 1994	1994 rank
Liquor	199.9	20.3	17
Insurance & Real Estate	198.8	13.6	16
Household Equipment & Supplies	188.4	23.5	18
Household Furnishings	179.7	1.4	15
Electronic Entertainment Equipment	171.9	21.2	19
Building Materials & Fixtures	143.5	25.2	20
Top 20 total	10,295.0		

Source: "Top Advertising Categories." *Brandweek,* 4 March 1996, p. 27. Primary source: Competitive Media Reporting.

★ 319 ★

Advertising

Top Magazine Advertisers, 1995

Company	Spending ($ mil.)	Pages
General Motors Corp.	429.5	6,294
Phillip Morris Cos. Inc.	384.8	4,968
Procter & Gamble Co.	266.4	3,223
Ford Motor Co.	257.1	3,686
Chrysler Corp.	253.2	4,410
Nestle SA	138.7	2,061
Roll International Corp.	124.4	847
Toyota Motor Corp.	124.0	1,782
Sony Corp.	118.3	1,466
IBM Corp.	110.4	1,777
Time Warner Inc.	106.9	1,493
Johnson & Johnson	98.7	1,220
Bertelsmann AG	93.3	1,361
Unilever PLC	91.0	1,351
National Syndications Inc.	90.6	96
Bradford Exchange	89.6	672
Benckiser Joh A. GMBH	78.2	1,326
BAT Industries, PLC	72.4	840
Seagram Co., Ltd.	70.6	1,143
Microsoft Corp.	70.4	1,135

[Continued]

★ 319 ★

Top Magazine Advertisers, 1995
[Continued]

Company	Spending ($ mil.)	Pages
Top 20 total	3,068.5	41,151
All companies total	11,025.9	214,876

Source: "Top Magazine Spending by Company." *Brandweek,* 4 March 1996, p. 27. Primary source: Competitive Media Reporting.

★ 320 ★

Advertising

Top Magazine Advertisers, 1996

Advertisers are ranked by magazine advertising spending in millions of dollars.

[In dollars]

Company	1995 ($ mil.)	1996 ($ mil.)	% Change
General Motors Corp.	$410.6	$456.4	11.2
Phillip Morris Co.	373.8	343.1	-8.2
Procter & Gamble Co.	243.2	280.2	15.2
Ford Motor Co.	254.3	280.2	10.2
Chrysler Corp.	231.1	269.5	16.6
Time Warner	118.6	156.4	31.8
Johnson & Johnson	87.2	154.6	77.2
Toyota Motor Corp.	121.1	126.1	4.1
Unilever	109.5	125.2	14.4
Nestle	152.9	118.9	-22.2
IBM Corp.	109.2	84.1	-23.0
Joh. A Benckiser	78.0	81.5	4.4
Walt Disney Co.	76.7	78.4	2.2
Sony Corp.	73.4	77.2	5.2
B.A.T. Industries	70.4	75.6	7.4
Glaxo Wellcome	51.0	74.3	45.8
Estee Lauder Inc.	62.5	74.0	18.3
Microsoft Corp.	69.7	67.7	-2.9
Honda Motor Co.	62.6	65.9	5.2
Revlon Inc.	49.0	63.5	29.7
American Express Co.	30.2	62.1	105.7
Bristol-Meyers Squibb Co.	43.0	61.1	42.2
American Home Products Corp.	52.2	56.0	7.3

[Continued]

★ 320 ★

Top Magazine Advertisers, 1996

[Continued]

Company	1995 ($ mil.)	1996 ($ mil.)	% Change
RJR Nabisco	52.7	56.0	6.1
Nike Inc.	48.5	55.6	14.6

Source: "100 Leading National Advertisers." *Advertising Age,* 29 September 1997, p. S46. Primary source: Competitive Media Reporting.

★ 321 ★

Advertising

Women's Magazine Ad Page Sales

Data show number of ad pages.

Magazine	September 1995 ad pages	September 1996 ad pages	Percent change
Vogue	443	517	+16.7
Elle	302	336	+11.3
W	180	325	+80.1
Harper's Bazaar	310	315	+1.6
Vanity Fair	145	249	+71.7
Glamour	161	198	+23.0
Allure	145	182	+25.5
Mademoiselle	143	181	+26.6
Marie Claire	146	180	+23.3
Seventeen	164	180	+9.8

Source: "The September Results." *Women's Wear Daily,* 16 August 1996, p. 12. *Note:* These numbers were supplied by the publishers.

Business Magazines

★ 322 ★

Business-to-Business Magazine Advertising

Category	Revenue			Pages		
	1996 ($ mil.)	1995 ($ mil.)	Change (%)	1996 count	1995 count	Change (%)
Computers	2,307.40	1,992.10	15.8	97,888.7	91,821.5	6.6
Business	687.30	93.30	636.4	18,305.0	7,539.8	142.8
E. engineering	464.60	403.30	15.2	46,142.0	44,481.5	3.7
Travel, retail	248.80	222.40	11.9	20,874.2	20,864.4	0.1
Radio & television	145.60	134.70	8.1	20,045.9	19,239.6	4.2
Ad & marketing	140.20	132.20	6.1	16,231.7	15,151	7.1
Restaurant & food	124.30	119.80	3.8	11,314.1	12,009.8	-5.8
Automotive	117.10	101.70	15.2	12,357.4	11,418.6	8.2
Financial	108.70	92.00	18.1	8,063.0	5,612.7	43.7
Motion pictures	96.50	83.30	15.9	18,755.4	17,864.3	5.0

Source: "Press Box: Strong Gains in '96 over '95." *Business Marketing* (May 1997), p. 6. Primary source: Competitive Media Reporting's Rome Reports.

★ 323 ★

Business Magazines

Top Business and Trade Magazines by Ad Pages

Magazine	Advertising pages		
	1995	1996	% change
Electronic Engineering Times	5,520.82	6,254.03	13.3
New England Journal of Medicine	3,939.00	5,702.00	44.8
Travel Weekly	5,278.91	5,096.33	-3.5
Travel Agent	4,604.56	4,868.06	5.7
Medical Economics	3,085.00	4,843.00	57.0
Journal of the AMA	3,233.00	4,360.00	34.9
Electronic Design	3,493.25	3,977.10	13.9
EDN	3,308.76	3,971.14	20.0
Electronic Buyer's News	3,338.16	3,582.18	7.3
Chronicle of Higher Education	3,159.00	3,429.29	8.6
Publisher's Weekly	2,745.00	2,827.89	3.0
Design News	2,611.86	2,704.29	3.5
Multichannel News	2,482.23	2,697.35	8.7

[Continued]

★ 323 ★

Top Business and Trade Magazines by Ad Pages
[Continued]

Magazine	Advertising pages		
	1995	1996	% change
Science	2,586.95	2,659.89	2.8
Nature	2,558.32	2,611.57	2.1

Source: *Advertising Age,* 16 June 1997, p. S23.

★ 324 ★

Business Magazines

Top Business and Trade Magazines by Ad Revenue

Revenues are shown in millions of dollars.

Magazine	Advertising revenue		
	1995	1996	% change
Electronic Engineering Times	$76.4	$94.2	23.3
Travel Weekly	77.3	84.5	9.3
Travel Agent	64.5	79.9	23.8
EDN	36.0	52.3	45.4
Electronic Buyer's News	39.5	46.8	18.3
Electronic Design	39.8	40.7	2.2
Restaurants & Institutions	38.6	36.4	-5.5
Barron's	25.7	35.4	37.7
SN-Supermarket News	32.4	31.5	-2.8
Design News	27.7	31.4	13.6
Advertising Age	23.3	30.3	29.8
Tour & Travel News/TTG North America	30.9	27.9	-9.6
Machine Design	27.0	27.7	2.7
Nation's Restaurant News	28.6	27.6	-3.5
Institutional Investor	24.7	26.1	5.7

Source: *Advertising Age,* 16 June 1997, p. S23.

Computer Magazines

★ 325 ★

Top Computer and Internet Magazines by Ad Pages

Magazine	Advertising pages		
	1995	1996	% change
Computer Shopper	7,912.00	9,145.00	15.6
Computer Reseller News	7,220.57	8,186.25	13.4
PC Week	6,517.14	6,350.58	-2.6
PC Magazine	6,632.57	6,069.80	-8.5
InfoWorld	4,059.00	4,188.00	3.2
Computerworld	4,748.67	4,064.82	-14.4
Information Week	3,501.84	3,708.06	5.9
MacWeek	3,122.35	3,166.57	1.4
Communications Week	2,632.80	2,856.84	8.5
Windows Magazine	3,402.95	2,788.25	-18.1
PC World	2,802.05	2,691.85	-3.9
NetworkWorld	2,404.75	2,677.95	11.4
PC/Computing	2,993.80	2,665.15	-11.0
VARBusiness	2,144.37	2,554.00	19.1
Windows Sources	2,152.41	2,502.00	16.2

Source: Advertising Age, 16 June 1997, p. S23.

★ 326 ★

Computer Magazines

Top Computer and Internet Magazines by Ad Revenue

Revenues are shown in millions of dollars.

Magazine	Advertising revenue		
	1995	1996	% change
PC Magazine	$331.1	$318.1	-3.9
PC Week	196.4	239.5	21.9
Computer Shopper	145.9	173.1	18.6
Computer Reseller News	121.2	148.1	22.2
Computerworld	143.4	134.5	-6.2
InfoWorld	109.4	125.4	14.7
PC World	114.5	125.1	9.3
PC/Computing	101.3	98.7	-2.5
InformationWeek	82.6	97.0	17.5

[Continued]

★ 326 ★

Top Computer and Internet Magazines by Ad Revenue
[Continued]

Magazine	Advertising revenue		
	1995	1996	% change
NetworkWorld	57.7	73.6	27.7
Windows Magazine	67.1	70.7	5.3
CommunicationsWeek	59.9	68.5	14.3
Macworld	61.9	60.4	-2.3
Network Computing	47.3	57.0	20.5
MacWeek	45.1	47.4	5.0

Source: Advertising Age, 16 June 1997, p. S23.

★ 327 ★

Computer Magazines

Top Computer Magazines

PC Magazine - 1,044

PC World - 929

PC Computing - 882

Macworld - 568

Computer Shopper - 505

Data show average circulation.

Magazine	Circulation (000)
PC Magazine	1,044
PC World	929
PC Computing	882
Macworld	568
Computer Shopper	505

Source: Washington Post, 29 March 1996, p. F2. Primary source: Simba Information and *San Jose Mercury News.*

★ 328 ★

Association Magazine Survey: ASAE Winners

The table shows the results of a survey of ASAE Gold Circle Award winners in 1993-95 competitions.

Magazine name	The American School Board Journal	AORN Journal	Association Management	California Schools	Carolina Alumni Review
Circulation					
members	37,000	47,000	23,464	6,000	50,000
others	-	4,000	2,000	1,500	3,000
Frequency	monthly	monthly	monthly	quarterly	every other month
Number of colors	4-color	4-color	4-color	4-color	4-color
Subscription price					
members (or imputed from dues)	$48	$27	$24	$15	$18
nonmembers	-	$80	$30	$20	-
Full-time staff equivalents					
editorial	6	6	5	1.50	1.75
production	1	2	3	.20	1.00
advertising	3	4	8	.25	1.00
administrative	4	2	2	.25	.25
Pages published per year					
editorial	390	1,400	696	122	336
advertising	150	1,000	891[3]	54	120
Number of advertisers annually	100	-	346	60	40
Manufacturing costs[1]					
per editorial page	$418	-	$337	$230	$560
per page/per copy[2]	.0113	-	.0132	.0307	.0106
Ad rate B/W full-page	$5,486	$1,500	$4,705	$1,196	$1,285
additional charge for two colors	$530	$400	$950	$350	$390
three colors	-	$600	$1,900	$600	-
four-color full-page ad rate	$6,971	$2,350	$6,500	$1,796	$2,250
fee for bleeds	$245	0	0	10%	0
Frequency discounts offered	3x, 6x,	6x, 12x,	3x, 6x,	2x, 4x	4x, 6x

[Continued]

★ 328 ★

Association Magazine Survey: ASAE Winners
[Continued]

Magazine name	The American School Board Journal	AORN Journal	Association Management	California Schools	Carolina Alumni Review
	12x, 24x	24x, 36x, 48x, 60x	12x, 24x		
Ad reps-independent, on staff, or both?	staff	staff	both	independent	staff
Ad reps' commission	2.5%	-	varies[4]	25-35%	-
Does the publisher earn an override on ad sales?	no	-	no	no	no
Gross income last year	$2.4 million	$1.5 million	$3.18 million	$75,000	-
Did you have a net income?	yes	yes	yes	no	-
Does the net include income from imputed dues?	no	yes	no	no	-

Source: Association Management (July 1996), p. 57. *Notes:* 1. Manufacturing costs include preparation, printing, paper, and mailing services (not postage). Two magazines survey calculate separate costs for editorial and advertising pages: *Association Management* - $337 per editorial page, $360 per advertising page; and the second anonymous magazine (member circulation 68,000) - $629 per editorial page, $558 per advertising page. 2. The per page/per copy cost was calculated by dividing the manufacturing cost per editorial page by the total circulation. Another way of expressing the figure is that it would cost *The American School Board Journal,* for example, $1.13 to produce one copy of a 100-page issue. 3. Includes advertorials. 4. Commission varies according to performance and whether inside or outside rep. Inside reps: average of 5 percent; outside reps: average of 20 percent.

★ 329 ★

Consumer Magazines

Association Magazine Survey: More ASAE Award Winners

Data show the results of a survey of ASAE Gold Circle Award winners in 1993-95 competitions.

Magazine name	On the Internet	Prime Times	Progressive Rentals	School Foodservice & Nutrition	Sonoma County Physician
Circulation members others	5,000 1,000	80,000 1,500	4,300 300	64,000 1,000	700 300
Frequency	every other month	quarterly	every other month	monthly[5]	every other month
Number of colors	2-color[7]	4-color	4-color	4-color	B/W[7]

[Continued]

★ 329 ★

Association Magazine Survey: More ASAE Award Winners
[Continued]

Magazine name	On the Internet	Prime Times	Progressive Rentals	School Foodservice & Nutrition	Sonoma County Physician
Subscription price					
members (or imputed from dues)	$35	$12	varies[4]	-	$18
nonmembers	$25	$15	$30	$125	$18
Full-time staff equivalents					
editorial	1.50	2	1.0	2.0	.50
production	1.00	2	.5	.5	.25
advertising	.75	1	1.0	.5	.50
administrative	.25	1	.5	1.0	-
Pages published per year					
editorial	309	120	204	497	130
advertising	75	24	124	406	70
Number of advertisers annually	8	10	55	102	50
Manufacturing costs[1]					
per editorial page	$450	$1,701[3]	$246	$1,000	$185
per page/per copy[2]	.0750	.0209	.0535	.0154	.1850
Ad rate B/W full-page	$600[4]	$2,500	$1,862	$4,350	$525
additional charge for two colors	$200	-	$250	$650[6]	-
three colors	$600	-	$500	$1,300[6]	-
four-color full-page ad rate	$1,700	$3,000	$2,462	$6,560	$1,300
fee for bleeds	0	0	0	0	0
Frequency discounts offered	12x	4x	3x, 6x	3x, 6x, 11x, 18x, 22x, 30x	3x, 6x
Ad reps-independent, on staff, or both?	staff	both	staff	independent	staff
Ad reps' commission	30%	15%	5%	20%	-
Does the publisher earn an override on ad sales?	yes	yes	no	no	no
Gross income last year	-	-	$197,468	$1.13 million	$37,000
Did you have a net income?	-	-	yes	no	yes

[Continued]

★ 329 ★

Association Magazine Survey: More ASAE Award Winners
[Continued]

Magazine name	On the Internet	Prime Times	Progressive Rentals	School Foodservice & Nutrition	Sonoma County Physician
Does the net include income from imputed dues?	-	-	no	no	no

Source: Association Management (July 1996), p. 57. *Notes:* 1. Manufacturing costs include preparation, printing, paper, and mailing services (not postage). Two magazines survey calculate separate costs for editorial and advertising pages: *Association Management* - $337 per editorial page, $360 per advertising page; and the second anonymous magazine (member circulation 68,000) - $629 per editorial page, $558 per advertising page. 2. The per page/per copy cost was calculated by dividing the manufacturing cost per editorial page by the total circulation. Another way of expressing the figure is that it would cost *The American School Board Journal,* for example, $1.13 to produce one copy of a 100-page issue. 3. Includes design. 4. Subscription rate for member companies varies depending on number of sites. 5. Produced 11 times annually. 6. Rate for PMS color; rates vary by type of color. 7. B/W inside with 4-color cover.

★ 330 ★

Consumer Magazines

Popular In-Flight Magazines

Data show the number of copies distributed per month.

Airline	Title	Copies/ month
Delta	*Sky*	500,000
United	*Hemispheres*	500,000
US Airways	*US Airways*	440,000
Continental	*Continental*	350,000
Northwest	*World Traveler*	350,000
American	*American Way*	301,500
Southwest	*Spirit*	261,978
TWA	*Ambassador*	185,000
America West	*America West Magazines*	130,000
Alaska	*Alaska Air*	50,000

Source: "In-Flight Magazines." *USA TODAY*, 8 April 1997, p. 10B.

★ 331 ★

Consumer Magazines

Top Consumer Magazines by Ad Pages

Magazine	1995	1996	% change
Hemmings Motor News	9,454.00	9,808.00	-3.6
Forbes	4,548.18	4,542.13	0.1
Business Week	3,885.10	3,816.36	1.8
People	3,708.28	3,328.21	11.4
Fortune	3,336.59	3,184.37	4.8
Bride's Magazine	3,062.18	2,931.32	4.5
TV Guide	3,038.96	3,228.84	-5.9
New York Times Magazine	3,007.15	2,807.86	7.1
Sports Illustrated	2,870.06	2,627.71	9.2
Economist, The	2,830.83	2,850.92	-0.7
Modern Bride	2,723.84	2,734.48	-0.4
Vogue	2,545.91	2,450.32	3.9
Newsweek	2,533.30	2,299.79	10.2
New York	2,491.45	2,497.71	-0.3
Time	2,392.92	2,322.55	3.0

Source: "Magazines: The Advertising Age 300," *Advertising Age,* 16 June 1997, p. S 22.

★ 332 ★

Consumer Magazines

Top Consumer Magazines by Ad Pages Growth

Magazine	1995	1996	% change
George	354.10	689.80	94.8
Marie Claire	619.50	998.90	61.2
InStyle	510.34	774.25	51.7
Martha Stewart Living	598.79	855.43	42.9
Town & Country	860.58	1,205.11	40.0
Northwest Airlines World Traveler	830.34	1,081.58	30.3
Sports Illustrated For Kids	310.10	385.01	24.2
American Heritage	408.84	505.32	23.6
Runner's World	427.10	525.83	23.1
Soap Opera Digest	683.06	827.27	21.1
Departures	461.90	558.87	21.0
Fitness	487.63	587.05	20.4
Vibe	735.76	883.96	20.1
Entertainment Weekly	1,555.23	1,847.92	18.8
Soap Opera Weekly	335.90	398.80	18.7

Source: "Magazines: The Advertising Age 300," *Advertising Age,* 16 June 1997, p. S 22.

★ 333 ★

Consumer Magazines

Top Consumer Magazines by Ad Revenue

Magazine	1995 ($ mil.)	1996 ($ mil.)	% change
People	437.7	525.6	20.1
Sports Illustrated	435.7	522.2	19.8
Parade	515.6	494.0	-4.2
Time	404.5	439.6	8.7
TV Guide	406.9	403.0	-1.0
Newsweek	331.9	383.8	15.6
Better Homes & Gardens	274.4	335.5	22.2
Business Week	267.6	298.6	11.7
USA Weekend	229.6	228.6	-0.4
U.S. News & World Report	222.4	227.5	2.3
Forbes	205.7	222.4	8.1
Woman's Day	197.5	216.9	9.8
Reader's Digest	186.6	201.6	8.0
Fortune	179.5	198.9	10.8
Good Housekeeping	238.7	184.8	-22.6

Source: "Magazines: The Advertising Age 300," *Advertising Age,* 16 June 1997, p. S 22.

★ 334 ★

Consumer Magazines

Top Consumer Magazines by Ad Revenue Growth

Magazine	1995	1996	% change
Marie Claire	14.0	31.3	124.3
InStyle	12.6	25.8	104.5
Martha Stewart Living	33.3	65.6	97.1
George	5.3	10.3	94.8
Vibe	10.6	20.7	94.7
Fitness	13.6	19.8	46.0
Town & Country	28.8	41.7	45.0
Northwest Airlines World Traveler	15.5	22.3	43.8
W	44.4	63.3	42.8
Entertainment Weekly	88.9	124.2	39.6
Family Life	9.3	12.9	39.1
Runner's World	11.7	16.3	38.7
Sun	0.6	0.9	37.8
Departures	14.3	19.7	37.5
American Heritage	6.3	8.7	37.5

Source: "Magazines: The Advertising Age 300," *Advertising Age,* 16 June 1997, p. S 22.

★ 335 ★
Consumer Magazines

Top Magazines by Circulation, 1995

Data do not include Sunday newspaper magazines or association publications. Figures are for the last six months of 1995.

Magazine	Average total paid 1995	% change vs. 1994
Reader's Digest	15,103,830	0.2
TV Guide	13,175,549	-6.1
National Geographic	8,988,444	-2.3
Better Homes & Gardens	7,603,207	-0.1
Good Housekeeping	5,372,786	2.8
Ladies Home Journal	5,045,644	0.0
Family Circle	5,007,542	0.0
Woman's Day	4,707,330	-0.4
McCall's	4,520,186	-2.0
Time	4,083,105	0.5
People Weekly	3,321,198	-3.0
Playboy	3,283,272	-2.6
Prevention	3,252,115	-5.1
Redbook	3,173,313	-6.7
Sports Illustrated	3,157,303	-2.9
Newsweek	3,155,155	-0.1
Cosmopolitan	2,569,186	1.6
Southern Living	2,471,170	-0.1
U.S. News & World Report	2,220,327	-0.9
Seventeen	2,172,923	9.8
YM	2,165,079	12.0
Smithsonian	2,151,172	-2.9
Glamour	2,141,752	-1.5
Field & Stream	2,001,875	-0.1
Ebony	1,927,675	0.2
Money	1,922,737	-3.0
Parents	1,848,008	-0.2
Country Living	1,838,808	-4.7
Popular Science	1,805,525	-0.1
Popular Mechanics	1,586,137	-3.1
Life	1,556,189	-2.5
Golf Digest	1,501,525	2.6
Sunset	1,451,846	-3.1
Martha Stewart Living	1,449,744	52.8

[Continued]

★ 335 ★

Top Magazines by Circulation, 1995

[Continued]

Magazine	Average total paid 1995	% change vs. 1994
Soap Opera Digest	1,372,316	-3.6
Woman's World	1,363,240	16.8
'Teen	1,360,411	6.1
Outdoor Life	1,358,647	-9.6
Discover	1,320,701	30.9
Men's Health	1,314,802	4.5
Golf Magazine	1,283,925	1.3
Mademoiselle	1,280,169	-2.6
New Woman	1,262,003	-3.1
Consumers Digest	1,254,879	3.8
First for Women	1,237,449	0.1
Boys' Life	1,229,052	-1.1
Cooking Light	1,213,158	-2.9
Self	1,211,024	2.0
Us	1,201,377	2.0
Entertainment Weekly	1,195,926	7.0

Source: "The Big Books." *Adweek-Midwest Edition,* 4 March 1996, p. 26. Primary source: Audit Bureau of Circulation.

★ 336 ★

Consumer Magazines

Top Magazines by Circulation, 1996

Top paid circulation magazines for the second half of 1996 (compared with the same period in 1995) based on Audit Bureau of Circulations and BPA International figures. ABC and BPA also audit non-paid circulation.

Publication	Circulation	Percent change	Publication	Circulation	Percent change
Modern Maturity	20,528,786	-2.5	*Nation's Business*	857,343	-0.7
Reader's Digest	15,072,260	-0.2	*American Health for Women*	850,308	4.2
TV Guide	13,013,938	-1.2	*The New Yorker*	847,208	0.0
National Geographic	9,025,003	0.4	*Food & Wine*	841,872	5.5
Better Homes & Gardens	7,605,325	0.0	*Working Mother* [1]	835,273	1.0
The Cable Guide	5,260,421	11.0	*Midwest Living*	826,097	-1.5
Family Circle	5,239,074	4.6	*Sports Illustrated for Kids* [1]	817,436	2.5
Good Housekeeping	4,951,240	-7.8	*FamilyFun*	815,858	14.5
Ladies' Home Journal	4,544,416	-9.9	*Architectural Digest*	812,748	-1.7
Woman's Day	4,317,604	-8.3	*Flower & Garden*	805,390	33.5
McCall's	4,290,216	-5.1	*Conde Nast Traveler*	805,205	-5.0
Time	4,102,168	0.5	*Organic Gardening*	804,341	-0.6
People	3,449,852	3.9	*Tennis*	803,825	-0.3

[Continued]

★ 336 ★

Top Magazines by Circulation, 1996

[Continued]

Publication	Circulation	Percent change	Publication	Circulation	Percent change
Prevention	3,311,244	1.8	Traditional Home	799,871	0.0
Playboy	3,236,517	-1.3	Forbes	789,871	1.2
Newsweek	3,194,769	1.4	American Legion Aux. National News	787,152	-3.6
Sports Illustrated	3,173,639	0.5	Sport	784,266	0.2
Redbook	2,926,702	-7.8	Fortune	775,031	2.2
The American Legion Magazine	2,777,351	-2.6	Hot Rod	768,497	-6.2
Home & Away	2,719,931	23.4	Fitness	768,055	40.8
Avenues	2,549,695	-8.2	Windows Magazine	758,088	13.5
Southern Living	2,490,542	0.8	Road & Track	749,309	1.5
Cosmopolitan	2,486,393	-3.2	Inside Sports	737,947	4.8
National Enquirer	2,480,349	-5.1	Child	736,326	10.0
Seventeen	2,442,090	12.4	Harper's Bazaar	736,095	-5.5
Motorland	2,376,974	1.8	Allure	735,693	0.5
U.S. News & World Report	2,260,857	1.8	Traveler	719,179	-0.8
Star	2,220,711	-6.5	Yankee	715,002	4.3
NEA Today	2,168,447	0.6	North American Hunter	705,857	2.4
YM	2,153,815	-0.5	SmartMoney	702,997	17.5
Glamour	2,115,488	-0.5	Total TV	698,386	11.8
Smithsonian	2,095,819	-2.6	GQ	694,543	-1.1
Martha Stewart Living	2,025,182	39.7	Scientific American	666,631	4.7
Money	1,993,119	3.7	Working Woman	666,164	-12.8
V.F.W. Magazine	1,980,947	-1.6	Inc. Magazine	664,608	0.6
Ebony	1,803,566	-4.0	Eating Well	652,773	1.2
Popular Science	1,793,192	-0.7	Esquire	651,451	-6.3
Field & Stream	1,750,180	-12.3	Metropolitan Home	619,339	-0.6
Parents	1,737,249	-6.0	Automobile Magazine	615,732	0.4
Country Living	1,674,925	-8.8	Mirabella	611,763	6.7
Life	1,601,069	2.9	Wood	610,152	-6.2
American Rifleman	1,545,242	-7.3	Marie Claire	609,559	N/A
Gold Digest	1,515,829	1.0	Premiere	608,639	-1.2
Woman's World	1,504,067	10.3	The Walking Magazine	606,418	18.0
Soap Opera Digest	1,468,333	6.3	New Choices	602,438	0.2
Sunset	1,431,549	-1.4	Junior Scholastic	585,252	6.6
Popular Mechanics	1,428,356	-9.9	Guns & Ammo	583,622	4.9
Cooking Light	1,379,055	13.7	True Story	582,549	-17.5
Men's Health	1,373,817	4.5	Arthritis Today	574,981	8.0
Secure Retirement [1]	1,363,086	-4.3	Travel Holiday	574,604	-4.7
Outdoor Life	1,353,061	-0.5	Sierra	556,571	7.7
First for Women	1,331,399	7.6	Game & Fish Magazine	550,319	7.1
'Teen	1,327,893	-2.4	Computer Shopper	550,174	1.5
Rolling Stones	1,298,631	10.0	Country Sampler	550,138	-10.2
Golf Magazine	1,292,980	-0.2	Ducks Unlimited	549,290	6.4
Entertainment Weekly	1,280,230	6.0	The Sporting News	547,239	2.6
Boys' Life	1,267,283	3.0	Worth	540,154	2.3
Consumer Digest	1,259,422	0.4	Colonial Homes	530,244	-8.5
The Elks Magazine	1,250,475	-1.5	Macuser	529,907	0.8
Discover	1,228,111	-7.0	North American Fisherman	524,034	5.1
New Woman	1,222,143	-3.2	The Rotarian	523,389	1.5

[Continued]

★ 336 ★

Top Magazines by Circulation, 1996
[Continued]

Publication	Circulation	Percent change	Publication	Circulation	Percent change
Mademoiselle	1,206,054	-5.3	National Examiner	517,885	-2.4
Bon Appetit	1,197,505	6.0	Details	516,409	6.9
Vogue	1,190,018	6.6	Outside	515,764	4.4
Self	1,159,305	-2.9	Barney Family Magazine	514,249	0.5
PC Magazine	1,151,473	4.0	Your Money	512,541	8.8
Kiplinger's Personal Finance	1,148,760	12.1	Entrepreneur Magazine	510,216	17.7
Car & Driver	1,122,047	1.2	Soap Opera Weekly	508,960	5.7
Vanity Fair	1,115,760	-4.5	American How-To	508,656	74.8
The American Hunter	1,114,553	-14.5	Natural History	507,560	-1.0
Scholastic Parent & Child	1,095,681	5.6	Catholic Digest	503,521	-1.0
PC World	1,091,987	7.4	Byte Magazine	501,527	-1.9
The Family Handyman	1,089,755	4.1	Workbench	490,724	-13.8
Us	1,083,639	-9.8	Muscle & Fitness	485,452	7.7
Endless Vacation	1,083,582	7.8	Men's Journal	482,964	27.5
Scouting	1,062,843	2.0	Family Life	478,799	18.1
Parenting Magazine	1,060,360	8.2	Successful Farming	477,518	-1.9
Country Home	1,043,599	1.3	Mutual Funds Magazine	474,518	29.9
Sesame Street Magazine	1,032,627	1.1	Sports Afield	465,929	-7.5
Home	1,017,227	2.6	Financial World	463,153	-8.0
Motor Trend	1,013,326	5.4	Home PC	462,570	15.0
PC/Computing	1,005,213	4.2	Home Office Computing	461,353	2.4
Penthouse	1,005,006	-8.7	The Atlantic Monthly	459,868	0.0
Essence	1,000,208	0.7	Macworld[1]	459,267	-3.4
Travel & Leisure	990,115	-2.0	Popular Photography	459,043	0.6
Disney Adventures	977,349	2.0	Vibe	458,673	25.8
Weight Watchers Magazine	976,063	-2.5	Stereo Review	456,893	1.4
In Style	950,680	34.8	Audubon	454,099	-0.2
Health	943,543	-1.0	The Saturday Evening Post	450,104	-0.2
Victoria	943,125	-1.9	Town & Country	448,714	-6.3
Shape	931,893	7.7	Success	444,583	-5.7
American Homestyle & Gardening	930,155	25.6	Runner's World	443,633	1.8
Jet	925,308	-2.6	Elle Decor	436,732	-2.0
Elle	924,242	0.3	Crayola Kids Magazine	436,380	16.0
Globe	905,338	-6.2	The Tennessee Magazine	432,011	4.6
Country America	902,122	-6.1	Weekly World News	431,795	-8.3
Today's Homeowner	901,266	-9.8	New York Magazine	425,996	1.0
Business Week	893,771	1.3	Kentucky Living	420,345	1.9
House Beautiful	886,323	-9.6	Scholastic Scope	413,362	0.0
Gourmet	880,744	-1.7	Ski Magazine	407,384	-9.9

Source: "Consumer Magazine Paid Circulation." Advertising Age, 24 February 1997, p. 14. Primary source: Audit Bureau of Circulations and BPA International. Notes: 1. The following magazines also reported non-paid circulation; Macworld, 167,877; Secure Retirement, 252,783; Sports Illustrated for Kids, 186,750; Working Mother, 102,382.

★ 337 ★

Consumer Magazines

Top Single-Copy Selling Magazines, 1994

The table shows the average number of single copies of magazines sold, in millions. Data are for the eight months ended July 1994.

Magazine	Sales
TV Guide	5.310
Woman's Day	3.185
Family Circle	2.966
National Enquirer	2.901
Star	2.569
Cosmopolitan	2.008
People	1.664
Good Housekeeping	1.296
First For Women	1.269
Woman's World	1.216

Source: *Supermarket Business* (December 1994), p. 66. Primary source: Magazine Publishers of America.

★ 338 ★

Consumer Magazines

Top Single-Copy Selling Magazines, 1996

Figures are for the last six months of 1996.

Title	Single-copy sales (000)	Total circulation (mil.)
TV Guide	4,058.5	13.0
Family Circle	2,275.5	5.2
Woman's Day	2,171.7	4.3
National Enquirer	2,164.9	2.5
Star	1,910.1	2.2
Cosmopolitan	1,676.9	2.5
Woman's World	1,504.0	1.5
People	1,440.2	3.5
Good Housekeeping	1,376.9	5.0
First for Women	1,185.8	1.3
Glamour	1,067.1	2.1
Soap Opera Digest	868.5	1.5
Globe	863.8	NA
Reader's Digest	777.0	15.1
Redbook	720.1	2.9

[Continued]

★ 338 ★

Top Single-Copy Selling Magazines, 1996
[Continued]

Title	Single-copy sales (000)	Total circulation (mil.)
Seventeen	700.7	2.4
Penthouse	699.8	NA
YM	660.0	2.2
Vogue	637.8	NA
In Style	635.9	NA
Ladies Home Journal	628.2	4.5
Playboy	608.3	3.2
Prevention	582.8	3.3
Mademoiselle	570.3	NA
Country Living	520.7	1.7

Source: *Supermarket Business* (May 1997), p. 134. Primary source: Audit Bureau of Circulation. *Note:* NA = not available.

★ 339 ★

Consumer Magazines

Top Women's Magazines

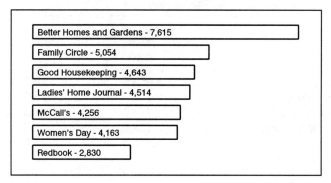

Better Homes and Gardens - 7,615
Family Circle - 5,054
Good Housekeeping - 4,643
Ladies' Home Journal - 4,514
McCall's - 4,256
Women's Day - 4,163
Redbook - 2,830

Name	Circulation (000)
Better Homes and Gardens	7,615
Family Circle	5,054
Good Housekeeping	4,643
Ladies' Home Journal	4,514
McCall's	4,256
Women's Day	4,163
Redbook	2,830

Source: Hainer, Cathy. "Better Homes and Gardens Still Comfy at 75." *USA TODAY,* 10 September 1997, p. 6D. Primary source: Audit Bureau of Circulations; *Advertising Age.*

Foreign Markets

★ 340 ★

Canada: Best-Selling Magazines

Chatelaine - 892	
TV Guide - 830	
Canadian Living - 565	
Macleans - 556	
Time - 329	
	Canadian Geographic - 246

Title	Circulation (000)
Chatelaine	892
TV Guide	830
Canadian Living	565
Macleans	556
Time	329
Canadian Geographic	246

Source: "Fighting Words." *Montreal Gazette,* 14 January 1995, p. D1. Primary source: Audit Bureau of Circulation.

★ 341 ★

Foreign Markets

Canada: Trends in the Magazine Industry

Year	Number of titles	Ad revenue (C$ mil.)
1990-91	1,503	565.3
1991-92	1,440	NA
1992-93	1,400	NA
1993-94	1,331	485.2
1994-95	1,404	521.8

Source: Shofield, John. "Publish or Perish: Canada's Magazine Industry Faces an Uncertain Future." *Maclean's,* 2 June 1997, p. 45. Primary source: Statistics Canada. *Note:* NA = not available.

★ 342 ★

Foreign Markets

Canada's Magazine Industry

The magazine business now has annual sales of $850 million. The table gives facts on the industry.

Item	Value
Number of Canadian periodicals	1,440
Full-time employees	4,583
Part-time employees	1,690
Unpaid volunteers	4,046
Portion of editorial content produced by Canadians (%)	92.3
Portion of Illustration/photography produced by Canadians (%)	92.7
Advertising sales as a percentage of total revenue	64
Subscription sales as a percentage of total revenue	22
Newsstand (single copy) sales as a percentage of total revenue	7
Profit before taxes as percentage of total revenue	2.4

Source: "Fighting Words." *Montreal Gazette,* 14 January 1995, p. D1. Primary source: Statistics Canada.

★ 343 ★

Foreign Markets

Information Technology Magazines in Spain

As new technologies like the Internet and CD-ROMs become more popular, circulation is expected to increase.

Publication	Average circulation
PC World Espana	63,648
PC Actual	49,372
PC Mania	43,674
Micromania	39,070
PC Magazine	38,180
Byte Espana	19,060
PVD-Distribuidor de Informatica	12,233
Datamation	10,688
Computer World Espana	7,901
Macworld Espana	7,474
Redes Lan	5,962
Communicaciones World	5,062
Open Systems	4,443

Source: "Spain - Computer Magazines." *National Trade Data Bank:* The Export Connection CD-ROM, STAT-USA, U.S. Department of Commerce, Washington, D.C. 20302, 21 May 1996, p. IMI960510.

★ 344 ★

Foreign Markets

Latin America: Selected Periodical Subscriptions

Serials are in the local language.

Publication	Circulation
AmericaEconomia	85,758
The Wall Street Journal Americas	1.4 million
Buenhogar (Good Housekeeping)	226,689
Cosmopolitan	493,240
Elle	95,278
Eres	543,974
Geomundo	164,305
Harper's Bazaar	103,556
Ideas Para Tu Hogar	237,677
Marie Claire	188,630
Mecanica Popular	185,517
Men's Health en espanol	223,000
PC Magazine	196,016
Tu	309,740
T.V. y Novelas	935,777
Vanidades	542,579
e³	126,000[1]
Computer World	80,000
PC World	336,000
Reader's Digest Latin America	1.6 million
Viajero VIP	10,100
Vision	110,000
Newsweek en espanol	55,000

Source: "Ad Age International's Latin America Print Media Lineup." *Advertising Age International* (January 1997), p. 131. *Note:* 1. Published every two months.

★ 345 ★

Foreign Markets

Most Read Magazines in France, 1994

Data show millions of readers, based on a survey of 12,492.

Title	Readers
Tele-7 Jours	10,978
TV Magazine	10,919
Femme actuelle	8,409
Tele-Star	6,461

[Continued]

★ 345 ★

Most Read Magazines in France, 1994
[Continued]

Title	Readers
Tele Z - Tele Journal	6,228
TV Hebdo	6,126
Tele Poche	6,093
Tele Loisirs	5,819
Geo	5,483
Prima	5,355
Modes et Travaux	4,830
Sante Magazine	4,810
L'Action Auto-Moto	4,748
Paris-Match	4,540
Notre Temps	4,436
Top Sante	4,435
Selection	4,236
Maxi	4,181
Marie Claire	4,127
Parents	4,016

Source: "Top 20 Magazines." *Le Nouvel Economiste,* 4 March 1994, p. 41.

★ 346 ★

Foreign Markets

Top General Interest Magazines in Europe

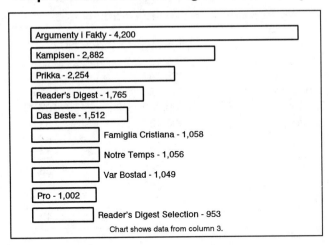

| Argumenty i Fakty - 4,200 |
| Kampisen - 2,882 |
| Prikka - 2,254 |
| Reader's Digest - 1,765 |
| Das Beste - 1,512 |
| Famiglia Cristiana - 1,058 |
| Notre Temps - 1,056 |
| Var Bostad - 1,049 |
| Pro - 1,002 |
| Reader's Digest Selection - 953 |

Chart shows data from column 3.

Title	Country	Frequency	Circulation (000)
Argumenty i Fakty	Russia	Weekly	4,200
Kampisen	Netherlands	Monthly	2,882
Prikka	Finland	Ten a year	2,254
Reader's Digest	United Kingdom	Monthly	1,765
Das Beste	Germany	Monthly	1,512
Famiglia Cristiana	Italy	Weekly	1,058
Notre Temps	France	Monthly	1,056
Var Bostad	Sweden	Monthly	1,049
Pro	Switzerland	Monthly	1,002
Reader's Digest Selection	France	Monthly	953

Source: Short, David. "Succeeding in Title Role." *The European,* 8-14 August 1996, p. 26. Primary source: *World Magazine Trends, 1996.*

★ 347 ★

United Kingdom: Fastest-Growing Magazines

Year-on-year gains are shown for the last six months of 1996.

Title	Circulation	Year-on-year rise (%)
FHM	365,341	217.6
Top of the Pops	292,824	141.6
Auto Trader	30,762	107.7
Cable Guide	908,187	92.9
Loaded	323,115	84.9
Live & Kicking	200,186	80.8
Period Living	84,386	58.5
Maxim	150,261	53.2
Total Guitar	42,647	46.6
Sugar	456,939	43.7

Source: "The Information." *The Observer,* 16 February 1997, p. 47.

★ 348 ★

United Kingdom: Fastest-Growing Men's Magazines

Title	Publisher	Jan-June 1995	Jan-June 1996	% change
FHM	Wagadon	90,607	181,581	+100.4
Loaded	NatMags	127,677	127,677	+87.2
Arena	Emap	76,879	93,513	+21.6
Men's Health	Conde Nast	114,975	131,887	+14.7
GQ	IFC	127,276	131,074	+3.0
Esquire	Dennis	110,798	107,058	-3.4
Maxim	Rodale	NA	113,264	NA

Source: "Men's Magazines." *The Observer,* 11 August 1996, p. 16. Primary source: Audit Bureau of Circulation.

★ 349 ★

Foreign Markets

United Kingdom: Magazine Circulation, 1996

Data show the change in circulation from the first six months of 1995 over the same period in 1996.

Title	Publisher	Jan-Jun 1996 circulation	Period on period %	Year on year %
Men's				
Loaded	IPC	238,955	+36.7	+87.2
FHM	Emap	181,581	+57.8	+100.4
Men's Health	Rodale	131,887	+9.6	+14.7
GQ	Conde Nast	131,074	+1.8	-3.0
Maxim	Dennis	113,264	+15.5	NA
Esquire	Nat Mags	107,058	+0.9	-3.4
Arena	Wagadon	93,513	+10.3	+21.6
Women's monthlies (selected)				
Cosmopolitan	Nat Mags	460,141	+0.8	+0.9
Marie Claire	IPC	455,477	+0.7	+0.1
Company	Nat Mags	291,078	+0.3	-4.8
She	Nat Mags	245,839	-2.5	-9.9
New Women	Emap	231,657	-12.1	-11.5
Elle	Emap	191,243	-6.9	-14.2
Options	IPC	156,531	-3.0	-5.3
Woman's Journal	IPC	149,641	-4.9	-6.7
Teenage/Pop				
Sugar	Attic Futura	361,764	+13.7	+37.8
It's Bliss	Emap	322,063	+22.6	NA
TV Hits	Attic Futura	204,154	+6.3	+11.4
Smash Hits	Emap	202,202	-17.4	-33.1
Top of the Pops	BBC	192,674	+58.9	NA
Big!	Emap	175,049	-7.9	-26.5
Just Seventeen	Emap	162,490	-12.2	-33.6
Sky	Emap	154,281	-4.6	-3.8
Mizz	IPC	150,889	-18.8	-17.9
Live & Kicking	BBC	141,833	+28.1	+3.1

Source: "Going Up, Coming Down." *The Guardian,* 5 August 1996, p. 15. Primary source: Audit Bureau of Circulation.

★ 350 ★

Foreign Markets

United Kingdom: Popular Cricket Titles

Data show estimated number of readers.

Title	Circulation
The Cricketer	35,124
Wisdom Cricket Monthly	35,000
Cricket World	23,000
Johnny Miller 96 Not Out	15,000

Source: "Media Focus." *Campaign,* 13 May 1994, p. 24.

★ 351 ★

Foreign Markets

United Kingdom: Popular Gardening Titles

Data show estimated number of readers.

Title	Circulation
Amateur Gardening	65,896
Gardender's World	272,580
The Garden	181,603
Garden Answers	136,757
Garden News	87,284
The Gardener	41,000
Practical Gardening	66,881
Your Garden	102,444

Source: "Media Focus." *Campaign,* 15 April 1994, p. 29.

★ 352 ★

Foreign Markets

United Kingdom: Popular Government Titles

Data show estimated number of readers.

Title	Circulation
Local Government Chronicle	9,407
Local Government News	21,294
Municipal Journal	8,855
Public Service and Local Government	18,278

Source: "Media Focus." *Campaign,* 24 September 1993, p. 25.

★ 353 ★

Foreign Markets

United Kingdom: Popular Religious Titles

Magazine	Circulation
Occultist	
Fortean Times, journal of strange phenomena	60,872
Prediction	24,368
Horoscope	20,000
Reincarnation International	2,000
UFO Times	1,500
Religious	
The War Cry	78,000
Jewish Chronicle	48,000
Catholic Herald	22,000
Christianity	10,000
New Moon	6,000

Source: "God's Squad." *The Observer,* 24 November 1996, p. 6.

★ 354 ★

Foreign Markets

United Kingdom: Popular Secretarial Titles

Data show estimated number of readers.

Title	Circulation
Girl About Town	95,000
Midweek	95,000
Ms. London Weekly	95,000
Nine to Five	125,000

Source: "Media Focus." *Campaign,* 20 August 1993, p. 18.

★ 355 ★

Foreign Markets

Women's Magazine Sales in Russia

Glossy magazines for women have become one of the most developed segments in the printing industry in Russia. *Cosmo*, which began selling there in 1994, now sells nearly 400,000 a month. *Elle*'s circulation has jumped to nearly 200,000 in its first seven months.

Source: "Read All About It." *The Wall Street Journal,* 11 November 1996, p. A10.

Chapter 8
MUSIC PUBLISHING

With the exception of audio books (covered in Chapter 3), the publishing of music is the most important non-print segment of the Publishing industry—although electronic publishing is a growing contender. Music publishing is covered in this chapter under the topics of *Sales and Distribution*, *Bestsellers*, *Companies*, *Costs*, *Royalties*, and *Foreign Markets*.

Sales and Distribution

★ 356 ★

Music Publishing: Dollar Shipments by Year

Data show manufacturer shipments in millions of dollars.

Segment	1992	1993	1994	1995	1996
CD	5,326.5	6,511.4	8,464.5	9,377.4	9,934.7
CD single	45.1	45.8	56.1	110.9	184.1
Cassette	3,116.3	2,915.8	2,976.4	2,230.6	1,905.3
Cassette single	298.8	298.5	274.9	236.3	189.3
Vinyl LP/EP	13.5	10.6	17.8	25.1	36.8
Vinyl single	66.4	51.2	47.2	46.7	47.5
Music video	157.4	213.3	231.1	220.3	236.1
Total value	9,024.0	10,046.6	12,068.0	12,320.3	12,533.8

Source: "Flash Report—Recorded Music." *Discount Merchandiser* (August 1997), p. 114. Primary source: Recording Industry Association of America.

★ 357 ★

Sales and Distribution

Music Publishing: Unit Shipments by Year

Data show manufacturer shipments in millions of units.

Segment	1992	1993	1994	1995	1996
CD	407.5	495.4	662.1	722.9	778.9
CD single	7.3	7.8	9.3	21.5	43.2
Cassette	366.4	339.5	345.4	272.6	225.3
Cassette single	84.6	85.6	81.1	70.7	59.9
Vinyl LP/EP	2.3	1.2	1.9	2.2	2.9
Vinyl single	19.8	15.1	11.7	10.2	10.1
Music video	7.6	11.0	11.2	12.6	16.9
Total units	895.5	955.6	1,122.7	1,112.7	1,137.2

Source: "Flash Report—Recorded Music." *Discount Merchandiser* (August 1997), p. 114. Primary source: Recording Industry Association of America.

★ 358 ★

Sales and Distribution

Music Sales by Age

Distribution is shown based on dollar value.

[In percent]

Age	1992	1993	1994	1995	1996
10-14 years	8.6	8.6	7.9	8.0	7.9
15-19 years	18.2	16.7	16.8	17.1	17.2
20-24 years	16.1	15.1	15.4	15.3	15.0
25-29 years	13.8	13.2	12.6	12.3	12.5
30-34 years	12.2	11.9	11.8	12.1	11.4
35-39 years	10.9	11.1	11.5	10.8	11.1
40-44 years	7.4	8.5	7.9	7.5	9.1
45 + years	12.2	14.1	15.4	16.1	15.1

Source: "Flash Report—Recorded Music." *Discount Merchandiser* (August 1997), p. 114. Primary source: Recording Industry Association of America.

★ 359 ★

Sales and Distribution

Music Sales by Format

Distribution is shown based on dollar value.

[In percent]

Format	1992	1993	1994	1995	1996
Full-length CDs	46.5	51.1	58.4	65.0	68.4
Full-length cassettes	43.6	38.0	32.1	25.1	19.3
Singles (all types)	8.6	9.2	7.4	7.5	9.3
Music videos	1.0	1.3	0.8	0.9	1.0
Vinyl LPs	1.3	0.3	0.8	0.5	0.6
Other	0.1	0.1	0.5	2.0	1.4

Source: "Flash Report—Recorded Music." *Discount Merchandiser* (August 1997), p. 114. Primary source: Recording Industry Association of America.

★ 360 ★

Sales and Distribution

Music Sales by Outlet

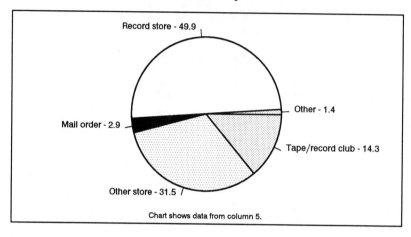

Chart shows data from column 5.

Distribution is shown based on dollar value.

[In percent]

Channel	1992	1993	1994	1995	1996
Record store	60.0	56.2	53.3	52.0	49.9
Other store	24.9	26.1	26.7	28.2	31.5
Tape/record club	11.4	12.9	15.1	14.3	14.3
Mail order	3.2	3.8	3.4	4.0	2.9
Other	0.5	1.0	1.5	1.5	1.4

Source: "Flash Report—Recorded Music." *Discount Merchandiser* (August 1997), p. 114. Primary source: Recording Industry Association of America.

★ 361 ★

Sales and Distribution

Printed Music Market

The strongest segment of the printed music market was in educational products, such as method books and choral and band scores. Figures are in millions of dollars.

Year	Wholesale ($ mil.)	Retail ($ mil.)
1991	181.51	330.36
1992	190.65	347.00
1993	203.80	370.50
1994	216.02	400.05

[Continued]

★ 361 ★

Printed Music Market
[Continued]

Year	Wholesale ($ mil.)	Retail ($ mil.)
1995	226.82	420.05
1996	228.00	425.00

Source: "The Music Industry Census." *Music Trades,* (April 1997), p. 104.

★ 362 ★
Sales and Distribution

U.S. Music Sales by Genre

Rock - 33
Other - 22
Country - 15
R&B - 12
Pop - 9
Rap - 9

Chart shows data from column 2.

Record sales reached $12.53 billion between 1995-96. Sales are shown by type.

[In percent]

Type	1987	1996
Rock	45	33
Country	11	15
R&B	9	12
Pop	14	9
Rap	4	9
Other	17	22

Source: Rawsthorn, Alice. "Changing the Tune in U.S. Music." *Financial Times,* 27 September 1997, p. 23. Primary source: Recording Industry Association of America.

★ 363 ★

Sales and Distribution

Vinyl Record Sales by Year

| 1997 - 2,200,000 |
| 1996 - 1,100,000 |
| 1995 - 794,000 |
| 1994 - 625,000 |

Despite digital technology, vinyl LP sales continue to prosper. Top buyers include jazz aficionados who want vinyl reissues and club DJs. Sales in 1997 are as of June 29, 1997.

Year	Sales
1994	625,000
1995	794,000
1996	1,100,000
1997	2,200,000

Source: "Datapoint." *Time,* 14 July 1997, p. 20. Primary source: Soundscan Inc.

Bestsellers

★ 364 ★

Best-Selling Albums, 1996

Data show the top sellers in millions of units.

Artist	Title	Copies sold
Alanis Morissette	*Jagged Little Pill*	7.38
Celine Dion	*Falling Into You*	6.13
Fugees	*The Score*	4.51
No Doubt	*Tragic Kingdom*	4.36
Mariah Carey	*Daydream*	3.08
2Pac	*All Eyes on Me*	3.00
Metallica	*Load*	2.96
Toni Braxton	*Secrets*	2.89
Shania Twain	*Woman In Me*	2.78
Oasis	*(What's the Story) Morning Glory?*	2.63
Tracy Chapman	*New Beginning*	2.56

[Continued]

★ 364 ★

Best-Selling Albums, 1996

[Continued]

Artist	Title	Copies sold
Soundtrack	*Waiting to Exhale*	2.55
Bone Thugs-N-Harmony	*E.1999 Eternal*	2.46
LeAnn Rimes	*Blue*	2.46
Bush	*Sixteen Stone*	2.27
Hootie & the Blowfish	*Fairweather Johnson*	2.14
Keith Sweat	*Keith Sweat*	2.10
Dave Matthews Band	*Crash*	1.99
Smashing Pumpkins	*Mellon Collie and the Infinite Sadness*	1.94
Hootie & the Blowfish	*Cracked Rear View*	1.72

Source: Wilman, Chris. "The Top 20." *Entertainment Weekly,* 17 January 1997, p. 34. Primary source: Soundscan.

★ 365 ★

Bestsellers

Top 10 Singles of All Time

Data show worldwide sales. Elton John's tribute to Princess Diana, *Candle in the Wind 1997,* is expected to take the top spot.

[In millions]

Titles	Performer	Amount
White Christmas	Bing Crosby	30
Rock Around the Clock	Bill Haley & His Comets	17
I Want to Hold Your Hand	The Beatles	12
It's Now or Never	Elvis Presley	10
I Will Always Love You	Whitney Houston	10
Hound Dog/Don't Be Cruel	Elvis Presley	9
Diana	Paul Anka	9
Hey Jude	The Beatles	8
I'm a Believer	The Monkees	8
Can't Buy Me Love	The Beatles	7
Do They Know It's Christmas	Band Aid	7
We Are the World	USA for Africa	7

Source: "Songs That Rocked Around the World." *The Christian Science Monitor,* 16 August 1996, p. 2. Primary source: *The Top 10 of Everything.*

★ 366 ★

Music Industry Leaders

| Warner Music - 20.30 |
| BMG - 15.88 |
| Sony Music - 15.43 |
| PolyGram - 12.56 |
| EMI Music - 9.08 |
| Universal Music - 7.66 |

Chart shows data from column 1.

Market shares are shown in percent.

[In percent]

Company	1996[1]	1997[1]
Warner Music	20.30	17.30
Universal Music	7.66	14.91
EMI Music	9.08	13.50
BMG	15.88	13.21
PolyGram	12.56	11.82
Sony Music	15.43	11.61

Source: Reilly, Patrick M. "Universal Music Charts a Comeback with Hot Artists." *The Wall Street Journal,* 29 May 1997, p. B4. *Note:* 1. From January 1 through mid-May.

★ 367 ★
Companies

Top Country Music Distributors

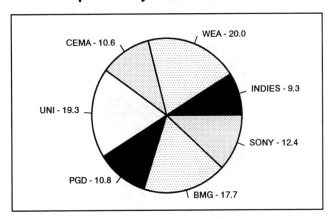

Market shares are shown for the first three months of 1996.

[In percent]

Company	Share
WEA	20.0
UNI	19.3
BMG	17.7
SONY	12.4
PGD	10.8
CEMA	10.6
INDIES	9.3

Source: Christman, Ed. "Indie Sector Nears Top With 1st. Quarter Market Share Gain." *Billboard,* 27 April 1996, p. 63. Primary source: Soundscan.

★ 368 ★

Companies

Top R&B Music Distributors

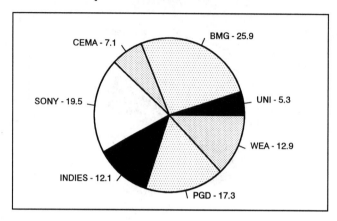

Market shares are shown for the first three months of 1996.

[In percent]

Company	Share
BMG	25.9
SONY	19.5
PGD	17.3
WEA	12.9
INDIES	12.1
CEMA	7.1
UNI	5.3

Source: Christman, Ed. "Indie Sector Nears Top With 1st. Quarter Market Share Gain." *Billboard,* 27 April 1996, p. 63. Primary source: Soundscan.

★ 369 ★

The Cost of a CD

In the early 1990's, the record industry enjoyed double-digit annual sales growth. However, in 1994, growth fell from 20% to approximately 2% in 1995 and 1996. The figures for revenue growth are not much brighter. The early market growth can largely be attributed to people making the switch from vinyl and cassettes to CDs. The sudden dropoff in the market in 1995 (CDs were introduced in 1983) surprised retailers. Many have filed for bankruptcy. Competition has become fierce in the market, with prices varying as much as 30%. On average, the consumer pays $12.70 for a CD. The table shows the distribution of the average $10.30 wholesale cost of a CD.

[In dollars]

Segment	Cost
Manufacturing and packaging	1.00
Marketing	2.00
Distribution	1.50
Promotion	1.00
Artist royalty	1.50-3.00
Reserves for returns	1.50-2.00
Profit	1.00-2.00

Source: O'Donnell, Jayne and David Lieberman. "Pricing Probe Could Play Out in Full Investigation." *USA TODAY,* 12 August 1997, p. B1. Primary source: Veronis, Suhler & Associates and industry sources.

★ 370 ★

Music Publishing Royalties, 1993

The ownership of copyrights to music is a $5.0 billion a year global business. Public performance refers to music played in clubs, bars, hotels, amusement parks and health clubs. Royalties are shown in millions of dollars.

Segment	($ mil.)	% Growth
Reproduction	1,506	+6
Public performance	1,008	+32
TV, cable, satellite	608	+12
Printed music sales	489	+13
Radio	474	+12
Synchronization	259	+7
Other	705	-21

Source: Sandler, Adam. "Publishing Discovers Revenue Avenue." *Variety,* 23 October 1995, p. 27. Primary source: National Music Publishers Association.

★ 371 ★

Australia's Music Sales

Australia's Copyright Act has been driving up prices in the recording industry. It bans the commercial importation of music by anyone other than the Australian copyright holder. Critics argue this gives multinational a lucrative and far too controlling influence in the market. Sales are shown in millions of units.

[In millions]

Segment	1991	1992	1993	1994	1995
CDs	21.4	25.50	26.40	28.80	34.30
Singles	7.7	8.60	10.20	9.30	8.50
Cassettes	15.9	12.90	10.10	8.60	6.60
LPs	0.4	0.03	0.02	0.03	0.02

Source: Tait, Nikki. "Australians in a Spin Over Cost of Music." *Financial Times,* 21 March 1997, p. 7. Primary source: International Federation of the Phonographic Industry.

★ 372 ★

Foreign Markets

Classical Music Leaders in the United Kingdom

Polygram - 36.0	
Others - 26.6	
EMI - 21.8	
	Independents - 11.1
	Sony - 4.5

Chart shows data from column 2.

Market shares are shown in percent.

[In percent]

Company	1991	1996
Polygram	60.2	36.0
EMI	24.0	21.8
Sony	2.5	4.5
Independents	4.3	11.1
Others	9.0	26.6

Source: Clark, Andrew. "All Shook Up Over Classical Music." *Financial Times,* 23 March 1997, p. 7. Primary source: British Photographic Industry.

★ 373 ★

Foreign Markets

Europe's Music Market, 1996

The top markets are shown in billions of dollars.

Country	($ bil.)
Germany	3.18
U.K.	2.71
France	2.32
Netherlands	0.66
Italy	0.64
Spain	0.59

Source: Rawsthorn, Alice. "Parallel CD Imports Prompt Pricing Rethink." *Financial Times,* 10 October 1997, p. 8. Primary source: International Federation of the Phonographic Industry.

★ 374 ★

Foreign Markets

Global Music Sales by Format, 1996

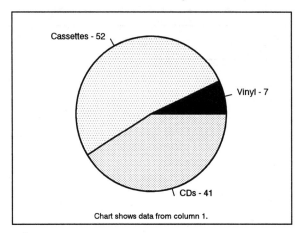

Cassettes - 52

Vinyl - 7

CDs - 41

Chart shows data from column 1.

[In percent]

Format	1991	1996
CDs	41	58
Cassettes	52	41
Vinyl	7	1

Source: Rawsthorn, Alice. "Big Five Adjust the Volume." *Financial Times,* 5 November 1996, p. 15. Primary source: International Federation of the Phonographic Industry.

★ 375 ★

Foreign Markets

Global Music Sales by Region, 1995

[In percent]

Country	Share
Europe	34
North America	33
Japan	19
Asia	5
Latin America	5
Australia	2
Africa	1
Middle East/Turkey	1

Source: Rawsthorn, Alice. "Big Five Adjust the Volume." *Financial Times,* 5 November 1996, p. 15. Primary source: International Federation of the Phonographic Industry.

★ 376 ★

Foreign Markets

Global Music Sales by Region, 1996

The global market grew from $27.15 billion in 1991 to $39.83 billion in 1996. Distribution is shown by region.

[In percent]

Region	1991	1996
Europe	42	34
North America	32	33
Asia	20	23
Latin America	4	6
Others	2	4

Source: Rawsthorn, Alice. "Music Groups Dream of Capturing Global Market." *Financial Times,* 23 August 1997, p. 2. Primary source: International Federation of the Phonographic Industry.

★ 377 ★

Foreign Markets

Latin America: Music Sales by Country

Sales are shown in millions of U.S. dollars. All figures include estimated piracy sales.

Country	($ mil.)
Brazil	1,171.9
Mexico	384.3
Argentina	310.5
Colombia	218.9
Chile	86.6
Venezuela	48.0
Peru	25.9
Uruguay	22.1
Paraguay	20.1
Ecuador	10.7

Source: "Samba Time." *Latin Trade* (November 1996), p. 15. Primary source: International Federation of the Phonographic Industry.

★ 378 ★

Foreign Markets

Music Sales in Leading Countries, 1996

Data show wholesale sales in millions of units. These countries represent two thirds of the global music market.

Country	Singles	LPs	Tapes	CDs	Wholesale sales ($ mil.)
Belgium	4.5	0.1	0.5	16.5	201.8
Brazil	NA	1.6	4.5	88.8	874.3
Canada	0.5	NA	12.7	41.4	402.2
France	30.4	0.07	17.3	97.4	1,289.6
Italy	1.0	0.5	14.3	27.7	292.3
Japan[1]	139.4	0.9	20.5	259.2	4,643.6
Netherlands	7.6	0.05	1.0	35.7	313.4
Portugal	0.1	NA	4.1	7.6	91.3
US	120.8	1.5	166.7	448.4	7,901.4
Total	304.3	4.82	241.6	1,028.1	16,075.4

Source: Rawsthorn, Alice. "Music Industry Sales Static." *Financial Times,* 31 January 1997, p. 4. Primary source: *Music & Copyright. Note:* 1. These figures are for 11 months only.

★ 379 ★

Foreign Markets

Online Music Sales Worldwide

Sales are estimated in millions of dollars.

Year	Sales
1997	47
1998	110
1999	240
2000	505
2001	958
2002	1,640

Source: Rawsthorn, Alice. "Internet Music Retailers Hear an Upbeat Tempo." *Financial Times,* 5 December 1997, p. 17. Primary source: Jupiter Communications.

★ 380 ★

Foreign Markets

World Music Sales

Year	Value ($ bil.)	Units (bil.)
1986	14.00	1.96
1987	17.00	2.13
1988	20.30	2.42
1989	21.50	2.68
1990	24.10	2.68
1991	26.75	2.58
1992	29.00	2.97
1993	30.78	3.09
1994	36.13	3.40
1995	39.68	3.49

Source: Rawsthorn, Alice. "Big Five Adjust the Volume." *Financial Times,* 5 November 1996, p. 15. Primary source: International Federation of the Phonographic Industry.

Chapter 9
NEWSPAPER PUBLISHING

Will newspapers be overwhelmed by a mounting tide of electronic publishing, cable broadcasting, and other forms of "virtual" news reporting? The data presented in this chapter would indicate otherwise. This major segment of publishing is profiled under the topics of *Industry Statistics*, *Trends*, *Sales and Markets*, *Companies*, *Rankings*, *Circulation*, *Reader Profiles*, and *Foreign Markets*. Related information, on magazines and journals, is presented in Chapter 7. For a full treatment of electronic newspapers, please see Gale's *By-the-Numbers: Electronic and Online Publishing*.

★ 381 ★

General Statistics on the Newspaper Industry, 1982-1998

Year	Com-panies	Establishments		Employment			Compensation	
		Total	With 20 or more employees	Total (000)	Production workers (000)	Hours (mil.)	Payroll ($ mil.)	Wages ($ hr.)
1982	3,144	3,328	690	94.0	17.4	31.9	1,986.1	7.62
1983	NA	NA	NA	93.4	17.3	31.9	2,073.7	8.03
1984	NA	NA	NA	93.5	16.2	28.8	2,231.7	8.71
1985	NA	NA	NA	95.8	16.2	28.4	2,554.5	9.59
1986	NA	NA	NA	98.1	14.2	24.9	2,710.9	11.60
1987	3,757	4,020	876	110.0	18.3	32.4	2,982.7	11.06
1988	NA	NA	NA	111.4	19.1	33.8	3,152.1	11.99
1989	NA	4,101	872	115.9	20.7	32.6	3,422.8	12.45
1990	NA	NA	NA	115.2	21.6	35.4	3,658.5	13.09
1991	NA	NA	NA	110.6	20.7	35.4	3,661.0	13.21
1992	4,390	4,699	991	116.2	20.1	39.0	4,074.5	13.40
1993	NA	NA	NA	117.1	19.7	37.4	4,305.3	12.51
1994	NA	NA	NA	116.4	18.3	34.5	4,273.9	12.97
1995	NA	NA	NA	123.2[1]	20.9[1]	37.7[1]	4,618.7[1]	14.65[1]
1996	NA	NA	NA	125.6[1]	21.2[1]	38.3[1]	4,827.0[1]	15.14[1]
1997	NA	NA	NA	127.9[1]	21.6[1]	39.0[1]	5,035.3[1]	15.62[1]
1998	NA	NA	NA	130.3[1]	21.9[1]	39.7[1]	5,243.6[1]	16.11[1]

Source: 1997 *Manufacturing STATROM* [machine-readable data files]. MStat97. Editorial Code and Data, Inc., Detroit, Michigan, 1997. Primary source: 1982, 1987, 1992 *Economic Census*; *Annual Survey of Manufactures*, 1983-1986, 1988-1991, 1993-1994. Establishment counts for non-Census years are from *County Business Patterns*; establishment values for 1983-1984 are extrapolations. Industries reclassified in 1987 will not have data for prior years. *Notes:* NA = Not available. 1. Items are projected by the editors.

★ 382 ★

Industry Statistics

General Indices of Change in the Newspaper Industry, 1982-1998

Year	Com-panies	Establishments		Employment			Compensation	
		Total	With 20 or more employees	Total (000)	Production workers (000)	Hours (mil.)	Payroll ($ mil.)	Wages ($ hr.)
1982	111	102	97	96	109	110	62	71
1983	NA	NA	NA	97	111	112	67	76
1984	NA	NA	NA	96	110	112	70	79
1985	NA	NA	NA	99	112	113	75	83
1986	NA	NA	NA	101	112	115	80	84
1987	110	105	100	104	110	111	86	88
1988	NA	NA	NA	104	108	111	89	89
1989	NA	99	108	103	109	108	94	92
1990	NA	NA	NA	106	110	107	99	96
1991	NA	NA	NA	103	107	107	98	95
1992	100	100	100	100	100	100	100	100
1993	NA	NA	NA	98	97	95	99	100
1994	NA	NA	NA	98	99	93	101	104
1995	NA	NA	NA	103[1]	100[1]	97[1]	110[1]	107[1]
1996	NA	NA	NA	103[1]	99[1]	95[1]	114[1]	109[1]
1997	NA	NA	NA	103[1]	98[1]	94[1]	117[1]	112[1]
1998	NA	NA	NA	104[1]	97[1]	92[1]	120[1]	114[1]

Source: 1997 *Manufacturing STATROM* [machine-readable data files]. MStat97. Editorial Code and Data, Inc., Detroit, Michigan, 1997. Primary source: 1982, 1987, 1992 *Economic Census*; *Annual Survey of Manufactures*, 1983-1986, 1988-1991, 1993-1994. Establishment counts for non-Census years are from *County Business Patterns*; establishment values for 1983-1984 are extrapolations. Industries reclassified in 1987 will not have data for prior years. Values reflect change from the base year, 1992. Values above 100 mean greater than 1992, values below 100 mean less than 1992, and a value of 100 in the 1982-1991 or 1993-1998 period means same as 1992. *Notes:* NA = Not available. 1. Items are projected by the editors.

★ 383 ★

Industry Statistics

General Production Statistics on the Newspaper Industry, 1982-1998

Year	Production ($ million)			
	Cost of materials	Value added by manufacture	Value of shipments[1]	Capital investment
1982	4,568.1	6,910.9	11,478.0	194.8
1983	4,603.6	7,868.9	12,436.7	251.7
1984	5,117.6	8,943.9	14,052.6	267.4
1985	5,579.8	9,678.1	15,246.4	339.7
1986	5,558.1	10,196.0	15,719.4	274.1
1987	5,872.7	11,452.1	17,329.2	246.4
1988	6,201.9	12,439.6	18,611.8	246.1
1989	6,581.0	13,248.4	19,787.2	272.2
1990	6,579.6	13,847.7	20,396.7	274.8
1991	6,459.0	13,794.4	20,345.1	223.0
1992	6,200.9	15,833.0	22,033.9	234.4
1993	6,391.2	16,271.9	22,652.5	289.5
1994	5,903.1	15,821.4	21,723.3	306.6
1995	6,638.9[2]	17,793.6[2]	24,431.2[2]	278.7[2]
1996	6,895.1[2]	18,480.2[2]	25,373.9[2]	280.9[2]
1997	7,151.3[2]	19,166.8[2]	26,316.7[2]	283.2[2]
1998	7,407.5[2]	19,853.5[2]	27,259.5[2]	285.4[2]

Source: 1997 *Manufacturing STATROM* [machine-readable data files]. MStat97. Editorial Code and Data, Inc., Detroit, Michigan, 1997. Primary source: 1982, 1987, 1992 *Economic Census*; *Annual Survey of Manufactures*, 1983-1986, 1988-1991, 1993-1994. Establishment counts for non-Census years are from *County Business Patterns*; establishment values for 1983-1984 are extrapolations. Industries reclassified in 1987 will not have data for prior years. *Notes:* 1. "Industry Shipments" and "Product Shipments" are rarely the same value.

Industry Statistics

Materials Consumed by the Newspaper Industry

Material	Delivered cost ($ mil.)
Materials, ingredients, containers, and supplies	5,850.3
Newsprint, basis wt. 30 lb.	3,202.2
Newspaper, other basis wt.	629.5
Coated paper	37.9
All other paper, except light sensitive	43.9
Letterpress printing inks, including news	33.7
Lithographic (offset) printing inks	114.9
Other printing inks, including gravure, flexographic, and screen process	24.3
Lithographic (offset) printing plates, exposed, prepared for printing	23.7
Letterpress printing plates, exposed, prepared for printing	17.1
Other printing plates, exposed, prepared for printing	11.0
Lithographic (offset) printing plates, unexposed photosensitive	33.1
Letterpress printing plates, unexposed photosensitive	18.7
Other printing plates, unexposed photosensitive	3.5
Light sensitive films	52.5
Light sensitive papers (including photographic paper and diffusion transfer paper)	18.9
All other materials and components, parts, containers, and supplies	472.5
Materials, ingredients, containers, and supplies, nsk	1,112.8

Source: 1997 *Manufacturing STATROM* [machine-readable data files]. MStat97. Editorial Code and Data, Inc., Detroit, Michigan, 1997. Primary source: 1992 *Economic Census.* Explanation of symbols used: nsk: Not specified by kind.

★ 385 ★

Industry Statistics

Product Share Details in the Newspaper Industry

Product code	Shipments ($ mil.)	% of total	Product name
2711	32,261.5	100.00	NEWSPAPERS
27111	6,541.6	20.28	Daily and Sunday newspapers (receipts from subscriptions and sales)
2711101	462.4	7.07	Morning papers (no Sunday editions)
2711111	278.1	4.25	Evening papers (no Sunday editions)
2711122	3,533.5	54.02	Morning and Sunday combination papers
2711132	554.7	8.48	Evening and Sunday combination papers
2711142	15.8	0.24	Morning and evening combination papers (no Sunday editions)
2711152	1,091.1	16.68	Morning, evening, and Sunday combination papers
2711100	605.1	9.25	Daily and sunday papers, n.s.k.
27112	20,123.8	62.38	Daily and Sunday newspapers (receipts from advertising)
2711201	907.9	4.51	Morning papers (no Sunday editions)
2711211	792.5	3.94	Evening papers (no Sunday editions)
2711222	11,845.7	58.86	Morning and Sunday combination papers
2711232	1,585.8	7.88	Evening and Sunday combination papers
2711242	35.1	0.17	Morning and evening combination papers (no Sunday editions) (receipts from advertising)
2711252	3,462.6	17.21	Morning, evening, and Sunday combination papers
2711200	1,494.1	7.42	Daily and Sunday papers, n.s.k.
27113	645.5	2.00	Weekly and other newspapers (receipts from subscriptions and sales)
2711362	512.1	79.33	Weekly papers, including those issued on Sunday only
2711398	114.3	17.71	Other papers
2711300	19.1	2.96	Weekly and other newspapers, n.s.k.
27114	2,108.3	6.54	Weekly and other newspapers (receipts from advertising)
2711462	1,496.4	70.98	Weekly newspapers, including those issued on Sunday only
2711498	462.3	21.93	Other newspapers
2711400	149.7	7.10	Weekly and other papers, n.s.k.
27110	2,842.4	8.81	Newspapers, n.s.k.

Source: 1997 *Manufacturing STATROM* [machine-readable data files]. MStat97. Editorial Code and Data, Inc., Detroit, Michigan, 1997. Primary source: 1992 *Economic Census*. The values shown are percent of total shipments in an industry. Values of indented subcategories are summed in the main headings. The abbreviation n.s.k. stands for 'not specified by kind' and n.e.c. for 'not elsewhere classifieds.

Industry Statistics

Production: Indices of Change in the Newspaper Industry, 1982 - 1998

Year	Production ($ million)			
	Cost of materials	Value added by manufacture	Value of shipments[1]	Capital investment
1982	87	56	62	62
1983	87	63	68	59
1984	94	69	74	65
1985	96	75	79	86
1986	102	81	86	78
1987	110	89	93	91
1988	117	91	96	98
1989	120	95	100	119
1990	118	97	102	113
1991	111	96	99	92
1992	100	100	100	100
1993	100	102	102	76
1994	102	106	105	80
1995	111[2]	114[2]	114[2]	103[2]
1996	114[2]	118[2]	117[2]	106[2]
1997	117[2]	121[2]	121[2]	108[2]
1998	121[2]	125[2]	124[2]	111[2]

Source: 1997 *Manufacturing STATROM* [machine-readable data files]. MStat97. Editorial Code and Data, Inc., Detroit, Michigan, 1997. Primary source: 1982, 1987, 1992 *Economic Census; Annual Survey of Manufactures,* 1983-1986, 1988-1991, 1993-1994. Establishment counts for non-Census years are from *County Business Patterns;* establishment values for 1983-1984 are extrapolations. Industries reclassified in 1987 will not have data for prior years. Values reflect change from the base year, 1992. Values above 100 mean greater than 1992, values below 100 mean less than 1992, and a value of 100 in the 1982-1991 or 1993-1998 period means same as 1992. *Notes:* 1. "Industry Shipments" and "Product Shipments" are rarely the same value. 2. Items are projected by the editors.

★ 387 ★

Industry Statistics

Occupations Employed by the Newspaper Industry

Occupation	% of total 1994	Change to 2005
Sales & related workers, nec	13.5	-1.0
Reporters & correspondents	8.2	-10.9
Writers & editors, including technical writers	8.0	-1.0
Hand packers & packagers	3.9	-6.6
Driver/sales workers	3.8	18.9
Truck drivers light & heavy	2.6	2.1
Advertising clerks	2.6	-10.9
Paste-up workers	2.4	-35.6
General office clerks	2.2	-15.5
General managers & top executives	2.2	-6.0
Offset lithographic press operators	2.1	-1.0
Printing press machine setters, operators	2.1	-20.8
Blue collar worker supervisors	2.0	-8.3
Machine feeders & offbearers	1.9	-10.9
Bookkeeping, accounting, & auditing clerks	1.8	-25.7
Marketing, advertising, & PR managers	1.7	-0.9
Marketing & sales worker supervisors	1.7	-1.0
Adjustment clerks	1.7	18.9
Duplicating, mail, & office machine operators	1.6	-42.2
Photographers	1.6	-1.9
Artists & commercial artists	1.5	9.8
Secretaries, ex-legal & medical	1.5	-9.8
Helpers, laborers, & material movers, nec	1.4	-1.0
Managers & administrators, nec	1.3	-1.0
Clerical supervisors & managers	1.3	1.3
Letterpress operators	1.3	-75.2
Typesetting & composing machine operators	1.1	-75.2
Janitors & cleaners, including maids	1.1	-20.8
Electronic pagination systems workers	1.1	58.5

Source: 1997 *Manufacturing STATROM* [machine-readable data files]. MStat97. Editorial Code and Data, Inc., Detroit, Michigan, 1997. Primary source: *Industry-Occupation Matrix*, Bureau of Labor Statistics. These data relate to one or more 3-digit SIC industry groups rather than to a single 4-digit SIC. The change reported for each occupation to the year 2005 is a percent of growth or decline as estimated by the Bureau of Labor Statistics. The abbreviation nec stands for 'not elsewhere classified.'

★ 388 ★

Industry Statistics

Selected Ratios for the Newspaper Industry

For 1992	Average of all manufacturing	Newspaper publishing	Index
Employees per establishment	46	48	105
Payroll per establishment	1,332,320	1,210,554	91
Payroll per employee	29,181	25,195	86
Production workers per establishment	31	16	50
Wages per establishment	734,496	350,209	48
Wages per production worker	23,390	22,465	96
Hours per production worker	2,025	1,743	86
Wages per hour	11.55	12.89	112
Value added per establishment	3,842,210	3,139,417	82
Value added per employee	84,153	65,341	78
Value added per production worker	122,353	201,382	165
Cost per establishment	4,239,462	792,027	19
Cost per employee	92,853	16,484	18
Cost per production worker	135,003	50,806	38
Shipments per establishment	8,100,800	3,931,824	49
Shipments per employee	177,425	81,833	46
Shipments per production worker	257,966	252,212	98
Investment per establishment	278,244	192,119	69
Investment per employee	6,094	3,999	66
Investment per Production worker	8,861	12,324	139

Source: 1997 *Manufacturing STATROM* [machine-readable data files]. MStat97. Editorial Code and Data, Inc., Detroit, Michigan, 1997. Primary source: 1982, 1987, 1992 *Economic Census; Annual Survey of Manufactures*, 1983-1986, 1988-1991, 1993-1994. Establishment counts for non-Census years are from *County Business Patterns*; establishment values for 1983-1984 are extrapolations. Industries reclassified in 1987 will not have data for prior years. Values reflect change from the base year, 1992. Values above 100 mean greater than 1992, values below 100 mean less than 1992, and a value of 100 in the 1982-1991 or 1993-1998 period means same as 1992. The 'Average of All Manufacturing' column represents the average of all manufacturing industries reported for the most recent complete year available. The Index shows the relationship between the Average and the Analyzed Industry. For example, 100 means that they are equal; 500 that the Analyzed Industry is five times the average; 50 means that the Analyzed Industry is half the national average.

★ 389 ★
Industry Statistics

State Level Data for the Newspaper Industry

The states are presented in ranked order by level of shipments.

State	Establish-ments	Shipments total ($ mil.)	% of U.S.	Per establish-ment	Employ-ment total number	% of U.S.	Per establ.	Wages ($/hour)	Cost as % of shipments	Investment per employee ($)
California	692	4,443.4	13.0	6.4	52,300	12.5	76	12.93	20.0	2,843
New York	504	3,341.4	9.8	6.6	31,600	7.6	63	18.34	21.0	5,927
Florida	329	2,189.3	6.4	6.7	22,800	5.5	69	12.51	19.7	2,162
Texas	634	1,938.4	5.7	3.1	20,800	5.0	33	10.33	24.8	1,572
Illinois	430	1,788.3	5.2	4.2	19,700	4.7	46	13.25	19.3	3,386
Pennsylvania	306	1,677.1	4.9	5.5	21,900	5.3	72	14.85	20.4	12,484
Ohio	286	1,364.0	4.0	4.8	16,600	4.0	58	12.63	20.0	7,446
Massachusetts	188	1,191.2	3.5	6.3	14,800	3.5	79	14.82	17.7	2,203
New Jersey	186	1,134.6	3.3	6.1	11,900	2.9	64	17.18	23.1	5,689
Virginia	174	1,065.6	3.1	6.1	11,300	2.7	65	10.24	22.2	1,699
Michigan	230	1,025.4	3.0	4.5	14,100	3.4	61	14.27	22.9	3,745
Washington	186	720.1	2.1	3.9	10,400	2.5	56	15.35	18.1	3,538
Georgia	233	695.6	2.0	3.0	10,200	2.4	44	10.28	20.8	4,833
North Carolina	215	671.9	2.0	3.1	9,900	2.4	46	11.27	19.7	1,737
Missouri	292	665.3	1.9	2.3	8,200	2.0	28	12.40	21.7	2,512
Wisconsin	235	624.8	1.8	2.7	10,900	2.6	46	10.80	20.5	1,541
Indiana	208	621.1	1.8	3.0	10,300	2.5	50	11.81	19.1	2,981
Minnesota	287	596.6	1.7	2.1	8,500	2.0	30	13.87	18.9	1,776
Arizona	110	592.3	1.7	5.4	6,300	1.5	57	12.10	19.0	NA
Connecticut	91	525.7	1.5	5.8	7,200	1.7	79	14.33	16.8	1,861
Tennessee	167	489.0	1.4	2.9	7,400	1.8	44	9.92	17.3	1,500
Maryland	86	486.6	1.4	5.7	4,900	1.2	57	15.92	16.7	2,673
Colorado	150	482.0	1.4	3.2	6,800	1.6	45	13.25	24.2	10,353
Iowa	241	375.9	1.1	1.6	6,100	1.5	25	10.06	20.3	1,738
Oregon	121	370.8	1.1	3.1	4,800	1.2	40	13.67	22.3	5,000
Louisiana	107	342.5	1.0	3.2	4,300	1.0	40	11.74	23.8	2,977
Oklahoma	175	337.1	1.0	1.9	4,700	1.1	27	11.46	18.7	3,128
Kentucky	156	320.9	0.9	2.1	4,400	1.1	28	10.50	19.5	2,250
South Carolina	105	309.7	0.9	2.9	4,500	1.1	43	9.63	19.4	2,511
Alabama	132	302.5	0.9	2.3	4,100	1.0	31	8.94	18.0	1,610
Hawaii	23	261.4	0.8	11.4	1,500	0.4	65	17.25	11.6	3,333
Kansas	184	220.7	0.6	1.2	4,100	1.0	22	10.17	17.1	1,171
Nevada	37	199.3	0.6	5.4	1,600	0.4	43	12.40	17.9	1,438
Nebraska	139	194.2	0.6	1.4	3,200	0.8	23	8.67	20.2	1,594
Arkansas	117	188.7	0.6	1.6	3,500	0.8	30	8.08	22.5	2,000
Mississippi	105	165.7	0.5	1.6	2,600	0.6	25	8.89	22.6	1,923
Utah	58	163.6	0.5	2.8	2,800	0.7	48	8.63	19.6	1,143
Rhode Island	22	162.4	0.5	7.4	2,300	0.6	105	17.75	23.2	NA
West Virginia	80	151.6	0.4	1.9	2,900	0.7	36	9.88	19.7	1,379
Maine	68	140.9	0.4	2.1	2,400	0.6	35	12.36	18.2	1,417
New Mexico	57	140.3	0.4	2.5	2,100	0.5	37	9.00	18.5	2,524
New Hampshire	55	118.4	0.3	2.2	2,100	0.5	38	12.50	17.3	1,238
Idaho	60	97.3	0.3	1.6	1,700	0.4	28	10.10	17.6	1,294
Montana	76	94.9	0.3	1.2	1,500	0.4	20	8.33	17.1	1,533
Delaware	18	94.8	0.3	5.3	900	0.2	50	11.40	20.0	NA

[Continued]

★ 389 ★

State Level Data for the Newspaper Industry
[Continued]

State	Establish-ments	Shipments total ($ mil.)	% of U.S.	Per establish-ment	Employ-ment total number	% of U.S.	Per establ.	Wages ($/hour)	Cost as % of shipments	Investment per employee ($)
North Dakota	68	85.2	0.2	1.3	1,500	0.4	22	9.18	17.0	1,067
South Dakota	91	81.5	0.2	0.9	1,600	0.4	18	8.11	19.6	1,500
Vermont	53	67.9	0.2	1.3	1,100	0.3	21	10.00	18.6	NA
Alaska	37	55.4	0.2	1.5	1,200	0.3	32	11.40	22.4	1,833
Wyoming	42	(D)	NA	NA	750[1]	0.2	18	NA	NA	NA
District of Columbia	33	(D)	NA	NA	3,750[1]	0.9	114	NA	NA	2,667

Source: 1997 *Manufacturing STATROM* [machine-readable data files]. MStat97. Editorial Code and Data, Inc., Detroit, Michigan, 1997. Primary source: 1992 *Economic Census*. The states are in descending order of shipments or establishments (if shipment data are missing for the majority). The symbol (D) appears when data are withheld to prevent disclosure of competitive information. States marked with (D) are sorted by number of establishments. *Notes:* NA = Not available. 1. Indicates the midpoint of a range.

★ 390 ★

Industry Statistics

Newspaper Industry: States with Most Activity

The table shows the industry by leading sectors.

State	Shipments as % of U.S.	Employment as % of U.S.	Payroll as % of U.S.	Cost of Materials as % of U.S.	Investment as % of U.S.
California	13.10	12.50	10.70	13.00	13.10
New York	9.70	7.60	7.40	9.80	9.70
Florida	6.40	5.50	5.60	6.40	6.40
Texas	5.40	5.00	5.50	5.70	5.40
Illinois	5.30	4.70	4.70	5.20	5.30
Pennsylvania	4.90	5.30	5.50	4.90	4.90
Ohio	4.00	4.00	4.50	4.00	4.00
Massachusetts	3.60	3.50	3.30	3.50	3.60
New Jersey	3.20	2.90	2.40	3.30	3.20
Virginia	3.00	2.70	2.40	3.10	3.00
Michigan	2.90	3.40	3.20	3.00	2.90
Washington	2.20	2.50	2.70	2.10	2.20
Georgia	2.00	2.40	2.30	2.00	2.00
North Carolina	2.00	2.40	2.60	2.00	2.00
Missouri	1.90	2.00	2.00	1.90	1.90
Indiana	1.80	2.50	2.70	1.80	1.80
Wisconsin	1.80	2.60	2.40	1.80	1.80
Minnesota	1.80	2.00	2.10	1.70	1.80
Arizona	1.80	1.50	1.60	1.70	1.80
Connecticut	1.60	1.70	1.30	1.50	1.60

Source: 1997 *Manufacturing STATROM* [machine-readable data files]. MStat97. Editorial Code and Data, Inc., Detroit, Michigan, 1997. Primary source: *Economic Census for 1992* and earlier years. The *Economic Census* is conducted by the Bureau of the Census, U.S. Department of Commerce, Washington, DC 20233.

★ 391 ★

Declining Newspaper Industry

From the source: "Daily newspapers are currently one of the country's most profitable industries. Not long ago, a monopoly newspaper in a medium-sized market could command a profit margin of 20 percent to 40 percent! Last year, the profit margin for the industry still averaged about 12.5 percent, almost twice the profit margin of a typical Fortune 500 company.

Ironically, the very factors that increased profits and prevented direct competition among papers—the huge infrastructure of a daily newspaper with its printing plant, its distribution network and expensive reporting staff—will lead to their demise by turning them into the monsters that cannot find enough to eat.

About 15 years ago, it became apparent that baby boomers' children were not picking up the daily newspaper-reading habit like their parents and grandparents. In fact, a recent study conducted for the American Society of Newspaper Editors found that so-called "Gen-Xers" are about a third less likely than baby boomers and far more likely to agree that reading is old-fashioned."

Source: Von Kaenel, Jeff. "Daily Dinosaurs." *Metro Times,* 1-7 January 1997, p. 11.

Growth of the Alternative Newsweeklies Market

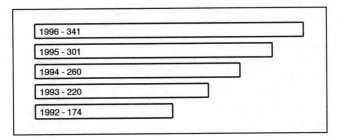

1996 - 341
1995 - 301
1994 - 260
1993 - 220
1992 - 174

While circulation is declining among daily newspapers, alternative newspapers have been experiencing healthy growth. Since 1990, trade sources report that circulation and revenue have more than doubled among the nation's more than 100 alternatives. Alternatives have become popular, in part, because of in-depth treatments of the arts and pop culture. As well, the writing is more loose and irreverent.

Year	Revenue ($ mil.)
1992	174
1993	220
1994	260
1995	301
1996	341

Source: Miller, James P. "Hip and Irreverent, Alternative Papers Grab Readers." *The Wall Street Journal,* 28 July 1997, p. B1. Primary source: Association of Alternative Newsweeklies.

Sales and Markets

Newspapers: Daily Sales, 1995

State	Sales
Arkansas	
Northwest Arkansas Times	13,500
California	
Barstow Desert Dispatch	8,000
Contra Costa Times	93,300
Antioch Ledger Dispatch	21,800

[Continued]

Newspapers: Daily Sales, 1995
[Continued]

State	Sales
Pleasanton Valley Times	37,500
Richmond West County Times	32,500
Madera Tribune	8,000
Merced Sun-Star	19,400
Los Banos Enterprise	3,000
Atwater Signal	12,000
Chowchilla News	3,000
Dos Palos Star	34,000
Gustine Standard	4,300
Livingston Chronicle	8,100
Escondido Times Advocate	40,000
Temecula Californian	12,000
Fallbrook Enterprise	7,600
Watsonville Register-Pajaronian	11,000
Connecticut	
Milford Citizen	6,500
East Haven Advertiser	4,100
Avon News	1,900
Banford Review	5,700
Bloomfield Journal	1,900
Clinton Recorder	3,900
Dolphin	10,800
Farmington News	2,000
Foothills Trader	55,700
Hamden Chronicle	8,500
Milford Reporter	7,100
Newington Town Crier	3,600
Orange/Woodbride/Bethany Bulletin	5,800
Pictorial Gazette	8,800
New Haven/Wallingford Post	4,300
Regional Standard	8,400
Regional Blanket	9,200
Rocky Hill Post	1,800
Simbury News	3,100
Shore Line Times	9,600
The Standard Times	6,600
Stratford Bard	6,100

[Continued]

★ 393 ★

Newspapers: Daily Sales, 1995
[Continued]

State	Sales
Tradewinds	48,000
West Hartford News	9,700
West Haven News	7,700
Wethersfield Post	4,200
Windsor Journal	4,500
Chariho Times	2,700
Narragansett Times	11,200
The Pendulum	3,300
The Standard Times	6,600
Florida	
Leesburg Daily Commercial	31,700
Georgia	
Carrollton Times Georgian	10,800
Douglas County Sentinel	9,300
Sevierville Mountain Press	9,900
Bowdon Bulletin	2,900
Bremen Gateway Beacon Villa Rican	2,500
Illinois	
Jacksonville Journal Courier	15,300
Sterling/Rock Falls Daily Gazette	15,000
Indiana	
New Albany Tribune	11,800
Kansas	
Leavenworth Times	8,600
Olathe Daily News	8,700
Kentucky	
Corbin Times Tribune	7,600
Richmond Register	9,000
Madisonville Messenger	10,700
Owensboro Messenger Inquirer	33,000

[Continued]

★ 393 ★

Newspapers: Daily Sales, 1995
[Continued]

State	Sales
Massachusetts	
Berkshire Eagle	32,000
Middletown Press	13,900
Bennington Banner	7,700
Brattleboro Reformer	11,220
Manchester Journal	3,000
Southbridge News	5,500
Auburn News	2,560
Blackstone Valley Tribune	4,400
Spencer New Leader	3,600
Webster Times	7,500
Minnesota	
Worthington Daily Globe	13,400
Mississippi	
Corinth Daily Corinthian	8,500
Missouri	
Fulton Sun	4,700
Mexico Ledger	9,100
Sikeston Standard Democrat	10,200
Nebraska	
Nebraska City News Press	2,700
New Jersey	
Woodbridge News Tribune	54,000
New York	
Herkimer Evening Telegram	6,900
Olean Times Herald	21,000
Oswego Palladium Times	11,000
Journal of Commerce	21,000

Source: "1995 Daily Newspaper Sales." *Editor & Publisher,* 6 January 1996, pp. 52-54.

Non-Daily Newspaper Sales, 1995

State	Sales
Alabama	
Dothan Progress	3,000
Heflin Cleburne News	2,259
Alaska	
Alaska Journal of Commerce	5,100
California	
Gonzales Tribune	800
King City Rustler	3,200
Soledad News	1,400
Healdsburg Tribune	4,400
Windsor Times	1,500
Sebastopol Times & News	4,300
Guerneville Russian River News	2,000
Colorado	
Snowmass Sun	4,200
Florida	
Florida Mariner	20,000
Georgia	
Twiggs County New Era	1,700
Illinois	
Amboy News	2,200
Indiana	
Greenwood Gazette	14,000
Iowa	
Dunlap Reporter	1,300
Lime Springs Herald	900
Staceyville Monitor Review	1,300
Kansas	
Linn County News	3,000
Yates Center News	2,000

[Continued]

★ 394 ★

Non-Daily Newspaper Sales, 1995
[Continued]

State	Sales
Kentucky	
Hickman County Gazette	2,200
Massachusetts	
Abington Rockland Mariner	2,100
Braintree Forum	3,600
Canton Journal	2,700
Cohasset Mariner	1,700
Hanover Mariner	4,000
Hingham Mariner	4,000
Holbrook Sun	1,800
Kingston Mariner	3,000
Mariner Pennysavers	51,400
Marshfield Mariner	4,000
Norwell Mariner	2,100
Pembroke Mariner	1,300
Pennysaver Publishing Of Cape Cod	164,000
Randolph Mariner	1,200
Scituate Mariner	3,700
Stoughton Journal	1,600
Weymouth News	4,100
Nantucket Beacon	6,000
Minnesota	
Freeborn County Register & Shopper	24,000
Mower County Register & Shopper	24,000
Leroy Independent	1,200
Mississippi	
Booneville Banner Independent	5,400
Missouri	
Appleton City Journal	1,800
Humansville Star Leader	1,700
Osceola Buyers Guide	2,200
Doniphan Prospect News	5,400

[Continued]

★ 394 ★

Non-Daily Newspaper Sales, 1995
[Continued]

State	Sales
Nebraska	
Red Cloud Chief	2,100
New Hampshire	
Franklin Tilton Telegram	1,660
Oklahoma	
Stillwell Democrat Journal	6,000
South Carolina	
Hartsville Messenger	6,200
Texas	
Burnet Bulletin	3,500
Marble Falls Highlander	6,100
Clay County Leader	3,150
Washington	
Cashmere Valley Record	1,500
Leavenworth Echo	2,400
Issaquah Press and Shopper	19,500
Sedro Woolley Courier Times	2,500
Skagit River Times	2,500
Vashon Beachcomber	4,400
Wisconsin	
Colfax Messenger	1,500
Enterprise Newspapers	178,000

Source: "1995 Nondaily Newspaper Sales." *Editor & Publisher,* 6 January 1996, pp. 58-60.

★ 395 ★

Sales and Markets

Tabloid Market

Circulation is shown in millions.

Tabloid	1993 (mil.)	1997 (mil.)
National Enquirer	3.1	2.5
Star	2.6	2.2
Globe	1.1	1.0
National Examiner	0.7	0.5
Weekly World News	0.6	0.4

Source: "Tabloid Tally," *Business Week,* 15 September 1997, p. 42. Primary source: Audit Bureau of Circulation and Data Company Reports.

Companies

★ 396 ★

Tabloid Leaders

Circulation is shown in millions.

Magazine	Circulation
United States[1]	
National Enquirer	2.7
Star	2.2
Globe	1.0
Britain	
The Sun	4.0
Daily Mirror	2.5
Daily Mail	2.0

Source: "Celebrities Lucrative Angle for Photographers. *Los Angeles Times,* 4 September 1997, p. A 14. Primary source: Audit Bureau of Circulation: Benn's Media; *Editor & Publisher Yearbook. Notes:* 1. U.S. tabloids published weekly; others are dailies unless otherwise indicated.

★ 397 ★
Companies

Times Mirror's Major Newspapers

Data show circulation leaders as of March 1997.

Newspaper	Daily circulation
Los Angeles Times	1,068,812
Newsday (Long Island, NY)	559,233
Baltimore Sun	326,636
Hartford (Conn.) Courant	217,759
Allentown (Pa.) Morning Call	130,102
Stamford (Conn.) Advocate	28,357
Greenwich (Conn.) Time	12,887

Source: Consoli, John. "Hands-on at Times Mirror." *Mediaweek,* 22 September 1997, p. 8. Primary source: Audit Bureau of Circulation.

Rankings

★ 398 ★

Top 10 Largest Newspapers Owned by Knight-Ridder

Knight-Ridder is the nation's second largest newspaper company.

Newspaper	Average daily paid circulation in 1996
Philadelphia Inquirer	458,000
Miami Herald	366,000
Detroit Free Press	363,000
Kansas City Star	291,000
San Jose Mercury News	287,000
Fort Worth Star-Telegram [1]	240,000
Charlotte Observer	237,000
Saint Paul Pioneer Press	208,000
Contra Costa Newspapers	237,000
Philadelphia Daily News	190,000

Source: "Knight-Ridder to Buy 4 Newspapers From Disney for $1.65 Billion," *New York Times,* 5 April 1997, p. C35. Primary source: Knight-Ridder Inc. and Associated Press. *Note:* 1. Includes Arlington Star-Telegram.

★ 399 ★

Rankings

Top 20 Daily Newspapers: Advertising in Selected Retail Categories[1]

January 1997 - Full run ROP (run of press), excluding preprints.

Newspaper	Department stores	Discount stores	Drug stores	Food stores	Furniture and accessories	Jewelry stores	Office supply stores	Sports and toys
New York Times	5,895	42	-	35	5,384	1,331	685	563
Los Angeles Times	19,343	1,246	65	3,942	5,008	141	2,541	3,916
Washington Post	14,147	1,299	153	5,182	11,308	333	1,382	1,307
New York Daily News	5,349	112	42	1,764	5,038	124	412	378
Chicago Tribune	5,336	1,398	315	821	7,837	102	1,853	1,441
Newsday	6,163	679	127	168	4,803	84	2,124	1,005
Houston Chronicle	18,265	1,441	172	1,093	15,010	393	1,101	2,532
Chicago Sun-Times	2,116	746	182	380	2,187	131	330	597
San Francisco Chronicle	10,203	814	437	-	3,554	28	2,350	866
Dallas Morning News	17,840	1,738	94	7,366	11,644	243	2,535	1,497
Boston Globe	9,784	2,029	378	1,520	3,438	303	1,081	2,361
New York Post	-	391	20	280	1,971	68	161	302
Philadelphia Inquirer	14,080	482	306	314	7,733	208	1,096	591
Newark Star-Ledger	6,096	958	158	1,134	8,148	209	1,472	817
Cleveland Plain Dealer	7,363	675	224	5,793	5,524	147	1,290	509
Phoenix Arizona Republic	10,978	742	181	1,234	12,587	190	767	1,272
San Diego Union-Tribune	14,661	626	95	3,961	7,424	317	1,305	4,412
Minneapolis/St. Paul Star Tribune	4,393	1,538	126	737	6,552	140	1,401	1,556
Detroit Free Press	3,688	324	180	216	1,501	31	1,553	668
Orange County Register	16,092	499	76	7,104	11,981	265	2,597	5,846

Source: "Top 20 Daily Newspapers Ad Inches in Selected Retail Categories." *Editor & Publisher,* 5 April 1997, p. 45. Primary source: Competitive Media Reporting. *Notes:* 1. Newspapers are listed by circulation based on Audit Bureau FAS-FAX report for the period ending September 30, 1996.

★ 400 ★

Rankings

Top 20 Daily Newspapers: Advertising in Selected Retail Categories[1]

January 1997 - Full run ROP (run of press), excluding preprints.

Newspaper	Total	Apparel and accessories	Auto supply/ repair	Books and stationery	Building materials	Computer stores	Consumer electronics
New York Times	23,158	3,162	-	1,108	38	3,305	1,610
Los Angeles Times	51,805	1,185	1,557	174	179	1,811	10,697
Washington Post	48,842	3,239	374	108	926	2,752	6,332
New York Daily News	26,238	1,393	1,671	-	400	225	9,330
Chicago Tribune	28,612	2,420	113	330	548	1,950	4,148
Newsday	28,582	1,477	548	84	566	954	9,800
Houston Chronicle	52,997	2,983	676	329	1,171	1,498	6,333

[Continued]

★ 400 ★

Top 20 Daily Newspapers: Advertising in Selected Retail Categories
[Continued]

Newspaper	Total	Apparel and accessories	Auto supply/ repair	Books and stationery	Building materials	Computer stores	Consumer electronics
Chicago Sun-Times	14,573	1,688	1,218	1	796	179	4,022
San Francisco Chronicle	22,399	506	279	270	93	1,000	1,999
Dallas Morning News	55,522	4,703	99	313	389	2,445	4,616
Boston Globe	28,973	2,059	58	744	271	1,425	3,522
New York Post	10,865	1,122	81	14	89	485	5,881
Philadelphia Inquirer	31,967	1,747	582	41	185	2,968	1,634
Newark Star-Ledger	35,523	2,753	534	30	284	1,055	11,875
Cleveland Plain Dealer	26,011	1,441	331	177	332	189	2,016
Phoenix Arizona Republic	34,632	1,112	522	-	774	583	3,690
San Diego Union-Tribune	48,134	650	789	158	554	3,116	10,066
Minneapolis/St. Paul Star Tribune	23,843	1,885	221	140	612	1,009	3,533
Detroit Free Press	15,872	841	300	-	804	323	5,443
Orange County Register	63,911	1,094	4,255	72	1,072	1,806	11,152

Source: "Top 20 Daily Newspapers Ad Inches in Selected Retail Categories." *Editor & Publisher,* 5 April 1997, p. 45. Primary source: Competitive Media Reporting. *Notes:* 1. Newspapers are listed by circulation based on Audit Bureau FAS-FAX report for the period ending September 30, 1996.

★ 401 ★
Rankings

Top 20 Daily Newspapers, by Selected National Categories[1]

January 1997 - Full run ROP (run of press), excluding preprints.

Newspaper	Total	Airlines	Auto dealer associates	Factory automotive	Banks	Computers and software	Credit Cards
New York Times	42,699	2,280	333	971	2,323	1,750	1,009
Los Angeles Times	50,338	1,553	4,663	963	1,228	792	516
Washington Post	23,587	1,634	2,525	319	3,819	609	528
New York Daily News	15,072	1,029	231	504	1,128	252	-
Chicago Tribune	23,831	1,895	2,737	1,175	2,579	864	504
Newsday	17,970	713	867	532	4,191	327	-
Houston Chronicle	17,056	1,947	1,323	129	1,015	272	258
Chicago Sun-Times	13,984	876	1,635	770	1,656	140	-
San Francisco Chronicle	16,122	1,089	642	230	644	840	516
Dallas Morning News	18,159	972	1,047	126	1,514	504	507
Boston Globe	23,604	1,299	451	523	1,418	666	693
New York Post	14,232	816	229	730	1,497	-	-
Philadelphia Inquirer	16,994	1,512	303	973	3,285	549	252
Newark Star-Ledger	14,582	1,771	266	959	3,444	31	-
Cleveland Plain Dealer	10,163	1,040	559	179	1,861	-	-
Phoenix Arizona Republic	15,338	945	3,237	129	581	323	-

[Continued]

★ 401 ★

Top 20 Daily Newspapers, by Selected National Categories
[Continued]

Newspaper	Total	Airlines	Auto dealer associates	Factory automotive	Banks	Computers and software	Credit Cards
San Diego Union Tribune	18,091	261	2,161	29	813	793	258
Minneapolis/St. Paul Star Tribune	11,657	679	405	126	1,020	661	-
Detroit Free Press	9,001	316	1,217	373	338	401	-
Orange County Register	16,746	486	3,216	297	826	604	-

Source: "Top 20 Daily Newspapers Ad Inches in Selected National Categories." *Editor & Publisher,* 5 April 1997, p. 44. Primary source: Competitive Media Reporting. *Notes:* 1. Newspapers are listed by circulation based on Audit Bureau FAS-FAX report for the period ending September 30, 1996.

★ 402 ★

Rankings

Top 20 Daily Newspapers, by Selected National Categories[1]

January 1997 - Full run ROP (run of press), excluding preprints.

Newspaper	Food and household	Hotels and resorts	Insurance	Investments	Motion pictures	Travel and tourism	Utilities and comms.
New York Times	412	994	330	2,977	22,307	535	6,478
Los Angeles Times	541	624	766	935	32,508	261	4,988
Washington Post	277	769	210	922	6,492	508	4,975
New York Daily News	-	544	525	168	7,363	294	3,034
Chicago Tribune	633	845	158	709	7,146	331	4,255
Newsday	126	83	547	404	6,566	692	2,922
Houston Chronicle	36	4	919	144	5,364	31	5,614
Chicago Sun-Times	338	486	243	42	5,133	239	2,426
San Francisco Chronicle	385	812	674	524	7,235	318	2,213
Dallas Morning News	224	1,215	316	622	5,353	430	5,329
Boston Globe	463	2,654	1,689	999	6,294	701	5,754
New York Post	-	802	458	335	5,468	1,767	2,130
Philadelphia Inquirer	374	504	444	38	5,998	38	2,724
Newark Star-Ledger	153	295	1,073	256	3,342	171	2,821
Cleveland Plain Dealer	303	153	401	129	3,074	55	2,409
Phoenix Arizona Republic	146	255	1,600	225	4,198	360	3,339
San Diego Union Tribune	16	377	528	563	5,395	184	6,713
Minneapolis/St. Paul Star Tribune	419	879	-	901	4,327	466	1,774
Detroit Free Press	206	48	-	68	4,328	96	1,610
Orange County Register	17	158	690	-	6,412	205	3,835

Source: "Top 20 Daily Newspapers Ad Inches in Selected National Categories." *Editor & Publisher,* 5 April 1997, p. 44. Primary source: Competitive Media Reporting. *Notes:* 1. Newspapers are listed by circulation based on Audit Bureau FAS-FAX report for the period ending September 30, 1996.

Rankings

Top 20 Sunday Newspapers: Advertising in Selected Retail Categories[1]

January 1997 - Full run ROP (run of press), excluding preprints.

Newspaper	Department stores	Discount stores	Drug stores	Food stores	Furniture and accessories	Jewelry stores	Office supply stores	Sports and toys
New York Times	3,433	6	-	-	2,089	415	54	51
Los Angeles Times	3,327	113	-	1,035	948	56	482	495
Washington Post	2,800	481	528	3,253	1,746	135	100	185
Chicago Tribune	1,820	162	257	2	1,884	29	715	240
New York Daily News	806	35	458	2,604	2,170	-	-	21
Philadelphia Inquirer	2,509	163	756	531	3,453	34	194	131
Detroit News & Free Press	805	10	40	-	782	-	440	172
Dallas Morning News	5,325	120	-	8,735	2,781	21	276	3,110
Boston Globe	3,067	118	378	21	3,420	248	335	856
Houston Chronicle	5,294	244	2	1,907	5,167	46	214	3,576
Atlanta Journal	2,504	2,921	278	1,111	2,062	2	212	162
Minneapolis/St. Paul Star-Tribune	1,105	1,068	378	1,883	1,072	-	181	291
Newsday	1,176	337	-	-	3,083	84	394	280
San Francisco Examiner & Chronicle	3,286	166	-	19	1,488	41	255	140
Newark Star-Ledger	1,476	292	383	2,646	1,847	-	407	226
Phoenix Arizona Republic	2,965	239	55	1,017	417	194	122	1,149
St. Louis Post-Dispatch	2,491	156	-	608	706	-	330	52
Cleveland Plain Dealer	1,661	215	756	756	384	12	638	258
Seattle Times/Post-Intelligencer	1,145	235	135	135	609	28	237	105
Baltimore Sun	1,706	936	756	3,019	1,580	35	94	299

Source: "Top 20 Sunday Newspapers Ad Inches in Selected Retail Categories." *Editor & Publisher,* 5 April 1997, p. 45. *Notes:* 1. Newspapers are listed by circulation based on Audit Bureau FAS-FAX report for the period ending September 30, 1996.

Rankings

Top 20 Sunday Newspapers: Advertising in Selected Retail Categories[1]

January 1997 - Full run ROP (run of press), excluding preprints.

Newspaper	Total	Apparel and accessories	Auto supply/ repair	Books and stationery	Building materials	Computer stores	Consumer electronics
New York Times	8,237	567	-	254	6	522	840
Los Angeles Times	9,282	389	863	390	100	237	847
Washington Post	11,654	780	882	316	72	252	124
Chicago Tribune	7,594	329	780	489	132	485	270
New York Daily News	10,782	134	674	-	-	588	3,292
Philadelphia Inquirer	13,491	304	979	74	123	315	3,925
Detroit News & Free Press	4,329	68	132	-	456	94	1,230
Dallas Morning News	27,234	696	987	98	51	693	4,341
Boston Globe	11,119	803	230	102	634	425	482
Houston Chronicle	22,628	922	861	260	437	681	3,017
Atlanta Journal	11,908	303	954	62	30	334	973
Minneapolis/St. Paul Star-Tribune	6,749	164	308	38	98	99	64

[Continued]

★ 404 ★

Top 20 Sunday Newspapers: Advertising in Selected Retail Categories
[Continued]

Newspaper	Total	Apparel and accessories	Auto supply/ repair	Books and stationery	Building materials	Computer stores	Consumer electronics
Newsday	8,539	329	14	-	206	198	2,438
San Francisco Examiner & Chronicle	6,891	273	448	322	18	139	296
Newark Star-Ledger	11,761	642	483	44	99	1,025	2,191
Phoenix Arizona Republic	8,107	59	637	-	92	599	562
St. Louis Post-Dispatch	5,046	25	369	37	182	90	-
Cleveland Plain Dealer	6,116	209	540	-	545	-	142
Seattle Times/Post-Intelligencer	5,457	67	348	133	108	576	1,596
Baltimore Sun	13,793	118	1,341	42	21	243	3,603

Source: "Top 20 Sunday Newspapers Ad Inches in Selected Retail Categories." Editor & Publisher, 5 April 1997, p. 45. Primary source: Competitve Media Reporting Notes: 1. Newspapers are listed by circulation based on Audit Bureau FAS-FAX report for the period ending September 30, 1996.

★ 405 ★

Rankings

Top 20 Sunday Newspapers, by Selected National Categories[1]

January 1997 - Full run ROP (run of press), excluding preprints.

Newspaper	Food and household	Hotels and resorts	Insurance	Investments	Media pictures	Travel and tourism	Utilities and comms.
New York Times	110	4,524	34	2,391	7,922	7,607	1,463
Los Angeles Times	185	3,647	-	454	7,005	3,246	1,544
Washington Post	-	1,103	132	110	1,720	2,582	815
Chicago Tribune	-	2,140	252	340	1,874	4,609	2,076
New York Daily News	-	1,176	-	168	1,991	1,601	1,026
Philadelphia Inquirer	122	1,118	274	183	1,552	3,014	1,002
Detroit News & Free Press	-	356	-	11	1,185	2,215	851
Dallas Morning News	-	1,338	287	234	1,450	3,095	2,330
Boston Globe	13	2,870	450	366	1,425	4,614	2,146
Houston Chronicle	-	395	120	271	1,119	2,010	1,812
Atlanta Journal Constitution	-	475	128	422	1,389	3,412	717
Minneapolis/St. Paul Star Tribune	32	1,386	253	380	1,080	3,093	892
Newsday	-	1,380	253	-	1,857	2,831	535
San Francisco Examiner & Chronicle	63	2,790	63	594	1,547	2,983	858
Newark Star-Ledger	24	2,327	3	594	878	2,957	1,062
Phoenix Arizona Republic	-	1,470	1,448	304	1,072	1,872	1,870
St. Louis Post-Dispatch	-	265	-	50	990	1,428	1,012
Cleveland Plain Dealer	89	362	514	18	834	2,757	1,112
Seattle Times/Post-Intelligencer	-	859	65	184	1,439	3,749	1,277
Baltimore Sun	15	292	464	110	839	1,440	614

Source: "Top 2o Sunday Newspapers Ad Inches in Selected National Categories." Editor & Publisher, 5 April 1997, p. 44. Primary source: Competitive Media Reporting. Notes: 1. Newspapers are listed by circulation based on Audit Bureau FAS-FAX report for the period ending September 30, 1996.

★ 406 ★

Rankings

Top 20 Sunday Newspapers, by Selected National Categories[1]

January 1997 - Full run ROP (run of press), excluding preprints.

Newspaper	Total	Airlines	Auto dealer associates	Factory automotive	Banks	Computers and software	Credit Cards
New York Times	31,135	2,013	1,764	1,377	990	-	940
Los Angeles Times	20,354	846	2,396	323	677	-	31
Washington Post	8,579	755	218	-	1,078	-	66
Chicago Tribune	14,086	942	678	840	335	-	-
New York Daily News	6,893	364	84	84	378	21	-
Philadelphia Inquirer	11,743	653	878	361	2,523	-	63
Detroit News & Free Press	7,283	672	1,561	199	201	-	32
Dallas Morning News	10,276	653	229	-	610	50	-
Boston Globe	14,439	528	470	98	1,316	17	126
Houston Chronicle	6,780	463	-	-	551	25	14
Atlanta Journal Constitution	7,707	426	-	310	411	-	17
Minneapolis/St. Paul Star Tribune	8,580	677	32	-	755	-	-
Newsday	8,300	672	56	84	582	32	18
San Francisco Examiner & Chronicle	9,689	404	65	-	290	32	-
Newark Star-Ledger	11,894	716	202	225	2,889	-	15
Phoenix Arizona Republic	9,447	447	339	44	708	73	-
St. Louis Post-Dispatch	5,173	307	509	65	547	-	-
Cleveland Plain Dealer	7,387	500	243	-	958	-	-
Seattle Times/Post-Intelligencer	8,917	816	172	-	324	32	-
Baltimore Sun	5,417	668	299	-	676	-	-

Source: "Top 20 Sunday Newspapers Ad Inches in Selected National Categories." *Editor & Publisher,* 5 April 1997, p. 44. Primary source: Competitive Media Reporting. *Notes:* 1. Newspapers are listed by circulation based on Audit Bureau FAS-FAX report for the period ending September 30, 1996.

★ 407 ★

Rankings

Top National Newspaper Advertisers, 1996

Advertisers are ranked by national newspaper advertising in millions of dollars.

Company	1995	1996	% Change
General Motors Corp.	28.0	29.1	4.0
Dow Jones & Co.	23.0	27.4	18.9
Fidelity Investment Co.	20.5	27.2	32.3
IBM Corp.	32.7	21.3	-35.0
American Express Co.	9.7	21.2	118.0
Ford Motor Co.	21.9	21.1	-4.0

[Continued]

★ 407 ★

Top National Newspaper Advertisers, 1996
[Continued]

Company	1995	1996	% Change
Charles Schwab Corp.	14.0	20.2	43.8
Circuit City Stores	0.5	18.4	3,299.1
Toyota Motor Corp.	16.8	16.9	0.8
Chrysler Corp.	13.8	16.0	16.2
Merrill Lynch & Co.	9.9	15.1	53.5
U.S. Government	9.3	14.8	59.0
AT&T Corp.	14.4	13.5	-5.8
Compaq Computer Corp.	6.2	12.7	106.2
Washington Mint	13.1	11.9	-8.6
Microsoft Corp.	9.2	11.0	18.8
Canon	4.4	10.6	143.3
Travelers Group	4.0	9.7	143.8
America West Airlines	4.6	9.5	105.8
Time Warner	4.9	9.3	89.7
Northwest Airlines Corp.	8.1	9.1	12.1
Nissan Motor Co.	5.5	8.6	55.7
ITT Corp.	8.4	8.2	-3.0
HFS	6.7	8.0	19.8
Sprint Corp.	12.4	8.0	-35.1

Source: "100 Leading National Advertisers." *Advertising Age,* 29 September 1997, p. S46. Primary source: Competitive Media Reporting.

★ 408 ★

Rankings

Top Newspaper Advertisers, 1996

Advertisers are ranked by local newspaper advertising in millions of dollars.

Company	1995	1996	% Change
Federated Department Stores	340.1	339.5	-0.2
May Department Stores Co.	296.6	326.1	9.9
Circuit City Stores	206.2	250.3	21.4
Sears, Roebuck & Co.	185.4	193.1	4.1
Dayton Hudson Corp.	154.9	158.8	2.5
Dillard Department Stores	108.3	126.9	17.2
Time Warner	231.6	124.0	-46.5
Walt Disney Co.	219.9	118.7	-46.0
J.C. Penney Co.	91.8	105.2	14.6
Kmart Corp.	113.6	97.9	-13.8
AT&T Corp.	75.8	95.1	25.6

[Continued]

★ 408 ★

Top Newspaper Advertisers, 1996
[Continued]

Company	1995	1996	% Change
Tandy Corp.	65.6	82.3	25.4
General Motors Corp.	60.0	74.1	23.5
The Wiz	62.5	68.1	8.9
Montgomery Ward & Co.	72.6	67.1	-7.5
Viacom	115.9	64.0	-44.8
Bell Atlantic Corp.	39.3	63.5	61.7
Best Buy Co.	31.0	56.7	82.5
Sony Corp.	0.0	55.0	NA
Ford Motor Co.	60.5	52.4	-13.5
Mazda Motor Corp.	60.7	46.2	-23.9
Walgreen Co.	32.6	40.8	25.1
Office Depot	24.2	39.1	61.4
Lib/Go Travel	31.0	38.5	24.4
Koninklijke Ahold	37.8	38.4	1.6

Source: "100 Leading National Advertisers." *Advertising Age,* 29 September 1997, p. S46. Primary source: Competitive Media Reporting.

★ 409 ★

Rankings

Top Newspapers by Circulation, 1996

Figures are for the six months ended September 30, 1996, compared with the same period last year. Rank is based on Monday-Friday circulation, except where noted. When papers report separate circulations for some weekdays, the number used is the weighted average. In some cases, Sunday papers have different names.

Newspaper	Circulation	Change	Sunday circulation	Change
The Wall Street Journal	1,783,532	1.2	None	-
USA Today[1]	1,591,629	4.5	2,008,940	3.8
The New York Times	1,071,120	-1.0	1,652,800	-0.9
Los Angeles Times	1,029,073	2.2	1,349,889	-4.3
The Washington Post	789,198	-0.6	1,122,276	-0.5
Daily News	734,277	0.5	888,759	-9.2
Chicago Tribune	680,535	-0.6	1,046,777	-3.4
Newsday[4]	564,754	1.5	656,895	1.0
Houston Chronicle[2]	545,348	0.7	748,082	0.6
The Dallas Morning News[3]	502,893	-4.1	785,934	-1.8
Chicago Sun-Times	496,030	1.6	442,905	-4.3
San Francisco Chronicle	486,977	-0.5	633,513	-2.0

[Continued]

★ 409 ★

Top Newspapers by Circulation, 1996
[Continued]

Newspaper	Circulation	Change	Sunday circulation	Change
The Boston Globe	471,024	-5.6	763,135	-3.8
New York Post[4]	429,642	3.9	291,497	NA
The Philadelphia Inquirer	427,175	-9.0	876,669	-3.3
The (Newark, N.J.) Star-Ledger	405,869	-7.0	605,627	-6.3
Cleveland Plain Dealer[2]	386,256	-2.7	518,196	-2.9
Arizona Republic	382,122	4.4	553,192	-1.1
Minneapolis Star Tribune[5]	375,278	-3.7	678,001	1.5
San Diego Union-Tribune[1]	372,081	-2.0	450,984	-0.9
Detroit Free Press[6]	363,385	N/A	789,666	NA
Orange County Register[2]	353,812	1.1	415,553	0.8
The Miami Herald[2]	344,363	-6.3	466,024	-4.4
Portland Oregonian	338,586	1.5	439,704	-0.3
The Denver Post[2]	334,436	10.3	461,837	1.2

Source: "National Papers Record Healthy Circulation Gains." *Advertising Age,* 11 November 1996, p. 55. Primary source: Audit Bureau of Circulations. *Notes:* 1. USA Today's Friday circulation is listed in Sunday column. 2. Rank based on Monday-Saturday circulation. 3. Figures adjusted by Ad Age to indicate weekday average circulation. 4. Change in publishing plan and/or frequency. 5. Figures adjusted by Ad Age to indicate comparable Monday-Saturday figures for 1996 compared to 1995. 6. Detroit Free Press did not report numbers for year-ago period.

★ 410 ★

Rankings

Top Publications Covering the U.S. Congress

Title	Circulation
The Hill	21,000
Roll Call	17,505
Congressional Quarterly	11,000
National Journal	6,200

Source: Henneberger, Melinda. "Seeing Politics, and Mirrors, in the Coverage of Capitol Hill." *The New York Times,* 6 October 1997, p. C1. Primary source: The magazines and *Ulrich's International Periodicals Directory.*

Circulation

★ 411 ★

Los Angeles County: Daily Newspaper Circulation

Figures are for the six months ended March 31, 1997.

Paper	Period	1996	1997
L.A. Times	M-F	1,021,121	1,068,812
L.A. Times	Sun.	1,391,074	1,361,988
Investor's Business Daily	M-F	210,942	228,039
Daily News	M-F	204,220	204,493
Daily News	Sun.	217,652	215,881
San Gabriel Valley Group	M-Sat.	119,102	119,460
San Gabriel Valley Group	Sun.	119,354	120,137
Copley L.A.	M-Sat.	117,151	116,451
Copley L.A.	Sun.	112,465	111,376
Press-Telegram	M-F	107,255	109,515
Press-Telegram	Sun.	125,577	124,920
La Opinion	M-F	101,891	103,048
La Opinion	Sun.	61,967	62,099
Hollywood Reporter	M, W, Th, F	24,103	24,936
Hollywood Reporter	Tues.	34,770	36,205

Source: Turner, Dan. "L.A. Times Leads U.S. Papers in Readership Growth." *Los Angeles Business Journal,* 13 May 1997, p. 17. Primary source: Audit Bureau of Circulation.

★ 412 ★

Circulation

Newspaper Circulation in Selected Countries, 1994

Country	Circulation (per 1,000 people)
Hong Kong	817
Norway	607
Czech Republic	582
Russia	580
Japan	576
Iceland	517
Finland	511
Sweden	510

[Continued]

★ 412 ★

Newspaper Circulation in Selected Countries, 1994
[Continued]

Country	Circulation (per 1,000 people)
Chile	455
South Korea	412
Kuwait	343
Singapore	330
New Zealand	305
Australia	263
Israel	242
North Korea	221
Malaysia	117
Mongolia	91
Brunei	75
Thailand	73

Source: "Vital Signs: News Junkies." *Asiaweek*, 16 August 1996, p. 10. Primary source: World Bank.

Reader Profiles

★ 413 ★

Newspapers: A Profile of Suburban Readers

Figures are based on a survey of 1,300 phone interviews. Data was then projected to a 14 market adult population of 5,821,000.

- Average household income exceeds $76,000.

- Median home value is $141,000.

- 39 percent of the population is college educated.

- 27 percent are white collar workers.

- 71 percent of households are owner occupied.

- 53 percent have children under the age of 18 living at home.

Source: "Results Exceed Expectations." *Mediaweek*, 20 October 1997, p. 5. Primary source: Simmons Market Research.

★ 414 ★

Reader Profiles

Newspapers: Who Reads and Why

Papers seek more personal connection with readers.

Segment	Readers (%)
Adults who read newspapers in 1990.	62
Adults who read newspapers in 1996.	59
Women who read newspapers.	55
Men who read newspapers.	62
Persons age 18-24 who read newspapers.	45
Persons age 55-64 who read newspapers.	70
Reasons readers buy single-copy Sunday paper.	
Advertising	46
News and features	32
Other	22

Source: "Rethinking the News." *New York Times*, 19 May 1997, p. C1. Primary source: 1996 Scarborough Report Top 50 DMA Markets, Simmons Market Research Bureau, Minnesota Opinion Research Inc. (MOR) and Gollin Research, as reported in Single-Copy.

Foreign Markets

★ 415 ★

Australia: Sunday Newspaper Circulation, 1996

Newspaper	Circulation
The Sunday Telegraph	701,651
The Sunday Mail (Qld)	581,000
The Sun-Herald	548,393
The Sunday Herald Sun	506,082
The Sunday Times (WA)	347,961
Sunday Mail (SA)	337,615
The Sunday Age	200,000
The Sunday Tasmanian	53,705
The Canberra Times	39,597
The Sun Territorian (NT)	25,117

Source: Hornery, Andrew. "Papers Power Ahead on Continued Growth." *Sydney Morning Herald,* 7 February 1997, p. 29.

★ 416 ★

Foreign Markets

Germany: Top Weeklies

Stern - 1,231	
Der Spiegel - 1,034	
Focus - 802	
Die Zeit - 469	
	Die Woche - 119

Data show circulation.

Title	Circulation (000)
Stern	1,231
Der Spiegel	1,034
Focus	802
Die Zeit	469
Die Woche	119

Source: "Germany's Press: Through a Glass Sharply." *The Economist,* 11 January 1997, p. 47. Primary source: IVW.

★ 417 ★

Foreign Markets

Indonesia: Daily Newspaper Readers

Monthly household spending	Readership (%)
Over $382	83
$255-382	75
$170-254	59
$128-169	51
$85-127	41
$64-84	29
Below $64	16

Source: "Indicators." *Far Eastern Economic Review,* 21 November 1996, p. 15. Primary source: AC Nielsen and SRG.

★ 418 ★
Foreign Markets

Ireland: Popular Newspapers Among Business People

Figures shown are based on a survey of 700 business people on both sides of the border who were asked: "What publications is it important for you to read in your job?" The businesses covered were industrial and commercial enterprises with 250 or more employees, as well as other leading companies, in terms of turnover, employing 150 people or more. Data show average issue readership.

Newspaper	Republic %	North %	Combined %
Dailies			
The Irish Times	83	19	65
Irish Independent	56	5	42
Financial Times	33	25	31
Belfast Telegraph	1	80	23
The Examiner	14	0	10
News Letter (London)	0	36	10
The Times (London)	7	17	9
Daily Telegraph	4	19	8
Daily Mail	3	21	8
Irish News	2	13	5
Daily Express	1	11	4
The Guardian	3	1	2
Independent (London)	1	2	1
Weeklies			
Business This Week (The Irish Times)	71	14	55
Sunday Independent	64	6	48
Sunday Times	45	44	45
Business & Finance	55	12	43
Sunday Business Post	51	9	39
Sunday Tribune	49	7	37
Business Supplement (Irish Independent)	47	5	35
Business Telegraph (Belfast Telegraph)	1	71	21
The Economist	16	11	15
Time	12	10	10

Source: "Over 80% of Top Business People Read Irish Times" *Irish Times,* 15 September 1997, p. 3. Primary source: *Irish Business Readership Survey,* 1997.

★ 419 ★

Foreign Markets

Latin America: Top Newspapers

Newspapers	Country	Circulation	
		Mon.-Sat.	Sunday
Clarin	Argentina	624,000	1,200,000
Folha de S. Paulo	Brazil	490,000	1,150,000
O Globo	Brazil	465,000	1,050,000
O Estado de Sao Paulo	Brazil	355,000	700,000
El Tiempo	Colombia	257,771	409,885
La Nacion	Argentina	240,000	310,000
La Tercera	Chile	180,000	220,000
El Nacional	Venezuela	170,000	220,000
El Espectador	Colombia	157,959	205,810
El Universo	Ecuador	148,065	230,000

Source: "Extra!! Extra!!" *Latin Trade* (January 1997), p. 12.

★ 420 ★

Foreign Markets

Leading Newspaper Reading Countries

The table shows the daily newspaper circulation in leading countries. Circulation has been calculated with morning and evening editions as one subscription. Figures are per capita per 1,000 people.

Country	Circulation	Per capita (000)
Japan	71,690,000	377
U.S.	60,164,000	296
Russia	57,367,000	387
China	58,520,000	43
India	27,500,000	31
Germany	25,952,000	323
U.K.	22,100,000	383
Rep. of Korea	18,000,000	412
France	11,695,000	205
Mexico	10,231,000	116

Source: Sakuya, Fujiwara. "Fear and Favor in the Japanese Print Media." *Look Japan* (May 1997), p. 35. Primary source: *Unesco Statistical Yearbook*.

★ 421 ★

Foreign Markets

Newspaper Circulation by Country, 1996

Country	(mil.)
Germany	25.2
Great Britain	19.3
Italy	6.0
France	8.4
Netherlands	4.8
Spain	4.2
Sweden	3.9

Source: "Turning Off the Presses." *The Economist,* 11 October 1997, p. 74. Primary source: *World Press Trends, 1997.*

★ 422 ★

Foreign Markets

Newspaper Reading in Canada

Data show the amount of time devoted to newspaper reading. Figures refer to respondents 18 years and older.

[In minutes]

Location	Weekday time spent reading	Weekend time spent reading
National	46	86
British Columbia	45	66
Prairies	44	84
Ontario	46	88
Quebec	47	98
Atlantic	44	63

Source: Primary source: *NADbank-Marketing Magazine supplement,* 14 October 1996, p. 4.

★ 423 ★

Foreign Markets

Popular Newspapers in Russia

Data show the most frequently read newspapers in Russia. Figures are shown based on a survey of 4,000 adults from a survey conducted June-December 1996. The table includes the circulation claimed by each newspaper.

Newspaper	Percentage (%)	Circulation (mil.)
Argumenty i Fakty	32	3.4
Komsomolskaya Pravda	14	1.4
Moskovsky Komsomolyets	7	0.9
Trud	6	1.4
Izvestia	5	0.6
Rossiskaya Gazyeta	4	0.5
Kommersant	2	0.1
Pravda 5	1	0.3
Sevodnya	1	0.1
None	21	NA

Source: "All the News That Fits." *The Economist,* 15 February 1997, p. 50. Primary source: Russian media reports and Russian Market Research Company.

★ 424 ★

Foreign Markets

Quebec: Widely Read Newspapers

The table shows the most widely read newspapers in Quebec, based on a survey of 1,005 Quebecois.

Newspapers	Percentage (%)
Le Journal de Montreal	33.8
La Presse	21.0
The Gazette	13.5
Le Journal de Quebec	11.1
Le Soleil	7.8
Le Devoir	2.8
Globe and Mail	0.2

Source: Marketing Magazine, 6 February 1995, p. 19. Primary source: Le Groupe Leger & Leger Inc.

★ 425 ★

Foreign Markets

Quebec's Top Newspapers

Quebecois read mostly French dailies: 11 of the 13 dailies published in Quebec are French, and these account for 85% of Quebec dailies. Of those listed, only *The Gazette* is in English. Circulation is shown in thousands.

Dailies	Circulation (000)
Le Journal de Montreal	278.8
La Presse	176.1
The Gazette	148.0
Le Journal de Quebec	99.7
Le Soleil	91.7
Le Devoir	30.5

Source: "Welcome to Media Paradise!" *Marketing in Quebec,* Special Supplement, p. 15. Primary source: NAD bank.

★ 426 ★

Foreign Markets

South Africa: Newspapers with the Fastest Growing Circulations, 1986-1996

Newspaper	1986	1996
Business Day	27,998	38,146
The Citizen	110,746	138,071
Daily Dispatch	32,707	39,147
D.F. Advertiser	7,194	7,368
E.P. Herald	28,051	31,629
Sowetan	113,675	211,688
Beeld	92,503	118,220
Burger	71,584	97,630
Volksblad	24,048	28,210
Mail & Guardian	16,013	30,745
Rapport	393,922	398,852
City Press	162,084	271,228
Ilanga	112,480	119,657

Source: "Newspaper Circulations: The Winners." *Mail & Guardian,* 24 January 1997, p. B7. Primary source: Audit Bureau of Circulation.

★ 427 ★
Foreign Markets

South Africa's Newspaper Market

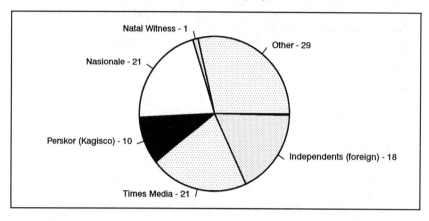

Data show who controls the newspaper market. Distribution is shown in percent.

Company	Share
Nasionale	21
Times Media	21
Independents (foreign)	18
Perskor (Kagisco)	10
Natal Witness	1
Other	29

Source: Warman, Janice. "Journalists Cry Freedom Again in South Africa," *The Observer,* 16 February 1997, p. 7.

Chapter 10
THE PRINTING INDUSTRY

Publishing, like many other industries, is a multi-tiered activity. The Printing Industry, profiled in this chapter, is the most important second tier, supporting the primary publishers. The next chapter, *Suppliers of the Industry*, provides additional data on a third tier. Topics covered here include *Markets*, *Companies*, *Employment*, *Book Printing*, *Business Forms* (which is actually a primary industry), *Commercial Printing*, *Digital Printing*, *Typesetting*, *Capital Expenditures*, *Mergers and Acquisitions*, *Print-on-Demand*, and *Foreign Markets*.

★ 428 ★

In-Plants: Frequently Printed Materials

Data show the items produced by in-plants, based on a survey of 66 respondents.

Product	% of respondents
Newsletters	95
Brochures	82
Business forms	82
Manuals	82
Reports	74
Stationery	74
Directories	72
Envelopes	69
Tags/labels	67
Pamphlets	66
Posters	61
Direct mail pieces	56
Price books	52
Proposals	48
Business cards	44
Folders	39
Calendars	36
Catalogs	34
Point of purchase	33
Packaging	15
Annual reports	13
Engineering drawings	8
Magazines	8

Source: "Making the Best Look Better." *In-Plant Graphics,* (January 1996), p. 13.

★ 429 ★

Markets

Markets with the Greatest Print Potential in 1997

Category	Size ($ bil.)	Growth (%)	% to printing	Print potential ($ bil.)
Computer software	89	14.3	10.4	9.3
Health care services	1,300	0.0	0.6	7.8
Motor vehicles	1,155	-2.8	0.6	6.9
Beverages	139	17.8	4.9	6.8
Publishing	52	15.5	13.1	6.8
Home improvements	260	14.0	2.2	5.7
Telecommunications equipment/services	415	18.3	1.4	5.7
Packaged foods	448	12.2	0.1	5.4
Medical products/pharmaceuticals	90	15.4	6.0	5.4
Financial services	835	11.5	0.5	4.1
Fashion	188	7.5	1.9	3.7
Leisure-activity products	96	21.4	3.1	3.0
Consumer electronics	578	20.5	0.5	2.9
Travel/hospitality	546	4.0	0.5	2.7
Amusements	80	35.8	2.4	1.9
Recorded entertainment	36	16.1	5.3	1.9
Restaurants, clubs	345	8.5	0.5	1.9
Higher education	38	21.0	4.2	1.6
Television/radio	41	4.0	3.7	1.5
Chemicals/petroleum	555	19.3	0.1	1.5
Cosmetics/toiletries	50	21.8	2.2	1.1
Real estate	501	2.2	0.5	1.1
Discount retailing	268	9.1	0.45	1.0
Religion/charity	178	14.0	0.1	1.0
Federal/state government	NA	10.6	0.1	1.0

Source: "The Hot Markets for 1997." *American Printer* (December 1996), p. 35. Primary source: PB/BA Acquisitions Corporation.

★ 430 ★

Markets

Printing Industry by Segment

Sales are shown in billions of dollars.

Segment	($ bil.)
Commercial printing	42.8
Package printing	17.6
Prepress services	6.9
Business forms printing	5.9
Book printing	5.2
Quick printing	4.4
Other specialty	5.4

Source: "Sizing Up the U.S. Printing Industry." *Graphic Arts Monthly* (September 1997), p. 87. Primary source: Printing Industries of America.

★ 431 ★

Markets

Printing Industry: Value of Shipments by State

Data show shipments in millions of dollars for 1996.

State	Shipments ($ mil.)	Rank
Alabama	973.2	32
Alaska	165.2	50
Arizona	1,412.7	27
Arkansas	1,261.7	28
California	11,516.8	1
Colorado	1,922.1	24
Connecticut	2,509.1	18
Delaware	251.9	47
District of Columbia	277.3	44
Florida	3,822.5	13
Georgia	3,415.0	14
Hawaii	254.0	46
Idaho	514.6	40
Illinois	9,670.0	3
Indiana	4,315.9	12
Iowa	2,115.7	23
Kansas	1,920.2	25
Kentucky	2,316.4	21
Louisiana	1,261.3	29

[Continued]

★ 431 ★

Printing Industry: Value of Shipments by State
[Continued]

State	Shipments ($ mil.)	Rank
Maine	901.8	33
Maryland	2,434.3	20
Massachusetts	4,956.1	9
Michigan	4,331.5	11
Minnesota	4,627.7	10
Mississippi	696.3	37
Missouri	2,473.9	19
Montana	286.5	43
Nebraska	1,025.2	31
Nevada	475.5	41
New Hampshire	870.6	34
New Jersey	6,371.0	5
New Mexico	290.6	42
New York	10,067.7	2
North Carolina	3,158.2	15
North Dakota	188.3	49
Ohio	6,185.7	6
Oklahoma	1,098.9	30
Oregon	1,649.8	26
Pennsylvania	7,652.6	4
Rhode Island	651.6	38
South Carolina	847.4	36
South Dakota	240.8	48
Tennessee	2,875.9	16
Texas	6,025.3	7
Utah	870.0	35
Vermont	539.8	39
Virginia	2,563.1	17
Washington	2,240.4	22
West Virginia	276.5	45
Wisconsin	5,263.1	8
Wyoming	111.4	51
Total	132,142.7	

Source: "Sizing Up the U.S. Printing Industry." *Graphic Arts Monthly* (September 1997), p. 89. Primary source: Printing Industries of America.

★ 432 ★

Markets

Printing Market by Type of Firm

Data show the printing/imaging industry by type of printer.

Segment	No. of firms
Commercial printing	25,035
Quick printing	7,385
Prepress services	5,832
Package printing	1,745
Business forms printing	797
Book printing	355
Other specialty	901

Source: "Sizing Up the U.S. Printing Industry." *Graphic Arts Monthly* (September 1997), p. 87. Primary source: Printing Industries of America.

★ 433 ★

Markets

Top Printing Markets, 1995

Segments are ranked by the printing potential in billions of dollars. The market is expected to reach $83 billion.

Segment	Amount
Health care	10.7
Software	7.9
Motor vehicles	7.2
Packaged foods	5.8
Home improvements	5.7
Beverages	5.5
Book publishing	4.3
Medical products	4.1
Telecommunications equipment/services	4.0
Housing	3.6

Source: American Printer (December 1994), p. 37. Primary source: American Management.

★ 434 ★

Markets

Top Printing Markets by City, 1996

Cities are ranked by revenues in billions of dollars.

City	($ bil.)
Boston, MA	4.3
New York, NY	4.2
Atlanta, GA	3.9
Cincinnati, OH	3.9
Chicago, IL	3.9
Dallas, TX	3.9
Minneapolis, MN	3.9
Los Angeles, CA	3.9
Newark, NJ	3.9
Philadelphia, PA	3.7

Source: "Sizing Up the U.S. Printing Industry." *Graphic Arts Monthly* (September 1997), p. 88.
Primary source: Printing Industries of America.

★ 435 ★

Markets

Top Printing Markets by State, 1996

California - 11.5
New York - 10.0
Illinois - 9.6
Pennsylvania - 7.6
New Jersey - 6.3
Ohio - 6.1
Texas - 6.0
Wisconsin - 5.2
Massachusetts - 4.9
Minnesota - 4.6

States are ranked by revenues in billions of dollars.

State	($ bil.)
California	11.5
New York	10.0
Illinois	9.6
Pennsylvania	7.6
New Jersey	6.3
Ohio	6.1
Texas	6.0
Wisconsin	5.2
Massachusetts	4.9
Minnesota	4.6

Source: "Sizing Up the U.S. Printing Industry." *Graphic Arts Monthly* (September 1997), p. 88.
Primary source: Printing Industries of America.

★ 436 ★

Markets

U.S. Book Printing Market, 1997

The value of each market is shown in millions of dollars.

[In dollars]

End use	Value ($ mil.)
General trade books, print & bind	1,550.5
Tech, scientific, professional print & bind	1,387.3
Textbooks, print & bind	853.9
Pamphlets, print & bind	498.4
Religious, print & bind	270.5
Book printing only, no binding	133.8
Other books, print & bind	812.3
All other book printing	605.6
Total	6112.3

Source: "Total Size of U.S. Book Printing." *American Printer* (February 1997), p. 10.

Companies

★ 437 ★

Fastest-Growing Printers

Company	Key market	% Sales growth 1994-96	Sales	
			1994 ($000)	1996 ($000)
The Peerless Group[1] Little Rock, AR	Advertising, packaging, retail	2,510	77	2,002
Express Press Fargo, ND	Quick printing	300	800	3,200
E&G Printing Service Madison Heights, MI	Advertising, auto retail	235	10,963	36,724
BeaverPrints/Global Village Press Bellwood, PA	Marketing, direct mail	196	1,025	3,031

[Continued]

★ 437 ★

Fastest-Growing Printers
[Continued]

Company	Key market	% Sales growth 1994-96	Sales	
			1994 ($000)	1996 ($000)
Baker Press Dallas, TX	Advertising, corporate, commercial	163	3,800	10,000
Consolidated Graphics Houston, TX	Commercial	152	57,200	144,100
Offset Atlanta Norcross, GA	Corporate, manufacturing	134	1,516	3,549
Mercury Print Productions Rochester, NY	Corporate	104	5,910	12,073
AmeriPrint Graphics Neenah, WI	Financial, corporate, insurance	100	1,200	2,400
K-B Offset Printing State College, PA	Corporate	100	1,800	3,600
Moran Printing Company Orlando, FL	Corporate	95	22,000	43,000
Cedar Graphics Hiawatha, IA	Corporate, education	84	10,800	19,900
Port Printing Lake Charles, LA	Commercial	81	1,275	2,302
IBF Industries Tampa, FL	Insurance, corporate Telecommunications	76	744	6,307
APS International San Francisco, CA	Legal, financial, corporate	75	4,000	7,000
NLS Thomasville, GA	Retail, corporate, insurance	75	1,029	1,800

[Continued]

★ 437 ★

Fastest-Growing Printers
[Continued]

Company	Key market	% Sales growth 1994-96	Sales 1994 ($000)	1996 ($000)
Professional Printers West Columbia, SC	Commercial	72	1,800	3,100
Web Express Printing Royal Oak, MI	Print resellers	69	3,245	5,489
Peczuh Printing Price, UT	Mining, corporate transportation	68	1,583	2,664
Webtrend Vista, CA	Commercial, direct mail	65	11,542	19,057

Source: "On the Fast Track." *American Printer* (June 1997), p. 38. *Note:* 1. Figures include print business.

★ 438 ★

Companies

Largest Digital Prepress Leaders, 1997

Firms are ranked by annual sales in millions of dollars.

Company	Sales ($ mil.)
Wace USA	200.0
Applied Graphics Technologies	133.0
Black Dot Group	132.7
Schawk	90.8
American Color	75.0
The Enteron Group	68.0
IVA, Ltd.	66.0
Kwik International Color	44.0
Color Associates	37.6
Graphic Technologies	30.0
Quality House of Graphics	26.5
Kreber Graphics	24.0
TSI Graphics	23.0
PrepSAT	22.3
Gamma One	22.0
NEC	22.0
Graphic Art Service	21.0

[Continued]

★ 438 ★

Largest Digital Prepress Leaders, 1997
[Continued]

Company	Sales ($ mil.)
Blanks Color Imaging	20.8
H&S Graphics	19.4
Horan Imaging Solutions	19.0
Rex Three	19.0
Flying Color Graphics	18.7
Tukaiz Communications	18.5
Primary Color	18.3
Phototype Color Graphics	16.3

Source: "Prepress Leaders Adapting." *Graphic Arts Monthly* (September 1997), p. 47.

★ 439 ★

Companies

Printing Industry: Number of Firms by State

Data are for 1996.

State	Number	Rank
Alabama	516	30
Alaska	77	51
Arizona	663	25
Arkansas	362	33
California	6,564	1
Colorado	855	19
Connecticut	807	21
Delaware	110	49
District of Columbia	130	47
Florida	2,430	5
Georgia	1,143	16
Hawaii	112	48
Idaho	181	41
Illinois	3,443	3
Indiana	1,200	14
Iowa	690	23
Kansas	576	28
Kentucky	585	27
Louisiana	517	29
Maine	234	38
Maryland	796	22
Massachusetts	1,567	10

[Continued]

★ 439 ★

Printing Industry: Number of Firms by State
[Continued]

State	Number	Rank
Michigan	1,824	9
Minnesota	1,267	12
Mississippi	272	36
Missouri	1,152	15
Montana	163	44
Nebraska	398	32
Nevada	171	43
New Hampshire	278	35
New Jersey	2,333	8
New Mexico	233	39
New York	3,902	2
North Carolina	1,254	13
North Dakota	142	46
Ohio	2,415	7
Oklahoma	643	26
Oregon	669	24
Pennsylvania	2,418	6
Rhode Island	242	37
South Carolina	453	31
South Dakota	181	42
Tennessee	910	17
Texas	3,429	4
Utah	307	34
Vermont	143	45
Virginia	855	20
Washington	910	18
West Virginia	195	40
Wisconsin	1,296	11
Wyoming	84	50
Total	52,097	

Source: "Sizing Up the U.S. Printing Industry." Graphic Arts Monthly (September 1997), p. 89.
Primary source: Printing Industries of America.

★ 440 ★

Companies

Top 10 Capital Investors

Firms are ranked by investments in millions of dollars.

Company	Capital investment	Prepress sales
Quad/Graphics	71.2	99.6
American Color	53.0	74.0
Schawk, Inc.	50.0	91.0
Intaglio Vivi-Color Alliance	42.0	60.0
World Color Digital Services	22.6	51.9
Black Dot Group	20.0	126.2
PrepSAT	18.2	21.5
Kwik International Color Inc.	17.7	41.2
Wace USA	16.5	150.0
Color Associates, Inc.	16.0	40.0

Source: From the Internet by mediacentral at: http://www.mediacentral.com/Magazines/Pre/97pre100/charts.htm. Primary source: *Pre Magazine.*

★ 441 ★

Companies

Top 10 Prepress and PrePublishing Companies, 1997

Firms are ranked by sales in millions of dollars.

Company	Prepress sales	Capital investment	Number of facilities
Wace USA	150.0	16.5	13
Applied Graphics Tech.	130.0	3.5	13
Black Dot Group	126.2	20.0	19
Schawk, Inc.	91.0	50.0	12
American Color	74.0	53.0	17
Enteron Group	61.0	5.0	4
Intaglio Vivi-Color	60.0	42.0	13
Banta Digital Group	52.0	6.5	5
Kwik International Color	41.2	17.7	1
Color Associates, Inc.	40.0	16.0	1

Source: From the Internet by mediacentral at: http://www.mediacentral.com/Magazines/Pre/97pre100/charts.htm. Primary source: *Pre Magazine.*

★ 442 ★

Companies

Top Book Printers, 1997

R.R. Donnelley & Sons - 725.89	
Quebecor Printing - 560.00	
Banta Corp. - 238.48	
	Bertelsmann Industries U.S. - 162.80
	Golden Books Publishing - 152.40
	Courier Corp. - 131.00
	Taylor Publishing - 99.00
	Maple-Vail Book Mfg. - 80.00
	Webcrafters - 75.00
	Landoll Inc. - 71.00

Chart shows data from column 1.

Publishers, faced with very high return rates, have begun to cut back on the size of book orders. The market is expected to experience growth, particularly in the children's and religious books segments. Firms are ranked by book printing sales in millions of dollars.

Company	Segment Sales ($ mil.)	Total Sales ($ mil.)
R.R. Donnelley & Sons	725.89	6,599.00
Quebecor Printing	560.00	3,500.00
Banta Corp.	238.48	1,084.00
Bertelsmann Industries U.S.	162.80	220.00
Golden Books Publishing	152.40	254.00
Courier Corp.	131.00	131.00
Taylor Publishing	99.00	99.00
Maple-Vail Book Mfg.	80.00	80.00
Webcrafters	75.00	75.00
Landoll Inc.	71.00	71.00

Source: Bak, Carolyn R. "Not-So-Great Expectations." *Printing Impressions,* (December 1997), p. 34.

★ 443 ★

Companies

Top Catalog Mail Printers, 1997

Some of the factors driving market growth include targeted offerings, shorter production cycles and more effective buying incentives. Firms are ranked by direct mail sales in millions of dollars.

Company	Segment Sales ($ mil.)	Total Sales ($ mil.)
R.R. Donnelley & Sons	1,319.80	6,599.00
Quebecor Printing	525.00	3,500.00
Quad/Graphics	479.32	1,042.00
World Color Press	443.07	1,641.00
Banta Corp.	216.80	1,084.00
Arandell Corp.	141.22	153.50
Brown Printing	125.00	500.00
Perry Graphic Communications	59.50	170.00
Hess Management	56.00	140.00
Avanti/Case-Hoyt	56.00	112.00

Source: Greenlaw, Dawn. "Capitalizing on Convenience." *Printing Impressions,* (December 1997), p. 30.

★ 444 ★
Companies

Top Direct Mail Printers, 1997

Quebecor Printing - 385.00	
Banta Corp. - 216.80	
	World Color Press - 147.69
	Wallace Computer Services - 117.82
	The Instant Web Cos. - 84.80
	General Business Forms - 56.81
	Clondalkin Group - 55.30
	Japs-Olson - 36.00
	Solar Communications - 35.75
	Berlin Industries - 34.00

Chart shows data from column 1.

The direct mail industry is expected to have a good year in 1998, with sales expected to grow 5 to 7 percent. There has been shift in the industry from large, blanket mailings to having more personalized relationships with customers. Printers are producing shorter length runs, more versions of mail pieces and more codes. Many firms have become involved much earlier in the graphic communications process. Firms are ranked by direct mail sales in millions of dollars.

Company	Segment Sales ($ mil.)	Total Sales ($ mil.)
Quebecor Printing	385.00	3,500.00
Banta Corp.	216.80	1,084.00
World Color Press	147.69	1,641.00
Wallace Computer Services	117.82	906.30
The Instant Web Cos.	84.80	106.00
General Business Forms	56.81	87.40
Clondalkin Group	55.30	553.00
Japs-Olson	36.00	90.00
Solar Communications	35.75	55.00
Berlin Industries	34.00	85.00

Source: Greenlaw, Dawn. "This Time it's Personal." *Printing Impressions,* (December 1997), p. 27.

★ 445 ★

Companies

Top Financial Printers, 1997

The financial printing market has a very successful year as a result of the stock market and numerous mergers and acquisitions. Firms are ranked by financial printing sales in millions of dollars.

Company	Segment Sales ($ mil.)	Total Sales ($ mil.)
R.R. Donnelley & Sons	461.93	6,599.0
Bowne & Co.	303.75	675.00
Merrill Corp.	141.60	354.00
Daniels Printing	42.60	71.00
Cadmus Communications	42.34	384.90
Global Financial Press	37.00	37.00
Northstar Computer Forms	32.20	46.00
Applied Printing Technologies	21.60	90.00
Packquisition Corp.	19.80	33.00
PGI Co.	15.96	38.00

Source: Janda, Jerry. "Running with the Bulls." *Printing Impressions,* (December 1997), p. 40.

★ 446 ★

Companies

Top Prepress Houses by Annual Prepress Sales

Company	Total annual sales ($ mil.)	Annual prepress sales ($ mil.)
Wace USA	200.00	180.00
Applied Graphics Technologies	132.00	132.00
Black Dot Group	126.19	126.19
Schawk	NA	90.80
American Color	72.00	72.00
Intaglio Vivicolor Alliance	66.00	66.00
Enteron Group	67.00	58.00
Color Associates	38.70	38.70
Multi-Ad Services	32.40	32.40
Kwik International Color	44.00	32.40
Graphic Technology	31.00	24.40
TSI Graphics	23.00	23.00

[Continued]

★ 446 ★

Top Prepress Houses by Annual Prepress Sales
[Continued]

Company	Total annual sales ($ mil.)	Annual prepress sales ($ mil.)
Prepsat	21.70	21.70
Gamma One	22.00	21.50
Spectrum	21.50	21.50
Quality House of Graphics	26.40	21.10
Graphic Art Service	21.00	21.00
Kreber Graphics	24.00	20.00
Graphtec	30.00	19.00
Horan Imaging Solutions	19.00	19.00
Primary Color	18.20	18.20
Integrated Imaging Center	NA	18.00
H&S Graphics	20.70	17.70
Flying Color Graphics	18.70	17.60
Tukaiz Communications	17.50	17.50
NEC	17.00	17.00
Blanks Color Imaging	20.80	15.80
Accu-Color	15.70	15.70
Colorhouse	15.70	15.70
Magna Graphic	14.80	14.80
Carey Color	14.50	14.50
Deluxe Engraving	14.50	14.50
Colorbrite	13.00	13.00
Katz Digital Technologies	15.60	12.60
Unitech Prepress Solutions	12.20	12.20
Color Concepts	12.00	12.00
Stevenson Photo Color	12.00	12.00
The Peerless Group	11.20	11.20
The Clarinda Co.	11.00	11.00
EMR Systems Communication	11.25	10.00
Baum Printing	29.00	9.70
ASG Sherman Graphics	10.38	9.60
Digital Color Image	11.60	9.60
One Color Communications	9.20	9.20
Eastern Rainbow	9.60	9.10
Computer Graphics (CGI)	8.70	8.70
Professional Graphics	8.60	8.60

[Continued]

★ 446 ★

Top Prepress Houses by Annual Prepress Sales
[Continued]

Company	Total annual sales ($ mil.)	Annual prepress sales ($ mil.)
Imaging Systems	8.40	8.40
The Argus Press	24.69	8.00
Rex Three	19.00	8.00

Source: "Top 50 Prepress Houses." *Printing Impressions* (August 1997), p. 62.

★ 447 ★

Companies

Top Printing Firms by Percent Sales Increase
[In percent]

Company	Percent increase
CST Office Products	110.7
St. Ives	71.9
Landoll, Inc.	71.4
Consolidated Graphics	69.2
DEC International	56.1
American Banknote Corp.	49.9
Merrill Corp.	44.5
Big Flower Press Holdings	34.0
Champion Industries	33.9
Data Business Forms, Ltd.	33.9
Wisconsin Label Corp.	32.4
Mail-Well, Inc.	30.5
Great Western Publishing	30.0
Taylor Corp.	29.2
Reynolds & Reynolds/Bus. Syst.	27.7
Bowne & Co.	27.6
World Color	32.1
Wallace Computer Services	20.9
Cadmus Communications	20.4
Clondalkin Group	18.8

Source: "Ranking the Leaders." *American Printer* (July 1997), p. 42.

★ 448 ★

Companies

Top Printing Firms by Sales Per Employee

[In dollars]

Company	Sales
CST Office Products	561,905
Valassis Communications	549,250
Instant Web	416,000
Paris Business Products	337,647
Anderson Lithograph	323,077
E&D Web	315,152
Tweddle Litho Co.	281,081
Stevens Graphics	279,583
Arandell Corp.	264,655
Sandy Alexander	261,176
Century Graphics Corp.	252,941
Multi-Color Corp.	244,444
Sullivan Communications	238,636
NCR Systemedia Group	253,417
Rhodes, Inc.	228,333
Sonoco/Engraph	226,667
ColorGraphics	226,667
L.P. Thebault	220,000
O.E.I. Business Forms	215,881
Groupe Interweb	213,023

Source: "Ranking the Leaders." *American Printer* (July 1997), p. 42.

★ 449 ★

Companies

Top Printing Firms in North America

Company/location	Total sales 1996	Percent change	Top executive	Number of employees	Primary business	Number of plants
R.R. Donnelley & Sons Co., Chicago, IL.	6,600.0	1.5	William M. Davis	38,000	CAT, INS, PUB BK	80
Quebecor Printing, Inc., Montreal PQ, ON, CAN	3,100.0	3.2	Jean Neveu	26,000	PUB, INS, BK, CAT	107
Moore Corp. Ltd., Toronto ON, CAN	2,500.0	-3.8	Reto Braun	19,000	BF, SPC, DIR, COM	100
Deluxe Corp., Shoreview, MN	1,896.0	2.0	J.A. Blanchard III	19,643	SPC, BF	81
World Color, Greenwich, CT	1,600.0	23.1	Robert G. Burton	12,500	PUB, CAT, COM, SPC	36
Big Flower Press Holdings, Inc., New York, NY	1,202.0	34.0	Theodore Ammon	6,410	INS, PUB, SPC	34
Banta Corp., Menasha, WI	1,084.0	6.0	Donald D. Belcher	6,100	COM, BK, CAT, PUB	35
Quad/Graphics, Inc., Pewaukee, WI	1,042.0	4.0	Harry V. Quadracci	9,386	CAT, PUB, INS, BK	18
Standard Register, Dayton, OH	944.0	4.5	Peter S. Redding	6,481	BF, SPC	48
Wallace Computer Services, Inc., Lisle, IL	862.0	20.9	Robert J. Cronin	4,100	BF, SPC, COM, CAT	24
Mail-Well, Inc., Englewood, CO	779.0	30.5	Gerald F. Mahoney	6,100	SPC, COM	52
Taylor Corp., North Mankato, MN	775.0[1]	29.2	Glen Taylor	12,000	COM, SPC, BF, INS	40
Valassis Communications, Inc., Livonia, MI	659.1	7.4	David A. Brandon	1,200	INS, SPC	3
UARCO, Inc., Barrington, IL	650.0[1]	-3.7	Robert Harbage	4,000	BF, SPC	29
American Business Products, Atlanta, GA	631.6	-0.4	Robert W. Gundeck	3,520	SPC, BK, CAT, INS	13
John H. Harland Co., Decatur, GA	609.4	8.5	Robert J. Amman	7,000	SPC, BF, COM, FIN	40
Reynolds & Reynolds/Business Syst. Div, Dayton, OH	595.1	27.7	David R. Holmes	6,000	BF	24

[Continued]

★ 449 ★

Top Printing Firms in North America
[Continued]

Company/location	Total sales 1996	Percent change	Top executive	Number of employees	Primary business	Number of plants
Transcontinental Printing Inc., Saint-Laurent, PQ, CAN	582.5	7.4	Serge De Paoli	4,800	INS, COM, PUB, CAT	26
NCR Systemedia Group, Miamisburg, OH	565.0	2.7	Daniel J. Enneking	2,400	BF, COM	16
Sullivan Communications, Inc., Stamford, CT	525.0	-0.9	Stephen Dyott	2,200	INS, COM, BK, PUB	10
Bowne & Co., Inc., New York, NY	501.0	27.6	Robert M. Johnson	4,300	FIN, COM, SPC	16
Brown Printing Co., Waseca, MN	480.0	10.3	Dan Nitz	3,300	PUB, CAT, INS	5
Clondalkin Group Inc., Philadelphia, PA	449.0	18.8	Henry Lund	3,195	PKG, SPC, COM, BF	33
Graphic Industries, Inc., Atlanta, GA	437.1	4.7	Mark C. Pope III	3,348	COM, FIN, SPC, PUB	20
Shorewood Packaging Corp., New York, NY	394.4	10.5	Marc P. Shore	2,700	PKG, SPC	9
Merrill Corp., St. Paul, MN	354.0	44.5	John W. Castro	2,700	FIN, COM	6
Cadmus Communications Corp., Richmond, VA	337.0	20.4	Steve Gillispie, Jr.	3,234	PUB, COM, FIN, PKG	8
American Banknote Corp., New York, NY	309.0	49.9	Morris Weissman	3,260	SPC	8
CST Office Products Inc., Wheeling, IL	295.0	110.7	Keith C. Koski	525	BF	10
Clarke American Checks, Inc., San Antonio, TX	278.0	3.3	Charles L. Korbell, Jr.	2,552	SPC, BF	23
Golden Books Family Entertainment Inc., Racine, WI	277.1[1]	-25.1	Richard E. Snyder	1,470	BK, SPC, COM, INS	2
Sonoco/Engraph Inc., Atlanta, GA	272.0[1]	10.0	Maurice Richardson	1,200	SPC	10
Devon Group, Inc., Stamford, CT	264.4	6.2	Marne Obernauer, Jr.	2,200	PUB, COM, CAT, INS	21
New England Business Service, Inc., Groton, MA	255.0	-3.3	Robert J. Murray	2,014	BF, SPC	5
Data Documents, Inc., Omaha, NE	246.5	1.8	Walter J. Kearns	1,300	BF, PKG, COM, SPC	12
Jostens, Inc., Minneapolis, MN	217.0	6.8	Robert C. Buhrmaster	5,500	SPC, COM	5
Stevens Graphics, Inc., Atlanta, GA	201.3	11.2	William J. Davidson	720	DIR, CAT	2
Queens Group, Inc., Long Island City, NY	195.0	0.5	Eric Kaltman	1,098	PKG, COM, SPC, INS	5
Ivy Hill Corp., New York, NY	187.0	-3.1	Ellis Kern	1,100	PKG	5
Data Business Forms Ltd., Brampton ON, CAN	170.0	33.9	John Conway	1,160	BF, SPC	11
Perry Graphic Communications, Waterloo, WI	170.0	1.2	Craig A. Hutchinson	1,200	PUB, CAT, INS	2
Bertelsmann Printing & Manufacturing, New York, NY	166.7[1]	2.0	Wayne D. Taylor	2,000	BK, SPC	5
Miami Systems Corp., Cincinnati, OH	160.0	8.1	Samuel L. Peters	1,300	BF, SPC, COM	9
Ennis Business Forms, Inc., Ennis, TX	153.7	8.2	Kenneth A. McCrady	1,550	BF, COM, SPC	16
Arandell Corp., Menomonee Falls, WI	153.5	5.5	F. Edward Treis	580	CAT, INS	1
Publishers Printing Co. Inc., Shepersdville, KY	152.8	8.4	Nicholas X. Simon	1,700	PUB, DIR, INS	2
Judd's, Inc., Washington, DC	152.6	8.1	John J. Broderick	1,027	PUB, BK, CAT, DIR	2
Consolidated Graphics Inc., Houston, TX	144.0	69.2	Joe R. Davis	1,450	COM, DIR, FIN, CAT	19
Avanti/Case Hoyt, Miami, FL	130.0	6.6	Joe R. Arriola	800	COM, FIN, CAT, SPC	2
Century Graphics Corp., Metairie, LA	129.0	18.3	Michael D. Moffitt	510	INS	4
Bagcraft Corp. of America, Chicago, IL	128.0	-1.5	Mark F. Santacrose	1,100	PKG	3
Anderson Lithograph Co., Los Angeles, CA	126.0	-0.8	John C. Fosmire	390	CAT, FIN, COM, INS	1
Courier Corp., North Chelmsford, MA	125.0	4.2	James F. Conway III	1,100	BK	6
Fleming Packaging Corp., Peoria, IL	123.6	1.3	Gregory P. Fulford	800	PKG, SPC	12
Hart Graphics, Inc., Austin, TX	120.0[1]	9.2	David E. Hart	850	BK, BF, PUB, COM	5
The Lehigh Press, Inc., Cherry Hill, NJ	120.0	-9.1	John D. DePaul	650	BK, COM, INS, CAT	5
Mebane Packaging Group, Mebane, NC	118.0	10.3	George F. Krall	1,000	PKG, INS	6
J.J. Keller & Assoc., Inc., Neenah, WI	116.4	2.9	Robert L. Keller	750	PUB, BF, BK, SPC	1

Source: American Printer (July 1997), p. 40. *Notes:* 1. Estimated sales figures; BF-Business Forms; CAT-Catalogs; DIR-Directories; INS-Inserts; PUB-Publications; BK-Book Publishing; COM-Commercial; FIN-Financial; PKG-Packaging; SPC-Speciality Printing.

★ 450 ★

Companies

Top Publications Printers, 1995

Printers are ranked by publications sales in millions of dollars. The companies print such items as consumer, business, and trade magazines; farm magazines; Sunday newspaper magazine supplements, comic books and newspaper supplements; tabloids; scholarly journals and corporate publications and various forms of newspapers.

Company	Sales ($ mil.)
R.R. Donnelley & Sons Inc.	670.0
World Color Press Inc.	397.0
Quebecor Printing Inc. USA	360.0
Quad/Graphics Inc.	245.0
Brown Printing Co.	220.0
Ringier America Inc.	160.0
Cadmus Communications Corp.	125.0
Publishers Press Inc.	116.0
American Signature	113.3
Banta Corp., Publications Group	97.4
Treasure Chest Advertising	90.3
Custom Printing Co.	90.0
KTB Associates Inc.	90.0
Spartan Printing Co.	78.0
Mack Printing Group	77.0

Source: High-Volume Printing (April 1995), p. 34. Primary source: Trade & Technology Press 1991/1992 Print Markets.

★ 451 ★

Companies

Top Publications Printers, 1997

| R.R. Donnelley & Sons - 1,121.80 |
| Quebecor Printing - 1,015.00 |
| World Color Press - 475.89 |
| Quad/Graphics - 416.80 |
| Cadmus Communications - 230.94 |
| Brown Printing - 200.00 |
| Publishers Printing/Publishers Press - 151.00 |
| Banta Corp. - 119.24 |
| Judd's Inc. - 94.86 |
| Perry Graphic Communications - 93.50 |

Chart shows data from column 1.

The market is expected to experience most of its growth in the fields of special-interest and trade publications. Concerns in the market include the fall of single-copy sales, declines in efficiency as returns increase, and the rapidly increasing number of titles on newsstands. Print runs for traditionally large titles have begun to shrink. More specialized titles with smaller print runs have steadily merged. Firms are ranked by publication printing sales in millions of dollars.

Company	Segment Sales ($ mil.)	Total Sales ($ mil.)
R.R. Donnelley & Sons	1,121.80	6,599.00
Quebecor Printing	1,015.00	3,500.00
World Color Press	475.89	1,641.00
Quad/Graphics	416.80	1,042.00
Cadmus Communications	230.94	384.90
Brown Printing	200.00	500.00
Publishers Printing/Publishers Press	151.00	151.00
Banta Corp.	119.24	1,084.00
Judd's Inc.	94.86	153.00
Perry Graphic Communications	93.50	170.00

Source: Alonso, Marie Ranoia. "Celebrating...but Cautious." *Printing Impressions,* (December 1997), p. 36.

Employment

★ 452 ★

Occupations Employed by Printing Trade Services

The three digit standard industrial code 277, which is reported below, covers the Greeting Card Industry.

Occupation	% of total 1994	Change to 2005
Strippers, printing	7.2	-8.6
Sales & related workers, nec	5.4	6.3
Electronic pagination systems workers	4.2	63.7
Typesetting & composing machine operators	4.2	-74.3
Printing workers, precision, nec	3.8	37.9
General managers & top executives	3.8	-1.5
Hand packers & packagers	3.7	3.0
Artists & commercial artists	2.6	10.7
Proofreaders & copy markers	2.4	-33.2
Production, planning, & expediting clerks	2.3	22.2
Photoengravers	2.3	-28.4
Camera operators	2.1	-18.1
Bookkeeping, accounting, & auditing clerks	2.0	-21.2
Paste-up workers	1.9	-33.3
Machine feeders & offbearers	1.8	7.5
Printing press machine setters, operators	1.7	-9.0
Adjustment clerks	1.6	34.4
Data entry keyers, composing	1.6	-74.3
Secretaries, ex legal & medical	1.6	0.1
General office clerks	1.6	-8.4
Freight, stock, & material movers, hand	1.5	-4.4
Assemblers, fabricators, & hand workers, nec	1.4	15.4
Messengers	1.4	-20.6
Clerical supervisors & managers	1.4	10.7
Management support workers, nec	1.4	19.5
Platemakers	1.3	-27.7
Offset lithographic press operators	1.3	1.4
Printing, binding, & related workers, nec	1.3	14.9
Traffic, shipping, & receiving clerks	1.2	7.2
Industrial production managers	1.2	5.4

[Continued]

★ 452 ★

Occupations Employed by Printing Trade Services
[Continued]

Occupation	% of total 1994	Change to 2005
Bindery machine operators & set-up operators	1.2	9.9
Data entry keyers, ex composing	1.1	-16.6

Source: 1997 *Manufacturing STATROM* [machine-readable data files]. MStat97. Editorial Code and Data, Inc., Detroit, Michigan, 1997. Primary source: *Industry-Occupation Matrix*, Bureau of Labor Statistics. These data relate to one or more 3-digit SIC industry groups rather than to a single 4-digit SIC. The change reported for each occupation to the year 2005 is a percent of growth or decline as estimated by the Bureau of Labor Statistics. The abbreviation nec stands for 'not elsewhere classified.'

★ 453 ★

Employment

Printing Industry: Employment by State

Data are for 1996.

State	Employment	Rank
Alabama	8,012	31
Alaska	1,198	50
Arizona	11,134	27
Arkansas	8,780	30
California	95,862	1
Colorado	14,220	24
Connecticut	19,029	18
Delaware	1,994	47
District of Columbia	2,293	45
Florida	31,548	12
Georgia	24,992	14
Hawaii	1,949	48
Idaho	3,558	40
Illinois	76,204	3
Indiana	30,745	13
Iowa	15,735	22
Kansas	13,575	25
Kentucky	14,699	23
Louisiana	9,119	28
Maine	5,602	36
Maryland	18,849	19
Massachusetts	36,960	9
Michigan	33,900	10

[Continued]

★ 453 ★

Printing Industry: Employment by State

[Continued]

State	Employment	Rank
Minnesota	32,974	11
Mississippi	4,978	38
Missouri	20,575	17
Montana	2,304	44
Nebraska	7,583	32
Nevada	3,343	41
New Hampshire	5,886	35
New Jersey	48,336	6
New Mexico	2,921	42
New York	80,778	2
North Carolina	24,300	15
North Dakota	1,781	49
Ohio	47,214	7
Oklahoma	8,908	29
Oregon	12,227	26
Pennsylvania	55,285	4
Rhode Island	5,335	37
South Carolina	7,241	33
South Dakota	2,263	46
Tennessee	20,949	16
Texas	50,244	5
Utah	6,741	34
Vermont	3,712	39
Virginia	18,829	20
Washington	17,049	21
West Virginia	2,577	43
Wisconsin	37,893	8
Wyoming	1,053	51
Total	1,013,234	

Source: "Sizing Up the U.S. Printing Industry." *Graphic Arts Monthly* (September 1997), p. 89.
Primary source: Printing Industries of America.

★ 454 ★

Employment

Printing Market by Employment

Data show the top sectors for employment in the printing/imaging industry.

Segment	Employment
Commercial printing	355,606
Package printing	116,771
Prepress services	75,552
Quick printing	46,080
Business forms printing	41,148
Book printing	28,891
Other specialty	36,110

Source: "Sizing Up the U.S. Printing Industry." *Graphic Arts Monthly* (September 1997), p. 87. Primary source: Printing Industries of America.

Book Printing

★ 455 ★

Book Printing: Employment Statistics, 1987-1998

Data for 1993 and beyond are projected by the editor.

Years	Total establish-ments	Employ-ment (000)	Production workers (000)	Payroll ($ mil.)	Payroll per employee ($)	Hours per production worker
1987	561	43.5	34.4	961.4	22,101	1,968
1988	535	NA	NA	1,108.6	NA	NA
1989	507	46.5	37.7	1,077.5	23,172	1,936
1990	498	47.1	37.5	1,162.7	24,686	1,992
1991	515	48.5	37.9	1,185.8	24,449	1,916
1992	623	50.9	38.8	1,360.7	26,733	1,964
1993	632	49.8	38.3	1,378.8	27,687	2,037
1994	529	46.4	35.6	1,351.7	29,131	2,093
1995	521	NA	NA	1,444.2	NA	NA
1996	512	NA	NA	1,498.6	NA	NA
1997	503	NA	NA	1,553.0	NA	NA
1998	495	NA	NA	1,607.3	NA	NA

Source: 1997 *Manufacturing STATROM* [machine-readable data files]. MStat97. Editorial Code and Data, Inc., Detroit, Michigan, 1997. Primary source: *Economic Census* for 1992 and earlier years. The Economic Census is conducted by the Bureau of the Census, U.S. Department of Commerce, Washington, DC 20233. *Note:* NA = Not available.

★ 456 ★

Book Printing

Book Printing: General Statistics, 1987-1998

[In millions of dollars]

Year	Cost of materials	Value added by manufacture	Value of shipments[1]	Capital investment
1987	1,269.3	1,996.5	3,256.3	154.4
1988	1,555.8	2,026.6	3,565.9	NA
1989	1,624.8	2,212.7	3,838.8	179.8
1990	1,740.8	2,400.9	4,132.0	211.7
1991	1,752.8	2,388.0	4,140.0	163.5
1992	1,868.4	2,833.6	4,687.9	198.2
1993[2]	1,895.7	2,903.7	4,810.1	173.8
1994[2]	1,869.7	2,840.2	4,698.5	281.2
1995[2]	2,030.3	3,084.2	5,102.2	NA
1996[2]	2,115.1	3,213.0	5,315.2	NA
1997[2]	2,199.9	3,341.7	5,528.2	NA
1998[2]	2,284.6	3,470.5	5,741.2	NA

Source: 1997 *Manufacturing STATROM* [machine-readable data files]. MStat97. Editorial Code and Data, Inc., Detroit, Michigan, 1997. Primary source: *Economic Census* for 1992 and earlier years. The Economic Census is conducted by the Bureau of the Census, U.S. Department of Commerce, Washington, DC 20233. *Notes:* NA = Not available. 1. "Industry Shipments" and "Product Shipments" are rarely the same value. 2. Data on this line are projected by the editors.

Business Forms

★ 457 ★

Business Form Shipments

Data show the demand for business forms in the United States. While sales continue to fall, the industry has seen increased need for non-forms (commercial web, sheet printing) and converted products (blank or stock format cut sheet, label, and tag). The industry is deeply affected by changes in printing methods and the cost of paper. Figures are in millions of dollars.

Segment	1996	1997	1998	1999	2000	2001
Custom continuous	3,493	3,336	3,149	2,929	2,779	2,612
Multi-part mailer	240	228	212	195	176	154
Form/label combos	275	309	343	372	419	450
Other	2,978	2,799	2,594	2,361	2,184	2,008
Stock continuous	1,378	1,275	1,166	1,038	945	850

[Continued]

★ 457 ★

Business Form Shipments
[Continued]

Segment	1996	1997	1998	1999	2000	2001
Unit sets	1,529	1,477	1,412	1,322	1,269	1,193
Salesbks, pegboard	313	296	276	251	236	217
Total forms	6,713	6,384	6,003	5,540	5,229	4,872
Cut sheet	641	670	692	709	737	761
Labels	828	886	939	970	1,027	1,084
Total	8,182	7,940	7,634	7,219	6,993	6,717

Source: "Demand for Forms Continues Tumble, Despite Low Prices." *Purchasing,* 6 November 1997, p. 80. Primary source: International Business Forms Industries.

Commercial Printing

★ 458 ★

Commercial Printing: Employment Statistics, 1987-1998

Data for 1993 and beyond are projected by the editor.

Years	Total establish-ments	Employ-ment (000)	Production workers (000)	Payroll ($ mil.)	Payroll per employee ($)	Hours per production worker
1987	24,980	403.0	292.9	9,132.1	22,660	1,982
1988	23,460	405.2	293.2	9,524.3	23,505	2,001
1989	22,623	414.7	306.3	10,149.0	24,473	2,009
1990	22,535	410.1	307.3	10,606.7	25,864	2,053
1991	23,622	400.1	290.8	10,386.6	25,960	2,045
1992	29,344	439.9	317.4	12,047.5	27,387	2,057
1993	27,996	437.6	319.1	12,298.9	28,105	2,052
1994	28,606	439.8	319.3	12,618.2	28,691	2,082
1995	29,620	466.2	337.7	13,476.5	28,907	2,100
1996	30,634	478.0	345.7	14,082.8	29,460	2,113
1997	31,648	489.9	353.7	14,689.2	29,987	2,125
1998	32,662	501.7	361.7	15,295.6	30,489	2,137

Source: 1997 *Manufacturing STATROM* [machine-readable data files]. MStat97. Editorial Code and Data, Inc., Detroit, Michigan, 1997. Primary source: *Economic Census* for 1992 and earlier years. The Economic Census is conducted by the Bureau of the Census, U.S. Department of Commerce, Washington, DC 20233.

★ 459 ★

Commercial Printing

Commercial Printing: General Statistics, 1987-1998

[In millions of dollars]

Years	Cost of materials	Value added by manufacture	Value of shipments[1]	Capital investment
1987	14,581.7	18,162.1	32,698.2	1,537.3
1988	15,758.3	18,997.0	34,727.0	1,435.4
1989	16,727.9	20,416.1	37,128.0	1,627.6
1990	17,623.2	21,230.3	38,877.4	1,662.4
1991	16,788.0	20,952.4	37,718.9	1,370.0
1992	18,723.1	24,842.5	43,588.2	1,629.4
1993[2]	19,304.5	25,406.9	44,704.2	1,682.2
1994[2]	19,432.4	26,473.9	45,846.8	1,958.8
1995[2]	20,973.1	28,572.9	49,481.8	1,897.0
1996[2]	21,964.0	29,922.9	51,819.6	1,960.9
1997[2]	22,954.9	31,272.8	54,157.4	2,024.7
1998[2]	23,945.8	32,622.7	56,495.2	2,088.6

Source: 1997 *Manufacturing STATROM* [machine-readable data files]. MStat97. Editorial Code and Data, Inc., Detroit, Michigan, 1997. Primary source: *Economic Census* for 1992 and earlier years. The Economic Census is conducted by the Bureau of the Census, U.S. Department of Commerce, Washington, DC 20233. *Notes:* 1. "Industry Shipments" and "Product Shipments" are rarely the same value. 2. Data on this line are projected by the editors.

Digital Printing

★ 460 ★

Digital Color Printing

From the source: "Xerox Corporation has announced that its DocuColor 40 system has become the world's leading digital color production system, accounting for more than half of worldwide installations within eight months of its launch last May.

In 1996, Xerox reports, it placed more than 1,200 DocuColor 40 units, accounting for 65% of such placements during the year. Another 7% of 1996 placements were Scitex Spontane units, which are based on the same print engine as the DocuColor 40.

[Continued]

★ 460 ★

Digital Color Printing
[Continued]

More than one-third of the units were installed in the U.S.: Europe, Africa, and the Middle East accounted for about 30%, about the same as Japan, Southeast Asia, and Australia. Remaining units went to Latin America and Canada.

Moreover, the placements were evenly split between the graphic arts industry and corporate and governmental inplant reproduction departments."

Source: "DocuColor 40 Leads Digital Color Market." *Graphic Arts Monthly* (April 1997), p. 26.

★ 461 ★

Digital Printing

Leading Digitally Printed Products

Data show the materials produced on electronic digital printers, based on a survey of 88 respondents. While most in-plants do not have digital printing, they are adding the capabilities to do so. An average of 387,500 pages per month are produced digitally, compared with 1,896,750 printed through non-digital methods.

Product	% of respondents
Reports	72
Manuals	68
Brochures, business forms	61
Direct mail letters	58
Newsletter, policy/procedure booklets	57
Directories	53
Instruction booklets	52
Employee benefit booklets	52
Course documents	50
Pamphlets	48
Proposals	44
Books	39
Labels	38
Annual reports	36
Operation plans	31
Product data sheets	30
Price book/lists	26
Folders, stationery	25
Business cards	23
Package inserts	20

Source: "Digital Printing Here to Stay." *In-Plant Graphics* (April 1997), p. 16.

████████████████ **Typesetting** ████████████████

★ 462 ★

Typesetting: Employment Statistics, 1987-1998

Data for 1993 and beyond are projected by the editor.

Years	Total establishments	Employment (000)	Production workers (000)	Payroll ($ mil.)	Payroll per employee ($)	Hours per production worker
1987	3,364	37.6	29.5	809.2	21,521	1,980
1988	3,157	NA	NA	866.2	NA	NA
1989	2,920	36.1	25.0	796.8	22,072	2,172
1990	2,843	34.2	25.1	826.9	24,178	2,112
1991	2,727	29.6	22.1	743.6	25,122	2,095
1992	2,517	26.1	19.7	687.6	26,345	2,000
1993	2,297	25.4	19.2	678.8	26,724	1,969
1994	2,533	21.9	17.7	631.0	28,813	1,989
1995	2,474	NA	NA	765.3	NA	NA
1996	2,415	NA	NA	773.6	NA	NA
1997	2,355	NA	NA	782.0	NA	NA
1998	2,296	NA	NA	790.3	NA	NA

Source: 1997 *Manufacturing STATROM* [machine-readable data files]. MStat97. Editorial Code and Data, Inc., Detroit, Michigan, 1997. Primary source: *Economic Census* for 1992 and earlier years. The Economic Census is conducted by the Bureau of the Census, U.S. Department of Commerce, Washington, DC 20233. *Note:* NA = Not available.

★ 463 ★

Typesetting

Typesetting: General Statistics, 1987-1998

[In millions of dollars]

Years	Cost of materials	Value added by manufacture	Value of shipments[1]	Capital investment
1987	309.7	1,471.1	1,783.7	73.9
1988	333.2	1,587.1	1,919.8	NA
1989	294.0	1,483.0	1,775.7	83.3
1990	351.2	1,605.7	1,957.4	72.7
1991	320.3	1,487.8	1,812.5	49.8
1992	286.3	1,323.6	1,611.9	60.9

[Continued]

★ 463 ★

Typesetting: General Statistics, 1987-1998
[Continued]

Years	Cost of materials	Value added by manufacture	Value of shipments[1]	Capital investment
1993[2]	316.9	1,320.9	1,635.4	50.6
1994[2]	291.4	1,250.1	1,546.8	57.6
1995[2]	346.2	1,485.3	1,837.8	NA
1996[2]	351.7	1,508.9	1,867.1	NA
1997[2]	357.2	1,532.6	1,896.3	NA
1998[2]	362.8	1,556.2	1,925.6	NA

Source: 1997 *Manufacturing STATROM* [machine-readable data files]. MStat97. Editorial Code and Data, Inc., Detroit, Michigan, 1997. Primary source: *Economic Census* for 1992 and earlier years. The Economic Census is conducted by the Bureau of the Census, U.S. Department of Commerce, Washington, DC 20233. *Notes:* NA = Not available. 1. "Industry Shipments" and "Product Shipments" are rarely the same value. 2. Data on this line are projected by the editor.

Capital Expenditures

★ 464 ★

Pre-Press Capital Spending, 1998

Data show the percent of companies planning on purchasing each item in 1998. Companies plan to spend an average of 4.9 percent of company sales for pre-press capital equipment. Figures are based on a survey.

Product	% of companies
Digital proofing	55.0
Networks	45.0
Archiving	35.0
Desktop workstations	30.0
MIS	27.5
Digital presses	22.5
Digital camera	20.0
CTP platesetters	17.5
High-res design systems	12.5
Drum scanners	12.5
Desktop imagesetters	10.0
Photo CD devices	5.0
Input devices	5.0

[Continued]

★ 464 ★

Pre-Press Capital Spending, 1998
[Continued]

Product	% of companies
High-res scanners	5.0
Flatbed scanners	5.0

Source: "PrePress Shopping List for 1998." *American Printer* (November 1997), p. 11. Primary source: National Association of Printers and Lithographers/International Prepress Association *Prepress Market Watch.*

Mergers and Acquisitions

★ 465 ★

Printing Industry Mergers by Year

An estimated 500 to 1,000 printing firms leave the industry each year.

Year	No. of deals
1989	143
1990	92
1991	55
1992	34
1993	41
1994	50
1995	58
1996	80

Source: "Merger Myths." *American Printer* (April 1997), p. 10.

★ 466 ★

Print-On-Demand Market

From the source: "The publication print-on-demand market is expected to grow from $10.1 billion in 1996 to $17.7 billion in 2001, according to a study recently completed by Strategies on Demand. The study also notes that significant growth opportunities still are available in one-color printing.

The one-color market is driven by growth in the overall demand for print products and increasing penetration of the eligible print-on-demand segment by digital printing.

Electronic printing will see growth in the one-color segment from $3.9 billion in 1996 to $7.5 billion in 2001, a 14 percent compound annual growth rate (CAGR). The growth will come primarily through replacement of offset printing and duplicating.

The study also concludes that the total eligible color publication print-on-demand segment (including both electronic and offset printing) will grow from $5.1 billion in 1996 to $9.8 billion in 2001. Although the volume of electronic color printing in this segment is expected to grow at 40 percent CAGR, the value of print shipments is expected to reach only $3.8 billion. This is primarily due to declines in print cost and pricing as well as competition from offset printing."

Source: "Print on Demand Markets Growing." *American Printer* (July 1997), p. 10.

★ 467 ★

Mexico: Books Printed in 1994

Kind of printing	Titles		Issues	
	Number	%	Number (mil.)	%
First edition	4,674	38	37.7	41
Subsequent editions	1,162	9	13.1	14
Reprints	6,633	53	41.3	45

Source: "Mexico - Educational Equipment and Supplies." *National Trade Data Bank:* The Export Connection CD-ROM, STAT-USA, U.S. Department of Commerce, Washington, D.C. 20302, 26 August 1996, p. ISA960301.

★ 468 ★

Foreign Markets

Mexico: Printing of Periodicals by Frequency

Over the last decade, the number of magazine titles have doubled. Mexican companies and advertising agencies have turned increasingly to printed media.

Publication	Titles	Copies (mil.)
Daily	53	450.9
Weekly	151	295.8
Every 14 days	69	74.8
Every 15 days	41	26.4
Monthly	223	82.7
Every 2-6 months	292	8.8
Annually	46	5.2
Irregular	36	1.9

Source: "Mexico - Printing and Graphic Arts." *National Trade Data Bank:* The Export Connection CD-ROM, STAT-USA, U.S. Department of Commerce, Washington, D.C. 20302, 12 September 1996, p. ISA960801. Primary source: Camara Nacional de la Industria Editorial Mexicana.

★ 469 ★

Foreign Markets

Spain: Production of Printed Matter

Product	Value ($ mil.)
Commercial forms	2,047.02
Newspapers and magazines	1,853.91
Books and booklets	1,621.15
Stationery	341.77
Official forms	216.38
Other	484.38

Source: "Spain - Printing Equipment Market Overview." *National Trade Data Bank:* The Export Connection CD-ROM, STAT-USA, U.S. Department of Commerce, Washington, D.C. 20302, (October 1995), p. IMI951020.

Chapter 11
SUPPLIERS OF THE INDUSTRY

This chapter covers industrial sectors that support publishing activities. Included are *Industry Statistics*, *Bookbinding*, *Chemicals*, *Computer Equipment*, *Ink*, *Machinery*, *Paper*, and *Photographic Equipment*. The printing industry is covered separately in Chapter 10.

★ 470 ★

Publishing Supplier Industries: Number of Companies, 1987 and 1992

Industry	Companies		% Change 1987 to
	1987	1992	1992
Commercial printing, lithographic	24,328	28,489	17.10
Typesetting	3,317	2,481	-25.20
Bookbinding & related work	1,009	1,071	6.14
Photographic equipment & supplies	719	831	15.58
Book Printing	520	575	10.58
Computer peripheral equipment, nec	520	748	43.85
Printing trades machinery	408	461	12.99
Paper industries machinery	256	298	16.41
Printing ink	224	220	-1.79
Magnetic & optical recording media	181	239	32.04
Paper mills	122	127	4.10
Computer terminals	122	186	52.46
Computer storage devices	100	163	63.00

Source: 1997 Manufacturing STATROM [machine-readable data files]. MStat97. Editorial Code and Data Inc., Detroit, Michigan, 1997. Primary source: Economic Census for 1992 and earlier years. The Economic Census is conducted by the Bureau of the Census, U.S. Department of Commerce, Washington DC 20233.

★ 471 ★

Industry Statistics

Supplier Industries: Employment, 1987-1998

Data for 1993 and beyond are projected by the editor.

[In thousands]

Industry	Employment							
	1987	1988	1989	1990	1992	1994	1996	1998
Commercial printing, lithographic	403.0	405.2	414.7	410.1	439.9	439.8	478.0	501.7
Paper mills	129.1	130.4	130.1	130.1	130.6	122.8	127.0	126.5
Photographic equipment & supplies	88.0	87.5	87.0	79.3	77.5	64.8	58.9	51.2
Computer peripheral equipment, nec	76.2	67.8	77.2	78.1	59.3	57.6	49.7	43.7
Book printing	43.5	NA	46.5	47.1	50.9	46.4	NA	NA

[Continued]

★ 471 ★

Supplier Industries: Employment, 1987-1998
[Continued]

Industry	Employment							
	1987	1988	1989	1990	1992	1994	1996	1998
Computer storage devices	43.3	56.1	44.7	41.7	40.8	39.8	36.5	34.0
Typesetting	37.6	NA	36.1	34.2	26.1	21.9	NA	NA
Bookbinding & related work	29.6	NA	31.2	30.8	27.7	27.9	NA	NA
Magnetic & optical recording media	25.6	25.1	25.5	25.5	22.6	23.7	22.1	21.2
Printing trades machinery	25.0	25.6	29.3	22.1	18.7	21.1	17.1	15.0
Paper industries machinery	17.1	17.3	18.2	19.5	18.2	17.4	19.0	19.5
Computer terminals	15.0	15.8	15.8	13.5	9.3	6.6	4.1	1.3
Printing ink	11.1	11.1	12.2	11.5	12.3	13.2	13.2	13.8

Source: 1997 *Manufacturing STATROM* [machine-readable data files]. MStat97. Editorial Code and Data, Inc., Detroit, Michigan, 1997. Primary source: *Economic Census* for 1992 and earlier years. The Economic Census is conducted by the Bureau of the Census, U.S. Department of Commerce, Washington, DC 20233. *Notes:* NA = Not available. nec means not elsewhere classified.

★ 472 ★

Industry Statistics

Supplier Industries: Payroll per Employee, 1987-1998

Data for 1993 and beyond are projected by the editor.

[In dollars]

Industry	Payroll per employee							
	1987	1988	1989	1990	1992	1994	1996	1998
Paper mills	35,608	36,603	37,872	38,905	41,505	44,944	47,484	50,363
Computer peripheral equipment, nec	34,454	34,375	25,806	23,784	36,690	41,385	42,422	47,467
Computer storage devices	33,316	35,221	37,680	35,734	44,005	41,470	46,982	50,969
Photographic equipment & supplies	32,708	33,867	36,026	37,042	39,604	41,923	47,940	54,233
Printing trades machinery	30,064	31,488	28,461	37,158	35,075	38,431	42,055	46,920
Computer terminals	29,447	28,576	28,513	30,585	37,000	39,455	55,549	136,205
Paper industries machinery	29,368	31,110	34,330	33,246	35,813	39,730	40,506	42,492
Printing ink	28,009	30,333	29,246	30,817	33,122	34,735	36,275	37,690
Magnetic & optical recording media	24,945	26,378	25,533	25,565	30,752	32,848	35,135	38,077
Commercial printing, lithographic	22,660	23,505	24,473	25,864	27,387	28,691	29,460	30,489
Book printing	22,101	NA	23,172	24,686	26,733	29,131	NA	NA
Typesetting	21,521	NA	22,072	24,178	26,345	28,813	NA	NA
Bookbinding & related work	16,774	NA	16,647	18,289	19,816	21,384	NA	NA

Source: 1997 *Manufacturing STATROM* [machine-readable data files]. MStat97. Editorial Code and Data, Inc., Detroit, Michigan, 1997. Primary source: *Economic Census* for 1992 and earlier years. The Economic Census is conducted by the Bureau of the Census, U.S. Department of Commerce, Washington, DC 20233. *Notes:* nec means not elsewhere classified. NA = Not available.

★ 473 ★

Industry Statistics

Supplier Industries: Wages per Production Worker, 1987-1998

Data for 1993 and beyond are projected by the editor.

[In dollars]

Industry	Wages per production worker							
	1987	1988	1989	1990	1992	1994	1996	1998
Paper mills	34,296	34,956	36,078	37,229	39,010	42,686	44,964	47,647
Photographic equipment & supplies	27,322	27,713	29,600	30,503	33,725	35,278	39,147	43,359
Printing trades machinery	25,300	26,402	26,855	28,065	29,155	30,308	32,155	33,725
Paper industries machinery	24,890	27,067	29,007	28,434	30,822	33,549	35,213	37,264
Printing ink	24,658	27,232	26,221	26,299	28,457	28,554	31,789	33,513
Computer terminals	22,567	20,805	23,486	24,418	24,457	24,748	25,692	26,117
Computer peripheral equipment, nec	22,113	21,450	21,698	21,119	22,655	27,050	NA	NA
Computer storage devices	21,865	22,017	23,642	23,179	28,088	33,123	34,210	37,267
Commercial printing, lithographic	20,097	20,731	21,240	22,012	24,194	24,860	26,239	27,556
Magnetic & optical recording media	19,881	20,767	20,795	22,019	24,097	27,681	28,959	31,216
Book printing	19,641	NA	20,002	21,255	23,803	25,301	NA	NA
Typesetting	19,143	NA	21,286	21,876	23,520	25,416	NA	NA
Bookbinding & related work	14,586	NA	15,693	15,344	17,228	18,075	NA	NA

Source: 1997 Manufacturing STATROM [machine-readable data files]. MStat97. Editorial Code and Data, Inc., Detroit, Michigan, 1997. Primary source: *Economic Census* for 1992 and earlier years. The Economic Census is conducted by the Bureau of the Census, U.S. Department of Commerce, Washington, DC 20233. *Notes:* nec means not elsewhere classified. NA = Not available.

★ 474 ★

Industry Statistics

Supplier Industries: Manufacturing Value Added, 1987-1998

Data for 1993 and beyond are projected by the editor.

[In millions of dollars]

Industry	Value added by manufacturing							
	1987	1988	1989	1990	1992	1994	1996	1998
Commercial printing, lithographic	18,162.1	18,997.0	20,416.1	21,230.3	24,842.5	26,473.9	29,922.9	32,622.7
Paper mills	14,021.9	16,866.2	17,100.6	16,599.8	14,847.7	15,012.3	16,737.7	17,747.7
Photographic equipment & supplies	12,908.0	14,223.2	15,804.2	14,527.2	14,885.4	16,057.0	16,751.2	17,468.6
Computer peripheral equipment, nec	6,918.1	5,928.0	4,726.6	3,923.0	5,034.8	5,422.4	4,874.5	4,938.1
Computer storage devices	3,268.5	4,208.6	3,666.7	4,359.0	4,658.8	4,364.6	4,550.4	4,935.3
Book printing	1,996.5	2,026.6	2,212.7	2,400.9	2,833.6	2,840.2	3,213.0	3,470.5
Magnetic & optical recording media	1,687.2	1,593.5	1,542.8	1,675.6	2,091.5	2,615.2	2,821.0	3,075.9
Printing trades machinery	1,606.6	1,739.8	1,948.7	1,808.2	1,266.4	1,573.3	1,473.2	1,409.5
Typesetting	1,471.1	1,587.1	1,483.0	1,605.7	1,323.6	1,250.1	1,508.9	1,556.2
Paper industries machinery	1,027.0	1,022.5	1,208.8	1,118.7	1,273.8	1,407.5	1,574.9	1,716.9
Computer terminals	1,014.3	1,210.3	726.1	728.5	800.2	516.2	536.9	483.1
Printing ink	985.1	947.9	1,038.5	1,035.7	1,114.0	1,266.2	1,381.2	1,497.7
Bookbinding & related work	905.2	939.3	941.8	1,035.8	1,017.3	1,087.3	1,223.1	1,305.8

Source: 1997 Manufacturing STATROM [machine-readable data files]. MStat97. Editorial Code and Data, Inc., Detroit, Michigan, 1997. Primary source: *Economic Census* for 1992 and earlier years. The Economic Census is conducted by the Bureau of the Census, U.S. Department of Commerce, Washington, DC 20233. *Note:* nec means not elsewhere classified.

★ 570 ★

Industry Statistics

Supplier Industries: Value Added per Employee, 1987-1998

Data for 1993 and beyond are projected by the editor.

[In dollars]

Industry	Value added per employee							
	1987	1988	1989	1990	1992	1994	1996	1998
Photographic equipment & supplies	146,682	162,551	181,657	183,193	192,070	247,793	284,587	341,287
Paper mills	108,613	129,342	131,442	127,593	113,688	122,250	131,778	140,285
Computer peripheral equipment, nec	90,789	87,434	61,225	50,230	84,904	94,139	98,097	112,963
Printing ink	88,748	85,396	85,123	90,061	90,569	95,924	104,470	108,761
Computer storage devices	75,485	75,020	82,029	104,532	114,186	109,663	124,653	144,974
Computer terminals	67,620	76,601	45,956	53,963	86,043	78,212	130,346	379,976
Magnetic & optical recording media	65,906	63,486	60,502	65,710	92,544	110,346	127,917	145,212
Printing trades machinery	64,264	67,961	66,509	81,819	67,722	74,564	85,907	94,035
Paper industries machinery	60,058	59,104	66,418	57,369	69,989	80,891	82,741	87,934
Book printing	45,897	NA	47,585	50,975	55,670	61,211	NA	NA
Commercial printing, lithographic	45,067	46,883	49,231	51,769	56,473	60,195	62,597	65,028
Typesetting	39,125	NA	41,080	46,950	50,713	57,082	NA	NA
Bookbinding & related work	30,581	NA	30,186	33,630	36,726	38,971	NA	NA

Source: 1997 *Manufacturing STATROM* [machine-readable data files]. MStat97. Editorial Code and Data, Inc., Detroit, Michigan, 1997. Primary source: *Economic Census* for 1992 and earlier years. The Economic Census is conducted by the Bureau of the Census, U.S. Department of Commerce, Washington, DC 20233. *Notes:* nec means not elsewhere classified. NA = Not available.

★ 568 ★

Industry Statistics

Supplier Industries: Shipments, 1987-1998

Data for 1993 and beyond are projected by the editor.

[In millions of dollars]

Industry	Value of shipments							
	1987	1988	1989	1990	1992	1994	1996	1998
Commercial printing, lithographic	32,698.2	34,727.0	37,128.0	38,877.4	43,588.2	45,846.8	51,819.6	56,495.2
Paper mills	28,915.5	33,545.8	35,387.1	35,321.8	32,786.4	35,071.3	39,102.1	41,461.6
Photographic equipment & supplies	19,240.5	20,545.8	22,737.8	21,018.2	22,149.8	23,367.6	24,377.9	25,421.9
Computer peripheral equipment, nec	13,965.5	13,213.3	9,625.2	9,146.3	12,156.5	13,665.9	12,285.0	12,445.3
Computer storage devices	6,394.8	9,543.9	7,612.5	8,751.1	9,544.3	11,004.5	11,473.0	12,443.5
Magnetic & optical recording media	3,504.0	3,630.7	3,644.2	4,032.1	4,641.3	5,256.3	5,670.0	6,182.3
Book printing	3,256.3	3,565.9	3,838.8	4,132.0	4,687.9	4,698.5	5,315.2	5,741.2
Printing trades machinery	2,857.8	3,313.1	3,691.9	3,538.2	2,591.9	3,015.4	2,823.5	2,701.5
Printing ink	2,391.7	2,447.2	2,637.2	2,754.4	3,075.1	3,366.0	3,671.7	3,981.3
Paper industries machinery	1,867.1	2,012.1	2,579.8	2,770.4	2,524.2	2,812.5	3,147.0	3,430.8
Computer terminals	1,799.0	2,332.6	1,969.2	1,790.0	2,070.7	1,427.5	1,484.8	1,336.0
Typesetting	1,783.7	1,919.8	1,775.7	1,957.4	1,611.9	1,546.8	1,867.1	1,925.6
Bookbinding & related work	1,176.3	1,218.2	1,240.2	1,363.4	1,321.3	1,378.5	1,550.7	1,655.5

Source: 1997 *Manufacturing STATROM* [machine-readable data files]. MStat97. Editorial Code and Data, Inc., Detroit, Michigan, 1997. Primary source: *Economic Census* for 1992 and earlier years. The Economic Census is conducted by the Bureau of the Census, U.S. Department of Commerce, Washington, DC 20233. *Note:* nec means not elsewhere classified.

★ 477 ★

Industry Statistics

Supplier Industries: Shipments per Employee, 1987-1998

Data for 1993 and beyond are projected by the editor.

[In dollars]

Industry	Shipments per employee							
	1987	1988	1989	1990	1992	1994	1996	1998
Paper mills	223,978	257,253	271,999	271,497	251,044	285,597	307,856	327,729
Photographic equipment & supplies	218,642	234,809	261,354	265,047	285,804	360,611	414,157	496,671
Printing ink	215,468	220,468	216,164	239,513	250,008	255,000	277,718	289,124
Computer peripheral equipment, nec	183,274	194,886	124,679	117,110	205,000	237,255	247,231	284,696
Computer storage devices	147,686	170,123	170,302	209,859	233,929	276,495	314,289	365,523
Magnetic & optical recording media	136,875	144,649	142,910	158,122	205,367	221,785	257,100	291,861
Computer terminals	119,933	147,633	124,633	132,593	222,656	216,288	360,460	1,050,787
Printing trades machinery	114,312	129,418	126,003	160,100	138,604	142,910	164,649	180,228
Paper industries machinery	109,187	116,306	141,747	142,072	138,692	161,638	165,335	175,712
Commercial printing, lithographic	81,137	85,703	89,530	94,800	99,087	104,245	108,403	112,613
Book printing	74,857	NA	82,555	87,728	92,100	101,261	NA	NA
Typesetting	47,439	NA	49,188	57,234	61,759	70,630	NA	NA
Bookbinding & related work	39,740	NA	39,750	44,266	47,700	49,409	NA	NA

Source: 1997 *Manufacturing STATROM* [machine-readable data files]. MStat97. Editorial Code and Data, Inc., Detroit, Michigan, 1997. Primary source: *Economic Census* for 1992 and earlier years. The Economic Census is conducted by the Bureau of the Census, U.S. Department of Commerce, Washington, DC 20233. *Notes:* nec means not elsewhere classified. NA = Not available.

★ 478 ★

Industry Statistics

Supplier Industries: Capital Investment, 1987-1998

Data for 1993 and beyond are projected by the editor.

[In millions of dollars]

Industry	Capital investment							
	1987	1988	1989	1990	1992	1994	1996	1998
Paper mills	2,759.9	3,299.5	5,236.6	4,277.5	2,911.5	3,137.5	4,031.3	4,283.9
Commercial printing, lithographic	1,537.3	1,435.4	1,627.6	1,662.4	1,629.4	1,958.8	1,960.9	2,088.6
Photographic equipment & supplies	681.0	809.7	1,008.2	1,008.6	808.1	755.3	948.1	983.7
Computer peripheral equipment, nec	391.2	461.5	341.6	299.1	393.0	410.8	366.0	365.6
Computer storage devices	347.0	404.4	432.4	426.5	455.6	521.9	575.0	623.2
Magnetic & optical recording media	225.6	269.1	219.8	286.8	394.2	325.7	399.4	437.2
Book printing	154.4	NA	179.8	211.7	198.2	281.2	NA	NA
Printing trades machinery	114.2	86.3	99.5	89.6	59.6	70.7	41.3	26.8
Typesetting	73.9	NA	83.3	72.7	60.9	57.6	NA	NA
Computer terminals	58.0	42.7	69.3	45.4	44.4	41.7	29.7	23.5
Bookbinding & related work	48.3	NA	33.6	44.6	41.8	46.1	NA	NA
Paper industries machinery	45.6	60.0	84.6	72.0	65.4	49.3	78.6	85.9
Printing ink	37.8	32.7	46.6	44.3	46.0	55.4	55.8	60.0

Source: 1997 *Manufacturing STATROM* [machine-readable data files]. MStat97. Editorial Code and Data, Inc., Detroit, Michigan, 1997. Primary source: *Economic Census* for 1992 and earlier years. The Economic Census is conducted by the Bureau of the Census, U.S. Department of Commerce, Washington, DC 20233. *Notes:* nec means not elsewhere classified. NA = Not available.

███████████████ **Bookbinding** ███████████████

★ 479 ★

Bookbinding & Related: Employment Statistics, 1987 - 1998

Data for 1993 and beyond are projected by the editor.

Years	Total establish-ments	Employ-ment (000)	Production workers (000)	Payroll ($ mil.)	Payroll per employee ($)	Hours per production worker
1987	1,035	29.6	24.6	496.5	16,774	1,955
1988	1,009	NA	NA	507.5	NA	NA
1989	1,000	31.2	24.0	519.4	16,647	2,004
1990	1,033	30.8	26.4	563.3	18,289	1,977
1991	1,052	30.8	25.7	547.0	17,760	1,953
1992	1,098	27.7	22.7	548.9	19,816	1,978
1993	1,104	25.6	21.5	525.2	20,516	2,009
1994	1,086	27.9	23.5	596.6	21,384	2,013
1995	1,097	NA	NA	620.8	NA	NA
1996	1,107	NA	NA	640.5	NA	NA
1997	1,117	NA	NA	660.3	NA	NA
1998	1,127	NA	NA	680.0	NA	NA

Source: 1997 *Manufacturing STATROM* [machine-readable data files]. MStat97. Editorial Code and Data, Inc., Detroit, Michigan, 1997. Primary source: *Economic Census* for 1992 and earlier years. The Economic Census is conducted by the Bureau of the Census, U.S. Department of Commerce, Washington, DC 20233. *Note:* NA = Not available.

★ 480 ★
Bookbinding

Bookbinding & Related Work: General Statistics, 1987-1998

[In millions of dollars]

Years	Cost of materials	Value added by manufacture	Value of shipments[1]	Capital investment
1987	275.2	905.2	1,176.3	48.3
1988	282.7	939.3	1,218.2	NA
1989	294.2	941.8	1,240.2	33.6
1990	333.2	1,035.8	1,363.4	44.6
1991	314.5	1,009.7	1,328.3	28.5
1992	309.3	1,017.3	1,321.3	41.8

[Continued]

★ 480 ★

Bookbinding & Related Work: General Statistics, 1987-1998
[Continued]

Years	Cost of materials	Value added by manufacture	Value of shipments[1]	Capital investment
1993[2]	302.0	957.6	1,258.0	24.9
1994[2]	300.4	1,087.3	1,378.5	46.1
1995[2]	326.5	1,181.8	1,498.3	NA
1996[2]	337.9	1,223.1	1,550.7	NA
1997[2]	349.3	1,264.5	1,603.1	NA
1998[2]	360.8	1,305.8	1,655.5	NA

Source: 1997 *Manufacturing STATROM* [machine-readable data files]. MStat97. Editorial Code and Data, Inc., Detroit, Michigan, 1997. Primary source: *Economic Census* for 1992 and earlier years. The Economic Census is conducted by the Bureau of the Census, U.S. Department of Commerce, Washington, DC 20233. *Notes:* NA = Not available. 1. "Industry Shipments" and "Product Shipments" are rarely the same value. 2. Data on this line are projected by the editor.

Chemicals

★ 481 ★

U.S. Paper Chemical Consumption

Consumption of specialty chemicals is shown in billions of dollars.

Chemical	($ bil.)
Dyes & pigments	2.70
Printing inks	1.10
Paper additives	0.78

Source: "Specialties Shine to 1998." *Chemical Week,* 1 January 1997, p. 24. Primary source: Strategic Analysis Inc.

Computer Equipment

★ 482 ★

Computer Peripheral Equipment: General Statistics, 1987-1998

[In millions of dollars]

Years	Cost of materials	Value added by manufacture	Value of shipments[1]	Capital investment
1987	7,107.3	6,918.1	13,965.5	391.2
1988	7,761.3	5,928.0	13,213.3	461.5
1989	4,909.0	4,726.6	9,625.2	341.6
1990	5,239.3	3,923.0	9,146.3	299.1
1991	5,779.9	3,748.4	9,614.7	223.8
1992	7,166.4	5,034.8	12,156.5	393.0
1993[2]	8,184.2	5,182.6	13,366.6	415.1
1994[2]	8,293.2	5,422.4	13,665.9	410.8
1995[2]	7,406.6	4,842.7	12,204.9	366.2
1996[2]	7,455.2	4,874.5	12,285.0	366.0
1997[2]	7,503.8	4,906.3	12,365.1	365.8
1998[2]	7,552.5	4,938.1	12,445.3	365.6

Source: 1997 *Manufacturing STATROM* [machine-readable data files]. MStat97. Editorial Code and Data, Inc., Detroit, Michigan, 1997. Primary source: *Economic Census* for 1992 and earlier years. The Economic Census is conducted by the Bureau of the Census, U.S. Department of Commerce, Washington, DC 20233. *Notes:* 1. "Industry Shipments" and "Product Shipments" are rarely the same value. 2. Data on this line are projected by the editor.

★ 483 ★

Computer Equipment

Computer Peripherals: Employment Statstics, 1987 - 1998

Data for 1993 and beyond are projected by the editor.

Years	Total establish- ments	Employ- ment (000)	Production workers (000)	Payroll ($ mil.)	Payroll per employee ($)	Hours per production worker
1987	549	76.2	26.2	2,625.4	34,454	2,240
1988	663	67.8	24.0	2,330.6	34,375	1,950
1989	616	77.2	24.2	1,992.2	25,806	1,934
1990	597	78.1	25.4	1,857.5	23,784	1,965
1991	651	53.5	20.7	1,963.9	36,708	2,043
1992	772	59.3	23.5	2,175.7	36,690	2,060

[Continued]

★ 483 ★

Computer Peripherals: Employment Statstics, 1987 - 1998
[Continued]

Years	Total establish- ments	Employ- ment (000)	Production workers (000)	Payroll ($ mil.)	Payroll per employee ($)	Hours per production worker
1993	786	59.3	24.0	2,260.4	38,118	2,063
1994	800	57.6	23.1	2,383.8	41,385	2,095
1995	834	52.7	22.4	2,124.5	40,329	2,038
1996	869	49.7	22.0	2,108.0	42,422	2,036
1997	903	46.7	21.7	2,091.5	44,783	2,034
1998	937	43.7	21.3	2,075.0	47,467	2,032

Source: 1997 Manufacturing STATROM [machine-readable data files]. MStat97. Editorial Code and Data, Inc., Detroit, Michigan, 1997. Primary source: Economic Census for 1992 and earlier years. The Economic Census is conducted by the Bureau of the Census, U.S. Department of Commerce, Washington, DC 20233.

★ 484 ★

Computer Equipment

Computer Terminals: Employment Statistics, 1987 - 1998

Data for 1993 and beyond are projected by the editor.

Years	Total establish- ments	Employ- ment (000)	Production workers (000)	Payroll ($ mil.)	Payroll per employee ($)	Hours per production worker
1987	121	15.0	5.5	441.7	29,447	1,945
1988	129	15.8	5.9	451.5	28,576	1,898
1989	141	15.8	6.3	450.5	28,513	2,048
1990	138	13.5	4.8	412.9	30,585	2,042
1991	154	11.7	5.2	386.1	33,000	1,981
1992	190	9.3	4.2	344.1	37,000	1,905
1993	177	7.9	3.5	307.2	38,886	1,943
1994	193	6.6	2.7	260.4	39,455	1,926
1995	204	5.5	2.8	256.6	46,298	1,947
1996	215	4.1	2.3	228.8	55,549	1,938
1997	226	2.7	1.9	201.0	74,573	1,925
1998	237	1.3	1.4	173.2	136,205	1,904

Source: 1997 Manufacturing STATROM [machine-readable data files]. MStat97. Editorial Code and Data, Inc., Detroit, Michigan, 1997. Primary source: Economic Census for 1992 and earlier years. The Economic Census is conducted by the Bureau of the Census, U.S. Department of Commerce, Washington, DC 20233.

★ 485 ★

Computer Equipment

Computer Terminals: General Statistics, 1987-1998

[In millions of dollars]

Years	Cost of materials	Value added by manufacture	Value of shipments	Capital investment
1987	742.0	1,014.3	1,799.0	58.0
1988	1,159.2	1,210.3	2,332.6	42.7
1989	1,219.1	726.1	1,969.2	69.3
1990	1,035.5	728.5	1,790.0	45.4
1991	1,429.5	865.0	2,326.5	42.4
1992	1,288.2	800.2	2,070.7	44.4
1993[2]	807.8	615.8	1,435.0	29.3
1994[2]	894.7	516.2	1,427.5	41.7
1995[2]	977.2	563.8	1,559.1	32.8
1996[2]	930.6	536.9	1,484.8	29.7
1997[2]	884.0	510.0	1,410.4	26.6
1998[2]	837.4	483.1	1,336.0	23.5

Source: 1997 *Manufacturing STATROM* [machine-readable data files]. MStat97. Editorial Code and Data, Inc., Detroit, Michigan, 1997. Primary source: *Economic Census* for 1992 and earlier years. The Economic Census is conducted by the Bureau of the Census, U.S. Department of Commerce, Washington, DC 20233. *Notes:* 1. "Industry Shipments" and "Product Shipments" are rarely the same value. 2. Data on this line are projected by the editor.

★ 486 ★

Computer Equipment

Magnetic & Optical Recording: Employment Statistics, 1987-1998

Data for 1993 and beyond are projected by the editor.

Years	Total establishments	Employ-ment (000)	Production workers (000)	Payroll ($ mil.)	Payroll per employee ($)	Hours per production worker
1987	200	25.6	16.3	638.6	24,945	2,025
1988	191	25.1	16.2	662.1	26,378	2,012
1989	214	25.5	16.9	651.1	25,533	1,929
1990	215	25.5	16.1	651.9	25,565	1,950
1991	243	25.4	16.1	734.7	28,925	2,062
1992	261	22.6	15.1	695.0	30,752	2,132
1993	261	22.2	15.0	689.6	31,063	2,080
1994	277	23.7	15.5	778.5	32,848	1,955
1995	289	22.5	15.0	759.0	33,750	2,049

[Continued]

★ 486 ★

Magnetic & Optical Recording: Employment Statistics, 1987-1998

[Continued]

Years	Total establish-ments	Employ-ment (000)	Production workers (000)	Payroll ($ mil.)	Payroll per employee ($)	Hours per production worker
1996	302	22.1	14.8	774.9	35,135	2,056
1997	314	21.6	14.6	790.7	36,576	2,064
1998	327	21.2	14.4	806.6	38,077	2,072

Source: 1997 *Manufacturing STATROM* [machine-readable data files]. MStat97. Editorial Code and Data, Inc., Detroit, Michigan, 1997. Primary source: *Economic Census* for 1992 and earlier years. The Economic Census is conducted by the Bureau of the Census, U.S. Department of Commerce, Washington, DC 20233. *Note:* 1. Data on this line are projected by the editor.

★ 487 ★

Computer Equipment

Magnetic & Optical Recording Media: General Statistics, 1987-1998

[In millions of dollars]

Years	Cost of materials	Value added by manufacture	Value of shipments[1]	Capital investment
1987	1,836.6	1,687.2	3,504.0	225.6
1988	2,067.0	1,593.5	3,630.7	269.1
1989	2,080.0	1,542.8	3,644.2	219.8
1990	2,365.9	1,675.6	4,032.1	286.8
1991	2,734.8	1,959.9	4,615.9	305.2
1992	2,513.6	2,091.5	4,641.3	394.2
1993[2]	2,406.1	2,388.0	4,765.5	337.9
1994[2]	2,637.5	2,615.2	5,256.3	325.7
1995[2]	2,716.6	2,693.6	5,413.8	380.5
1996[2]	2,845.1	2,821.0	5,670.0	399.4
1997[2]	2,973.6	2,948.5	5,926.1	418.3
1998[2]	3,102.1	3,075.9	6,182.3	437.2

Source: 1997 *Manufacturing STATROM* [machine-readable data files]. MStat97. Editorial Code and Data, Inc., Detroit, Michigan, 1997. Primary source: *Economic Census* for 1992 and earlier years. The Economic Census is conducted by the Bureau of the Census, U.S. Department of Commerce, Washington, DC 20233. *Notes:* 1. "Industry Shipments" and "Product Shipments" are rarely the same value. 2. Data on this line are projected by the editor.

Ink

★ 488 ★

Printing Ink: Employment Statistics, 1987 - 1998

Data for 1993 and beyond are projected by the editor.

Years	Total establish- ments	Employ- ment (000)	Production workers (000)	Payroll ($ mil.)	Payroll per employee ($)	Hours per production worker
1987	504	11.1	6.2	310.9	28,009	2,097
1988	484	11.1	6.4	336.7	30,333	2,109
1989	498	12.2	6.3	356.8	29,246	2,079
1990	491	11.5	6.2	354.4	30,817	2,081
1991	495	10.8	5.9	358.1	33,157	2,119
1992	519	12.3	6.5	407.4	33,122	2,015
1993	517	12.2	6.8	404.9	33,189	2,088
1994	516	13.2	7.8	458.5	34,735	2,051
1995	519	12.9	7.2	459.9	35,523	2,077
1996	522	13.2	7.3	479.6	36,275	2,078
1997	525	13.5	7.4	499.3	36,997	2,078
1998	529	13.8	7.6	519.0	37,690	2,079

Source: 1997 *Manufacturing STATROM* [machine-readable data files]. MStat97. Editorial Code and Data, Inc., Detroit, Michigan, 1997. Primary source: *Economic Census* for 1992 and earlier years. The Economic Census is conducted by the Bureau of the Census, U.S. Department of Commerce, Washington, DC 20233.

★ 489 ★

Ink

Printing Ink: General Statistics, 1987-1998

[In millions of dollars]

Years	Cost of materials	Value added by manufacture	Value of shipments[1]	Capital investment
1987	1,410.5	985.1	2,391.7	37.8
1988	1,511.8	947.9	2,447.2	32.7
1989	1,602.5	1,038.5	2,637.2	46.6
1990	1,727.2	1,035.7	2,754.4	44.3
1991	1,761.7	1,032.9	2,825.7	29.2
1992	1,973.0	1,114.0	3,075.1	46.0

[Continued]

★ 489 ★

Printing Ink: General Statistics, 1987-1998

[Continued]

Years	Cost of materials	Value added by manufacture	Value of shipments[1]	Capital investment
1993[2]	2,084.1	1,134.5	3,209.9	55.8
1994[2]	2,110.0	1,266.2	3,366.0	55.4
1995[2]	2,204.6	1,322.9	3,516.8	53.7
1996[2]	2,301.6	1,381.2	3,671.7	55.8
1997[2]	2,398.7	1,439.4	3,826.5	57.9
1998[2]	2,495.7	1,497.7	3,981.3	60.0

Source: 1997 Manufacturing STATROM [machine-readable data files]. MStat97. Editorial Code and Data, Inc., Detroit, Michigan, 1997. Primary source: Economic Census for 1992 and earlier years. The Economic Census is conducted by the Bureau of the Census, U.S. Department of Commerce, Washington, DC 20233. Notes: 1. "Industry Shipments" and "Product Shipments" are rarely the same value. 2. Data on this line are projected by the editor.

★ 490 ★

Ink

Soy-based Inks: A Profile

457,000,000—estimated number of bushels of soybeans that went into printing inks in 1995, up from 9,000 in 1987, the first year soy-based inks went into commercial use.

3,000—number of U.S. newspapers using soy-based ink.

2,875—number of U.S. daily and weekly papers, out of a total of 8,714, using soy ink, overwhelmingly color.

2,200—percentage increase in consumption of soybean-based printing inks 1988-1994—for an average annual increase of 366%.

1,000—number of bushels of soybeans it takes to supply the *Los Angeles Times* with black and color ink every day.

90—percentage of U.S. dailies using some soy-based ink. The vast majority is color, but several papers, including the *L.A. Times,* have switched to soy black.

75—number of manufacturers producing inks with soy oils or proteins.

50—approximate percentage of news ink that is oil. Color ink contains less oil than black.

[Continued]

★ 490 ★

Soy-based Inks: A Profile
[Continued]

25—percentage extra it costs to buy black ink made from soybean oil instead of petroleum-based oils.

11—percentage of total U.S. printing ink consumption attributed to newspapers.

Source: Abramowitz, Harvey. "Oh, Soy, Can You Print." *Editor & Publisher,* 27 January 1996, p. 10P. Primary source: National Soy Ink Information Center.

★ 491 ★

Ink

Soy-based Printing Ink Consumption in the United States

Nearly one-third of the nation's 8,700 newspapers, including nine out of 10 dailies, use soy ink. Data are in millions of pounds.

Year	Lbs. (mil.)
1988	2
1989	15
1990	20
1991	30
1992	41
1993	44
1994	46

Source: Abramowitz, Harvey. "Oh, Soy, Can You Print!" *Editor & Publisher,* 27 January 1996, p. 8P. Primary source: National Soy Ink Information Center.

★ 492 ★

Ink

Top U.S. Ink Makers, 1996

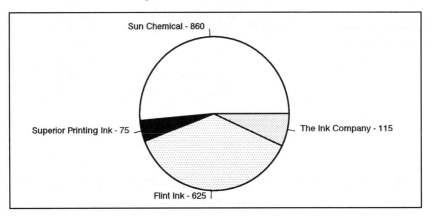

Firms are ranked by revenue from domestic sales. Figures are extrapolations for 1996 based on reported results through the first nine months of the year. The U.S. industry saw revenue grow 5% in 1996. Overall sales nearly reached $4 billion for the first time.

Company	Amount ($ mil.)
Sun Chemical	860
Flint Ink	625
The Ink Company	115
Superior Printing Ink	75

Source: "Moving Target for Industry Observers: Ranking the Ink Giants." *Graphic Arts Monthly* (March 1997), p. 70.

Machinery

★ 493 ★

Printing Trades Machines: Employment Statistics, 1987-1998

Data for 1993 and beyond are projected by the editor.

Years	Total establish- ments	Employ- ment (000)	Production workers (000)	Payroll ($ mil.)	Payroll per employee ($)	Hours per production worker
1987	438	25.0	12.1	751.6	30,064	2,091
1988	431	25.6	13.1	806.1	31,488	2,061
1989	428	29.3	13.6	833.9	28,461	2,103
1990	430	22.1	12.9	821.2	37,158	2,147
1991	443	24.0	12.1	799.9	33,329	2,107
1992	506	18.7	10.3	655.9	35,075	2,136
1993	514	18.9	10.3	683.8	36,180	2,068
1994	512	21.1	11.3	810.9	38,431	2,124
1995	526	18.2	10.3	730.1	40,055	2,126
1996	540	17.1	10.0	721.2	42,055	2,132
1997	554	16.1	9.6	712.2	44,324	2,138
1998	568	15.0	9.3	703.3	46,920	2,145

Source: 1997 *Manufacturing STATROM* [machine-readable data files]. MStat97. Editorial Code and Data, Inc., Detroit, Michigan, 1997. Primary source: *Economic Census* for 1992 and earlier years. The Economic Census is conducted by the Bureau of the Census, U.S. Department of Commerce, Washington, DC 20233.

★ 494 ★
Machinery

Printing Trades Machines: General Statistics, 1987-1998
[In millions of dollars]

Years	Cost of materials	Value added by manufacture	Value of shipments	Capital investment
1987	1,315.1	1,606.6	2,857.8	114.2
1988	1,600.1	1,739.8	3,313.1	86.3
1989	1,820.4	1,948.7	3,691.9	99.5
1990	1,752.8	1,808.2	3,538.2	89.6
1991	1,706.2	1,850.1	3,538.1	74.7
1992	1,267.6	1,266.4	2,591.9	59.6

[Continued]

★ 494 ★

Printing Trades Machines: General Statistics, 1987-1998

[Continued]

Years	Cost of materials	Value added by manufacture	Value of shipments	Capital investment
1993[2]	1,334.5	1,393.9	2,727.2	52.9
1994[2]	1,471.3	1,573.3	3,015.4	70.7
1995[2]	1,407.5	1,505.0	2,884.6	48.5
1996[2]	1,377.7	1,473.2	2,823.5	41.3
1997[2]	1,347.9	1,441.4	2,762.5	34.0
1998[2]	1,318.1	1,409.5	2,701.5	26.8

Source: 1997 *Manufacturing STATROM* [machine-readable data files]. MStat97. Editorial Code and Data, Inc., Detroit, Michigan, 1997. Primary source: *Economic Census* for 1992 and earlier years. The Economic Census is conducted by the Bureau of the Census, U.S. Department of Commerce, Washington, DC 20233. *Notes:* 1. "Industry Shipments" and "Product Shipments" are rarely the same value. 2. Data on this line are projected by the editor.

Paper

★ 495 ★

Largest Newsprint Companies in North America - 1996

Firms are ranked by annual capacity in thousands of metric tons. Total capacity reached 16 million metric tons.

Company	Canada	U.S.	Total	Share %
Abitibi-Price[1]	1,187	654	1,841	11.4
Avenor Inc.	1,163	242	1,405	8.7
Stone-Consolidated[2]	909	435	1,344	8.3
Donahue[3]	1,374	0	1,374	8.5
Bowater	230	1,072	1,302	8.1
Kruger	926	36	962	5.9
Fletcher Challenge Canada	759	0	759	4.7
North Pacific Paper	0	700	700	4.3
Champion International	0	700	700	4.3
Smurfit Newsprint	0	645	645	4.0
Southeast Paper	0	442	442	2.7
Daishowa Forest Products	399	0	399	2.4
Boise Cascade	0	396	396	2.4
MacMillan Bloedel	392	0	392	2.4
Spruce Falls	300	0	300	1.8

[Continued]

★ 495 ★

Largest Newsprint Companies in North America - 1996
[Continued]

Company	Canada	U.S.	Total	Share %
Kimberly-Clark	0	299	299	1.8
Alberta Newsprint	246	0	246	1.5
Newsprint South	0	233	233	1.4
Garden State Paper	0	225	225	1.3
James Maclaren Industries	218	0	218	1.3
Bear Island Paper	0	213	213	1.3
F.F. Soucy	211	0	211	1.3
Alliance Forest Products[4]	203	0	203	1.2
Irving Paper	202	0	202	1.2
Howe Sound Pulp & Paper	197	0	197	1.2

Source: "Industry at a Glance." *Editor & Publisher,* 11 October 1997, p. 31. Primary source: *Pulp & Paper Week,* Canadian Pulp and Paper Association and American Forest & Paper Association. *Notes:* 1. Abitibi-Price and Stone-Consolidated merged earlier this year. 2. Includes Rainy River Forest Products and Stone Container Corp's mill in Snowflake, AZ. 3. Includes the Duno Corp. mills; does not include Donohue's 50% stake in Finlay. 4. Includes Domtar's newsprint and uncoated groundwood business, acquired in 1995; does not include Coosa Pines, AL, mill, acquired from Kimberly-Clark in 1997.

★ 496 ★

Paper

Newsprint Consumption by Year

Newsprint prices reached a high of $750 a metric ton in January 1996 after doubling for the last two years. As of November 1996, the price had fallen to $500. Data show newsprint consumption by American dailies. Consumption has decreased because of fine-tuning inking systems, reducing waste at the start of press runs, eliminating systems, eliminating whole sections and, in some cases, cutting newspaper deliveries to uneconomical rural areas.

Year	Tons (mil.)
1994	9.4
1995	8.9
1996	8.2

Source: Peterson, Iver. "As the Cost of Newsprint Declines, Analysts Argue Over Who Will Benefit." *New York Times,* 11 November 1996, p. C7. Primary source: National Newspaper Association.

★ 497 ★

Paper

Paper Industries Machines: Employment Statistics, 1987 - 1998

Data for 1993 and beyond are projected by the editor.

Years	Total establish- ments	Employ- ment (000)	Production workers (000)	Payroll ($ mil.)	Payroll per employee ($)	Hours per production worker
1987	278	17.1	9.6	502.2	29,368	1,990
1988	272	17.3	10.4	538.2	31,110	2,135
1989	282	18.2	11.7	624.8	34,330	2,111
1990	285	19.5	12.2	648.3	33,246	2,156
1991	292	17.8	9.6	606.6	34,079	2,167
1992	333	18.2	10.2	651.8	35,813	2,088
1993	332	18.1	9.8	667.2	36,862	2,000
1994	329	17.4	9.7	691.3	39,730	2,082
1995	337	18.8	10.9	741.7	39,475	2,124
1996	346	19.0	11.0	771.0	40,506	2,133
1997	355	19.3	11.2	800.3	41,512	2,141
1998	363	19.5	11.4	829.7	42,492	2,149

Source: 1997 *Manufacturing STATROM* [machine-readable data files]. MStat97. Editorial Code and Data, Inc., Detroit, Michigan, 1997. Primary source: *Economic Census* for 1992 and earlier years. The Economic Census is conducted by the Bureau of the Census, U.S. Department of Commerce, Washington, DC 20233.

★ 498 ★

Paper

Paper Industry Machines: General Statistics, 1987-1998

[In millions of dollars]

Years	Cost of materials	Value added by manufacture	Value of shipments[1]	Capital investment
1987	868.8	1,027.0	1,867.1	45.6
1988	1,064.6	1,022.5	2,012.1	60.0
1989	1,410.1	1,208.8	2,579.8	84.6
1990	1,591.2	1,118.7	2,770.4	72.0
1991	1,200.0	987.8	2,206.3	62.6
1992	1,209.8	1,273.8	2,524.2	65.4
1993[2]	1,330.5	1,206.3	2,528.9	55.9
1994[2]	1,413.0	1,407.5	2,812.5	49.3
1995[2]	1,509.8	1,503.9	3,005.1	74.9

[Continued]

★ 498 ★

Paper Industry Machines: General Statistics, 1987-1998

[Continued]

Years	Cost of materials	Value added by manufacture	Value of shipments[1]	Capital investment
1996[2]	1,581.1	1,574.9	3,147.0	78.6
1997[2]	1,652.3	1,645.9	3,288.9	82.2
1998[2]	1,723.6	1,716.9	3,430.8	85.9

Source: 1997 *Manufacturing STATROM* [machine-readable data files]. MStat97. Editorial Code and Data, Inc., Detroit, Michigan, 1997. Primary source: *Economic Census* for 1992 and earlier years. The Economic Census is conducted by the Bureau of the Census, U.S. Department of Commerce, Washington, DC 20233. *Notes:* 1. "Industry Shipments" and "Product Shipments" are rarely the same value. 2. Data on this line are projected by the editor.

★ 499 ★

Paper

Paper Mills: Employment Statistics, 1987-1998

Data for 1993 and beyond are projected by the editor.

Years	Total establishments	Employment (000)	Production workers (000)	Payroll ($ mil.)	Payroll per employee ($)	Hours per production worker
1987	282	129.1	99.2	4,597.0	35,608	2,121
1988	NA	130.4	101.1	4,773.0	36,603	2,128
1989	316	130.1	100.6	4,927.1	37,872	2,127
1990	NA	130.1	98.6	5,061.5	38,905	2,136
1991	NA	130.3	99.4	5,223.5	40,088	2,134
1992	280	130.6	100.4	5,420.5	41,505	2,143
1993	NA	126.2	97.2	5,365.3	42,514	2,184
1994	NA	122.8	94.9	5,519.1	44,944	2,213
1995	NA	127.3	97.4	5,861.0	46,053	2,185
1996	NA	127.0	97.2	6,031.1	47,484	2,193
1997	NA	126.8	96.9	6,201.3	48,920	2,201
1998	NA	126.5	96.6	6,371.5	50,363	2,209

Source: 1997 *Manufacturing STATROM* [machine-readable data files]. MStat97. Editorial Code and Data, Inc., Detroit, Michigan, 1997. Primary source: *Economic Census* for 1992 and earlier years. The Economic Census is conducted by the Bureau of the Census, U.S. Department of Commerce, Washington, DC 20233. *Note:* NA = Not available.

★ 500 ★
Paper

Paper Mills: General Statistics, 1987-1998
[In millions of dollars]

Year	Cost of materials	Value added by manufacture	Value of shipments[1]	Capital investment
1987	14,856.0	14,021.9	28,915.5	2,759.9
1988	16,782.1	16,866.2	33,545.8	3,299.5
1989	18,481.0	17,100.6	35,387.1	5,236.6
1990	18,861.1	16,599.8	35,321.8	4,277.5
1991	17,983.1	15,510.3	33,344.0	3,637.7
1992	17,971.4	14,847.7	32,786.4	2,911.5
1993[2]	17,717.1	14,511.7	32,102.6	2,863.5
1994[2]	19,815.4	15,012.3	35,071.3	3,137.5
1995[2]	21,426.3	16,232.7	37,922.4	3,905.0
1996[2]	22,092.8	16,737.7	39,102.1	4,031.3
1997[2]	22,759.4	17,242.7	40,281.9	4,157.6
1998[2]	23,426.0	17,747.7	41,461.6	4,283.9

Source: 1997 *Manufacturing STATROM* [machine-readable data files]. MStat97. Editorial Code and Data, Inc., Detroit, Michigan, 1997. Primary source: *Economic Census* for 1992 and earlier years. The Economic Census is conducted by the Bureau of the Census, U.S. Department of Commerce, Washington, DC 20233. *Notes:* 1. "Industry Shipments" and "Product Shipments" are rarely the same value.

★ 501 ★
Paper

Paper Production by Year

Production is shown in thousands of tons. Data include newsprint, uncoated paper and packaging papers. Data for 1996-97 are estimated.

Year	Tons (000)
1992	40,973
1993	41,745
1994	43,355
1995	42,880
1996	42,036
1997	43,156

Source: "U.S. Paper Industry Will See More Globalization, Slower Growth in 1997." *Pulp & Paper* (January 1997), p. 55.

★ 502 ★

Paper

Publication Grades: How Lightweight Coated Stock is Used

Total production of coated paper reached 13.3 million tons in 1996. Production in North America should increase to 15.0 million tons in 1997. The table shows how the publication grade is used.

[In percent]

Segment	Share
Magazines	67.9
Catalogs	26.4
Inserts	3.8
Other	1.9

Source: "Coated Paper Alert: Prices Begin to Rise." *Graphic Arts Monthly,* (June 1997), p. 60.

★ 503 ★

Paper

Publication Grades: How Supercalendered Stock is Used

Of the 7.0 million tons of paper used annually for magazines and catalogs in the United States, very little is used in the United States. However, in Europe, almost half the magazines are printed on supercalendered paper. The table shows how the publication grade is used.

[In percent]

Segment	Share
Inserts	50.0
Catalogs	31.3
Magazines	6.3
Other	12.5

Source: "Coated Paper Alert: Prices Begin to Rise." *Graphic Arts Monthly,* (June 1997), p. 60.

★ 504 ★

Paper

Top Paper Companies in Canada

Firms are ranked by total pulp, paper and converted product sales. Figures are in millions of dollars.

Company	Sales
Abitibi-Price Inc.	2,590
Stone-Consolidated	2,129
Cascades	2,101
Fletcher Challenge	1,860
Domtar	1,672[1]
Avenor Inc.	1,656
MacMillan Bloedel Ltd.	1,626
Donohue Inc.	1,216
Repap Enterprises Inc.	1,213
Noranda Forest Inc.	1,029

Source: "Top North American Paper Companies: Annual Survey." *PIMA's Papermaker* (June 1997), p. 63. *Note:* 1. Estimate.

★ 505 ★

Paper

Top Coated Free-Sheet Producers in North America

Coated free-sheet papers are used in magazines, catalogs, and commercial printing uses such as advertising brochures and inserts. The table shows the market shares of the the leading providers, in percent. Shares are shown basd on total capacity of 5,471,861 short tons.

Company	Share
S.D. Warren	20.28
Westvaco	11.80
Champion International	10.82
Mead	9.59
Consolidated Papers	9.13
Repap	6.67
Potlatch	6.21
International Paper Co.	5.48
Simpson Paper	4.75
Appleton Papers	2.37
Other	13.0

Source: Routson, Joyce K. "Grade Profile." *Pulp & Paper,* (March 1997), p. 13.

★ 506 ★

Paper

Top Uncoated Free-Sheet Producers in North America

Uncoated free-sheet papers are used for office and business printing, business forms and envelopes, publishing (mostly text and adult trade), commercial printing and writing. The table shows the market shares of the leading providers, in percent. Total capacity is shown based on 15,858,000 short tons.

Company	Share
International Paper Co.	15.8
Georgia Pacific Co.	13.4
Champion International	9.6
Boise Cascade	7.7
Union Camp Corp.	7.6
Willamette Industries	6.1
Weyerhaeuser Co.	5.4
Domtar Inc.	5.3
Appleton Papers Inc.	3.6
James River Corp.	3.1
Noranda Forest Inc.	2.6
P.H. Glatfelter Co.	2.3
Other	22.0

Source: "Grade Profile." *Pulp & Paper,* (April 1997), p. 11.

★ 507 ★

Paper

Top U.S. Paper Companies

Firms are ranked by total pulp, paper and converted product sales. Figures are in millions of dollars.

Company	Sales
International Paper Company	14,003
Kimberly-Clark Corp.	13,149
Procter & Gamble Company	10,196
Unisource Worldwide	7,023
James River Corp.	5,690
Georgia-Pacific Corp.	5,609
Stone Container Corp.	5,142
Champion International	4,962
The Mead Corp.	4,707
Weyerhaeuser Company	4,648
Tenneco Packaging	3,602

[Continued]

★ 507 ★

Top U.S. Paper Companies
[Continued]

Company	Sales
Boise Cascade Corp.	3,584
Jefferson Smurfit Corp.	3,410
Union Camp Corp.	3,030
Sonoco Products	2,788
Westvaco Corp.	2,746
Willamette Industries	2,344
Temple-Inland Inc.	2,082
Bowater Inc.	1,616
Fort Howard Corp.	1,581
Consolidated Papers Inc.	1,545
Chesapeake Corp.	1,158
Riverwood International	1,146
Potlatch Corporation	1,079
Crown Vantage	925

Source: "Top North American Paper Companies: Annual Survey." *PIMA's Papermaker* (June 1997), p. 63.

Photographic Equipment

★ 508 ★

Photographic Equipment: Employment Statistics, 1987-1998

Data for 1993 and beyond are projected by the editor.

Years	Total establish-ments	Employ-ment (000)	Production workers (000)	Payroll ($ mil.)	Payroll per employee ($)	Hours per production worker
1987	787	88.0	44.8	2,878.3	32,708	2,056
1988	NA	87.5	43.9	2,963.4	33,867	2,114
1989	806	87.0	43.9	3,134.3	36,026	2,207
1990	NA	79.3	41.2	2,937.4	37,042	2,228
1991	NA	78.0	40.0	3,044.1	39,027	2,188
1992	904	77.5	39.4	3,069.3	39,604	2,302
1993	NA	75.7	38.0	2,881.0	38,058	2,279
1994	NA	64.8	34.8	2,716.6	41,923	2,233
1995	NA	62.7	31.7	2,844.8	45,371	2,424
1996	NA	58.9	29.6	2,821.8	47,940	2,497

[Continued]

★ 508 ★

Photographic Equipment: Employment Statistics, 1987-1998

[Continued]

Years	Total establishments	Employment (000)	Production workers (000)	Payroll ($ mil.)	Payroll per employee ($)	Hours per production worker
1997	NA	55.0	27.5	2,798.8	50,867	2,580
1998	NA	51.2	25.5	2,775.9	54,233	2,677

Source: 1997 *Manufacturing STATROM* [machine-readable data files]. MStat97. Editorial Code and Data, Inc., Detroit, Michigan, 1997. Primary source: *Economic Census* for 1992 and earlier years. The Economic Census is conducted by the Bureau of the Census, U.S. Department of Commerce, Washington, DC 20233. *Note:* NA = Not available.

★ 509 ★

Photographic Equipment

Photographic Equipment: General Statistics, 1987-1998

[In millions of dollars]

Years	Cost of materials	Value added by manufacture	Value of shipments[1]	Capital investment
1987	6,233.5	12,908.0	19,240.5	681.0
1988	6,638.0	14,223.2	20,545.8	809.7
1989	6,935.4	15,804.2	22,737.8	1,008.2
1990	6,439.2	14,527.2	21,018.2	1,008.6
1991	6,686.4	14,603.3	21,397.8	1,089.2
1992	7,058.7	14,885.4	22,149.8	808.1
1993[2]	6,750.5	15,916.8	22,367.8	775.4
1994[2]	7,011.4	16,057.0	23,367.6	755.3
1995[2]	7,157.9	16,392.6	23,855.9	930.3
1996[2]	7,314.5	16,751.2	24,377.9	948.1
1997[2]	7,471.2	17,109.9	24,899.9	965.9
1998[2]	7,627.8	17,468.6	25,421.9	983.7

Source: 1997 *Manufacturing STATROM* [machine-readable data files]. MStat97. Editorial Code and Data, Inc., Detroit, Michigan, 1997. Primary source: *Economic Census* for 1992 and earlier years. The Economic Census is conducted by the Bureau of the Census, U.S. Department of Commerce, Washington, DC 20233. *Notes:* 1. "Industry Shipments" and "Product Shipments" are rarely the same value. 2. Data on this line are projected by the editor.

Chapter 12
EMPLOYMENT, COMPENSATION, AND POSITIONS

Information on employment, occupations, income, and wages is presented throughout this book under the topic of *Industry Statistics* in a number of chapters, including occupational growth to the year 2005. The tables in this chapter are from trade sources and presented in one place to give additional career-related information.

★ 510 ★

Employment in the Publishing Industry

From the source: "Writers and editors held about 272,000 jobs in 1994. Nearly a third of salaried writers and editors work for newspapers, magazines, and book publishers. Substantial numbers also work in advertising agencies, in radio and television broadcasting, in public relations firms, and on journals and newsletters published by business and nonprofit organizations. Others develop publications for government agencies or write for motion picture companies. Many technical writers work for computer software firms or manufacturers of aircraft, chemicals, pharmaceuticals, and computers and other electronic equipment. Jobs with major book publishers, magazines, broadcasting companies, advertising agencies and public relations firms are concentrated in New York, Chicago, Los Angeles, Boston, Philadelphia, San Francisco and Washington D.C."

Source: "Writers and Editors." *Occupational Outlook Handbook 1996-97 Edition,* U.S. Department of Labor, Washington D.C., (January 1996), p. 185.

★ 511 ★

Editor/Executive Editor: Average Compensation by Responsibility

Data show the average salaries of editors or executive editors at consumer and business magazines. Figures are based on a survey of 504 respondents in editorial positions. Salaries increased approximately 7 percent over last year's survey, with reported salaries as low as $12,000 and as high as $150,000. Editors and executive editors are responsible for editorial direction and content including art, text and cover of one or more magazines.

Number of Magazines Supervised	Average	Average Business	Average Consumer
One magazine	$51,100	$53,200	$48,200
More than one	$47,600	$47,100	$48,100

Source: "Stressed for Success." *Folio,* 1 August 1997, p. 47.

★ 512 ★

Compensation

Editorial Directors: Average Compensation by Age

Data show the average salaries of editorial directors working at consumer and business magazines. Figures are based on a survey of 504 respondents in editorial positions. Salaries increased approximately 6 percent over last year's survey, with reported salaries as low as $30,000 and as high as $175,000. The Editorial Director or Editor in Chief set editorial policy; they may be in charge of other products and other departments in addition to editorial, and all editors report to this person.

Age Category	Average	Average Business	Average Consumer
Up to 29	$49,700	[1]	[1]
30 - 39	$64,368	$70,965	$55,756
40 - 49	$80,278	$77,880	$82,880
50 or more	$81,459	$77,580	$85,498

Source: "Stressed for Success." *Folio,* 1 August 1997, p. 47. *Note:* 1. Not enough information supplied to report results.

★ 513 ★

Compensation

Editorial Directors: Average Compensation by Total Pages Produced Annually

Editorial Director or Editor in Chief is defined as setting policy, may be in charge of other products and other departments in addition to editorial, and all editors report to this person.

Pages Produced Annually	Average	Average Business	Average Consumer
Up to 499	$63,612	$64,033	$63,100
500 - 999	$78,533	$76,242	$81,248
1,000 - 1,499	$66,233	[1]	$60,003
1,500 - 2,999	$72,531	[1]	[1]

Source: "Stressed for Success." *Folio,* 1 August 1997, p. 47. *Note:* 1. Not enough information supplied to report results.

★ 514 ★

Compensation

Managing Editors: Average Compensation by Circulation

Data show the average salaries of managing editors working at consumer and business magazines. Figures are based on a survey of 504 respondents in editorial positions. Salaries increased approximately 6 percent over last year's survey, with reported salaries as low as $22,000 and as high as $116,000. Managing editors coordinate editorial, art and production departments to ensure that the magazine is published on time and in acceptable form. Managing editors oversee the copy editing and proofreading functions.

Circulation	Average	Average Business	Average Consumer
Up to 19,999	$46,135	$39,373	[1]
20,000 - 49,999	$41,816	$43,452	$36,833
50,000 - 99,999	$45,466	$45,406	$45,557
100,000 - 499,999	$48,172	[1]	$48,812
500,000 or more	$81,737	[1]	$80,144

Source: "Stressed for Success." *Folio,* 1 August 1997, p. 47. *Note:* 1. Not enough information supplied to report results.

★ 515 ★

Compensation

Senior Editors: Average Compensation by Age

Data show the average salaries of senior editors working at consumer and business magazines. Figures are based on a survey of 504 respondents in editorial positions. Salaries increased approximately 4 percent over last year's survey, with reported salaries as low as $24,000 and as high as $130,000. Senior editors plan and write or assign features and other articles. They may head the editorial feature department and oversee other editorial employees.

Salary by Age	Average	Average Business	Average Consumer
Up to 29	$36,271	[1]	[1]
30-39	$59,223	$53,427	$64,613
40-49	$66,627	$60,872	$60,003
50 or more	$54,606	[1]	$53,157

Source: "Stressed for Success." *Folio,* 1 August 1997, p. 51. *Note:* 1. Not enough information supplied to report results.

★516★

Compensation

United Kingdom: Salaries of Selected Magazine Positions

Data show the range of potential salaries in women's and men's lifestyle magazines. Figures are in thousands of British pounds.

Job	Salary
Editor	30-100
Deputy Editor	30-49
Ad sales director	30-45
Ad sales manager	20-30
Production editor	25-35
Publisher	35-45
Sub-editor	20-28

Source: "Birt's Worth 354,000: How About You?" *The Guardian*, 14 July 1997, p. 5. Primary source: *BECTU/NUJ/CAMPAIGN* magazine.

★517★

Compensation

United Kingdom: Salaries of Selected Newspaper Positions

The table shows salaries in thousands of British pounds. Figures refer to National and regional newspapers.

Job	Regionals	Nationals
Editors	40-50	130 plus
Reporters	12-25	28-40
Specialist writer	25-30	35-55
Sub-editor	12-18	28-38

Source: "Birt's Worth 354,000: How About You?" *The Guardian*, 14 July 1997, p. 5. Primary source: *BECTU/NUJ/CAMPAIGN* magazine.

★518★

Canadian Book Promoters

From the source: "An informal salary survey by the Book Promoters Association of Canada has found that even though its members work an average of 49.5 hours a week, only 10% get paid overtime; 60% receive time off in lieu; and 30% receive nothing. Fewer than half of the 45 respondents receive regular employment reviews; half have access to a pension or RRSP plan; 10% get performance bonuses. Though most publicists are university-educated, they are hired at an average annual salary of $23,000."

Source: "Survey Says." *Quill & Quire,* (January 1996), p. 20.

★519★

Positions

Editorial Positions in Publishing, 1996

The average pay raise in the publishing industry was about 6 percent in 1995. The table is based on a survey of 327 people. The survey provided insight on several expected trends. The largest salaries were reported by people managing the largest companies—publishing companies with annual revenues of $100 million or more. Management positions carried higher salaries than those in editorial, sales and marketing, operations and rights. Outside of management, publishers were the best paid employees with larger mid-sized houses earning an average of $237,500.

[In dollars]

| Position | <$1 mil. | Company revenues | | |
		$1 mil.-$9.9 mil.	$10 mil.-$99.9 mil.	$100+ mil.
Net average	65,865	47,373	62,559	91,233
Ed. Director/Editor in Chief	74,833	53,670	88,400	125,000
Senior/Executive/Managing Editor	42,420	48,175	59,116	76,125
Editor	31,750	37,000	36,000	16,600
Associate Editor	57,700	35,000	NA	NA
Prod. Development Ed./Acquisitions	65,000	NA	56,266	NA
Copy Editor/Proofreader	NA	32,000	32,000	NA
Editorial Assistant	NA	31,500	30,000	NA

Source: Milliot, Jim. "The Corporate Payscale." *Publishers Weekly,* 19 August 1996, p. 38. *Note:* NA = Not available.

★ 520 ★
Positions

Management Positions in Publishing, 1996

Data show salaries of selected positions by size of company. Figures are based on a survey of 327 people.

[In dollars]

| Position | <$1 mil. | Company revenues | | $100+ mil. |
		$1 mil.-$9.9 mil.	$10 mil.-$99.9 mil.	
Net Average	76,375	78,758	130,118	160,167
President/CEO	106,108	128,167	249,525	330,000
Owner/Director	74,444	168,625	101,000	NA
Exec./Senior V.P.	67,600	118,000	102,900	200,000
V.P. General Manager	51,750	96,000	73,125	205,000
V.P. Fin./Controller	NA	63,500	61,500	150,000
V.P. Prod./Operations	NA	NA	225,000	126,375
Business/Office Manager	24,000	NA	NA	51,000

Source: Milliot, Jim. "The Corporate Payscale." *Publishers Weekly,* 19 August 1996, p. 39. *Note:* NA = Not available.

★ 521 ★
Positions

Operations Positions in Publishing, 1996

Figures show salaries for selected positions by size of company. Figures are based on a survey of 327 people.

[In dollars]

| Position | <$1 mil. | Company revenues | | $100+ mil. |
		$1 mil.-$9.9 mil.	$10 mil.-$99.9 mil.	
Net Average	NA	40,520	47,750	105,075
Dist./Fulfillment Director	NA	48,000	65,500	118,100
Prod./Director	NA	40,000	55,000	66,000
Art Director	NA	NA	NA	NA
Accounting Manager	NA	25,000	NA	NA

Source: Milliot, Jim. "The Corporate Payscale." *Publishers Weekly,* 19 August 1996, p. 39. *Note:* NA = Not available.

★ 522 ★

Positions

Rights Positions in Publishing, 1996

Data show salaries for selected positions by size of company. Figures are based on a survey of 327 people.

[In dollars]

| Position | <$1 mil. | Company revenues | | $100+ mil. |
		$1 mil.-$9.9 mil.	$10 mil.-$99.9 mil.	
Net Average	43,000	43,667	NA	104,000
Sub Rights Director/Manager	NA	53,000	NA	104,000
Licensing Director/Manager	43,000	NA	NA	NA
International Rights Director/Manager	NA	25,000	NA	NA

Source: Milliot, Jim. "The Corporate Payscale." *Publishers Weekly,* 19 August 1996, p. 39. *Note:* NA = Not available.

★ 523 ★

Positions

Sales and Marketing Positions in Publishing, 1996

Data show salaries for selected positions based on the size of the company. Figures are based on a survey of 327 people.

[In dollars]

| Position | <$1 mil. | Company revenues | | $100+ mil. |
		$1 mil.-$9.9 mil.	$10 mil.-$99.9 mil.	
Net Average	55,675	56,895	69,227	75,903
V.P. Sales/Marketing	78,000	48,250	85,333	175,000
Publisher	45,000	225,000	237,500	225,000
Associate Publisher	NA	56,000	NA	180,000
Sales Director/Manager	NA	58,688	66,500	79,500
Marketing Director/Manager	55,000	41,450	40,250	66,800
Promotion Director/Manager	29,400	24,000	51,500	NA
Sales Rep/Account Manager	83,000	45,000	45,322	55,891

Source: Milliot, Jim. "The Corporate Payscale." *Publishers Weekly,* 19 August 1996, p. 38. *Note:* NA = Not available.

Chapter 13
CRIME AND CENSORSHIP

The ten tables in this chapter provide a glimpse of illegal activities—primarily piracy of electronic and tape products—and some information about the censorship of printed products.

Crime

★ 524 ★

Leading Music Pirates

Countries are ranked by the number of CDs and cassettes illegally reproduced in millions of copies. Data include the share of the domestic market represented by pirated copies.

Country	Copies ($ mil.)	Share of market
Russia	222.3	73
China	145.0	54
India	128.4	30
Pakistan	75.4	94
Mexico	70.0	54
Brazil	62.4	45
United States	26.6	3
Italy	21.5	33
Romania	21.5	85
Turkey	16.4	30

Source: Tagliabue, John. "Fakes Blot a Nation's Good Names." *New York Times,* 15 July 1997, p. C1. Primary source: International Federation of the Phonographic Industry.

★ 525 ★

Crime

Leading Nations for Piracy

Countries are ranked by well organized piracy networks, weak laws and inadequate enforcement.

Country	Country
Turkey	Italy
China	Colombia
Thailand	

Source: Tagliabue, John. "Fakes Blot a Nation's Good Names." *New York Times,* 15 July 1997, p. C1. Primary source: European Brands Association.

★ 526 ★

Crime

Leading Software Pirates, 1996

Countries are ranked by the value of illegally copied software in millions of dollars. Data include the share of the domestic market represented by pirated copies.

Country	Value ($ mil.)	Share of market
United States	2,361	27
Japan	1,190	41
China	704	96
South Korea	516	70
Germany	498	36
France	412	44
Russia	383	91
Canada	357	42
Brazil	356	68
Italy	341	55

Source: Tagliabue, John. "Fakes Blot a Nation's Good Names." *New York Times,* 15 July 1997, p. C1. Primary source: Business Software Alliance.

★ 527 ★

Crime

Leading Video Pirates, 1995

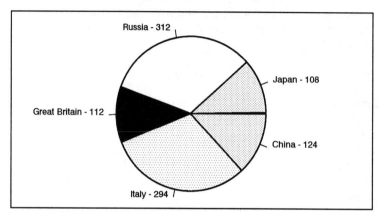

Countries are ranked by the value of illegally reproduced U.S. films. Figures are in millions of dollars.

Country	($ mil.)
Russia	312
Italy	294
China	124
Great Britain	112
Japan	108

Source: Tagliabue, John. "Fakes Blot a Nation's Good Name." *New York Times,* 15 July 1997, p. C1. Primary source: Motion Picture Industry of America.

★ 528 ★

Crime

U.S. Piracy Losses to China

Data show estimated annual losses in millions of dollars.

Product	Value ($ mil.)
Entertainment software	1,290
Records and music	300
Business software	250
Books	125
Motion pictures	124

Source: Brauchli, Marcus W. "In a Trade War, China Takes the Bigger Hit." *The Wall Street Journal,* 17 May 1996, p. A10. Primary source: Intellectual Property Alliance and Software Publishers Association.

★ 529 ★

Crime

U.S. Piracy Losses to Mexico, 1995

Data show the value of losses from the illegal reproduction of U.S. products. Mexico ranks fourth among countries where most piracy occurred. China lead the piracy market with $1.83 billion.

Product	Value ($ mil.)
Computer entertainment software	100
Records and music	85
Motion pictures	67
Books	33

Source: "The Counterfeit Story." *New York Times,* 20 April 1996, p. 20. Primary source: International Intellectual Property Alliance.

Censorship

★ 530 ★

Censorship Efforts in the United States

According to the source, 475 actions were recorded in 44 states last year. Attempts to censor books fell by 11% from 1994-1995, yet there were still 300 incidents. Broad challenges to the freedom to read, however, rose 46%; a third of the incidents directly or indirectly involved the religious right.

The book challenged most often was *I Know Why the Caged Bird Sings* by Maya Angelou, which reflects a three-year trend of a disproportionate number of attacks on books by African American women; such classics as *Of Mice and Men* and *The Catcher in the Rye* also appear on the list of most frequently challenged books.

Source: "In Banned Books Week, Censorship Still Thrives." *Publishers Weekly,* 23 September 1996, p. 12.

★ 531 ★

Censorship

Libraries and Community Standards

From the source: "Support for free speech increases with education and income, according to the 1996 National Household Education Survey. But it decreases with age: 88 percent of U.S. adults aged 18 to 39 would grant atheists the right to speak, compared with 86 percent of those aged 40 to 55, 77 percent of those aged 55 to 69 percent of those aged 70 and older. Free speech disturbs us more when it's in print and circulating to the public. A startling 73 percent of U.S. high school dropouts would ban a library book if most people disapproved of it, and so would 52 percent of adults with only a high school diploma. College is where those attitudes change. Only 39 percent of adults with some college experience would ban unpopular books from libraries, and only 24 percent of those with a bachelor's degree would do so."

Education	Percentage
Less than high school	73
High school diploma	52
Some college	39
College graduate	24

Source: "Who's Against Free Speech?" American Demographics (August 1997), p. 32.

★ 532 ★

Censorship

Most Banned or Challenged Books of 1996

1. *I Know Why the Caged Bird Sings*, by Maya Angelou, 1970. It's Angelou's first installment of her autobiography, the story of a black girl growing up during the Great Depression. Objections include Angelou's description of being raped as a child by her mother's boyfriend.

2. *Catcher in the Rye*, by J.D. Salinger, 1951. A prep-school dropout, adrift in New York City, learns to face the hypocrisy he finds in the adult world and his own weaknesses. Challenged in Florida, Maine, California, Georgia and Tennessee.

3. *The Chocolate War*, by Robert Cormier, 1974. Young adult novel about the battles of a Roman Catholic schoolboy and the school's efforts to generate income through the sale of chocolate candies using one-upmanship, backstabbing and power plays.

4. *Bridge to Terabithia*, by Katherine Paterson, 1977. Winner of the 1978 Newbery Medal, this novel tells about a friendship between a boy and girl from different cultural backgrounds and the imaginary kingdom they create.

[Continued]

★ 532 ★

Most Banned or Challenged Books of 1996
[Continued]

5. *Forever . . . A Novel*, by Judy Blume, 1975, involves a 17 year-old boy and girl and their first sexual experiences.

6. *It's Perfectly Normal: A Book About Changing Bodies, Growing Up, Sex, and Sexual Health*, by Robie Harris, 1994. Challenged in school and public libraries in Florida, New Jersey, New York and Washington.

7. *The Adventures of Huckleberry Finn*, by Mark Twain. Published in 1884 in Great Britain, 1885 in the United States. It describes the adventures of two runaway boys, one black, one white. Objections to language considered racially offensive.

8. *A Day No Pigs Would Die*, by Robert Newton Peck, 1972. Autobiographical novel about a Shaker boy and his father during hard times in rural Vermont in the 1920s.

9. *The Goosebumps* series, by R.L. Stine. More than 40 suspenseful horror stories written for children ages 8 to 13. Considered satanic, violent and disturbing by some parents.

10. *My Brother Sam is Dead*, by James Lincoln Collier and Christopher Collier, 1974. Revolutionary War novel. Objections included references to rape, drinking and battlefield violence.

Source: Young, Allison. "Book Banned, and Teacher Quit." *The Detroit Free Press,* 3 February 1997, p. 1A. Primary source: American Library Association.

Chapter 14
AWARDS, BESTSELLERS, PICKS

This chapter presents tabulations of award winners, lists of bestsellers, and "picks" of favorites by different groups or authorities.

Awards

★ 533 ★

Book Critics Circle Winners, 1997

Data show National Book Critics Circle Awards, winners by category.

Title	Author	Publisher
Fiction *Women in Their Beds*	Gina Berriault	Counterpoint
Criticism *Finding a Form*	William Gass	Knopf
Poetry *Sun Under Wood*	Robert Haas	Ecco
Biography/Autobiography *Angela's Ashes*	Frank McCourt	Scribner
General Nonfiction *Bad Land: An American Romance*	Jonathan Raban	Pantheon

Source: "Five Authors Honored by Book Critics Circle." *The Christian Science Monitor,* 21 March 1997, p. 2. Primary source: *Associated Press.*

★ 534 ★
Awards

Comic Industry Awards Winners

Here is a list of some of the winners of the 9th annual Will Eisner Comic Industry Awards:

Best Anthology - Batman: Black and White, Mark Chiarello and Scott Peterson, eds. (DC)

Best Writer - Alan Moore, From Hell (Kitchen Sink); Supreme (Maximum Press)

Best Writer/Artist-Humor - Don Rosa, Walt Disney's Comics & Stories; Uncle Scrooge (Gladstone)

Best Penciller - Steve Rude, Nexus: Executioner's Song (Dark Horse)

Best Inker - Al Williamson, Spider-Man, Untold Tales of Spider-Man #17-18 (Marvel)

Best Coloring - Matt Hollingsworth, Preacher; Death: The Time of Your Life (DC/Vertigo); Dr. Strangefate; Challengers of the Unknown (DC)

[Continued]

★ 534 ★

Comic Industry Awards Winners
[Continued]

Best Lettering - Todd Klein, The Sandman; Death; The Time of Your Life; House of Secrets; The Dreaming (DC/Vertigo); Batman; The Spectre; Kingdom Come (DC)

Best Editor - Dan Raspler, Kingdom Come; Hitman; The Spectre; Sergio Aragones Destroys the DC Universe (DC)

Hall of Fame - Gil Kane, Charles Schulz, Julius Schwartz and Curt Swan

Source: From the Internet, http://www.comicbookresources.com/news/eisner_0720.html, 20 July 1997.

★ 535 ★
Awards

Lambda Award Winners

The table shows selected award winners in the field of gay/lesbian literature.

- **Lesbian Fiction:** *Memory Mambo* by Achy Obejas.

- **Gay Men's Fiction:** *Funny Boy* by Shyam Selvadurai.

- **Lesbian Poetry:** (Tie) *All-American Girl* by Robin Becker and *Furious Cooking* by Maureen Seaton.

- **Gay Men's Poetry:** *What the Boy Told* by Rafael Campo.

- **Spirituality:** *The Good Book* by Peter Gomes.

- **Drama:** *Split Britches* by Sue-Ellen Case, Editor.

- **Children's/Young Adult Literature:** *Good Moon Rising* by Nancy Garden.

- **Editor's Choice:** *Tennessee Williams' Letters to Donald Windham 1940-1965* by Donald Windham, Editor.

- **Publisher's Service Award:** Norman Laurila.

- **Founders' Award:** Helaine Harris.

Source: "1996 Lammy Winners." *Lambda Book Report* (June 1997), p. 10.

★ 536 ★

Awards

National Book Award Finalists

Authors	Title
Fiction nominees	
Don DeLillo	*Underworld*
Charles Frazier	*Cold Mountain*
Diane Johnson	*Le Divorce*
Cynthia Ozick	*The Puttermesser Papers*
Nonfiction nominees	
Joseph J. Ellis	*American Sphinx*
David I. Kertzer's	*The Kidnapping of Egardo Mortara*
Jamaica Kincaid	*My Brother*
Thomas Lynch	*The Undertaking*
Sam Tanenhaus	*Whittaker Chambers*
Young people's literature nominees	
Brock Cole	*The Facts Speak for Themselves*
Adele Griffin	*Son of Liberty*
Mary Ann McGuigans	*Where You Belong*
Han Nolan	*Dancing on the Edge*
Tor Seidler	*Mean Magaret*
Poetry nominees	
John Balaban	*Locusts at the Edge of Summer*
Frank Bidart	*Desire*
Sarah Lindsay	*Primate Behavior*
William Meredith	*Effort at Speech*
Marilyn Nelson	The Fields of Praise

Source: Donahue, Deirdre. "DeLillo, Frazier Among Award Hopefuls." *USA TODAY,* 16 October 1997, p. 9D.

★ 537 ★

Awards

National Book Award Winners

Fiction: *Cold Mountain* by Charles Frazier.

Nonfiction: *American Sphinx: The Character of Thomas Jefferson* by Joseph J. Ellis

Young People Literature: *Dancing on the Edge* by Han Nolan

Poetry: *Effort at Speech: New & Selected Poems* by William Meredith.

Source: Minzesheimer, Bob. "'Mountain' Named Top Novel." *USA TODAY,* 19 November 1997, p. 22A.

★ 538 ★

Awards

National Magazine Award Finalists in Design

Finalists	Finalists
Entertainment Weekly *Garden Design* *I.D. Magazine*	*Martha Stewart Living* *Sports Afield*

Source: Hays, Constance L. "Award Puffs Magazines' Egos but Fails to Bolster Ad Sales." *New York Times,* 28 April 1997, p. C7. Primary source: American Society of Magazine Editors.

★ 539 ★

Awards

National Magazine Award Finalists in Essays and Criticism

Finalists	Finalists
The American Lawyer *Civilization*	*GQ* *The New Yorker*

Source: Hays, Constance L. "Award Puffs Magazines' Egos but Fails to Bolster Ad Sales." *New York Times,* 28 April 1997, p. C7. Primary source: American Society of Magazine Editors.

★ 540 ★

Awards

National Magazine Award Finalists in Feature Writing

Finalists	Finalists
GQ	*Rolling Stone*
The New Yorker	*Sports Illustrated*
Premiere	*Texas Monthly*

Source: Hays, Constance L. "Award Puffs Magazines' Egos but Fails to Bolster Ad Sales." *New York Times,* 28 April 1997, p. C7. Primary source: American Society of Magazine Editors.

★ 541 ★

Awards

National Magazine Award Finalists in Fiction

Finalists	Finalists
The Atlantic Monthly	*The New Yorker*
GQ	*Story*

Source: Hays, Constance L. "Award Puffs Magazines' Egos but Fails to Bolster Ad Sales." *New York Times,* 28 April 1997, p. C7. Primary source: American Society of Magazine Editors.

★ 542 ★

Awards

National Magazine Award Finalists in General Excellence for Magazines with Circulations of 100,000 to 400,000

Finalists	Finalists
Civilization	*This Old House*
Harper's Magazine	*W*
Saveur	*Wired*

Source: Hays, Constance L. "Award Puffs Magazines' Egos but Fails to Bolster Ad Sales." *New York Times,* 28 April 1997, p. C7. Primary source: American Society of Magazine Editors.

★ 543 ★

Awards

National Magazine Award Finalists in General Excellence for Magazines with Circulations of 400,000 to 1,000,000

Finalists	Finalists
Conde Nast Traveler	*Smart Money*
GQ	*Sports Afield*
Outside	

Source: Hays, Constance L. "Award Puffs Magazines' Egos but Fails to Bolster Ad Sales." *New York Times,* 28 April 1997, p. C7. Primary source: American Society of Magazine Editors.

★ 544 ★

Awards

National Magazine Award Finalists in General Excellence for Magazines with Circulations of Over 1,000,000

Finalists	Finalists
Business Week	*Sports Illustrated*
Discover	*Vanity Fair*
Entertainment Weekly	

Source: Hays, Constance L. "Award Puffs Magazines' Egos but Fails to Bolster Ad Sales." *New York Times,* 28 April 1997, p. C7. Primary source: American Society of Magazine Editors.

★ 545 ★

Awards

National Magazine Award Finalists in General Excellence for Magazines with Circulations Under 100,000

Finalists	Finalists
The American Lawyer	*I.D. Magazine*
Double Take	*Lingua Franca*
MHQ: The Quarterly Journal of Military History	*Poz*

Source: Hays, Constance L. "Award Puffs Magazines' Egos but Fails to Bolster Ad Sales." *New York Times,* 28 April 1997, p. C7. Primary source: American Society of Magazine Editors.

★ 546 ★
Awards

National Magazine Award Finalists in Personal Service

Finalists	Finalists
Title	*New York*
Seventeen	*Glamour*
Fortune	*Worth*

Source: Hays, Constance L. "Award Puffs Magazines' Egos but Fails to Bolster Ad Sales." *New York Times,* 28 April 1997, p. C7. Primary source: American Society of Magazine Editors.

★ 547 ★
Awards

National Magazine Award Finalists in Photography

Finalists	Finalists
Double Take	*Saveur*
Martha Stewart Living	*Vanity Fair*
National Geographic	

Source: Hays, Constance L. "Award Puffs Magazines' Egos but Fails to Bolster Ad Sales." *New York Times,* 28 April 1997, p. C7. Primary source: American Society of Magazine Editors.

★ 548 ★
Awards

National Magazine Award Finalists in Reporting

Finalists	Finalists
Fortune	*Outside*
GQ	*U.S. News & World Report*
The New Yorker	*The Washingtonian*

Source: Hays, Constance L. "Award Puffs Magazines' Egos but Fails to Bolster Ad Sales." *New York Times,* 28 April 1997, p. C7. Primary source: American Society of Magazine Editors.

★ 549 ★

Awards

National Magazine Award Finalists in Single Topic Issue

Finalists	Finalists
Life	*Scientific American*
Mother Jones	*Smart Money*
The New Yorker	*Sports Illustrated*

Source: Hays, Constance L. "Award Puffs Magazines' Egos but Fails to Bolster Ad Sales." *New York Times,* 28 April 1997, p. C7. Primary source: American Society of Magazine Editors.

★ 550 ★

Awards

National Magazine Award: Most Frequent Winners

Data show the top winners over the last 30 years. The award is intended to encourage quality in reporting, design and other areas.

Title	Awards
The New Yorker	19
The Atlantic Monthly	11
Esquire	9
Harper's Magazine	9
Life	8
Texas Monthly	8

Source: Hays, Constance L. "Award Puffs Magazines' Egos but Fails to Bolster Ad Sales." *New York Times,* 28 April 1997, p. C1. Primary source: American Society of Magazine Editors.

★ 551 ★

Awards

Xeric Award Winners

The Xeric Foundation has awarded over $641,000 to comic book creators and non-profit groups since September 1992. Xeric offers financial help to self-publishing comic book creators nationwide and qualified charitable and nonprofit organizations in Western Massachusetts. The Foundation recently awarded $25,942 to these comic book artists:

- Sarah Thornton - Cilla
- Fred Hofheinz and Lance Miller - Paper & Binding
- Kevin Quigley - Big Place Comics
- Fawn Gehweiler - Bomb Pop

[Continued]

★ 551 ★

Xeric Award Winners
[Continued]

- Robert Kirby - Curbside

Source: From the Internet, http://www.icomics.com/meanwhil.htm.

Bestsellers

★ 552 ★

All-Time Best-Selling Books on Politics

Title and author	Year	Weeks on list
Advise and Consent ~*Allen Drury*	1960	102
The Making of the President ~*Theodore H. White*	1961	56
Washington Confidential ~*Jack Lait, Lee Mortimer*	1950	40
The Best and the Brightest ~*David Halberstam*	1972	36
All the President's Men ~*Bob Woodward, Carl Bernstein*	1974	34

Source: Wines, Michael. "Successful Political Books Are Less Sober, More Pop." *New York Times,* 17 February 1997, p. 25.

★ 553 ★
Bestsellers

Best-Selling Books, 1996

Data show the best-selling books on *USA TODAY's* book list.

Title	Author
The Runaway Jury	John Grisham
Men Are From Mars, Women Are From Venus	John Gray
The Rainmaker	John Grisham
Snow Falling on Cedars	John Guterson
Primary Colors	Anonymous
Chicken Soup for the Soul	Jack Canfield, and Mark Victor Hansen
The Dilbert Principle	Scott Adams

[Continued]

★ 553 ★

Best-Selling Books, 1996
[Continued]

Title	Author
The Zone	Barry Sears and Bill Lawren
Executive Orders	Tom Clancy and Jack Ryan
The Green Mile, Part 1: The Two Dead Girls	Stephen King

Source: "Year's Best Seller: Grisham in a 'Runaway' On The Top Shelf." *USA TODAY,* 24 December 1996, p. 4D.

★ 554 ★

Bestsellers

Best-Selling Books on Politics, 1996

Title and author	Weeks on list
Primary Colors by Anonymous	25
Rush Limbaugh Is a Big Fat Idiot by Al Franken	23
My American Journey by Colin Powell	20
Unlimited Access by Gary Aldrich	19
Blood Sport by James B. Stewart	16

Source: Wines, Michael. "Successful Political Books Are Less Sober, More Pop." *New York Times,* 17 February 1997, p. 25.

★ 555 ★

Bestsellers

Best-Selling Classic Authors in the United Kingdom

The table show unit sales for classic authors for the four week period ending August 10, 1996.

Author	Titles in top 5,000	Sales
Jane Austen	21	13,288
Charles Dickens	16	5,268
Thomas Hardy	10	5,050
George Eliot	9	3,857
Charlotte Bronte	8	3,679
Joseph Conrad	7	2,042
J.R.R. Tolkien	7	2,302
Anthony Trollope	6	2,322

[Continued]

★ 555 ★

Best-Selling Classic Authors in the United Kingdom
[Continued]

Author	Titles in top 5,000	Sales
E.M. Forster	5	1,600
James Joyce	5	1,087

Source: Howard, Philip. "Old Austens Are Still Good Runners." *The Times,* 14 September 1996, p. 12.

★ 556 ★

Bestsellers

Longest-Running Hardcover Bestsellers, 1995

Title	Number of weeks on 1995 list	Number of weeks on 1994 list
FICTION		
The Celestine Prophecy[1] James Redfield. Warner	51	43
The Bridges of Madison County[1] Robert James Waller. Warner	40	51
Politically Correct Bedtime Stories[1] James Finn Garner. Macmillan	36	24
The Rainmaker[1] John Grisham. Doubleday	23	0
Beach Music[1] Pat Conroy. Doubleday	23	0
Ladder of Years Anne Tyler. Knopf	17	0
Moo Jane Smiley. Knopf	16	0
Coming Home	16	0

[Continued]

★ 556 ★

Longest-Running Hardcover Bestsellers, 1995
[Continued]

Title	Number of weeks on 1995 list	Number of weeks on 1994 list
Rosamunde Pilcher. St. Martin's		
Border Music Robert James Waller. Warner	15	0
NONFICTION		
Men Are From Mars, Women Are From Venus John Gray. HarperCollins	51	51
Midnight in the Garden of Good and Evil John Berendt. Random House	45	36
Sisters Carol Saline and Sharon Wohlmuth. Running Press	45	0
The Seven Spiritual Laws of Success Deepak Chopra. New World Library	45	0
The Hot Zone[1] Richard Preston. Random House	29	11
Mars and Venus in the Bedroom John Gray. HarperCollins	26	0
How to Argue and Win Every Time Gerry Spence. St. Martin's	26	0
The Death of Common Sense Philip K. Howard. Random House	25	0
A Good Walk Spoiled John Feinstein. Little Brown	21	0
In the Kitchen with Rosie	23	35

[Continued]

★ 556 ★

Longest-Running Hardcover Bestsellers, 1995
[Continued]

Title	Number of weeks on 1995 list	Number of weeks on 1994 list
Rosie Daley. Knopf		
The Beardstown Ladies' Commonsense Investment Guide Leslie Whitaker. Hyperion	17	0
New Passages Gail Sheehy. Random House	15	0
My Point...and I Do Have One Ellen DeGeneres. Bantam	16	0
Couplehood Paul Reiser. Bantam	15	16

Source: Maryles, Daisy. "Bestsellers 1995 Winning Combinations." *Publishers Weekly,* 1 January 1996, p. 51.
Notes: 1. These titles achieved the No. 1 spot during their 1995 presence on *Publishers Weekly* bestseller list.

★ 557 ★
Bestsellers

Longest-Running Paperback Bestsellers, 1995

Title	Number of weeks on 1995 list	Number of weeks on 1994 list
MASS MARKET		
The Alienist Caleb Carr. Bantam	26	0
The Chamber[1] John Grisham. Dell	25	0
Embraced by the Light Betty J. Eadie. Bantam	24	14
The Day After Tomorrow	21	0

[Continued]

★ 557 ★

Longest-Running Paperback Bestsellers, 1995
[Continued]

Title	Number of weeks on 1995 list	Number of weeks on 1994 list
Allan Folsom. Warner		
The Hot Zone[1] Richard Preston. Doubleday/Anchor	20	0
Circle of Friends Maeve Binchy. Dell	19	0
Congo[1] Michael Crichton. Ballantine	18	20
Tom Clancy's Op-Center[1] Tom Clancy. Berkley	17	0
The Body Farm[1] Patricia Cornwell. Berkley	16	0
Nothing Lasts Forever Sidney Sheldon. Warner	16	0
Debt of Honor[1] Tom Clancy. Berkley	15	0
TRADE		
7 Habits of Highly Effective People Stephen R. Covey. S&S/Fireside	51	51
Chicken Soup for the Soul Jack Canfield & Mark Hansen, eds. Health Communications	51	22
Ten Stupid Things Women Do to Mess Up Their Lives Laura Schlessinger. Harper-Perennial	45	0
What to Expect When You're Expecting	44	45

[Continued]

★ 557 ★

Longest-Running Paperback Bestsellers, 1995
[Continued]

Title	Number of weeks on 1995 list	Number of weeks on 1994 list
A. Eisenberg, H. Murkoff, S. Hathaway. Workman		
Reviving Ophelia Mary Pipher. Ballantine	36	0
A Second Helping of Chicken Soup for the Soul Jack Canfield & Mark Hansen, eds. Health Communications	35	0
Care of the Soul Thomas More. HarperPerennial	34	50
The Stone Diaries[1] Carol Shields. Penguin	34	0
The Shipping News[1] E. Annie Proulx. S&S/Touchstone	33	30
The Celestine Prophecy Experiential Guide James Redfield & Carol Adrienne. Warner	25	0
The Artist's Way Julia Cameron with Mark Bryan. Jeremy Tarcher	25	0
O.J.'s Legal Pad Henry Beard, John Boswell & Ron Barrett. Villard	22	0
What to Expect from the Toddler Years A. Eisenberg, H. Murkoff, S. Hathaway. Workman	19	0
Driven to Distraction Edward Hallowell & John J. Ratey. S&S/Touchstone	17	0
A Map of the World Jane Hamilton. Doubleday/Anchor	16	0

Source: Maryles, Daisy. "Bestseller 1995 Winning Combinations." *Publishers Weekly,* 1 January 1996, p. 52.
Notes: 1. These titles achieved the No. 1 during their 1995 presence on *Publishers Weekly* bestseller list.

★ 558 ★
Bestsellers

Top Business Books, 1997

Data show the best business books of the year, according to *Business Week.*

- *Apple: The Inside Story,* by Jim Carlton.

- *Car: A Drama of the American Workplace* by Mary Walton.

- *Cartels of the Mind: Japan's Intellectual Closed Shop* by Ivan P. Hall

- *The Colonel: The Life and Legend of Robert R. McCormick* by Richard Norton Smith.

- *Flying Blind, Flying Safe* by Mary Schiavo with Sabra Chartrand.

- *Inside Intel: Andy Grove and the Rise of the World's Most Powerful Chip Company* by Tim Jackson.

- *The Leadership Engine: How Winning Companies Build Leaders at Every Level* by Noel M. Tichy with Eli Cohen.

- *The Living Company: Habits for Survival in a Turbulent Business Environment* by Arie de Geus.

- *Frederick Winslow Taylor and the Enigma of Efficiency* by Robert Kanigel.

- *Personal History* by Katherine Graham.

Source: "The Best Business Books of 1997." *Business Week,* 15 December 1997, p. 18.

Lists

★ 559 ★

Big Money Book Deals

Author	Value ($ mil.)	Books
Jonathan Kellerman	20-25	Five-book deal (Random House)
Marcia Clark	4.2	*Without A Doubt* (Viking)
George Stephanopoulos	2.75	White House memoir (Little, Brown)
Dick Morris	2.5	*Behind the Oval Office* (Random House)
Margaret Cuthbert	2	*The Silent Cradle* and subsequent book (Pocket)
Liz Smith	1	Memoirs (Hyperion)

Source: Green, Hardy. "Superstores, Megabooks - And Humongous Headaches." *Business Week,* 14 April 1997, p. 92. Primary source: *Publishers Weekly*; Simon & Schuster; Joni Evans.

★ 560 ★

Lists

Book Printings of Popular Authors, 1995

The table ranks the initial printing of works of popular writers. Data are in millions of books.

Books	Amount
The Rainmaker by John Grisham	2.80
Debt of Honor by Tom Clancy	2.00
Insomnia by Stephen King	1.50
Border Music by Robert James Waller	1.15
Wings by Danielle Steel	1.10
Disclosure by Michael Crichton	0.90
Scarlett by Alexandra Ripley	0.75

Source: Variety, 8 May 1995, p. 6. publishers.

★ 561 ★
Lists

Largest Book Advances in the Trade Press

Title	Author	Publisher	Advance
Behind the Oval Office	Dick Morris	Thorndike	2.5 mil.
The Other Woman: My Years With O.J. Simpson	Paula Barbieri	Brown Little	3.0 mil.
Babyhood	Paul Reiser	William Morrow	5.6 mil.
Whoopi	Whoopi Goldberg	Rob Weisbach Books	6.0 mil.
My American Journey	Colin Powell	Random House	6.0 mil.

Source: "Middling (and Unloved) in Publishing Land." *New York Times,* 18 August 1997, p. C1.

★ 562 ★
Lists

Most-Influential Books of All Time

Figures are based on a survey of 1,000 adults.

Title	Author	Percentage
The Bible		79.8
Baby and Child Care	Dr. Benjamin Spock	4.7
Origin of the Species	Charles Darwin	4.1
1984	George Orwell	2.4
The Wealth of Nations	Adams Smith	0.8
The Prince	Niccolo Machiavelli	0.7
The Communist Manifesto	Karl Marx and Frederick Engels	0.5

Source: "The Bible, a Perennial, Runs Into Sales Resistance." *New York Times,* 28 October 1996, p. C10. Primary source: Barna Research via Tyndale House Publishers.

★ 563 ★
Lists

Odd Book Titles

From the source: "The British Bookseller's odd title award has gone this year to *The Greek Rural Postmen and Their Cancellation Numbers.* It fought off some tough competition from *God's Chewable Vitamin C for the Spirit* and *Tractors and the Men Who Love Them.* 'We feel this year's winner will be of lasting worth,' Horace Brent, chairman of the judges, said. Previous winners have ranged from *Oral Sadism and the Vegetarian Personality* to *Proceedings of the Second International Work Shop on Nude Mice.*"

Source: "Odd Book Titles." *USA TODAY,* 8 November 1996, p. 12A.

Picks

★ 564 ★

Best Books of the 20th Century According to the British

The list is based on a survey of 25,000 Britons.

Book	Book
The Lord of the Rings	*The Catcher in the Rye*
1984	*To Kill a Mockingbird*
Animal Farm	*100 Years of Solitude*
Ulysses	*The Grapes of Wrath*
Catch 22	*Trainspotting*

Source: "Jolly Good Hobbits." *USA TODAY,* 11 February 1997, p. D1. Primary source: Waterstone's booksellers.

★ 565 ★

Picks

Black History Month's Best Picks for Children

Title	Cost	Age
Nappy Hair	17.00	All
Jamaica Louis James	16.00	4-8
Allie's Basketball Dreams	15.00	4-8
Satchmo's Blues	16.00	6-10
Black Artists in Photography 1840-1940	17.00	10-up

Source: "Black History Month's Best Picks for Children." *The Christian Science Monitor,* 5 February 1997, p. 2.

★ 566 ★

Picks

Top 10 Books for 100 Years

Title	Author
Anne Frank: The Diary of a Young Girl	Anne Frank
Roots	Alex Haley
Brave New World	Aldous Huxley
Up From Slavery	Booker T. Washington
The Jungle	Upton Sinclair
Seven Pillars of Wisdom	T.E. Lawrence

[Continued]

★ 566 ★

Top 10 Books for 100 Years
[Continued]

Title	Author
The Story of My Life	Helen Keller
Dracula	Bram Stoker
The Jungle Books	Rudyard Kipling
Sexual Politics	Kate Millet

Source: New York Times, 28 October 1997, p. B2.

Chapter 15
TIMELINE

c.3500 BC

Pictographic writing in Sumer.

c.2500 BC

Use of papyrus by Egyptians.

2nd millenium BC

Phoenicians develop phonetic alphabet.

c.1860 BC

Development of early Semitic alphabet.

c.1100 BC

Phoenicians develop alphabetic script.

c.850 BC

Homer writes *Illiad* and *Odyssey*.

c. 8th century BC

Greeks adopt Phoenician alphabet, and add five symbols representing vowels, the basis of modern, fully alphabetic writing.

c.600 BC

Age of Greek lyric poetry.

4th century BC

Foundation of Library at Alexandria.

250 BC

The Seventy (Septuagint) translate the Jewish Bible into Greek at Alexandria.

196 BC

Foundation of Library at Pergamum.

180 BC

Aristarchus publishes edition of Homer, dividing the *Iliad* and *Odyssey* into 24 parts, the basis of the modern text.

c.50 BC

Julius Caesar writes account of Gallic Wars.

c.105

Paper manufacture begins in China.

120

Earliest Chinese dictionary, by Hsu Shen.

c.350

Gothic Bible produced.

c. 700

Chinese, Japanese, and Koreans devise printing methods using carved wooden blocks for 40,000-character ideographic alphabet.

8th Century

Zenith of manuscript illumination by the Celtic Church in Ireland.

c.860

Newspaper printed in China.

868

The first known book is produced in China.

c.1050

Invention of moveable type in China.

1086

Domesday Book completed.

1380

John Wycliffe's translation of the Bible into English appears.

c. 1445

Johannes Gutenberg in Europe develops printing press that uses moveable type (creates the business of publishing as we know it).

1454

Gutenberg prints the Bible in Mainz.

1475

William Caxton prints first book in English.

16th-18th centuries

Claude Garamond, William Caslon, Giambattista Bodoni, and John Baskerville design typefaces that form the backbone of modern typography.

1521

Books begin to be printed at Cambridge.

1525

William Tyndale's English translation of New Testament published.

1539

Word "encyclopedia" first used by Thomas Elyot.

1543

Nicolas Copernicus publishes *Of the Revolution of Celestial Bodies*.

1549

Book of Common Prayer issued.

1580s

The first university press books were published at Oxford and Cambridge.

1611

Authorized Version of the Bible issued.

1616

Death of William Shakespeare.

1617

Ben Jonson made first poet laureate of Britain.

1631

The first French newspaper, Theophraste Renaudot's *La Gazette*, appears.

1638

First printing press set up in America.

1687

Isaac Newton publishes his *Principia*.

1702

England's first daily newspaper issued, *The Daily Courant*.

1755

Publication of Samuel Johnson's *Dictionary*.

1762

Publication of Jean Jacques Rousseau's *Social Contract*.

1776

Publication of Adam Smith's *Wealth of Nations*.

1791

Death of Mozart.

1791

Publication of the first part of Thomas Paine's *The Rights of Man*.

1798

Aloys Senefelder develops lithography.

c. 1800

Metal presses replace wooden ones

Early 1800s

Development of continuous-roll paper — called the web.

1812

Invention of cylinder printing press.

1814

Freidrich Konig develops the steam-driven printing press.

1822

William Church invents the first typesetting machine.

1828

Publication of Noah Webster's *Dictionary* in USA.

1829

Braille invents system of touch-reading for blind.

1848

Communist Manifesto published.

1851

First publication of *The New York Times*.

1859

Publication of Charles Darwin's *The Origin of Species*.

c. 1865

Rotary-web-fed presses print newspapers at the rate of 10,000 impressions per hour.

1870

Death of Charles Dickens.

1878

The oldest continuously operating press in the United States was establised at The Johns Hopkins University.

1885

Ottmar Mergenthaler develops a hot metal composition machine, later known as the Linotype machine.

1886

First Linotype machine installed at a newspaper (New York Tribune).

1888

The first *National Geographic* magazine is published.

c. 1890

Introduction of Monotype and Linotype machines allows typesetter to sit at keyboard and type whole lines of type (hot type).

1894

First development of phototypesetting machine — was not commercially usable.

1900

Publication of Sigmund Freud's *The Interpretation of Dreams*.

1903

Publication of Bertrand Russell's *Principles of Mathematics*.

1920s

Four-color printing process is born of superimposed halftones.

1922

The first issue of *Fruit Garden and Home* is published. It is renamed *Better Homes and Gardens* in 1924.

1933

The first joint-operating newspaper was created in Albuquerque, New Mexico.

1933

The first recognized comic book, *Funnies on Parade*, appears. It was part of a promotional campaign.

1937

Knight Newspapers buys the *Miami Herald* for $2.5 million.

1937

Xerography (electrostatic dry photocopying) invented by Chester Carlson.

1938

The first appearance of Superman in Action Comics No. 1.

1940

Detroit Free Press acquired by Knight Newspapers for $3.1 million.

1946

Intertype Fotosetter, the first commercial phototypesetting machine, installed at U.S. Government Printing Office.

1950s

Phototypesetting (cold type) developed — optical process quickly replaces mechanical process in page composition.

1956

Better Homes and Gardens prints first microwave cooking article.

1956

Photon 2000, first successful electromechanical phototypesetter using lens, stroboscopic light, and rapidly moving sources of type characters developed by Rene Higonnet and Louis Moyround in France.

late 1950s

Copyflo machine developed for electrostatic printing of documents from microfilm.

1969

Knight Newspapers and Ridder Publications both go public.

c. 1970

Third-generation phototypesetting machines developed using electronic display of characters on a CRT.

1974

Knight-Ridder is formed by merger.

c. 1978

First digital typesetters appear — floppy disks replace photographic fonts.

1979

The American Newspaper Publishers Association (now the Newspaper Association of America) begins developing an alternative to petroleum-based oil as the vehicle, for delivering pigment to paper, in news inks.

c. 1980

Public and academic libraries begin computerizing their catalogs.

1985

Aldus Corporation releases PageMaker software for the Macintosh; Aldus founder Paul Brainerd first uses term "desktop publishing".

1985

CD-ROM brought out by Philips and Sony.

1987

Aldus introduces Pagemaker desktop publishing software for MS-DOS based PCs.

1987

The comics industry collapses. Black and white comics became the rage producing a false market and stranding collectors with pounds of worthless pulp.

1992

DC Comics publishes Superman No. 75, *The Death of Superman*. It becomes the lead story on radio and news programs.

1996

90% of U.S. dailies use some soy-based ink, overwhelmingly color, but a few, notably the *St. Petersburg Times* and *Los Angeles Times*, have switched to soy-based inks exclusively - color and black - added cost notwithstanding.

1997

Detective Comics No. 27, the first appearance of Batman, sells at auction for $68,500.

1997

Superman No. 17 sells for $36,800. It is a record price for any Golden Age cover.

Appendix I - Abbreviations and Acronyms

BBS

Bulletin board service: a computerized bulletin board accessible to those subscribing to it. Users can post and retrieve messages.

B/W

Advertising/newspaper abbreviation meaning "black and white," used to distinguish advertising rates and formats from "color"—which is typically more expensive.

CD-R

CD-Recordable — compact disk technology that lets users write or store their own information using a CD-R drive and disk. The disk material can only be written to once, although the user can store information in several sessions.

CD-ROM

Compact Disk-Read Only Memory — Storage disk which holds vast amounts of data (more than 650MB compared to 1.44MB on a 3.5 inch high-density disk). It is ideal for storing the entire contents of encyclopedias, for instance, or multimedia presentations. However, the technology does not allow the user to change the stored data, only to retrieve it.

CDs

Stands for Compact Disks used in publishing music. Sound is first digitized and then stored on the disk. CD players read the digital data and transform them into sound vibrations.

Cyberspace

Popular term encompassing all computer networks, including the Internet, online services, and private networks.

Desktop publishing

The activity of creating camera-ready materials without the help of commercial typesetting and layout companies/departments. Desktop publishing typically depends on programs which can merge text and graphics in an electronic layout to produce printed materials such as newsletters, ads, and educational materials. Users can select layout styles, fonts, and graphics, and actually see on-screen how the printed product will appear. Popular desktop publishing tools include Pagemaker, Quark Xpress, and Microsoft Publisher. A laser printer is usually required to give substance to the design effort.

ElHi

Abbreviation indicating the "elementary through high school" category. The abbreviation is used in publishing to indicate a particular audience.

E-mail address

Electronic location for sending and receiving e-mail, used to identify and contact users. Common form: username@company.com.

HTML

Hypertext markup language — coding convention for marking up text and referencing graphics and other pages on the World Wide Web. Conceptually simple, in practice quite involved, HTML coding is usually done using a specialized editor package or word processor capable of rendering a document so that it is in HTML format. HTML enables the page creator to embed graphics (by embedding the names of graphics files) and links to other pages. Browsers are designed to interpret HTML codes and to carry out embedded HTML commands. An HTML page created on any computer can be shown on any other if an appropriate browser is available, thus facilitating communications between machines that are technologically incompatible (e.g. Macintosh and PCs).

Internet

Global network of computer networks that lets users access information, transact business, send E-mail, and participate in discussions. Internet is the broadest definition of online communications between computers. The World Wide Web is a subset of the Internet; Gophers are another subset.

Intranet

Private network within a company or organization that allows users to consult organizational databases as well as the Internet. Intranets make use of HTML and browser packages; internal servers behave like Internet servers. Intranets can be designed to control access to its nodes (or the Internet).

K-8

Phrase indicating the educational level "kindergarden through 8th grade." This term is used in publishing to indicate an audience category.

Laser

Laser stands for Light amplification by stimulated emission of radiation. Laser devices excite or stimulate a gas or a solid crystal to emit light. Light is focused in the process so that it flows in one direction and in parallel waves, providing very high energy and precision. The resulting beam may be visible to the human eye or may be in the infrared range of the spectrum.

Laser technology is used extensively in printing and thus creates the possibilities for digital printing and desktop publishing.

LP/EP and LPs

Recording abbreviation meaning "long play/extended play" record (as in music). LPs are "long playing" records.

Modem

Device that allows a computer to access the Internet and transmit data over telephone lines. Digital information from the sending computer is first translated into sound (is *mod*ulated) so that it can travel using voice lines. At the receiving point, another modem translates the sound back into digital form (*dem*odulates).

NA

Used throughout *Publishing* to stand for "not available."

nec

Abbreviation used by the federal government in its census reports to indicate that a value is "not elsewhere classified." The nec label is usually appended to industrial categories that incorporate "miscellaneous" activities, i.e., activities too small to be placed into a 4-digit SIC category of their own.

Network

Group of computers linked by a common communications protocol. Networks are usually wired but need not be: radio links are possible and often used in wide-area data transmission.

n.s.k.

Abbreviation used by the federal government in its census reports to indicate that a product is "not specified by kind." The n.s.k. label is appended to product categories which are in the "miscellaneous" classification, meaning that they are not large enough to merit their own product code.

OEM

Original equipment manufacturer.

Online

Generic term for the Internet and online services.

Online service

Services such as America Online, CompuServe, Prodigy, and the Microsoft Network that provide members Internet access, e-mail, information, and discussion areas.

Pre-Press

Activity involved in preparing a publication before it is actually printed, including text preparation, scanning, photographic manipulation of images, typesetting, layout, platemaking, etc. The phrase usually excludes authoring and, in general, content preparation.

Print-on-Demand

A relatively new way to organize publishing activities so that printing of a document, image, book, etc. is undertaken only when there is demand for it. This contrasts to making a specific print run of, say, 1,000 copies, and hoping that 1,000 copies will actually sell. Print-on-Demand is made possible by new forms of digital data organization and digital printing on lasers.

ROP

Newspaper abbreviation meaning "run of press". The phrase "full run ROP" means the entire press run.

PC

Personal computer — also called a microcomputer, it is designed to serve a single user. The PC sits on a desktop and is equipped to handle software and peripherals (such as a printer) without relying on a mainframe computer. The acronym is usually applied to computers using one of the Intel CPUs (IBM PCs and clones). Macintosh PCs are usually referred to as Macs and workstations that run UNIX are called UNIX boxes.

R&B

Musical abbreviation meaning "rhythm and blues."

SIC

Standard Industrial Classification. A numerical scheme used by the federal government to classify industrial activities. Two-digit codes refer to major groups (e.g., SIC 27 is Printing and Publishing). Three-digit codes refer to industry groups (e.g., SIC 273 is Books). Four-digit codes are used for industries (e.g., SIC 2731 is Book Publishing). SIC codes are also widely used in academia and industry for classification of industrial information.

W/E

Abbreviation denoting "weeks ending", as in the phrase "52 W/E 3/9/96," the meaning of which is "[a period of] 52 weeks ending on 3/9/96".

Word processor

Type of software application used for writing and editing text. The user can produce letters, memos, reports, or even an entire book. Because documents created by word processing programs are electronic, changes and corrections can be quickly made on the screen before the document is printed. The electronic document can also be stored as a file for future use.

World Wide Web

Matrix of graphical information stored on server computers connected to the Internet. Servers store data and send it on receiving appropriate requests from qualified users.

Appendix II - Listing of Sources

This Listing of Sources shows all publications used in the preparation of *Publishing.* Each item is followed by one or more table references.

"100 Leading National Advertisers." *Advertising Age,* 29 September 1997. Tables: 320, 407-408.

"1995 Daily Newspaper Sales." *Editor & Publisher,* 6 January 1996, pp. 52-54. Table: 393.

"1995 Nondaily Newspaper Sales." *Editor & Publisher,* 6 January 1996, pp. 58-60. Table: 394.

"1996 Lammy Winners." *Lambda Book Report* (June 1997). Table: 535.

1997 *Manufacturing STATROM* [machine-readable data files]. MStat97. Editorial Code and Data, Inc., Detroit, Michigan, 1997. Tables: 2-78, 193-202, 277-282, 284-285, 287, 293-302, 381-390, 452, 455-456, 458-459, 462-463, 470-480, 482-489, 493-494, 497-500, 508-509.

"49th Annual Report on American Industry." *Forbes*, 13 January 1997. Tables: 86, 96.

"A Comic Is a Many Splendored Thing." *Non-Foods Merchandising* (December 1994). Table: 132.

"A Look at What's New." *New York Times,* 20 October 1997. Table: 312.

Abramowitz, Harvey. "Oh, Soy, Can You Print!" *Editor & Publisher,* 27 January 1996. Tables: 490-491.

"Ad Age International's Latin America Print Media Lineup." *Advertising Age International* (January 1997). Table: 344.

Adelson, Andrea. "Black-Owned Bookstores Defend Niche." *New York Times,* 6 October 1997. Table: 212.

Advertising Age, 14 August 1995. Table: 192.

Advertising Age, 16 June 1997. Tables: 323-326.

"All the News That Fits." *The Economist,* 15 February 1997. Table: 423.

"All-Time Best-Selling Children's Books." *Business and Society Review,* 1 July 1996. Table: 121.

"All You Need Is Fans." *Non-Foods Merchandising* (December 1994). Table: 142.

Alonso, Marie Ranoia. "Celebrating...but Cautious." *Printing Impressions* (December 1997). Table: 451.

American Printer (December 1994). Table: 433.

American Printer (July 1997). Table: 449.

Angel, Karen. "Black Booksellers Aim to Get Their Groove Market." *Publishers Weekly,* 15 September 1997. Table: 238.

Annicelli, Cliff. "Books Blossom in Toy Turf." *Playthings* (May 1997). Table: 127.

Applebome, Peter. "Publishers' Squeeze Making Tenure Elusive." *New York Times,* 18 November 1996. Table: 190.

Applebome, Peter. "Trends Conspire Against the Yearbook." *New York Times,* 3 December 1996. Table: 191.

Association Management (July 1996). Tables: 328-329.

"At Home Shoppers." *The Wall Street Journal*, 5 December 1997. Table: 269.

"Audiobook Clubs Offer New Markets." *Small Press (November/December 1997). Table: 112.*

Bak, Carolyn R. "Not-So-Great Expectations." *Printing Impressions* (December 1997). Table: 442.

"The Best Business Books of 1997." *Business Week,* 15 December 1997. Table: 558.

"Best-Selling Calendars of 1996: Do You Own One?" *The Christian Science Monitor,* 31 October 1996. Table: 119.

"The Bible, a Perennial, Runs Into Sales Resistance." *New York Times,* 28 October 1996. Tables: 171, 562.

"The Big Books." *Adweek-Midwest Edition,* 4 March 1996. Tables: 317, 335.

"Big Spenders on Books." *New York Times,* 24 February 1997. Table: 163.

Bird, Laura. "Beyond Mail Order: Catalogs Now Sell Image, Advice." *The Wall Street Journal,* 29 July 1997. Table: 268.

"Birt's Worth 354,000: How About You?" *The Guardian,* 14 July 1997. Tables: 516-517.

"BISG Predicts a 5% Gain in Book Sales in 1997." *Publishers Weekly,* 7 July 1997. Table: 80.

"Black History Month's Best Picks for Children." *The Christian Science Monitor,* 5 February 1997. Table: 565.

"Book Club Sales Grow." *USA TODAY,* 26 November 1997. Table: 215.

"Book Industry Forecast: Consumer Spending, Publishers' Manufacturing Expenditures." *High Volume Printing* (December 1996). Tables: 102, 241.

"Book Report." *The Christian Science Monitor,* 9 December 1997. Tables: 204, 208-209, 226, 236, 240.

Branwyn, Gareth. "Consumer Shopping Web Sites." *Wired* (March 1997). Table: 161.

Brauchli, Marcus W. "In a Trade War, China Takes the Bigger Hit." *The Wall Street Journal,* 17 May 1996. Table: 528.

Briggs, Rosland. "Adapting to the Press of Change." *Philadelphia Inquirer,* 23 February 1997. Table: 189.

Brogdon, Ken. "Reinventing the Academic Press." *Small Press* (May/June 1996). Table: 188.

"Buying the Book." *USA TODAY,* 4 September 1996. Table: 223.

"Can't Get Enough of Comic Books." *Non-Foods Merchandising* (December 1994). Table: 134.

"Card-Carrying Sports Fans." *USA TODAY,* 4 August 1997. Table: 184.

Carey, Anne R. and Gary Visgaitis. "Who Shops from Catalogs?" *USA TODAY,* 3 February 1997. Table: 270.

Carey, Anne R. and Marcy E. Mullins. "Age of Religious-Book Buyers." *USA TODAY,* 2 January 1997. Table: 167.

Carey, Anne R. and Suzy Parker. "Market for Christian Books." *USA TODAY,* 15 January 1997. Table: 168.

"The Case of the Bouncing Bunny." *The Economist,* 26 July 1997. Table: 88.

Catalog Age (August 1997). Table: 267.

"Celebrities Lucrative Angle for Photographers. *Los Angeles Times,* 4 September 1997. Table: 396.

"Chapter's New Verse." *Macleans,* 8 July 1996. Table: 251.

The Christian Science Monitor, 7 October 1997. Table: 217.

Christiana-Beaudry, Laura. "Who Buys Why?" *Catalog Age* (July 1996). Tables: 258, 262, 271.

Christman, Ed. "Indie Sector Nears Top With 1st. Quarter Market Share Gain." *Billboard,* 27 April 1996. Tables: 367-368.

Clark, Andrew. "All Shook Up Over Classical Music." *Financial Times,* 23 March 1997. Table: 372.

"Coated Paper Alert: Prices Begin to Rise." *Graphic Arts Monthly* (June 1997). Tables: 502-503.

Coleman, Calmetta Y. "Gibson Greetings Makes Headway in Turnaround Bid." *The Wall Street Journal,* 18 December 1997. Table: 290.

Consoli, John. "Hands-on at Times Mirror." *Mediaweek,* 22 September 1997. Table: 397.

"Consumer Magazine Paid Circulation." *Advertising Age,* 24 February 1997. Table: 336.

"The Counterfeit Story." *New York Times,* 20 April 1996. Table: 529.

"Datapoint." *Time,* 14 July 1997. Table: 363.

"Demand for Forms Continues Tumble, Despite Low Prices." *Purchasing,* 6 November 1997. Table: 457.

"Desktop Publishing Wave Brings Tide of New Authors to Bookstore Shelves." *The Christian Science Monitor,* 11 June 1996. Table: 1.

Deverell, John. "Chapters' Big Bookstores Try to Beat Rivals to Punch." *Toronto Star,* 8 February 1997. Table: 218.

"Digital Printing Here to Stay." *In-Plant Graphics* (April 1997). Table: 461.

DM (September 1996). Table: 292.

"Do-It-Yourself Publishing." *Detroit Free Press,* 20 January 1997. Table: 103.

"DocuColor 40 Leads Digital Color Market." *Graphic Arts Monthly* (April 1997). Table: 460.

Donahue, Deirdre. "DeLillo, Frazier Among Award Hopefuls." *USA TODAY,* 16 October 1997. Table: 536.

Engelson, Andy. "Book Festivals of Many Flavors." *Publishers Weekly,* 11 August 1997. Table: 232.

"Extending the Brand Name." *New York Times,* 18 November 1996. Table: 82.

"Extra!! Extra!!" *Latin Trade* (January 1997). Table: 419.

"Fads That Speak Volumes." *Financial Times,* 9 December 1996. Table: 117.

Ferguson, Tim and Josephine Lee. "Spiritual Reality." *Forbes,* 27 January 1997. Table: 169.

"Fiction for Kids." *USA TODAY,* 19 November 1997. Table: 128.

"Fiction's Story." *USA TODAY,* 24 December 1996. Table: 207.

"Fighting Words." *Montreal Gazette,* 14 January 1995. Tables: 340, 342.

"Five Authors Honored by Book Critics Circle." *The Christian Science Monitor,* 21 March 1997. Table: 533.

"Flash Report—Recorded Music." *Discount Merchandiser* (August 1997). Tables: 356-360.

"Folder for Bookworms." *Press und Sprache* (March 1996). Table: 244.

Folio, 1 October 1996. Table: 309.

"Fortune 1 Thousand Ranked Within Industries." *Fortune,* 28 April 1997. Table: 99.

Freedman, Eric. "Make the Bookstore Connection." *Folio,* 1 June 1996. Table: 101.

"From Marx to Mills and Boon." *The Economist,* 25 October 1997. Table: 253.

"From Similar Roots, but Bearing New Fruit." *New York Times,* 2 January 1997. Table: 306.

From the Internet, http://mediainfo.elpress.com/ephome/npaper/nphtm/stats.htm, 5 November 1997. Table: 156.

From the Internet, http://pubcouncil.ca/prof-ref-rev.html (August 1996). Table: 246.

From the Internet, http://simbanet.com/sources/pprsam.html#chart1, 9 May 1997. Table: 97.

From the Internet, http://www.bookwire.com/bisg/1997~study.html (November 1997). Table: 239.

From the Internet, http://www.bookwire.com/subtext/education.article, 25 June 1997. Tables: 175-176.

From the Internet, http://www.bookwire.com/subtext/international.article, 1 October 1997. Table: 181.

From the Internet, http://www.bookwire.com/subtext/international.article, 9 July 1997. Tables: 166, 186.

From the Internet, http://www.bookwire.com/sub-text/publishing.article, 10 September 1997. Tables: 95, 100.

From the Internet, http://www.comicbookresources.com/news/eisner_0720.html, 20 July 1997. Table: 534.

From the Internet, http://www.greetingcard.org/gca/facts.htm. Table: 288.

From the Internet, http://www.icomics.com/mean-whil.htm. Table: 551.

From the Internet, http://www.mediacentral.com/Magazines/Pre/9. Tables: 440-441.

From the Internet, *Science and Engineering Indicators,* at http://www.nsf. 19 September 1996. Tables: 313-314.

Fulford, Benjamin. "Comics in Japan Not Just Funny Business." *Nikkei Weekly,* 24 February 1997. Table: 135.

Gabriel, Trip. "Women Buy Fiction in Bulk and Publishers Take Notice." *New York Times,* 17 March 1997. Tables: 233, 235.

Garigliano, Jeff. "*Notorious* Lives Up to its Name." *Folio,* 1 Oct 1997. Table: 303.

Garrett, Alexander. "Local Boy Makes Good." *The Observer,* 21 September 1997. Table: 111.

"Germany's Press: Through a Glass Sharply." *The Economist,* 11 January 1997. Table: 416.

"Getting Into the American Market." *Publishers Weekly,* 23 September 1996, pp. 22-24. Table: 257.

Gill, Penny. "Limitless Possibilities." *HFN: Buyers Guide to Multimedia Computing,* 2 January 1995. Table: 149.

"God's Squad." *The Observer,* 24 November 1996. Table: 353.

"Going Up, Coming Down." *The Guardian,* 5 August 1996. Table: 349.

"Gospel According to Market." *USA TODAY,* 24 December 1996. Table: 170.

"Grade Profile." *Pulp & Paper (*April 1997). Table: *506.*

Green, Hardy. "Superstores, Megabooks - And Humongous Headaches." *Business Week,* 14 April 1997. Table: 559.

Greenlaw, Dawn. "Capitalizing on Convenience." *Printing Impressions* (December 1997). Table: 443.

Greenlaw, Dawn. "This Time it's Personal." *Printing Impressions* (December 1997). Table: 444.

"Greetings America." *American Demographics* (February 1997). Table: 286.

Grossman, Cathy Lynn. "Libraries are Torn Between Books, Bytes." *USA TODAY,* 17 July 1997. Table: 164.

Gussin, Lawrence. "The Consumer Title Publishing Business." *Online Inc.,* (January 1997). Table: 148.

Hainer, Cathy. "Better Homes and Gardens Still Comfy at 75." *USA TODAY,* 10 September 1997. Table: 339.

Hall, Cindy and Marcia Staimer. "Curling Up with a Gift Book." *USA TODAY,* 12 December 1996. Table: 234.

Hall, Cindy and Suzy Parker. "Top Sports for Trading Cards." *USA TODAY,* 29 November 1996. Table: 183.

"Harcourt Sales, Profits UP in 1996." *Publishers Weekly,* 10 March 1997. Table: 83.

Hays, Constance L. "Award Puffs Magazines' Egos but Fails to Bolster Ad Sales." *New York Times,* 28 April 1997. Tables: 538-550.

Henneberger, Melinda. "Seeing Politics, and Mirrors, in the Coverage of Capitol Hill." *New York Times,* 6 October 1997. Table: 410.

High-Volume Printing (April 1995). Table: 450.

Holmstrom, David. "Listening While the Miles Go By." *The Christian Science Monitor,* 27 March 1997. Table: 115.

Hornery, Andrew. "Papers Power Ahead on Continued Growth." *Sydney Morning Herald,* 7 February 1997. Table: 415.

"The Hot Markets for 1997." *American Printer* (December 1996). Table: 429.

Howard, Philip. "Old Austens Are Still Good Runners." *The Times,* 14 September 1996. Table: 555.

"Hyping Type." *New York,* 17 June 1996. Table: 242.

"In Banned Books Week, Censorship Still Thrives." *Publishers Weekly,* 23 September 1996. Table: 530.

"In-Flight Magazines." *USA TODAY,* 8 April 1997. Table: 330.

"Indicators." *Far Eastern Economic Review,* 10 October 1996. Table: 136.

"Indicators." *Far Eastern Economic Review,* 21 November 1996. Table: 417.

"Industry at a Glance." *Editor & Publisher,* 11 October 1997. Table: 495.

"The Information." *The Observer,* 16 February 1997. Table: 347.

"Italy - Catalog Retail Distribution." *National Trade Data Bank:* The Export Connection CD-ROM, STAT-USA, U.S. Department of Commerce, Washington, D.C. 20302, 10 May 1995. Tables: 274-275.

Ivanor, Mikhail. "What is Russia Reading?" *Russian Life* (July 1997). Table: 109.

Janda, Jerry. "Running with the Bulls." *Printing Impressions* (December 1997). Table: 445.

"Japan - Large Mail Order Companies." *National Trade Data Bank:* The Export Connection CD-ROM, STAT-USA, U.S. Department of Commerce, Washington, D.C. 20302, 19 December 1996. Table: 265.

"Jolly Good Hobbits." *USA TODAY,* 11 February 1997. Table: 564.

Kelly, Keith J. "1st Half Deliver Bad News for Most Consumer Titles." *Advertising Age,* 22 July 1996. Table: 316.

"Knight-Ridder to Buy 4 Newspapers From Disney for $1.65 Billion," *New York Times,* 5 April 1997. Table: 398.

Latin American Press, 16 May 1996. Table: 245.

"Lex Comment." *Financial Times,* 19 November 1997. Table: 261.

Liebeskind, Ken. "Consolidation Hits a Few Bumps." *Non-Foods Merchandising (September 1996). Table: 304.*

"Magazine Sales by Segment." *Supermarket Business* (February 1997). Table: 305.

"Magazines: The Advertising Age 300," *Advertising Age,* 16 June 1997. Tables: 331-334.

"Mail Order." *Direct Marketing* (August 1996). Table: 264.

"Making the Best Look Better." *In-Plant Graphics,* (January 1996). Table: 428.

Manzo, Kathleen Kennedy. "Glimmer of History Standards Shows Up in Latest Textbooks." *Education Week,* 8 October 1997. Table: 177.

Marketing Magazine, 6 February 1995. Table: 424.

Maryles, Daisy. "Bestseller 1995 Winning Combinations." *Publishers Weekly,* 1 January 1996. Tables: 90, 556-557.

Maryles, Daisy. "How the Winners Made It to the Top." *Publishers Weekly,* 6 January 1997. Tables: 91-92.

McDaniel, Jobeth. "Listen Up: Don't Drive Your Time Away." *Investor's Business Daily,* 13 January 1997. Table: 113.

"Media Focus." *Campaign,* 20 August 1993. Table: 354.

"Media Focus." *Campaign,* 24 September 1993. Table: 352.

"Media Focus." *Campaign,* 15 April 1994. Table: 351.

"Media Focus." *Campaign,* 13 May 1994. Table: 350.

"Men's Magazines." *The Observer,* 11 August 1996. Table: 348.

"Merger Myths." *American Printer* (April 1997). Table: 465.

"Mexico - Educational Equipment and Supplies." *National Trade Data Bank:* The Export Connection CD-ROM, STAT-USA, U.S. Department of Commerce, Washington, D.C. 20302, 26 August 1996. Tables: 250, 467.

"Mexico - Printing and Graphic Arts." *National Trade Data Bank:* The Export Connection CD-ROM, STAT-USA, U.S. Department of Commerce, Washington, D.C. 20302, 12 September 1996. Table: 468.

"Middling (and Unloved) in Publishing Land." *New York Times,* 18 August 1997. Table: 561.

Miller, James P. "Hip and Irreverent, Alternative Papers Grab Readers." *The Wall Street Journal,* 28 July 1997. Table: 392.

Miller, Matthew. "Surprise! National School Standards Exist." *U.S. News & World Report,* 17 November 1997. Table: 180.

Milliot, Jim. "Amazon.com Expects to Generate $34 Million from IPO." *Publishers Weekly,* 31 March 1997. Table: 213.

Milliot, Jim and Diane Roback. "Top Children's Publishers Post Modest Overall Gains." *Publishers Weekly,* 28 October 1996. Table: 129.

Milliot, Jim. "BISG Sees Only Modest Sales Gains for 1996." *Publishers Weekly,* 8 July 1996. Table: 79.

Milliot, Jim. "Chains Earned Profits of $233 Million in Fiscal 1997." *Publishers Weekly,* 26 May 1997. Table: 216.

Milliot, Jim. "Looking Down the Road to 2000." *Publishers Weekly,* 23 September 1996. Tables: 122-123.

Milliot, Jim. "Retail Sales, Media Vetures Spur Growth at Scholastic." *Publishers Weekly,* 23 September 1996. Table: 231.

Milliot, Jim. "Study Finds 69% of Canadians Bought a Book in 6-Mo. Period." *Publishers Weekly,* 1 January 1996. Table: 229.

Milliot, Jim. "The Corporate Payscale." *Publishers Weekly,* 19 August 1996. Tables: 519-523.

Milliot, Jim. "Value of Publishing Mergers Tripled in 1996." *Publishers Weekly,* 14 April 1997. Table: 104.

Milliot, Jim. "VS&A Sees Moderate Growth for Consumer Book Spending." *Publishers Weekly,* 28 July 1997. Table: 205.

Minzesheimer, Bob. "'Mountain' Named Top Novel." *USA TODAY,* 19 November 1997. Table: 537.

Monthly Retail Trade Survey, Services Division, Bureau of the Census, Washington, DC 20233. Tables: 224, 260.

"More Books 'Read' on Tape, *USA TODAY,* 14 August 1997. Table: 114.

Moukheiber, Zina. "The Price is Right." *Forbes,* 16 December 1996. Table: 214.

"Moving Target for Industry Observers: Ranking the Ink Giants." *Graphic Arts Monthly* (March 1997). Table: 492.

"Murder by the Numbers." *Small Press* (July/August 1996). Tables: 144-146.

Murray, Diana Dillaber. "Legislature Considers Relief from High Costs." *The Sunday Oakland Press,* 7 December 1997. Table: 178.

Murray, Diana Dillaber. "Throwing the Book at Competition." *The Sunday Oakland Press,* 7 December 1997. Table: 179.

"The Music Industry Census." *Music Trades* (April 1997). Table: 361.

Mutter, John and Elizabeth Bernstein. "Books Wherever You Look: The Mall as Market Microcosm." *Publishers Weekly,* 16 September 1996. Table: 228.

NADbank-Marketing Magazine supplement, 14 October 1996. Table: 422.

"National Papers Record Healthy Circulation Gains." *Advertising Age,* 11 November 1996. Table: 409.

National Trade Data Bank: The Export Connection CD-ROM, STAT-USA, U.S. Department of Commerce, Washington, D.C. 20230, 27 May 1996. Table: 108.

National Trade Data Bank: The Export Connection CD-ROM, STAT-USA, U.S. Department of Commerce, Washington, D.C., 20230, 8 August 1996. Table: 220.

National Trade Data Bank: The Export Connection CD-ROM, STAT-USA, U.S. Department of Commerce, Washington, D.C. 20280, 1 December 1996. Tables: 105-106.

National Trade Data Bank: The Export Connection CD-ROM, STAT-USA, U.S. Department of Commerce, Washington, D.C. 20302, 1 February 1997. Table: 243.

Nearman, Barry. "Daze of His Life: Putting Together A Blowout Calendar." *The Wall Street Journal,* 15 December 1997. Table: 120.

"New Magazine Launches." *American Demographics* (August 1997). Table: 311.

"New Study Puts Global Book Market at $80 Billion." *Publishers Weekly,* 14 October 1996. Table: 247.

New York Times, 28 October 1997. Table: 566.

"Newspaper Circulations: The Winners." *Mail & Guardian,* 24 January 1997. Table: 426.

Non-Foods Merchandising (December 1994). Table: 139.

"Odd Book Titles." *USA TODAY,* 8 November 1996. Table: 563.

"On the Fast Track." *American Printer* (June 1997). Table: 437.

"On the Shelf." *The Guardian,* 2 June 1997. Table: 227.

"Over 80% of Top Business People Read Irish Times" *Irish Times,* 15 September 1997. Table: 418.

O'Brien, Timothy L. "Justice Department Joins Lawsuit Against Leading Book Wholesaler." *The Wall Street Journal,* 4 February 1997. Table: 230.

O'Donnell, Jayne and David Lieberman. "Pricing Probe Could Play Out in Full Investigation." *USA TODAY,* 12 August 1997. Table: 369.

Peterson, Iver. "As the Cost of Newsprint Declines, Analysts Argue Over Who Will Benefit." *New York Times,* 11 November 1996. Table: 496.

Peterson, Iver. "Public Information, Business Rates." *New York Times,* 14 July 1997. Table: 157.

"Prepress Leaders Adapting." *Graphic Arts Monthly* (September 1997). Table: 438.

"PrePress Shopping List for 1998." *American Printer* (November 1997). Table: 464.

"Press Box: Strong Gains in '96 over '95." *Business Marketing* (May 1997). Table: 322.

"Print on Demand Markets Growing." *American Printer* (July 1997). Table: 466.

"Publish and Perish." *Macleans,* 17 October 1994, pp. 50-53. Table: 107.

Publishers Weekly, 1 May 1995. Table: 130.

Publishers Weekly, 21 August 1995. Table: 124.

"Publishers' Margins Show Surprising Strength in 1996." *Publishers Weekly,* 30 June 1997. Table: 87.

"Publishing End Market Indicators." *Graphic Arts Monthly* (April 1997). Table: 81.

"Ranking the Leaders." *American Printer* (July 1997). Tables: 447-448.

Rawsthorn, Alice. "A Giant Leap for CD-ROM." *Financial Times,* 7 October 1996. Table: 150.

Rawsthorn, Alice. "Big Five Adjust the Volume." *Financial Times,* 5 November 1996. Tables: 374-375, 380.

Rawsthorn, Alice. "Changing the Tune in U.S. Music." *Financial Times,* 27 September 1997. Table: 362.

Rawsthorn, Alice. "Internet Music Retailers Hear an Upbeat Tempo." *Financial Times,* 5 December 1997. Table: 379.

Rawsthorn, Alice. "Music Groups Dream of Capturing Global Market." *Financial Times,* 23 August 1997. Table: 376.

Rawsthorn, Alice. "Music Industry Sales Static." *Financial Times,* 31 January 1997. Table: 378.

Rawsthorn, Alice. "Parallel CD Imports Prompt Pricing Rethink." *Financial TImes,* 10 October 1997. Table: 373.

Rawsthorn, Alice. "World Book Market Faces Further Consolidation." *Financial Times,* 2 October 1996. Table: 94.

"Read All About it." *The Wall Street Journal,* 11 November 1996. Table: 355.

Reilly, Patrick M. "Universal Music Charts a Comeback with Hot Artists." *The Wall Street Journal,* 29 May 1997. Table: 366.

Report on Business Magazine (October 1996). Table: 93.

"Results Exceed Expectations." *Mediaweek,* 20 October 1997. Table: 413.

"Rethinking the News." *New York Times,* 19 May 1997. Table: 414.

Rohwedder, Cacilie." *The Wall Street Journal,* 6 January 1998. Table: 276.

"The Romance Novel Magazine That Has Them Swooning." *New York Times,* 10 December 1996. Table: 172.

"Romancing the Buck." *Forbes,* 2 June 1997. Table: 173.

Routson, Joyce K. "Grade Profile." *Pulp & Paper* (March 1997). Table: 505.

Ryle, Sarah. "Reed to Sell IPC Magazines." *The Guardian,* 28 October 1997. Table: 84.

Sakuya, Fujiwara. "Fear and Favor in the Japanese Print Media." *Look Japan* (May 1997). Table: 420.

"Sales Near $5 Billion at Top Bookstore Chains." *Publishers Weekly,* 31 March 1997. Table: 221.

"Samba Time." *Latin Trade* (November 1996). Table: 377.

Sandler, Adam. "Publishing Discovers Revenue Avenue." *Variety,* 23 October 1995. Table: 370.

Schiesel, Seth. "The Games People Play." *New York Times,* 27 October 1997. Table: 147.

Schulman, Richard D. "CD-ROM/CD-R in the Legal Labyrinth." *CD-ROM Professional* (November 1996). Tables: 151-152.

"Scrooge on the Way for Booksellers This Christmas?" *Publishers Weekly,* 21 October 1996. Table: 219.

"Sector Breakdown Shows Market Shares in Japan." *Nikkei Weekly,* 4 August 1997. Table: 85.

"The September Results." *Women's Wear Daily,* 16 August 1996. Table: 321.

Shofield, John. "Publish or Perish: Canada's Magazine Industry Faces an Uncertain Future." *Macleans,* 2 June 1997. Table: 341.

"Shopping by Mail." *USA TODAY,* 19 November 1997. Table: 259.

Short, David. "Succeeding in Title Role." *The European,* 8-14 August 1996. Table: 346.

Simon, Caulkin. "Are Business Books Hot Stuff? See the Sales Figures - They Speak Volumes." *The Observer,* 16 March 1997. Table: 118.

"Sizing Up the U.S. Printing Industry." *Graphic Arts Monthly* (September 1997). Tables: 430-432, 434-435, 439, 453-454.

Skriloff, Lisa. "A Diverse Netizenry." *Brandweek,* 17 February 1997. Table: 155.

"Songs That Rocked Around the World." *The Christian Science Monitor,* 16 August 1996. Table: 365.

"Spain - Book Distribution Channels." *National Trade Data Bank:* The Export Connection CD-ROM, STAT-USA, U.S. Department of Commerce, Washington, D.C. 20302, 21 October 1995. Table: 110.

"Spain - Computer Magazines." *National Trade Data Bank:* The Export Connection CD-ROM, STAT-USA, U.S. Department of Commerce, Washington, D.C. 20302, 21 May 1996. Table: 343.

"Spain - Printing Equipment Market Overview." *National Trade Data Bank:* The Export Connection CD-ROM, STAT-USA, U.S. Department of Commerce, Washington, D.C. 20302, (October 1995). Table: 469.

"Specialties Shine to 1998." *Chemical Week,* 1 January 1997. Table: 481.

"The State of Small Business 1997." *Inc.,* 20 May 1997. Table: 154.

"Statwrap." *Non-Foods Merchandising* (January 1995). Tables: 140-141, 222, 307.

"Stressed for Success." *Folio,* 1 August 1997. Tables: 511-515.

"Super Store Sales Rise 36% to More Than $3 Billion." *Publishers Weekly,* 19 May 1997. Table: 225.

Supermarket Business (December 1994). Table: 337.

Supermarket Business (May 1997). Table: 338.

"Survey Says." *Quill & Quire,* (January 1996). Table: 518.

Szadkowski, Joseph. "Comics Industry is a Serious Venture." *The Washington Times,* 29 September 1996. Tables: 131, 133, 137-138.

"Tabloid Tally," *Business Week,* 15 September 1997. Table: 395.

Tagliabue, John. "Fakes Blot a Nation's Good Name." *New York Times,* 15 July 1997. Tables: 524-527.

Tait, Nikki. "Australians in a Spin Over Cost of Music." *Financial Times,* 21 March 1997. Table: 371.

Taylor, Sally. "In Search of the Spanish Market." *Publishers Weekly,* 25 August 1997. Table: 187.

"Thailand - Book Publishing Industry." *National Trade Data Bank:* The Export Connection CD-ROM, STAT-USA, U.S. Department of Commerce, Washington, D.C. 20302, 30 October 1996. Table: 254.

Thomson, Adam "Most International Trader." *Latin Trade* (January 1997). Table: 125.

"Todays Top Sellers." *New York Times,* 14 March 1995. Table: 174.

"Top 20 Daily Newspapers Ad Inches in Selected National Categories." *Editor & Publisher,* 5 April 1997. Tables: 401-402.

"Top 20 Daily Newspapers Ad Inches in Selected Retail Categories." *Editor & Publisher,* 5 April 1997. Tables: 399-400.

"Top 20 Magazines." *Le Nouvel Economiste,* 4 March 1994. Table: 345.

"The Top 20 Sites." *Business Today,* 7 October 1996. Table: 160.

"Top 20 Sunday Newspapers Ad Inches in Selected National Categories." *Editor & Publisher,* 5 April 1997. Tables: 405-406.

"Top 20 Sunday Newspapers Ad Inches in Selected Retail Categories." *Editor & Publisher,* 5 April 1997. Tables: 403-404.

"Top 50 Prepress Houses." *Printing Impressions* (August 1997). Table: 446.

"Top Advertising Categories." *Brandweek,* 4 March 1996. Table: 318.

"Top Magazine Publishing Companies." *Adweek,* 3 March 1997. Table: 308.

"Top Magazine Spending by Company." *Brandweek,* 4 March 1996. Table: 319.

"Top North American Paper Companies: Annual Survey." *PIMA's Papermaker* (June 1997). Tables: 504, 507.

"Top Publishing Companies." *Brandweek,* 4 March 1996. Table: 98.

"Top Software, Top Companies of 1996." *USA TODAY,* 6 February 1997. Table: 162.

"Total Size of U.S. Book Printing." *American Printer* (February 1997). Table: 436.

"Trading Cards." *Non-Foods Merchandising* (October 1996). Table: 185.

Turner, Dan. "L.A. Times Leads U.S. Papers in Readership Growth." *Los Angeles Business Journal,* 13 May 1997. Table: 411.

"Turning Off the Presses." *The Economist,* 11 October 1997. Table: 421.

"U.S. Book Buying Growth." *USA TODAY*, 6 September 1995. Table: 210.

"U.S. Book Exports Edge Up 1.5%." *Publishers Weekly*, 9 September 1996. Table: 211.

U.S. News & World Report, 24 June 1996. Table: 153.

"U.S. Paper Industry Will See More Globalization, Slower Growth in 1997." *Pulp & Paper* (January 1997). Table: 501.

"USA Snapshots." *USA TODAY*, 4 August 1995. Table: 165.

"USA Snapshots." *USA TODAY*, 4 September 1997. Table: 310.

"USA Snapshots." *USA TODAY*, 15 October 1997. Table: 126.

"USA Snapshots." *USA TODAY*, 23 October 1997. Table: 182.

"USA Snapshots." *USA TODAY*, 17 December 1997. Tables: 272-273.

"USA Snapshots." *USA TODAY*, 24 December 1997. Table: 116.

"USA Snapshots." *USA TODAY*, 31 December 1997. Table: 203.

"Valentine's Day Rings Up Big Sales for Retailers." *The Christian Science Monitor*, 13 February 1997. Table: 291.

Variety, 8 May 1995. Table: 560.

"Vital Signs: News Junkies." *Asiaweek*, 16 August 1996. Table: 412.

"Volume Trading." *The Warsaw Voice*, 24 August 1997. Tables: 89, 249, 252.

"Volumes of Money." *Latin Trade* (October 1997). Table: 248.

Von Kaenel, Jeff. "Daily Dinosaurs." *Metro Times*, 1-7 January 1997. Table: 391.

Warman, Janice. "Journalists Cry Freedom Again in South Africa," *The Observer*, 16 February 1997. Table: 427.

Washington Post, 29 March 1996. Table: 327.

"Web Ads Trail Net Radio by Far." *Advertising Age*, 2 September 1996. Tables: 158-159.

"Welcome to Media Paradise!" *Marketing in Quebec*, Special Supplement. Table: 425.

"What Teens Want to Read." *USA TODAY*, 10 December 1997. Table: 237.

"Where the Readers Are." *The Christian Science Monitor*, 28 October 1996. Table: 255.

"Who's Against Free Speech?" *American Demographics* (August 1997). Table: 531.

Wilke, Michael. "Gay Press Sets Pace with 19.6% Ad Increase." *Advertising Age*, 9 September 1996. Table: 315.

Wilman, Chris. "The Top 20." *Entertainment Weekly*, 17 January 1997. Table: 364.

Wines, Michael. "Successful Political Books Are Less Sober, More Pop." *New York Times*, 17 February 1997. Tables: 552, 554.

"Wired Top 10." Wired (February 1996). Table: 266.

Woodyard, Chris. "Father's Day Cards Evolve With Times." *USA TODAY,* 12 June 1997. Table: 289.

Woodyard, Chris. "Wisconsin Cataloger Plows Through Storm." *USA TODAY,* 15 December 1997. Table: 263.

"The Word on Discount Books." *USA TODAY,* 9 October 1997. Table: 206.

"World-Class Book Buyers." *USA TODAY,* 27 November 1996. Table: 256.

"Writers and Editors." *Occupational Outlook Handbook 1996-97 Edition,* U.S. Department of Labor, Washington D.C., (January 1996). Table: 510.

"The Year in Review Top 10 Cookbooks." *Nation's Restaurant News,* 23 December 1996. Table: 143.

"Year's Best Seller: Grisham in a 'Runaway' On The Top Shelf." *USA TODAY,* 24 December 1996. Table: 553.

Young, Allison. "Book Banned, and Teacher Quit." *The Detroit Free Press,* 3 February 1997. Table: 532.

Keyword Index

This index provides access to all subjects covered in *By-the-Numbers: Publishing* including topics, geographical locations, occupations, company names, etc. Page references are provided; table references are also given inside brackets, e.g., [14]. Page references do not necessarily identify the page on which a table begins. In the cases where tables span two or more pages, references point to the page on which the index term appears—which may be the second or subsequent page of a table. Frequent cross-references have been added to index citations to facilitate the location of related topics and tables.

Numbers following p. or pp. are page references. Numbers in [ ] are table references.

Numbers following p. or pp. are page references. Numbers in [ ] are table references.

Numbers following p. or pp. are page references. Numbers in [ ] are table references.

Keyword Index

Numbers following p. or pp. are page references. Numbers in [ ] are table references.

Numbers following p. or pp. are page references. Numbers in [ ] are table references.

Keyword Index

Numbers following p. or pp. are page references. Numbers in [ ] are table references.

471

Numbers following p. or pp. are page references. Numbers in [ ] are table references.

Numbers following p. or pp. are page references. Numbers in [ ] are table references.

473

Numbers following p. or pp. are page references. Numbers in [ ] are table references.

Numbers following p. or pp. are page references. Numbers in [ ] are table references.

475

Numbers following p. or pp. are page references. Numbers in [ ] are table references.

Keyword Index

Numbers following p. or pp. are page references. Numbers in [ ] are table references.

477

Numbers following p. or pp. are page references. Numbers in [ ] are table references.

Keyword Index

Numbers following p. or pp. are page references. Numbers in [ ] are table references.

Numbers following p. or pp. are page references. Numbers in [ ] are table references.

Numbers following p. or pp. are page references. Numbers in [ ] are table references.

Keyword Index

Numbers following p. or pp. are page references. Numbers in [ ] are table references.

Numbers following p. or pp. are page references. Numbers in [ ] are table references.

484

Keyword Index

Numbers following p. or pp. are page references. Numbers in [ ] are table references.

486

Numbers following p. or pp. are page references. Numbers in [ ] are table references.

Numbers following p. or pp. are page references. Numbers in [ ] are table references.

Numbers following p. or pp. are page references. Numbers in [ ] are table references.

489

Numbers following p. or pp. are page references. Numbers in [ ] are table references.

Numbers following p. or pp. are page references. Numbers in [ ] are table references.

491

Keyword Index

Numbers following p. or pp. are page references. Numbers in [ ] are table references.

492

Numbers following p. or pp. are page references. Numbers in [ ] are table references.

493

Numbers following p. or pp. are page references. Numbers in [ ] are table references.

Numbers following p. or pp. are page references. Numbers in [ ] are table references.

Keyword Index

Numbers following p. or pp. are page references. Numbers in [ ] are table references.

Numbers following p. or pp. are page references. Numbers in [ ] are table references.

Numbers following p. or pp. are page references. Numbers in [ ] are table references.

Numbers following p. or pp. are page references. Numbers in [ ] are table references.

499

Numbers following p. or pp. are page references. Numbers in [ ] are table references.

Keyword Index

Numbers following p. or pp. are page references. Numbers in [ ] are table references.

Numbers following p. or pp. are page references. Numbers in [ ] are table references.

Numbers following p. or pp. are page references. Numbers in [ ] are table references.

Keyword Index

Keyword Index

Numbers following p. or pp. are page references. Numbers in [ ] are table references.

Keyword Index

Numbers following p. or pp. are page references. Numbers in [ ] are table references.

Keyword Index

Numbers following p. or pp. are page references. Numbers in [ ] are table references.

509